Praise for *A Lincoln Legacy*

"Being a member of the Western District of Michigan has meant learning from heroes and making lifelong friends. It is not just about the rule of law; it is also about the rule of honor, courtesy, and civility among rivals. With our history, we write our future."

—William W. Jack, Jr., Esq.

"*A Lincoln Legacy* masterfully guides readers through the origins of jurisprudence in the Western District of Michigan to the modern-day construct. The carefully chronicled legal, political, and human elements instruct historical details within eloquent storytelling to bring life to the court Lincoln created."

—Kim Clarke, Partner, Varnum, LLP

"In *A Lincoln Legacy*, Brenneman and Chardavoyne provide a comprehensive, informative, and thoroughly enjoyable history of the U.S. District Court for the Western District of Michigan and of the state writ large. From its examination of the post-colonial, pre-statehood territorial period to the modern day, the authors walk us through some of the most substantial cases. The discussion of the interplay between the state and federal government and between the three branches of government, including the appointments and funding process, is as timely today as it was in 1863 when President Lincoln established the Court. A must-read for all lawyers and judges but also for any citizen seeking to understand our state's history and the interworkings and interrelationships of the governments which serve us."

—Judge James Robert Redford, Michigan Court of Appeals

"*A Lincoln Legacy* is an extraordinary contribution to the story of Michigan. In recounting the history of the United States District Court in exquisite detail, *A Lincoln Legacy* brings to life the judges, cases, and characters that have shaped the law in West Michigan for more than a century and a half."

—Chris Yates, Kent County Circuit Court Judge

"Relying (harmlessly) on a little hearsay and inadmissible character evidence, *A Lincoln Legacy* is a clear and convincing winner."

—Terry Dillon, former Assistant United States Attorney in the Western District of Michigan

A LINCOLN LEGACY

A Lincoln Legacy

The History of the U.S. District Court for the
Western District of Michigan

David Gardner Chardavoyne

with Hugh W. Brenneman, Jr.

WAYNE STATE UNIVERSITY PRESS

DETROIT

Great Lakes Books

*A complete listing of the books in this series can be found online
at wsupress.wayne.edu*

Editor
Thomas Klug
Sterling Heights, Michigan

ISBN: 978-0-8143-4804-8 (jacketed cloth); ISBN: 978-0-8143-4805-5 (ebook)

Library of Congress Control Number: 2020938181

Wayne State University Press
Leonard N. Simons Building
4809 Woodward Avenue
Detroit, Michigan 48201–1309

Visit us online at wsupress.wayne.edu

CONTENTS

Seven score and seventeen years ago, on March 10, 1863, President Abraham Lincoln nominated Solomon Withey to be the first judge of the newly created Western District of Michigan. Congress and the President had created the Western District in February, over the objection of two federal officials from Detroit who wrote to Lincoln urging him to hold the bill "until Tuesday when bill will be shown to you to be absurd." Lincoln signed the bill anyway and promptly followed through with his nomination of Withey. The Senate confirmed the nomination the next day, and Lincoln signed the commission immediately. Thank God for Lincoln!

Eight months later, on November 19, 1863, Lincoln delivered his Gettysburg Address. He stirred listeners at the time, and readers today, to honor the monumental sacrifice of that battle—and by extension the entire Civil War—by resolving "that government of the people, by the people, for the people, shall not perish from the earth." This court and its sister districts throughout the nation have worked to realize and secure that resolution in the daily work of deciding cases, large and small, under the Constitution and laws of these United States.

Taking stock of history is an especially fitting enterprise for a court. Honest histories inform and constrain those presently in power. The tyrants who ran Orwell's Oceania in the fictional dystopia of *1984* exploited memory holes to arrogate to themselves the writing and rewriting of their imagined histories, rather than live within the bounds of a single honest one. In contrast, as lawyers and jurists we look reflexively to history as an integral part of our methodology, humbly acknowledging in the process the limits of our own power and understanding, as well as the wisdom of our predecessors in office.

But honest histories inspire, too. We can see ordinary men and women step up to the challenges of their time, as reflected in the cases presented to them, and work faithfully to apply the law without regard to political, social, or economic pressure. These stories of courage in office refresh the commitment of each new generation of lawyers and jurists, and humbly remind us of the ever-growing legacy upon which we build for the short time it is entrusted to our care.

So in both constraint and inspiration, honest history is first of all humbling. And it is in that spirit that our bench and bar offer this chronicle of the first 157 years of the Western District of Michigan, and of its even longer pedigree through the Territorial Court of Michigan (1805–1837), and the original District of Michigan (1837–1863). Long may the Western District thrive and prosper in its efforts to preserve Lincoln's Gettysburg vision for generations to come.

Robert J. Jonker
Chief United States District Judge
Western District of Michigan

The birth of our district—on February 24, 1863—occurred at a remarkable confluence of historical events. This was the midpoint of the Civil War, during perhaps the most perilous year in American history and at the low point of the Union's prospects for victory. Two difficult years of war remained—although, at the time, it seemed as if the end might never come. And it was far from clear then that the Union would even survive.

The events of the time were truly momentous. This was six months after the Battle of Antietam, the bloodiest day of the Civil War, weeks after President Lincoln's Emancipation Proclamation took effect, and days after the Union draft was signed into law. And it occurred just before the start of the spring campaigns, two months before the Confederate victory at Chancellorsville, four months before Gettysburg and the surrender of Vicksburg, and eight months before Lincoln delivered the Gettysburg Address. In an amazing historical coincidence, the new federal courtroom, where the Imperial Room of the Amway Grand Plaza Hotel now stands, opened on the first day of the Battle of Gettysburg, some 500 miles away.

And it was on March 10, 1863 that Lincoln nominated Solomon Withey, a 42-year-old Grand Rapids lawyer, as the first District Judge. Judge Withey served with distinction for 23 years and, during his entire tenure, he was the Western District's only federal judge.

On March 12, 2013, The Historical Society sponsored a magnificent gala celebrating the 150th anniversary of the Western District. The memorable evening at the Amway Grand Plaza, attended by some 400 guests, included Civil War–era music, Civil War reenactors, the mini documentary *Thank God for Michigan*, narrated by Grand Rapids Historian Gordon Olson, Presentation of the Colors, remarks by President Abraham Lincoln, the keynote address by presidential historian Richard Norton Smith, and perhaps, most remarkably, the attendance by Harold Becker, then age 95, whose father—yes, father! —fought in the Civil War.

It was this celebration of our 150-year history that inspired The Historical Society to commission a book chronicling the district's fascinating history. We approached attorney and historian David Chardavoyne, who had authored a 2012 book on the history of the Eastern District of Michigan. He was interested in researching and writing this one. And six years later, after much hard work and generous contributions, we celebrate its publication by Wayne State University Press.

The Historical Society is proud of this accomplishment and wishes to thank Mr. Chardavoyne, Court Historian and retired Magistrate Judge Hugh W. Brenneman, Jr., Chief Judge Robert J. Jonker and all of the District, Magistrate and Bankruptcy Judges, as well as The Peter C. and Emajean Cook Foundation, which generously provided a $20,000 grant for publication. We hope that members of the bar and bench enjoy this journey into their profession's rich past.

David J. Gass, President
The Historical Society for the U.S. District
Court for the Western District of Michigan

The Western District of Michigan

❧

THIS BOOK IS A history of the United States District Court for the Western District of Michigan. Congress created the Western District in 1863 when it passed a law that split the District of Michigan into two districts. Initially, the Western District included counties in the western half of the Lower Peninsula and portions of four counties in the Upper Peninsula located on the northern shore of Lake Michigan. The Eastern District retained counties in the eastern half of the Lower Peninsula as well as the rest of the Upper Peninsula, including those touching the southern shore of Lake Superior.

In 1878, Congress changed the district borders so that the Western District gained all of the counties in the Upper Peninsula. With minor geographical adjustments in 1878 and 1954, the Western District now consists of forty-nine counties, which includes 63 percent of Michigan's land area but only 35 percent of the state's population because the Upper Peninsula's fifteen counties are so sparsely populated. The 1863 statute creating the Western District designated Grand Rapids, in Kent County, as the place of holding the Western District's federal courts, the U.S. District Court and the U.S. Circuit Court. Since then, the judges of those courts have conducted court, with the authority of Congress, in federal courthouses in Marquette and Sault Ste. Marie in the Upper Peninsula and in Kalamazoo and Lansing in the Lower Peninsula.

Although this is a story of one federal court, telling that story also requires telling some aspects of four defunct courts that provided, at various times, the judicial power and the presence of the federal government in western Michigan: the Supreme Court for the Territory of Michigan (1805 to 1836); the United States District and Circuit Courts of the District of Michigan (both 1837 to 1863); and the United States Circuit Court for the Western District of Michigan (1863 to 1911).

CHAPTER 1

The Supreme Court of the Territory of Michigan, 1805 to 1836

FROM 1805 TO 1836, the Supreme Court of the Territory of Michigan consisted of a panel of three judges appointed by the President of the United States with the advice and consent of the U.S. Senate, and wielded jurisdiction over civil and criminal cases arising within the Michigan Territory based on federal law, territorial statutes, and the common law. When Michigan became a state in 1837, Congress dissolved the Territorial Court, the state legislature created the Supreme Court of Michigan and a set of lower state courts, and Congress created the United States District Court for the District of Michigan. The District Court's single District Judge, also appointed by the President with the advice and consent of the Senate, was responsible for the entire state until 1863, when Congress split the District of Michigan into two District Courts: the United States District Court for the Eastern District of Michigan and the United States District Court for the Western District of Michigan. But the story of federal courts in western Michigan begins much earlier, with one singular provision of the treaty between the United States and Great Britain negotiated in Paris, France, to end the American Revolutionary War.

The 1783 Treaty and the Northwest Territory

Peace negotiations between the United States and Great Britain began in April 1782, sponsored by France, which had entered the war as the key ally of the Americans but whose treasury was emptying at a terrifying pace as a result. American delegates included Benjamin Franklin, John Adams, and John Jay, while the French were led by Charles Gravier, comte de Vergennes.

After several months of fruitless bickering, a desperate Vergennes proposed a solution in which the United States would gain its independence and all territory east of the Appalachians, while Great Britain would retain Canada and all land west of Pennsylvania, north of the Ohio River, and east of the Mississippi River.[1]

Feeling that they were being betrayed by the French, the Americans decided to negotiate directly with Great Britain, whose negotiators realized that American independence was a fait accompli and useless as leverage for negotiation. Similarly, the British prime minister, William Petty, Earl of Shelburne, realized that Britain and her merchants could profit by a commercial and trade relationship between the two nations. Consequently, the British offered the new nation what its negotiators really wanted: a treaty provision in which Great Britain agreed to cede any claim to all of the land east of the Mississippi River, north of Florida, and south of Canada. The American delegation accepted, Spain got Florida, Britain and France got peace, and the United States got both peace and an enormous land grant.

Although acquiring vast tracts of wilderness in the west through the treaty was very favorable to the United States, it also created one of the first troubling internal arguments in the new nation. The issue was what to do with the land ceded by Great Britain, in particular the land north of the Ohio River, constituting what are now the states of Ohio, Indiana, Illinois, Michigan, Wisconsin, and the part of Minnesota east of the Mississippi. Relying on their colonial charter or Indian grants, some states claimed all or part of what they called the Northwest Territory. Virginia, for example, claimed all of the Northwest Territory while Massachusetts, Connecticut, and New York made competing claims to large tracts there.[2] On the other hand, states without western claims feared losing population and power in Congress to the claiming states.

In October 1780, after years of debate and negotiation in which some states refused to ratify the Articles of Confederation unless they prevailed on this issue, the last of the claimant states, Massachusetts and Connecticut, agreed to give up their western claims[3] and allow the Northwest Territory to be "settled and formed into distinct republican states which shall become members of the federal union, and have the same rights of sovereignty, freedom and independence, as the other states."[4]

At first, the Confederation Congress did not explain how and when such new states would be formed or how the western lands would be governed in the interim. In 1784, a committee chaired by Thomas Jefferson submitted to Congress "A Plan for Government of the Western Territory,"[5] most of which the Confederation Congress voted to adopt.[6] But Jefferson's plan was never put into action. It was not until July 13, 1787, that another session of the Confederation Congress enacted "An Ordinance for the Territory of the United States north-west of the River Ohio,"[7] which became known simply as the Northwest Ordinance. Two years later, on August 7, 1789, the new U.S. Congress, created by the U.S. Constitution, reenacted the Northwest Ordinance practically verbatim.[8]

Both enactments of the ordinance provided that, instead of starting as a single self-governing state or several such states, the Northwest Territory would begin as a single territory or "district," with the promise that, over time as populations grew, Congress would divide the Northwest Territory into independent territories and ultimately into three to five states to be admitted to the Union on equal terms with the original states. Initially, the Northwest Territory and its progeny territories would be governed by officials (a governor, a secretary, and three common-law judges) appointed by the federal government. In addition to their judicial responsibilities, the three territorial judges would also act, with the governor, as the territorial legislature. When any part of a territory achieved a population of "five thousand free male inhabitants of full age," it could elect a legislature, but its executive and judiciary would still be under the control of the federally appointed officials. Only when its population reached sixty thousand "free inhabitants" (not counting slaves or Indians) would the territory be eligible to become a state with all privileges of statehood.

The territorial structure established by the Northwest Ordinance was so successful that it was copied in territory after territory as the nation moved west. But even more significant to the nation's future were its "articles of compact" in which the original states made "unalterable" promises to the people of the Northwest Territory. These articles included guarantees of religious freedom; the protections of the common law, including habeas corpus and trial by jury; prohibitions of slavery and of cruel or unusual punishment; the encouragement of education; and good faith toward Indians.

In 1787, however, and as late as 1796, the details of governmental organization in the Northwest Territory were academic. Although it could be included on a map of the United States, the Northwest Territory had virtually no American inhabitants, and no American official exercised any practical authority there except for the single settlement at Marietta, near the confluence of the Muskingum and Ohio rivers. Despite the Treaty of Paris, Great Britain refused to evacuate its troops from the upper Northwest Territory, including forts at Detroit and Mackinac. To the contrary, Britain built new forts in northern Ohio to support the plans of Indian tribes to keep the Americans out.

What is now Ohio became a battleground between Indians and settlers. Although they had tolerated the French and British soldiers and traders who set up forts on their tribal lands, the tribes of the lower Northwest Territory were aware that the Americans were different. Whereas the French and British who set up forts and trading posts throughout the Northwest Territory had prohibited their citizens from settling there, the ability to own land on which to farm and settle, to the exclusion of Indians, was exactly what the Americans coming to Ohio wanted. Although the Northwest Ordinance required that Congress buy Indian lands rather than seize them, so that there were no legal American settlements north of Marietta, settlers pushed the boundaries constantly with the excuse that Ohio was now American. The Indians fought back with British assistance and won battles against settlers and American troops, but the settlers kept coming.

The end of organized resistance by the Ohio tribes began in August 1794 when Anthony Wayne defeated a force made up of many of the Ohio tribes at the Battle of Fallen Timbers, near Toledo. Three months later, in a treaty negotiated by John Jay,[9] Great Britain agreed that by June 1, 1796, the king would "withdraw all his troops and garrisons from all posts and places within the boundary lines assigned by the treaty of peace to the United States." Abandoned by the British and facing a growing American presence, the Ohio tribes gave up. In the Treaty of Greenville,[10] the United States acquired most of southern Ohio and other strategic locations in the Northwest Territory, including Detroit and Mackinac Island, all of which were now open to legal settlement.

Detroit's British troops and government did evacuate, by moving across the river to Canada before the Americans arrived there on July 11, 1796. At that time, Detroit was a different environment from what American officials were used to assimilating when they opened new areas for settlement. Despite the fact that it consisted of just a fort and about five hundred civilian inhabitants, it was an established European community in which the people considered themselves French or British.[11] The French population lived by subsistence farming, hunting, and trapping, while the British were mainly merchants and traders. Neither group was required to take an oath of allegiance to the United States, and both groups were of doubtful loyalty. There were also an unknown number of slaves.

The arrival of American forces did not mean that Detroit or Michigan became a separate territory, however. Between 1796 and 1805, what is now Michigan was governed by territorial governments located in Marietta and Chillicothe, Ohio, and in Vincennes, Indiana. The territorial judges of those governments were reluctant to travel to Detroit, so they held court in Detroit only twice in five years.[12] In 1800, Congress divided the Northwest Territory in two, forming the Indiana Territory and what was called the "eastern division" of the Northwest Territory. Their border was a line running from the Ohio River, at a point opposite the mouth of the Kentucky River, north-north-east to what is now the village of Fort Recovery, Ohio, on the Wabash River, then north to the Canadian border in Lake Superior.[13] The eastern half of Michigan's Lower Peninsula and the eastern tip of the Upper Peninsula remained in the Northwest Territory. The rest of Michigan, which had no American settlements, became part of the Indiana Territory with its capital at Vincennes on the lower reaches of the Wabash River.

In 1802, Congress authorized the organization of the state of Ohio. The remainder of the eastern division of the Northwest Territory, including the rest of lower Michigan, was added to the Indiana Territory effective February 19, 1803.[14] From the minute they became part of the Indiana Territory, the residents of Detroit complained loudly that they were being ignored and excluded from participating in territorial government by their distance from Vincennes. Because Indiana was still in the first stage of government, Michigan lost its legislative representative and was once more governed by a distant governor and judges. In March 1803, Detroiters petitioned Congress in two languages asking for their own government.[15] When the Indiana Territory passed to the second stage of government in December 1804, Detroit did not hear about the meeting of the General Assembly until it was too late to send a delegate.[16]

The distance from Detroit to Vincennes and the seeming disdain of the Indiana government for its northern constituents caused the people of Detroit and other nearby settlements to petition Congress, often and passionately, for another territorial split, this time severing Michigan from Indiana and affording the new territory its own government. On January 11, 1805, Congress granted their wish, dividing the Indiana Territory, effective the following June, and creating the Territory of Michigan, described as "all that part of the Indiana Territory, which lies north of a line drawn east from the southerly bend or extreme of Lake Michigan, until it shall intersect Lake Erie, and east of a line drawn from the said southerly [bend] through the middle of said lake to its northern extremity, and thence due north to the northern boundary of the United States. . . ."[17]

In 1809, Congress created the Illinois Territory by dividing the Indiana Territory (once more) along a line running north from the Ohio River, along the current western border of the state of Indiana, to the U.S. border on Lake Superior.[18] Under this act, Congress (intentionally or by mistake) left a large portion of the Upper Peninsula as well as the eastern end of Green Bay within the defined boundaries of the Indiana Territory but isolated from it by any land route.[19] The western portion of the Upper Peninsula was in the Territory of Illinois, and only the eastern tip of the Upper Peninsula was in the Territory of Michigan.

Congress did not alter the boundaries of the old Northwest Territory for another decade until, in 1816, Congress authorized the inhabitants of the Indiana Territory to form a state.[20] The act described the northern boundary of Indiana as "an east west line drawn through a point ten miles north of the southern extreme of Lake Michigan," a northward shift done apparently so that Indiana would have direct access to a port on Lake Michigan. As a result, the Indiana/Michigan border was moved ten miles north, while the Indiana Territory's portions of the Upper Peninsula and Green Bay were not included in the state's defined boundaries. Because Congress did not change the boundaries of the Illinois or Michigan territories to include them, apparently those parts of the Upper Peninsula were not part of any territory or state between April 1816 and April 1818.

On April 18, 1818, Congress authorized the inhabitants of Illinois to form a state with the same boundaries as today.[21] In the same act, Congress doubled the size of the Territory of Michigan by transferring to it "all that part of the territory of the United States lying north of the State of Indiana, and which was included in the former Indiana Territory, together with that part of the Illinois Territory which is situated north of and not included within the boundaries prescribed by this act. . . ."[22] Thus, the Michigan Territory added all of the rest of the Upper Peninsula and what are now the state of Wisconsin and part of Minnesota east of the Mississippi.

In 1834, Congress again doubled the size of the Territory of Michigan by extending the territorial borders outside the old Northwest Territory, west to the Missouri and White Earth rivers and south to the northern border of the state of Missouri.[23] This expansion included all of present-day Iowa and Minnesota as well as portions of South and North Dakota. Congress took this western extension as a temporary step in the process of creating the territory of Wisconsin in 1836, after which the Michigan Territory returned to its permanent state borders.[24]

After years of dispute, Michigan was admitted into the Union on January 26, 1837.[25] Michigan finally agreed to the Ohio Constitution border and retained, as compensation, the Upper Peninsula east of the Montreal and Menominee rivers.[26] The remainder of the Territory of Michigan became the territories of Wisconsin, which became a state in 1848, and Minnesota, approved as a state in 1858.

The Supreme Court of the Territory of Michigan

Section 4 of the Northwest Ordinance provided for the appointment of three territorial judges with a common-law jurisdiction "whose commissions shall continue in force during good behavior." Because Congress provided in 1805 that the government of the Michigan Territory was to be in all respects similar to that provided by the Northwest Ordinance, President Jefferson had the responsibility and opportunity to appoint a governor, a secretary, and three judges for Michigan. On March 2, 1805, he appointed his friend Augustus Brevoort Woodward as Chief Judge of the Michigan Territorial Court.[27]

Elias Brevoort Woodward was born in New York City in 1774 and graduated from Columbia College, now Columbia University, in 1793. Two years earlier he had changed his first name from Elias to Augustus, thinking it more dignified. When the federal government moved to the District of Columbia, he followed and established a prominent law practice and served on the first city council. In addition to English, he was fluent in Greek, Latin, French, and Spanish, and, like his great friend Thomas Jefferson, he had broad interests in the arts and sciences.[28]

Woodward arrived in Detroit on June 30, 1805, just three weeks after fire destroyed the town. With his characteristic energy, Woodward set himself up as the community's leader, rebuilding Detroit from the ashes. He joined Jefferson's second appointment to the Michigan bench, Detroit resident Frederick Bates, originally of Virginia and a family friend of both President Jefferson and Secretary of State James Madison. Bates, just twenty-seven years old, had made his living as an army quartermaster and as a storekeeper while

Judge Augustus Brevoort Woodward.
There is no known contemporary
image of Judge Woodward. This is a
modern portrait based on descriptions
of the judge in the historical record.

he studied law. There would not be a third judge until March 1806, but the
Northwest Ordinance allowed the court to operate with just two judges.
Accordingly, Woodward and Bates held the first session of the court, which
Woodward christened the Supreme Court of the Territory of Michigan, on
July 29, 1805.[29] Judge Bates left the court in 1806 to become the secretary of
the new Louisiana Territory, which included all of the Louisiana Purchase
north of the thirty-third parallel, which is now the southern border of the
state of Arkansas, and had its capital in St. Louis. He left that position in
1809, but in 1812, after the Louisiana Territory was renamed the Missouri
Territory, Bates served as its secretary until Missouri became a state in 1820.
In November 1824, he was elected the state's second governor, but he died in
office in August 1825.

President Jefferson replaced Bates on Michigan's Territorial Court with
John Griffin, the grandson of a Scottish laird and the son of a prominent
congressman and federal judge from Virginia. Jefferson had first appointed
John Griffin to be a judge of the Indiana Territorial Court in Vincennes, but
after a short residence there Griffin decided that the climate was bad for his

health, and he begged his father to petition Jefferson to find him a better job. Jefferson, who did not like either Griffin, chose to appoint John to the Michigan court, a job and location that came to please John even less, although he stayed in that office until 1823. In 1808, the court was finally filled with Jefferson's appointment of James Witherell of Vermont, a physician, judge, and veteran of the Revolutionary War.

Woodward, Griffin, and Witherell constituted the court for the next sixteen years. They were a disparate and uncomfortable trio. In 1822, Territorial Secretary William Woodbridge wrote to a friend that: "Our Chief Judge is a wild theorist, fitted principally for the extraction of sunbeams from cucumbers," while Griffin was a gentleman, tasteful and polite, "but with a mind lamentably inert." Griffin relied on Woodward and rarely acted contrary to him.[30] Judge Witherell, Woodbridge opined, was honest and intuitive, but he had an unfortunate defect for a common-law judge—"a deadly hostility to that common law that he is officially called upon to administer, because of its English descent."[31]

With the constant support of the hapless and permanently unhappy Griffin, Woodward controlled both the judicial and the legislative branches of the territorial government, able to count on a majority in the court and at least two of the four votes on the council. This power enraged both governors who served during Woodward's tenure in Michigan, William Hull and Lewis Cass. Woodward has historically been described as a "character," and he may have been eccentric and stubborn, but during the War of 1812 he proved that he was also brave. On August 16, 1812, Governor Hull surrendered all of the state's armed forces to the commander of the British forces in the west, General Isaac Brock. Brock sent Hull and other military officers to Montreal while he expelled most civil officials to Ohio and further east. The exception was Woodward, who insisted on remaining in Detroit to protect the rights of the residents. In his own particular way, he became a thorn in the side of Brock's successor, the much less competent General Henry Proctor, whom Woodward hectored and complained to about the condition of life in the occupied town. Woodward also managed to send intelligence to the American government and to hide the garrison's flag so that the British never found it. After months of dealing with Woodward, an exasperated Proctor expelled him from the territory. He returned when the war was over.

One of the subjects that Woodward was called to rule on early in his tenure was the status of slavery in the Michigan Territory.[32] One of the articles of compact in the Northwest Ordinance clearly promised that there would never be slavery in the Northwest Territory, but when the Americans arrived in Detroit, they discovered that the British population held dozens of African and Indian slaves. Judge Woodward was aware of the ordinance's compact barring slavery, but he also knew that an article of the Jay Treaty guaranteed that British residents of the Northwest Territory who decided to remain under the American government would "continue to enjoy, unmolested, all their property of every kind." Did that property include slaves, and if so, what law controlled their fate?

In 1807, Judge Woodward, sitting alone, had to decide if he could reconcile the ordinance and the treaty. A former slave, who had been freed by her owner, sued asking the Territorial Supreme Court to declare that her four children, whom her former owner still held as slaves, were themselves freed by the slavery compact in the ordinance. The owner responded that her property rights in the children were protected by the treaty. Woodward disliked slavery, but he also believed that he had to interpret the laws as written. After listening to the arguments of counsel, he ruled for the owner because the ordinance did not apply in Michigan until after the United States took control, whereas the treaty applied when it was ratified.

Woodward did limit his ruling, though, holding that the rights of the owner were only those acknowledged under Canadian law. In 1793, the parliament of Upper Canada had passed a law to gradually end slavery by emancipating all children born to slave mothers on their twenty-fifth birthday. Woodward used that law to hold that all persons born in Michigan on or after July 11, 1796, were born free, while those born to a slave mother after May 31, 1793, but before July 11, 1796, would be free on their twenty-fifth birthday. Thus, slavery ended slowly in the Michigan Territory, and the 1830 U.S. census was the last to record a slave within what are now Michigan's state boundaries.

Some of the eccentricity in Woodward's opinions might have been an attempt at humor. Michigan's Supreme Court was described as based on the common law, a set of rules that has developed over centuries and is constantly evolving. The issue in one case before Woodward's court was which version of the common law the court was bound to follow. One judge said one recent date, a second said another, and then Woodward, apparently with a straight face, insisted that the proper common law was the one current at the time of the coronation of "Richard, Coeur de Lion" (i.e., Richard the Lionheart, crowned king of England in the year 1189).

In another opinion, Woodward may have been showing off his scholarship playfully in resolving a simple issue that the attorneys for both sides actually agreed on. In an 1818 case,[33] the issue before the Supreme Court was whether the service of civil process on a Sunday was valid. Both sides agreed that such service was valid at common law, but Woodward disagreed. In what was then a mammoth opinion of approximately nine thousand words, he proved to his own satisfaction that the common law did indeed forbid Sunday service of process. He investigated the special status of Sunday from the time of Jesus, citing, among a multitude of authorities: the apostles John, Luke, and Paul; Byzantine emperors Theodosius, Constantine, and Anastasius; Pope Gregory; sixth-century kings Childebert of France and Gontran of Burgundy; and English kings Edward I, III, and VI, William I, Henry II, VI, and VIII, James I, and Charles II. He concluded the opinion with an alphabetical list of more than one hundred authorities—legal, historical, and ecclesiastical— supporting his conclusion. For a judge speaking literally in the wilderness, with no access to a library or college, this was an incredible feat of scholarship, but was it an elaborate joke by a scholar showing off his erudition?[34]

The Additional Judge of the Territory of Michigan

In April 1818, when Congress authorized the inhabitants of the Territory of Illinois to form a state, Congress also expanded the Michigan Territory by attaching to it what are now the Upper Peninsula of the state of Michigan, the state of Wisconsin, and the part of Minnesota east of the Mississippi River.[35] Six months later, on October 26, 1818, the governor of the Michigan Territory, Lewis Cass, issued a proclamation creating three new counties in that new Michigan land, named Michilimackinac, Brown, and Crawford counties.[36] Although Cass's proclamation described boundaries of the counties that enclosed extensive areas, the proclamation also provided that the counties would, in fact, include only land "in which the Indian title has been extinguished."[37] The Indian title to almost all of the land in the three new counties was not extinguished until 1836 or later. Thus, during the remainder of the Michigan Territory's existence, the three counties consisted of much less land than the boundaries suggested. Crawford County, the boundaries of which encompassed most of the western half of what is now the state of Wisconsin, in reality included just a number of non-Indian settlements on the upper Mississippi River. Brown County, whose boundaries encompassed the eastern half of Wisconsin, included only a few pioneer settlements around Green Bay on the western shore of Lake Michigan. Michilimackinac County, whose stated boundaries included the Upper Peninsula and a large area in the northcentral and northwestern parts of Michigan's Lower Peninsula, included only Mackinac Island, Sault Ste. Marie, and a few other settlements in the Upper Peninsula. In 1818, the total white population of all three counties was little more than a thousand residents, and twelve years later, in 1830, the total was just under three thousand.[38]

Despite the small actual area and white population of the three counties, it was not long before the white residents began to seek to bring federal or territorial justice closer to their homes and businesses. County courts presided over by justices of the peace could handle modest civil and criminal cases, but any matter within the exclusive jurisdiction of the Territorial Supreme Court had to be litigated in Detroit. Parties to such matters arising in the three counties might have to spend months traveling to the territorial capital and waiting for their cases to be tried. If a case was still pending when the Great Lakes froze, parties who were unable to return home might spend the winter in a hotel waiting for the Supreme Court to reconvene.

After years of petitioning by residents of the three counties, supported by Governor Cass, on January 30, 1823, Congress did authorize an "additional judge for the Michigan territory" to exercise jurisdiction within the three counties.[39] The statute authorized the additional judge to hold one term in each of the counties each year to exercise most of the jurisdiction of the Supreme Court, but not the Supreme Court's "original jurisdiction," and also to exercise the jurisdiction of the three county courts. The federal statute also granted the additional judge jurisdiction over two matters arising in Indian country, outside the three counties but within the Michigan Territory, which were of particular interest to county residents: federal laws regulating "trade and intercourse" between white merchants and Indians, and "all crimes and offences [sic] which shall be committed within that part of the Indian country lying north and west of Lake Michigan."

On January 20, 1824, President James Monroe nominated, to the position of "Additional Judge for the Territory of Michigan in the Counties of Michilimackinac, Brown and Crawford," James Duane Doty, a twenty-four-year-old Detroit lawyer and a Whig who was a protégé of Governor Cass. The Senate confirmed Doty the next day.[40] Because the statute required the additional judge to reside in one of the three counties, Doty moved with his new wife,

Sarah Collins Doty, to Prairie du Chien, and for the next eight years he held court in that town, in Green Bay, and on Mackinac Island. President John Quincy Adams, also a Whig, renewed Doty's appointment in 1828, but in April 1832 Democratic President Andrew Jackson refused to reappoint him. Doty later became a Wisconsin congressman, the second governor of the Wisconsin Territory, and the fifth governor of the Utah Territory, where he died in 1865.

To replace Doty, President Jackson appointed Democrat David Irvin, a native of Albemarle, Virginia. Irvin served as the additional judge until 1836 when Michigan's Territorial Courts were dissolved. In July 1836, Jackson appointed Irvin as judge of the Territorial Supreme Court of Wisconsin.[41] After Wisconsin became a state in 1848, Irvin moved to Texas where he became a state judge and a supporter of the Confederacy. He died in 1872.

Capital Punishment in the Territory of Michigan, 1821

Most of the cases brought in Michigan's Territorial Court arose from failed business transactions and matters related to transfers of real estate. A majority of the relatively few criminal cases dealt with postal theft, smuggling, and other nonviolent transgressions. However, three of the court's most remembered cases involved homicides and capital sentences carried out under the law of the territory or state of Michigan.[42] The defendants in two of those cases were Indians who in 1821 were hanged for having each killed a white man in separate incidents. The third was a white tavern keeper who killed his wife and was hanged in 1830.

On May 11, 1821, Dr. William S. Madison, an army surgeon assigned to the Third U.S. Infantry Regiment stationed at Green Bay, then part of the Michigan Territory, left that post on horseback with an escort of three soldiers to travel to Kentucky where his wife had recently given birth. The next day, shortly after the group crossed the Manitowoc River, they encountered Katakah, a Chippewa, standing near the trail. Although one of the soldiers, Elijah McCray, warned Dr. Madison that Katakah was held in low repute by other members of his tribe, Madison allowed him to join the group. A few miles later, they came to a cedar swamp, through which Katakah carried Dr. Madison's saddlebags, and then two deep ravines. The soldiers at the head of the column were descending the second ravine when they heard a shot and, looking back, saw Dr. Madison fall from his horse with a gunshot in his back. As Katakah ran into the woods, Dr. Madison shouted, "I have been shot by that Indian." Dr. Madison lived for two days, dying on Monday, May 14, 1821. Some days later, Katakah was arrested and brought to Green Bay where he gave a statement to Robert Irwin, Jr., justice of the peace, in which he admitted shooting Dr. Madison: "After traveling a short distance with the Doct[or] and his party, he concluded that he would kill one of the party and the Doct[or] happening at the time he then said Katakah formed the resolution to fall in the rear of the other whites, he leveled his gun, fired and discharged its contents, consisting of duck shot, into the Doct[or's] back somewhere he supposes between the shoulders."[43] One of Katakah's court-appointed attorneys, James Doty, later reported that Katakah told him that he shot Dr. Madison just "to see how *pretty* he would fall off the horse."[44]

At that time, Green Bay was part of the Territory of Michigan, in which the sole court with jurisdiction over all capital offenses, whether based on territorial or federal law, was the Supreme Court of the Territory of Michigan. With rare exceptions, the judges of the Supreme Court refused to sit anywhere except Detroit, where they held court for only one term each autumn.[45] Therefore, although there was a territorial Circuit Court that sat at Green Bay, Justice of the Peace Irwin sent Katakah and the witnesses to Detroit for trial. When he arrived in Detroit, Katakah was remanded to the Wayne County jail with another Indian awaiting trial for murder. Kewabishkim, a member of the Menominee Nation, had been arrested for the September 1820 murder of trapper Charles Ulrick, also in Green Bay.

So, when Judges Woodward, Griffin, and Witherell convened in Detroit's council house on September 17, 1821, for the court's annual term, they had two Indians in custody awaiting murder trials. There was, however, a question about which murder law, federal or territorial, should apply for each, a distinction that the judges found troubling. After some discussion, they decided that Kewabishkim was subject to territorial law because Ulrick had been killed on land that had been ceded to the United States under a treaty with a tribe and that Congress had added to the Michigan Territory. Katakah, on the other hand, was charged with shooting Dr. Madison on land that, although also within the boundaries of the Michigan Territory, was still owned by a tribe and not subject to the criminal laws of the territory. Instead, Madison's death came under an 1817 federal statute punishing capital crimes committed by Indians on non-Indians "within the United States, and within any town, district, or territory, belonging to any nation or nations, tribe or tribes, of Indians."[46] The Supreme Court decided that different laws required a separate trial for each defendant, with the court sitting as a Territorial Court in one trial and as a federal court in the other. However, the court also decided that the same grand jurors would consider indictments in both cases.[47]

On September 19, 1821, the court appointed attorney and future territorial judge James Duane Doty to represent Katakah and four attorneys—George Alexander O'Keeffe, Benjamin Franklin Hawkins Witherell (Judge Witherell's son), John L. Leib, and Spencer Coleman—to represent Kewabishkim. Charles Larned, Attorney General for the territory, prosecuted both cases, assisted by Solomon Sibley. The court also appointed people to translate the court proceedings, from English to French to Menominee for Kewabishkim, and from English to Chippewa for Katakah. However, the language skills of those translators were doubtful.

The trial of Kewabishkim was held on September 24, 1821, with all three Supreme Court judges presiding, as required by territorial law. The trial took less than a day from jury selection to a verdict of guilty of murder. Three or four witnesses testified for the prosecution and none, it seems, for the defense. Katakah's trial took place on October 2 and, although held under federal law, followed the same pattern of a short trial followed by the jury quickly returning a guilty verdict. Neither guilty verdict was a surprise because both of the defendants had admitted to the killings before trial. According to accounts in Detroit's only newspaper, the *Detroit Gazette*, the defense attorneys in both cases raised every jurisdictional and procedural objection they could, but the attorneys' objections were overruled.[48]

The court sentenced both defendants to be hanged on December 27, 1821, and both Katakah and Kewabishkim were hanged in Detroit as scheduled. The local militia regiment and federal troops provided security and an appearance of ceremonial formality. A large audience from Detroit and throughout southeastern Michigan gathered, some of the settlers walking for days to attend what they viewed as one of their few available and entertaining diversions. According to an eyewitness account in the *Detroit Gazette*, the defendants were "perfectly collected" throughout the proceedings. They approached the gallows and climbed its thirteen steps "in a manner peculiarly firm," asked the translators to apologize to the crowd, shook hands, and then "they launched into eternity."[49]

The Territorial Supreme Court after Woodward

Judges Woodward and Griffin continued in office until 1824. Their original appointments did not mention that their term of office had any limit, and they may have assumed that they were appointed for life, like judges of the U.S. District Courts.[50] However, in March 1823 Congress passed a law imposing a four-year term on Michigan's territorial judges, effective February 1, 1824.[51] Michiganders convinced President Monroe not to reappoint either Woodward or Griffin. The President did appoint Woodward to a U.S. District Court in Florida, where he died in 1827. Griffin anticipated Monroe, left town in the fall of 1823, and resettled in Philadelphia where he remained, still dissatisfied, until his death in 1849.[52] In their place, President Monroe appointed veteran Detroit attorneys John Hunt and Solomon Sibley.[53]

John Hunt left the territory in late 1826 and died in New York state in 1827. Until Hunt, all of Michigan's Supreme Court judges had been appointed by Jeffersonian presidents. However, the elections of 1824 proved to be a short-lived Whig landslide, and John Quincy Adams, a Whig like his father, was elected President. He replaced Judge Hunt with Whig Henry C. Chipman, a Detroit attorney and publisher of the local Whig newspaper.[54] In 1828, faced with the possibility that President Monroe might not reappoint him and worn out by his judicial duties, Judge Witherell switched offices with territorial secretary William Woodbridge, a Whig, who was tired of his boring job.[55]

The brief era of Whig ascendancy ended in 1828 when Democratic candidate Andrew Jackson won the presidency. Jackson believed in cementing the loyalty of the federal government by using the spoils system to replace Whig officeholders across the nation. The terms of the judges of Michigan's Supreme Court ended on February 1, 1832, and Jackson replaced Michigan's two Whig Supreme Court judges, Woodbridge and Chipman, with Democrats George Morell and Ross Wilkins.[56] Solomon Sibley, whose political affiliation was always ambiguous, somehow managed to avoid the political rumbles on and off the court, and he remained on the bench until the court ceased operations in anticipation of statehood on July 1, 1836.

George Morell (1786–1845) was an attorney, judge, and state assemblyman in New York before President Jackson appointed him as a territorial judge in Michigan. After his service on Michigan's Territorial Supreme Court, he was appointed to be the first justice of the Supreme Court of the State of Michigan. He later was the latter court's Chief Judge. He left the state Supreme

Judge Ross Wilkins

Court in 1843. Ross Wilkins stayed on the Territorial Court until it ceased operation. In 1837, Wilkins became Michigan's first U.S. District Judge; his biography is in chapter two.

Capital Punishment in the Territory of Michigan, 1830

Judges Woodbridge, Sibley, and Chipman presided over what was one of the most memorable trials of the territorial era: the 1830 murder prosecution of Stephen G. Simmons for killing his wife, Levana Simmons.[57] Stephen Simmons was a tall, burly fifty-year-old who had found no success as a soldier or farmer and who had emigrated from New York state to Michigan in 1825. He bought a tavern in what is now the city of Wayne, Michigan, on the Sauk Trail, now Ford Road, the main emigrant settler route from Detroit to the west. Simmons and his wife were no more successful as tavern keepers, largely because they were both alcoholics and violent bullies. In June 1830, Stephen Simmons returned home after winning a civil trial before Judges Woodbridge and Chipman, a victory he celebrated by getting drunk. While drunk, he accused Levana of having an affair with a stagecoach driver whose route brought him to the tavern frequently. When Levana denied Stephen's accusation, he proceeded to beat her to death with his fists.

The Simmonses' adult children arrested their father and took him and the body of their mother in a cart to Detroit. The children and some tavern guests testified in front of a grand jury, which issued an indictment charging Stephen with murder. The trial began in the territorial capitol building in Detroit on July 6, 1830. Benjamin F. H. Witherell prosecuted and George A. O'Keeffe, Witherell's cocounsel in defending Kewabishkim nine years earlier, defended. As in his defense of the Menominee, O'Keeffe's tactical options were limited. Simmons had no real defense on the facts: his children and the tavern guests would establish that he had killed Levana. The best O'Keeffe could hope for was a verdict of manslaughter, which might mean a sentence of one or two years in jail. If the jury found his client guilty of murder, the only legal sentence was death by hanging.

O'Keeffe began carrying out his plan during jury selection. In most cases tried in Detroit, jury selection took only an hour or so. O'Keeffe knew that the first panels of prospective jurors would be filled with the town's establishment, leading businessmen, politicians, and even law enforcement officers, ready to convict and having no sympathy for a country brawler and drunk. If O'Keeffe could force the sheriff to pull in more jury panels, though, he might be able to fill the jury box with farmers and other rough-hewn men from the country who just might go for manslaughter. So, using his peremptory challenges and challenges for cause, O'Keeffe forced the court to take three days and 128 jury candidates to seat twelve jurors. After this ploy, though, the trial took just one day and a half, and the jury deliberated for just a few hours before finding Stephen guilty of murder.

Stephen Simmons was hanged in front of the county jail, where the downtown Detroit Public Library now sits, on Friday, September 24, 1830. As had been the case in 1821, the hanging was a major attraction, and some two thousand people camped out in the nearby fields and then filled the stands erected by the city. A band played as the crowd waited, and then Stephen marched like a soldier out of the jail and up the stairs of the gallows in a new suit and boots. Minutes later, he died in the last execution under the law of Michigan in Detroit.[58] Seventeen years later, the Michigan legislature abolished capital punishment for murder.

The Territory of Michigan Becomes the State of Michigan

The Northwest Ordinance provided that a territory was eligible to seek statehood when it achieved a population of sixty thousand residents. The drafters of the ordinance probably did not imagine that a territory might remain in that lesser status for more than thirty years, but that was the case for Michigan. Ohio joined the Union in 1802, just two years after becoming a territory, Indiana waited seven years after reaching its present borders, and Illinois waited nine years. But the population of the Michigan Territory lagged behind those of its neighbors. This was in part due to the ease with which settlers could reach those other territories by the Ohio River compared to the difficulty of traveling to Michigan by land. The other impediment was another provision of the ordinance mandating that settlers could only buy land in the Northwest Territory from the United States and that the United States could obtain title to that land only by entering into treaties with Indian tribes. Although the 1795 Greenville Treaty opened most of southern Ohio to settlement, in Michigan the United States received basically only Detroit and Mackinac Island. The Detroit Treaty of 1807 allowed sales by the United States in southeastern Michigan, but the War of 1812 delayed any substantial settlement. Finally, from 1819 to 1821, with two treaties,[59] the United States purchased the rest of the southern Lower Peninsula and the Saginaw River basin as far west as what is now Lansing. However, most of the northwestern Lower Peninsula and all of the Upper Peninsula were not ceded to the United States, and thus were not available for settlement, until the Washington and Cedar Point treaties of 1836 and the La Pointe Treaty of 1842.

The lack of treaties was just one obstacle to the growth of Michigan's population. Another was months of difficult travel from the eastern states to Michigan. That obstacle was removed by two technological innovations of the mid-1820s, the Erie Canal and the steamboat, which ignited the great wave of Yankee immigration from New England and western New York state that transformed Michigan. Beginning in 1820, Michigan's population soared as hundreds of thousands of migrants headed west. Either from New England or from the "second New England" of western New York state,[60] they were on their way to settle and farm the southern half of Michigan's Lower Peninsula, which came to be called Yankeeland. Between 1820 and 1860, they added 740,000 people to Michigan's population, becoming a majority in every

Michigan county south of Saginaw as well as in Wisconsin, which was part of the Michigan Territory until 1836.

Michigan first applied for statehood in 1833, when its population was only about forty thousand, but growing. A census taken in 1835 found a population of eighty-five thousand, and so in May 1835 a convention of ninety-one elected delegates gathered in Detroit to draft a constitution for a state to consist of the Lower Peninsula and the eastern quarter of the Upper Peninsula. They completed the document in forty-five days, and in October the electorate overwhelmingly adopted it and elected a state governor and legislature. The convention stipulated that statehood must include the Toledo strip and the mouth of the Maumee River. The legislature met in November 1835 and then adjourned to see what Congress would do. On June 15, 1836, Congress called Michigan's bluff by ratifying the proposed constitution and declaring Michigan "to be one of the United States of America," but effective only when and if a new convention met and voted to accept Ohio's version of the border location, known as the Harris Line for its surveyor.[61]

As the weeks and months passed, Michiganders could look forward with some hope to statehood but also with considerable resentment toward Ohio and apprehension about how long they still had to wait. In September 1836, the legislature convened a ratification convention in Ann Arbor, but the delegates refused to give up the Toledo Strip. The political fight and the cost of keeping the militia in arms to protect against any armed incursion from Ohio were straining Michigan's finances to the limit, and several leading citizens organized a second convention in Ann Arbor in December 1836, without the consent of the legislature. Those delegates passed a resolution accepting the federal government's terms, and Congress formally admitted Michigan into the Union as the twenty-sixth state on January 26, 1837.[62]

CHAPTER 2

The U.S. District Court for the District of Michigan, 1836 to 1863

The Birth and Growth of the Courts of the United States, before 1836

A T THE BEGINNING OF the twenty-first century, Americans take for granted the existence of separate judicial systems, one for each state and one for the federal government, but few other nations with federal systems of government have federal trial courts. For Americans living during the first years of the nation, it was not a given that the federal government would have its own courts or that there would be parallel state and federal judiciaries. Logically, the federal government could have asserted authority over all courts, but that option was a political impossibility that was never under serious consideration. Alternatively, the enforcement of federal laws and protection of the federal government's interests could have been delegated entirely to the courts established by the states. That was, in fact, the solution in place from 1781 until 1789 under our first national compact, the Articles of Confederation, which provided for neither a federal supreme court nor federal trial courts. With a few specific exceptions, disputes involving the Articles or federal laws were resolved by state and local courts.[1] To its supporters, that system not only avoided the expense of a federal court system, it also insured that federal laws would be interpreted and executed by local judges instead of by officials of a distant and, they feared, tyrannical federal government.

Just a few years' experience proved that the Articles were unsatisfactory, as a whole and specifically regarding courts. The Articles relied on state officers to enforce decisions under federal law, both decisions by state courts and by the few federal tribunals, but too often those state officials did not.[2] Consequently, in 1789 delegates from every state gathered in Philadelphia to reform or replace the Articles of Confederation. Improvement of the judicial system was a source of debate among the delegates. A majority of states agreed on the necessity for a federal court of last resort to provide uniform interpretations of federal law, but a proposal to create a system of "inferior" courts to try cases involving federal laws or cases among citizens of different states (cases based on what is now called "diversity jurisdiction") divided the convention.

Some delegates, representing commercial and mercantile interests, noted the refusal of state courts to enforce contracts and collect debts during the economic panics that plagued the new nation from 1785 until 1797. They argued that only federal trial courts, immune to local pressure, could ensure national unity and protect the interests of out-of-state litigants. Their opponents were more concerned about federal tyranny than unity. George Mason of Virginia spoke for many Americans when he complained that a federal judicial system would "absorb and destroy the judiciaries of the several states, thereby rendering laws as tedious, intricate, and expensive, and justice as unattainable, by a great part of the community, as in England; and enabling the rich to oppress and ruin the poor."[3]

Elbridge Gerry, one of the signers of both the Declaration of Independence and the Articles of Confederation, refused to sign the Constitution that emerged from the convention because it did not include a bill of rights and because of his belief "that the judicial department will be oppressive."[4] The provisions on a federal judiciary that emerged from the convention in Article III of the Constitution did mandate a federal Supreme Court, but they did not create a federal court system. Instead, the convention delegates passed the buck to Congress by authorizing the legislative branch to decide whether and when to create federal "inferior courts."[5]

The first Congress convened under the Constitution accepted the drafters' invitation. On September 24, 1789, after months of sometimes bitter debate, it passed a law, now titled the Judiciary Act of 1789,[6] which established a federal judiciary still recognizable in the federal courts of the twenty-first century. This judiciary act divided the United States into thirteen judicial districts, one for each of the states that had ratified the Constitution, except that Massachusetts and Virginia were each assigned a second district (the districts of Maine and Kentucky), which included remote areas that Congress assumed would eventually become states. When North Carolina and Rhode Island finally ratified the Constitution (in November 1789 and May 1790, respectively), Congress added two new judicial districts[7] and did so again as each new state joined the Union. The Judiciary Act of 1789 created, for each district, "a court called a District Court," to consist of one judge "to be called a District Judge," who would "reside in the district for which he is appointed" and hold four District Court terms each year.

Thus, the District Judges were the permanent representatives of the federal judiciary in their districts, and they were the most visible evidence of the entire federal government in many districts. However, the Judiciary Act of 1789 also provided for another federal court, which brought the Justices of the U.S. Supreme Court to the districts every year. The Act grouped the District Courts, except those of Maine and Kentucky, into three circuits and provided for a Circuit Court to be held twice annually in each district, presided over by the District Judge and two Justices of the U.S. Supreme Court, known in this context as Circuit Justices. Although Congress gradually relieved the Circuit Justices of parts of that burden, the basic concept of a Justice of the Supreme Court spending a substantial portion of his life riding circuit from one district to another continued until the creation of the U.S. Circuit Courts of Appeal in 1891, although Justices only rarely rode circuit after the Civil War. From the beginning, the Justices resented attending Circuit Courts, which required them to complete thousands of miles of travel each year over terrible roads, where there were any roads at all.[8]

Besides creating the Supreme Court and authorizing inferior courts, Article III also affords the Justices and Judges of those courts, known as Article III Judges, a degree of job security unknown to most of the rest of the populace, providing the federal judiciary with a shield against political influence and popular pressure. Article III Judges are appointed, like many other federal officeholders, after being nominated by the President and confirmed by the Senate.[9] But unlike other federal officers, they hold their offices during good behavior, meaning, in practice, for life unless impeached by the House and convicted by the Senate for seriously criminal acts ("treason, bribery, and other high crimes and misdemeanors"). As a further shield from interference from Congress, Article III also guarantees that the pay of Article III Judges "shall not be diminished during their Continuance in Office."[10]

Article III defines "the judicial power of the United States," the outer limits of the types of cases which federal courts have the power (or "subject-matter jurisdiction") to entertain. The judicial power of the United States includes "all cases, in law and equity, arising under this Constitution, the

Laws of the United States, and Treaties," cases involving foreign diplomats, cases of admiralty and maritime law, cases involving the United States or between two or more states, what we now call diversity jurisdiction, cases between citizens of different states or between a state and citizens of another state or country, and citizens of the same state claiming land under grants issued by different states.

From the beginning, though, Congress has assumed that, as the creator of the inferior courts, it has the power to withhold some parts of that jurisdiction from them, although not from the Supreme Court. The choices Congress made in allocating this judicial power between the Circuit and District Courts evidence the compromises needed to pass the act. The District Courts, which were held by a single District Judge, received cases that were either minor (petty crimes against the United States, "cases where no other punishment than whipping, not to exceed thirty stripes, a fine not exceeding one hundred dollars, or a term of imprisonment not exceeding six months is to be inflicted") or clearly national in interest (admiralty cases, seizures of property by the United States, suits against foreign diplomats). The Circuit Courts, where the presence of Supreme Court Justices on the bench added authority to the decisions and moderated any tendency toward excess by a single judge, were allocated all other violations of federal criminal laws. In other areas, Congress provided for federal courts to share jurisdiction with state courts. For example, District Courts had concurrent jurisdiction over suits at common law in which the United States was a plaintiff and the amount in controversy exceeded $100. By implication, the federal government could bring smaller cases only in state courts likely to be closer to the defendant's home. However, for diversity cases and for cases brought by the United States as plaintiff, where the amount in controversy exceeded $500, the Circuit Courts had concurrent jurisdiction.

The substantial piece of the judicial power of the United States that Congress did *not* grant to either the Circuit or District Courts is further evidence of the compromises necessary in 1789 to pass the first judiciary act. It was not until 1875 that the federal trial courts were granted jurisdiction over the first types of cases listed in Article III: "all Cases, in Law and Equity, arising under this Constitution [and] the Laws of the United States." So, unless there was some other basis for asserting jurisdiction, such as diversity of citizenship or a specific grant of jurisdiction in a statute, the inferior federal courts were excluded from enforcing or interpreting the Constitution and the laws passed by Congress. Instead, those tasks were performed by state courts.

In March 1875, Congress finally gave the Circuit Courts full jurisdiction over cases arising under the Constitution or other federal laws.[11] When the Circuit Courts were dissolved on January 1, 1912, this jurisdiction passed to the District Courts. Today, general federal question jurisdiction constitutes a large and arguably the most important part of a District Court's docket.

The District Judge's Staff

Besides creating the inferior courts and their judges, the Judiciary Act of 1789 provided each District Court with a set of court officers to assist the judges in carrying out their judicial business. These officers included a clerk of the court, a marshal, and commissioners. The Act also provided for a District Attorney to represent the United States, but District Attorneys were not considered part of the judicial staff. They are discussed in chapter ten.

The Clerk of the Court

The Act authorized each District Judge to appoint a clerk to "enter and record all the orders, decrees, judgments, and proceedings" of the District and Circuit Courts and to summon jurors.[12] Congress was not more specific about the clerk's duties, but the position was well known in colonial America, and most of the first federal clerks were borrowed from local courts, so they knew how to go about their business. The federal clerk became the judge's factotum, doing whatever had to be done to keep the court running, from issuing arrest warrants to fixing the courthouse roof.[13] Until 1919, federal court clerks were compensated by the fees paid by litigants for the clerk's services[14] and by a per diem stipend and reimbursement for expenses if the court traveled.[15] The amount a clerk earned, therefore, depended on the amount of business that particular court attracted. Originally, the clerk was responsible for both the District and Circuit Courts, but, in 1839, Congress directed the judges of the Circuit Court (i.e., the District Judge and the Circuit Justice) to appoint a separate clerk for the Circuit Court,[16] although often the same person held both clerkships until the district's judicial business generated enough in fees, per diem, and travel expenses to support two clerks and their families. If a court's business grew sufficiently, a federal clerk could employ one or more deputies, but the clerk had to pay them from his fee income, so that most clerks kept deputies to a minimum or hired their children or their relatives as deputy clerks.

The U.S. Marshal

The 1789 Act also provided that "a Marshal shall be appointed in and for each district for the term of four years, but shall be removable from office at pleasure, whose duty it shall be to attend the District and Circuit Courts when sitting therein. . . . And to execute throughout the district, all legal precepts [orders, writs, warrants, attachments, etc.] directed to him and issued under the authority of the United States."[17] Although the Act did not specify who was to appoint the Marshal, Presidents seized that opportunity for political patronage. Besides providing security for the court, Marshals also paid the court's expenses, including "fuel, candles, and other contingencies," the fees and traveling expenses of witnesses, jurors, District Attorneys, and clerks of court, and the funds paid for housing federal prisoners in local jails and for the salaries of the bailiffs and court criers and for renting space for courtrooms.[18] Marshals were paid through the fees they earned for serving court papers, executing arrest warrants, and summoning jurors.

The Court Crier

The Act did not authorize employment of a court crier, but the Supreme Court quickly appointed one for itself. In 1799, Congress gave in and required District and Circuit Courts to appoint a crier, although the statute was silent as to a crier's duties.[19] Like federal clerks, criers in federal courts usually had experience in state courts and performed the same duties in the federal courts, "crying" any vocal announcement or direction needed and keeping order during court sessions.

Circuit Court Commissioners

In addition to the administrative assistance of the clerk of the court, the federal trial courts have always had quasi-judicial officers who relieved them of minor yet necessary chores. The 1789 Act authorized state magistrates or justices of the peace to arrest offenders against federal laws and to then imprison or release them on bail.[20] However, events like the Whiskey Rebellion of 1791 demonstrated that court officials who were elected and paid locally could not always be relied on to enforce unpopular federal laws. So, in 1793 Congress authorized the Circuit Courts (i.e., the District Judge and one or two

Supreme Court Justices) to appoint "discreet persons learned in the law . . . where, from the extent of the district, and remoteness of its parts from the usual residence of any of the above named officers, such provision shall, in the opinion of the court, be necessary."[21]

The initial authority of such "discreet persons" was merely to set bail for defendants charged with violating federal criminal laws. In 1812, Congress authorized those as yet untitled officers to take affidavits and acknowledgments of bail in civil cases.[22] In 1817, Congress, for the first time, gave those "discreet persons" a title, "commissioners," and authorized them to take the depositions of witnesses who were unable to appear in federal court.[23] Over the nineteenth century, Congress continued to add to the duties of the Commissioners, including adjusting seamen's wage disputes, enforcing the rights of slave masters under the Fugitive Slave Act of 1850, enforcing the rights of former slaves under the Civil Rights Act of 1866, and detaining and deporting illegal Chinese immigrants under the Chinese Exclusion Acts.

Masters in Chancery

Although the office was not provided for by statute, most federal District Courts appointed one or more masters in chancery to assist the judge by taking testimony in civil cases that did not require a jury and then making a report and recommendation to the judge. In the nineteenth and early twentieth centuries, masters in chancery were not employed directly by the court but instead were experienced private practitioners who were compensated by fees paid by the parties.

The District of Michigan and Its Only U.S. District Judge, Ross Wilkins

While Congress waited for Michigan to decide whether to accept the Harris Line, it did establish the basis for federal judicial power in the putative state. On July 1, 1836, Congress created the District of Michigan and, on the next day, President Jackson nominated and the Senate confirmed territorial judge Ross Wilkins as the first U.S. District Judge for the District of Michigan, although the district and the judicial appointment were not to take effect until Michigan became a state in January 1837.[24]

Judge Wilkins was born on February 19, 1799, in Pittsburgh, Pennsylvania, to Catherine (Stevenson) Wilkins and John Wilkins, Jr. After Judge Wilkins graduated from Dickinson College (AB, 1816), he returned to Pittsburgh to read law and was admitted to the Allegheny County bar. In 1821, he was elected to a two-year term as Pittsburgh's Prosecuting Attorney and opened a private practice that he continued until President Jackson appointed him to Michigan's Territorial Supreme Court in 1832. In 1829 and 1830, he was a member of Pennsylvania's House of Representatives.

Ross Wilkins was an easy choice for President Jackson's appointment to the District of Michigan for many reasons. First, Jackson had appointed him to Michigan's Territorial Supreme Court just four years earlier, so he was already a Michigan resident and judge. He was also known as a fervent supporter of both Jackson and the President's Republican-Democratic (later Democratic) Party. His father, John Wilkins, Jr., a veteran of the Revolution, had served as the Quartermaster General of the U.S. Army from 1796 to 1802, and his uncle, William Wilkins, was a prominent Republican-Democrat who had himself been a U.S. District Judge as well as a U.S. Senator, and who had recently been appointed by President Jackson as U.S. minister to Russia. William Wilkins would later serve as Secretary of War for President John Tyler.[25] Other strong support for Ross Wilkins's appointment as District Judge came from John Maugeridge Snowden, a Pittsburgh publisher and Jackson confidant who wrote to the President in November 1835 praising Judge Wilkins and reminding him of the Wilkins family's service to the party.[26]

Judge Wilkins did have another judicial option in 1836. On July 12, 1836, ten days after the Senate confirmed his appointment to the federal bench, he declined an offer from Michigan Governor Stevens T. Mason to be appointed to the new state Supreme Court.[27] The state position had serious disadvantages. The annual salary of a state justice, $1,500 per year,[28] was no more than he was to receive as a federal District Judge,[29] and he would have faced reelection every seven years.[30] Additionally, the legislature had passed a law dividing the state into three judicial circuits and requiring that one justice live in each of Detroit, Monroe, and Pontiac, with the Detroit justice also required to attend court in the Upper Peninsula.[31] It is not surprising that Wilkins chose a federal District Judge's lifetime tenure and the District of Michigan's single venue.

Although Ross Wilkins's family was wealthy, he was a firm opponent of wealth and privilege. Writing to William Seward in 1851, he remembered that: "In early life I became a politician from a conviction that the monied corporate power of the Bank of the United States was oppressive to the masses and perilous to civil liberty."[32] In his later years he warned that corporations, particularly railroads, posed the same menace. In addition to his other activities, Judge Wilkins was a Methodist lay preacher and a confirmed opponent of alcohol.[33]

In 1835, U.S. Attorney George C. Bates described the judge as:

About five feet ten inches in height, he was well proportioned, lithe and graceful, with fine features, long hair [and beard] and expressive eyes, magnificent teeth and a facial resemblance to Lord Byron and was one of the handsomest men of his day. His motions and intellect were both quick, and his reasoning was clear and lucid. While reading and studying the papers and evidence in the cases before him he was always moving restlessly in his chair, and when he was finished, he would rise and, going to the back of the courtroom, fill and light his long pipe and smoked as he walked around, always paying the keenest attention to the proceedings.[34]

Bates also noted that Judge Wilkins had a "splendid, majestic head, an eye like Mars, full of brilliancy, and as restless as the eagle's."[35] During his early days on the bench, on winter days when heating in his courtroom was not adequate, Judge Wilkins was known to bring his massive Newfoundland dog to lie at his feet and keep him warm. At the time of Wilkins's retirement from the federal court in 1870, when he was seventy-one years old, another Detroit lawyer described Wilkins as "[f]rank and impulsive, without cautious and calculating policy," and praised "the honesty of his heart and the sincerity of his convictions."[36] As for his approach to the law, one commentator described him as a jurist rather than a casuist, a believer in rules and laws, applied without regard to the facts or the circumstances.[37]

Judge Wilkins worried constantly about his finances. His federal salary remained insufficient throughout his tenure on the bench.[38] Although his annual salary would increase in steps to a peak of $3,500 in 1867, three years before he retired,[39] finding enough money to support his large extended family, including children, grandchildren, and servants,[40] was Judge Wilkins's chief concern throughout his tenure as District Judge, and his papers indicate a steady flow of pleas to his family and friends for loans.

Judge Wilkins's First District Court Staff
Clerk of the District Court John Winder

Judge Wilkins did not have to look far to find his clerk of the District Court. During the thirteen years since his arrival in Michigan, John Winder had made himself indispensable as clerk of the Supreme Court of the Territory of Michigan, Wayne County, and the Wayne County Circuit Court, Detroit's Board of Aldermen, and most other agencies of government in the territory. Winder was born in Uniontown, Pennsylvania, in 1804. He moved to Detroit in 1824, then a frontier village of about 1,500 residents, at the suggestion of the Michigan Territory's U.S. Marshal, Thomas Rowland, a friend of his father, to become Wayne County clerk. Winder was appointed clerk of the Territorial Supreme Court in 1826, a post he continued to hold until 1836 when he became clerk for Judge Wilkins. From 1837 to 1839, his appointment as clerk of the District Court also made him responsible for the Circuit Court, and when Congress authorized a Circuit Court clerk in 1839,[41] Wilkins and Circuit Justice John McLean appointed him to that position as well, a common practice then.[42] He kept both clerkships until 1848, and he served as clerk of one or both of the federal courts until he followed Judge Wilkins into retirement in April 1870.

U.S. Marshal Conrad ten Eyck

Accompanying Judge Wilkins's commission as District Judge was another presidential commission appointing Conrad ten Eyck as the District's U.S. Marshal.[43] "Coon" ten Eyck was, in fact, Michigan's fourth U.S. Marshal, after Thomas Rowland, John L. Leib, and Peter Desnoyers, who had served in the position while Michigan was a territory. Ten Eyck, born in Albany, New York, in 1782, emigrated to Detroit in 1801 and opened a store and later a tavern.[44] Active in politics, he served as Wayne County treasurer from 1817 to 1825, and he was a delegate to the state constitutional convention in 1835. His term as U.S. Marshal ended in March 1841 when Whig President William Henry Harrison was inaugurated. Conrad ten Eyck died on August 21, 1847.

The First Sessions of the District Court for the District of Michigan

For most of the nineteenth century, American courts, federal and state, were not in session continuously throughout the year. Instead, courts sat in "terms," which began on a certain date, usually set by the appropriate legislature, and ran until the judges adjourned court. Depending on the business of the court, a term might last for days or months. Congress directed the District Court for the District of Michigan to hold two regular terms each year, beginning on the first Mondays of May and October,[45] but Judge Wilkins was not about to wait three months after he received his commission to open his new court. Federal judges had the power to hold "special terms" at any time as circumstances required, so he scheduled a special term of the District Court to begin on Thursday, February 23, 1837. Before that could take place, though, he and ten Eyck had to find an appropriate space in which to hold court because, despite citizen petitions to Congress in 1836 praying for a federal "court-house and penitentiary in Detroit," there had been no response.[46] As District Judge Alfred Conkling of the Northern District of New York pointed out in 1831, the federal courts relied "upon the liberality of the local governments for the accommodation of the federal courts. . . . The Circuit and District Courts are generally held in public buildings belonging to the state, county or city where they sit, with the consent, either express or implied, of the proprietors," although the judge thought that, in the absence of an offer of free space, "it would doubtless be competent for the Marshal, under the direction of the court, to provide a suitable room at the expense of the United States."[47]

For his first session, Judge Wilkins was allowed to use Detroit's handsome new City Hall, located in the middle of what is now Cadillac Square.[48] This two-story brick, Greek Revival–style structure was fifty feet wide by one hundred feet long, topped by an octagonal belfry, which, interestingly enough, lacked a bell.[49] The spacious lower floor was sixteen feet high, while the total height from base to cornice was thirty-six feet. This stately building, designed by Alpheus White, a local architect who had trained in New Orleans, stood out in a town full of modest, single-story wooden construction. The project began in December 1833 as a new municipal market on the northern outskirts of town. By February 1835, it had evolved into "the new market and Council House," with space on the upper floor for Detroit's Common Council. By the time of the building's official inauguration, on November 18, 1835, it was officially known as the City Hall, although the lower floor was given over to the town's butchers. In October 1835, the Common Council allowed the Territorial Courts, which had been evicted from the territorial capitol by the new legislature, to use the City Hall's upper floor.[50] The Territorial Courts remained at City Hall until their last sessions in June 1836, and their state successors continued on there for a time.[51]

The first business of the District Court's first session was swearing in John Winder as clerk of the court and John Gibson as court crier. After Winder took his oath of office and posted a bond "for the faithful performance of the duties of his office," he read aloud Judge Wilkins's commission as well as those of District Attorney Goodwin and Marshal ten Eyck, and then both Goodwin and ten Eyck took their oaths of office. Wilkins directed Gibson to call the court's first case, a customs "libel," *The United States of America v. One piece ingrain carpeting and 13 yards grey cloth.* Goodwin made his appearance for the United States. After no one appeared to claim the goods, Judge Wilkins ordered that notice of the matter be posted in a Detroit newspaper, and he adjourned the matter to March 15. After five other cases were dealt with similarly, Winder swore in the first nine members of the Bar of the court: Daniel Goodwin, George E. Hand, Charles Cleland, Samuel Pitts, Henry N. Walker, Henry T. Backus, William Hale, Samuel G. Watson, and Asher B. Bates. The court adopted its first set of thirty-nine rules, ordered the naturalization of an immigrant, John McReynolds, and adjourned until March 15.[52] On that day, the court made its first ruling. As no one had appeared to claim the ingrain carpet, and "it appearing the goods were illegally imported from Upper Canada," Judge Wilkins ordered the carpet forfeited to the United States. He then made the same ruling as to a case involving the smuggling of a bay horse and shortly thereafter adjourned the special term.

At 10 a.m. on May 1, 1837, the first Monday in May, Crier Gibson called the District Court to order on the second floor of the City Hall for its first regular term. In all, the District Court was open for twenty-four days in 1837, although some days were very short, and on at least one day, November 9, the court convened but conducted no business at all.[53]

The First Sessions of the Circuit Court

The law creating the District of Michigan gave its District Judge "the same jurisdiction and powers which were by law given to the judge of the Kentucky district" by the Judiciary Act of 1789. That meant that Judge Wilkins was allowed to hold Circuit Court alone, and during the special term and the first few sessions of the regular term, he handled both District Court and Circuit Court cases. However, a week after the first special session in Detroit, Congress deleted that provision and assigned the District of Michigan to a new seventh judicial circuit.[54] When he learned of the new law during the District

Court's May term, Judge Wilkins had no choice but to open a second docket for Circuit Court cases[55] and to wait for the arrival of the Circuit Justice, John McLean, to hold the Circuit Court's inaugural term.

Circuit Justice John McLean

John McLean was born on March 11, 1785, in Morris County, New Jersey, to Fergus and Sophia Blackford McLean. The family moved to Virginia and Kentucky before settling in Ridgeville, Ohio. He read law and was admitted to the bar in 1807. He also established a Democratic-Republican newspaper in Lebanon, Ohio, and worked in the U.S. land office in Cincinnati. In 1812, he was elected to Congress as a Democratic-Republican and was reelected in 1814, but he left before the end of his term because he had been elected to the Ohio Supreme Court. In 1822, he returned to Washington when President James Monroe appointed him commissioner of the general land office and then Postmaster General. President Andrew Jackson nominated McLean to the U.S. Supreme Court on March 6, 1829, to the seat of Justice Robert Trimble, who had died.

After his appointment to the U.S. Supreme Court, McLean began to display both his ambition for the presidency and his independence. He associated himself with every party on the political spectrum, always moving further away from his Democratic-Republican beginnings. Although he owed his seat on the Court to Jackson, he split with the President over the treatment of Indians and slavery, flirted with the anti-Masons, Whigs, and Free-Soilers, and finally joined the Republican Party. Even as he sat on the Supreme Court, he often sought the presidential nomination of each of those parties, always unsuccessfully. Justice McLean's most famous opinion, his fierce dissent in *Dred Scott v. Sandford*,[56] increased his popularity nationally among abolitionists, so much so that a columnist for the *New York Times*, writing in April 1860, considered him to be the front-runner for the Republican presidential nomination.[57] Abraham Lincoln, not even mentioned in that *Times* article, won the nomination, of course, but McLean, despite his seventy-five years, received twelve votes at the Republican convention. In addition to his judicial service, Justice McLean is remembered for performing a vital service to the law and to historians by publishing six volumes of Circuit Court opinions, both his and those of the District Judges with whom he presided.[58] He died in Cincinnati on April 4, 1861, just before the beginning of the Civil War.

Justice McLean joined Judge Wilkins on the bench for the Circuit Court's first term on Monday, June 27, 1837. The relative unimportance of the federal courts at that time can be seen from the fact that Detroiters other than litigants and attorneys barely noticed the opening sessions of either court. In a town that organized Lucullan feasts for every public event of note, there is no evidence of any for either court's first term. Although McLean missed the June term in 1838, he did attend the November term that year,[59] and he returned for at least one term each year for the next two decades until 1860 when age and failing health precluded him from traveling.

With the District of Michigan and its courts in place, the business of federal jurisprudence in Michigan was ready to begin in earnest. From small beginnings—only seventy-three civil and criminal cases filed in 1837—the district would grow to almost three hundred cases filed in 1863, the year that it split into Eastern and Western Districts.

CHAPTER 3

The U.S. District Court for the Western District of Michigan, 1863 to 1900

Creating the Western District of Michigan

WITH TWO EXCEPTIONS, the Judiciary Act of 1789, which established the federal courts, created just one federal district and one District Judge for each of the states then in existence. As new states were admitted to the Union, Congress created for each a single district, and the President appointed a single District Judge. In 1814, the volume of work in the District of New York caused Congress to split that district in two, each with its own District Judge. Four years later, Congress did the same for Pennsylvania and in 1819 did so for Virginia. More splits followed, and, by 1862, a total of sixteen of the thirty-four states had more than one district, although three of those states still had only one District Judge.[1]

In 1840, the population of Michigan exceeded 200,000 and was growing at a rate that by 1850 would double the number of residents to 400,000. That population was spread across the state, particularly in the counties of the southern Lower Peninsula. For people in the western counties, attending the federal court of the District of Michigan, which held sessions only in Detroit, was onerous, requiring retention of Detroit attorneys and long journeys and stays in Detroit when cases came to trial.

On December 19, 1845, Michigan Congressman John Smith Chipman from Centreville, St. Joseph County, 150 miles southwest of Detroit, gave official notice that he would introduce a bill "to divide the state of Michigan into two United States judicial districts and the organization of the courts therein."[2] He did not introduce such a bill, but on February 24, 1846, Chipman did submit a petition by the bar of western Michigan "praying for a division of the State, and the organization of federal courts for the western part of said State."[3] However, a month later, on March 27, the House Judiciary Committee reported adversely to the petition, stating that "such a division is inexpedient."[4]

There was no further action in Congress on a second district until February 1857. With the state's population close to doubling again, the Michigan legislature adopted and sent to Congress a joint resolution requesting the division of the District of Michigan into two districts, eastern and western.[5] The resolution noted that Michigan was "fast settling in the north and northwestern portions" of the state, that citizens in such regions "now, and for some time past, have found it inconvenient, expensive, and otherwise onerous, to visit Detroit, where the United States courts for the District of Michigan are alone holden, for the transaction of business in said courts." Therefore, the legislature resolved "that we believe it to be the duty of the Congress of the United States, to divide our State into two districts, respectively embracing such territory as will best promote the interest of our citizens, and that Detroit should be made the term place of the eastern, and Grand Rapids of the western district." However, once again, on April 17, 1858, the House Judiciary Committee reported adversely on the resolution, stating that: "There is no necessity at this time for a division of the state into two judicial districts."[6]

However, just four years later, in 1862, Michigan's congressional delegation began another concerted campaign for legislation granting their state a second District Court with its own judge. The campaign was supported by Michigan's two U.S. senators, Zachariah Chandler and Jacob Howard, who were both close friends and loyal supporters of President Abraham Lincoln, as well as by Michigan's solid Lincoln Republican delegation in the House of Representatives,[7] one of whom, Kent County's Francis W. Kellogg, had raised three volunteer infantry regiments at the outset of the war. The time was ripe for a political reward. Besides, the proponents could point to a strong set of facts. Much of Michigan's population growth was in its western counties such as Kent (30,700 residents in 1860), Kalamazoo (25,000), St. Joseph (21,000), and Van Buren (15,000). At the same time, the amount of shipping on Lake Michigan soared, as did the number of collisions, mariners' wage disputes, and contract claims. Proponents of a western district with its own judge argued that in addition to relieving Judge Wilkins of some of his overloaded district and circuit dockets, the presence of a District Court conveniently close to Lake Michigan would surely divert many admiralty libels that now went to U.S. District Courts in Chicago or Milwaukee instead to the far-off

District Court in Detroit, which had only twenty admiralty libels in all of 1861. Among themselves, proponents smiled at the additional patronage a second district would create, an additional District Judge and staff as well as another U.S. Marshal and U.S. Attorney, plus more cases for western attorneys, particularly those in Grand Rapids, to litigate. The only negative, it seemed, was that it would also require the Sixth Circuit's Circuit Justice to attend one more Circuit Court.

On February 10, 1862, Michigan's entire delegation to the 37th Congress supported House Bill 267, introduced by Representative Kellogg, to split the District of Michigan into eastern and western districts, each with its own judge. The bill passed in the House easily on July 17, but ran into resistance in the Senate, despite being sponsored by the formidable Senator Howard. The Senate Committee on the Judiciary opposed the bill on principle. For more than a decade, the Senate had been bombarded with bills from practically every state with just one district seeking a division, and the Senate committee had opposed them all. Illinois, Missouri, Ohio, and Texas had eventually been successful, but many others had failed. The senators opposing the bill expressed concerns over the cost of funding another judge, set of court officers, district attorney, and courthouse, all of which were naturally part of the attraction for attorneys in western Michigan. Another argument against the bill was that more districts would result in more civil cases based on diversity and thus more decisions that the loser had an absolute right to appeal to an overworked U.S. Supreme Court, which was already two years behind in deciding appeals.

Disappointed in 1862, a year later, on February 17, 1863, Senator Howard brought a new bill to the floor, which, like its predecessor, was referred to the Senate Judiciary Committee, chaired by Senator Lyman Trumbull of Illinois. Although the bill "was reported adversely" by the committee, Senator Howard brought it forward for consideration in the full Senate. Trumbull expressed his continued opposition, sneering that: "I suppose it will be very convenient to have a court at Grand Rapids, which is a very flourishing town or city, on the western side of the State of Michigan. There is a railroad running right through there to Detroit. You may pass at any time from Grand Rapids to Detroit in ten hours. But still they urge that there is a great deal of maritime business and a great necessity for a court there. They always urge these considerations in every State."[8] Trumbull noted again the question of the cost of a second district as well as the likelihood that attorneys living near a new District Court would find ways to bring cases there that should have been filed in a state court, to the detriment of the Supreme Court.[9] Senator Howard responded by pleading for help for Judge Wilkins:

> I know quite well . . . that the excellent and learned district judge of that district is literally occupied the whole year, early and late, in hearing and determining cases, and in other matters concerned with the discharge of his duties, in which he is as faithful a man as ever I have met with in my life. He spends his whole time in the discharge of his duties; and the business is perpetually accumulating on his hands; and he does all this service learnedly, faithfully, and well, for the small pittance of $2,500 a year. I ought not to say that he does all the business of both of the courts, for the circuit judge comes and assists in holding a Circuit Court there ordinarily twice a year, but frequently only once a year, and remains there not to exceed a week or ten to twelve days. The great mass of business is thrown on the district judge. He ought to be relieved in some degree from the multitude of cases he is called upon to decide, admiralty cases as well as civil cases.[10]

Senator Morton S. Wilkinson of Minnesota voiced his support, but at the end of the day the Senate delayed consideration of the bill.

Not deterred, Senator Howard brought the bill forward again a week later, and other senators joined the debate. Lafayette S. Foster, of Connecticut, declared that although the people of Michigan were the "bone of [New England's] bone and flesh of our flesh," he had to oppose the bill, fearing that its passage would result in New York and Pennsylvania each demanding a third district and other states demanding a second.[11] William Pitt Fessenden, of Maine, offered his opinion that dividing districts was "rather a matter to make offices than to subserve any other purpose."[12] Senator Fessenden also doubted the need for a second court: "I cannot conceive how it is possible that the maritime business and the business peculiar to the United States courts in the State of Michigan should require anything like another court in that State."[13] New York City, he pointed out, had four times the business of all of Michigan, yet it got by with just one District Court. Iowa Senator James Wilson Grimes joked that if the new court was meant to serve citizens unable to get to Detroit easily, then it ought to be located at Copper Harbor on Lake Superior.[14]

However, enough other senators, such as Lazarus Whitehead Powell of Kentucky, who might have been anticipating their own states' needs for multiple federal courts,[15] supported the bill to make a majority. On February 21, the bill passed on a vote of twenty-five to eleven. It was signed by President Lincoln and became law on February 24, 1863.[16]

The Eastern and Western Districts of Michigan, 1863

Congress divided the District of Michigan into the Eastern and Western Districts of Michigan and assigned Judge Wilkins and his court officers to the Eastern District.[17] The act bisected the Lower Peninsula by a line running roughly north and south from the Straits of Mackinac, which assigned Ingham County and the state capital, Lansing, to the Eastern District. The Upper Peninsula was allocated to the eastern district except for Delta County on the north shore of Lake Michigan. The logic of this division was to assign Lake Michigan and its coastline located in Michigan on both peninsulas to the Western district so that its hoped-for large number of admiralty cases could be heard in Grand Rapids instead of more distant Detroit. Congress would, over the years, change the boundary separating the districts.

On February 26, President Lincoln nominated Grand Rapids attorney, state senator, and former probate judge Solomon Lewis Withey as the West-

Judge Solomon Lewis Withey

ern District's first District Judge. The Senate confirmed his appointment on March 11, 1863.[18]

Judge Withey's appointment took place at the midpoint of the Civil War, during the most perilous time in American history. The Battle of Antietam, fought on one day in Maryland six months earlier, had cost the contending armies more than 22,000 casualties, the bloodiest day of the Civil War. In the days and weeks leading up to Withey's appointment, President Lincoln's Emancipation Proclamation took effect, and the Union's first draft was signed into law. Two months after the appointment, the Union's Army of the Potomac was badly defeated at Chancellorsville, in Virginia, by Robert E. Lee's Army of Northern Virginia. Yet the months following Withey's appointment also saw the beginning of the ultimate victory of the Union. From July 1 to 3, that same Army of the Potomac defeated Lee's forces in the pivotal and bloody Battle of Gettysburg, and on July 4, General Ulysses S. Grant accepted the surrender of the Confederate garrison at Vicksburg, Mississippi, the last Confederate stronghold on the Mississippi River.

Not everybody in Michigan approved the district split, particularly eastern Michigan Democrats. On March 14, 1863, the *Detroit Free Press*, that city's ferociously Democratic, anti-Lincoln, and anti-African American newspaper, asserted that, in fact, there was no need for a second district, that there were few cases, "not one in fifty," that arose in what was now the Western District. Instead, the Western District "was created for the purpose of carrying out a contract made among politicians, and giving certain men office," and was "one of the most corrupt political jobs ever carried through Congress."[19] The *Free Press* also intimated that Solomon Withey, who was then a Michigan state senator, owed his new judgeship not to his legal skills, his judicial temperament, or even his services to the Republican Party, but instead to a desire "to pension him off so he would not interfere politically with some of the ambitious men in this part of the State." Further, the article went on to assert that "there is not a single truth" in Senator Howard's assertion that Judge Wilkins was overworked. The newspaper claimed that it had information from "one of the officers of the court, that all the business which comes before either the circuit or district can easily be performed by his Honor Judge Wilkins in three months."[20] Whatever the truth, the Western District was in existence, and Solomon L. Withey was its District Judge.

One last opposition attempt took place a year later, on February 5, 1864, when Congressman Augustus C. Baldwin, a Democrat from Pontiac, submitted a resolution requesting: "That the Committee on the Judiciary be instructed to inquire into the amount of business done in the United States District Court for the Western District of Michigan, and to report whether the public interests would not be best subserved by abolishing said district and incorporating the territory embraced therein with the Eastern District of Michigan."[21] The House did send the resolution to the committee, but nothing more was heard of it. Later that year, on June 20, Congress did make one adjustment by assenting to resolutions submitted by the supervisors of Branch County and citizens of Calhoun County to transfer their counties back to the Eastern District.[22]

U.S. District Judge Solomon Lewis Withey

Judge Solomon Lewis Withey was born to Solomon and Julia (Granger) Withey[23] on April 21, 1820, in St. Alban's Point, Vermont, near Lake Champlain. Because his father was also named Solomon, Judge Withey was called Lewis by his family and friends. Julia Withey died in March 1825, when Judge Withey was not quite five years old. In 1828, the family moved to St. Albans Bay, Vermont, where Judge Withey grew up and attended school.[24] This was the period of the great exodus of New Englanders to new lands in the west, and in September 1835 the Withey family joined that migration and moved to Cuyahoga Falls, Ohio, where the eldest son, William, was living. The following May, the family moved once more, this time to Grand Rapids, Michigan, where the elder Withey would become Kent County sheriff. In Detroit, however, Judge Withey, then sixteen years old, left the others to take a job as a mercantile clerk in a general store at Auberrys, near Chatham in Upper Canada. Several months later, he returned to Michigan and took a similar position in a grocery store in Ann Arbor. In March 1837, he rejoined his family briefly in Grand Rapids, but, deciding that he needed more education, he returned to Ohio to enroll in the Cuyahoga Falls Institute. In the summer of 1838, he returned again to Grand Rapids where he taught at a "select" school located on the east side of Kent Street near the corner of Kent and Bridge Streets.

In the fall of 1839, Judge Withey began to read law at the Grand Rapids offices of Alfred Day Rathbone, Kent County's first prosecuting attorney, and George Martin, a future chief justice of the Michigan Supreme Court. Their office was in the same building as the U.S. Post Office, and Withey worked as an assistant postmaster at night to support himself during his studies. On May 17, 1843, he and two other applicants were admitted to the bar of Kent County and in 1844 entered into a partnership with John Ball that lasted eight years.[25] In 1846 they were joined by George Martin as Ball, Martin, & Withey. Their practice included a large amount of collection work and some hard contested matters that presumably gave Withey experience in court.

On December 24, 1845, Withey married Marion Louise Hinsdill (1829–1912), the daughter of another emigrant family from Vermont; they had six children of whom four boys and a girl reached adulthood.[26] The Witheys built a home on the northeast corner of Fountain and Division Streets that reportedly had Michigan's first bathtub. As was common in those days, Withey practiced with a succession of lawyers over the next several years, always prospering. In addition to his private practice, he served as probate judge for Kent County (1848–1852). He was against liquor sales in the 1850s, and he campaigned for prohibition, but he later became convinced that enforcement was impossible and that taxing sales was a better strategy to limit drinking.[27] In 1860 he was elected to a two-year term in the state senate as a Republican, beginning January 1, 1861, just three months before the Civil War began. The war brought a multitude of railroad companies to the legislature seeking to be financed by a grant of state lands. Many of the companies were speculative and took title to the land grants without ever laying any track. Withey gained prominence statewide for pushing through a law that transferred title to the land only after the railroad track was completed.

Despite his federal appointment, Judge Withey remained active in local and state affairs. From 1869 until his death, he was president and later a director of the First National Bank of Grand Rapids and its successor, Old National Bank. In 1867, he was a delegate from Kent County to that year's convention, which was called to draft a replacement for Michigan's 1851 constitution; he served as chair of the convention's judiciary committee. When the electorate rejected the convention's proposed constitution, he was one of eighteen commissioners appointed in 1873 to a state constitutional commission by Michigan Governor Henry H. Crapo to investigate proposals for amending the 1851 constitution; he chaired the judiciary committee again. Unlike modern federal judges, Withey was also involved in many businesses.

Judge Withey apparently had bad health for much of his life. As a young man, soon after settling in Grand Rapids, he was afflicted by "a severe and painful illness," possibly malaria or erysipelas, both of which were then endemic in Michigan and afflicted most immigrants.[28] Frail in physique, he was described as having a pale, dignified, and kindly appearance. During his last years, however, Judge Withey suffered from a "physical infirmity,"[29] which affected his heart such that he had to be carried upstairs to his third-floor courtroom to hold court. In March 1885, "Judge Withey was, while on the bench, taken with a sinking feeling caused by some degeneration of the heart, and had been unable since then to attend to the active duties of his office. In January 1886, the judge in company with his wife, daughter, and several friends went to California in the hopes that it would improve his health."[30] The party wintered in Pasadena, then traveled on to San Diego. At dinner on the night of Easter Sunday, April 25, 1886, he complained of chest pains and had to be carried to his hotel room where he died at 7:30 p.m., at the age of sixty-six.[31] Judge Withey's body was returned to Grand Rapids where he was eventually buried in the family mausoleum in Oak Hill Cemetery. He was survived by his wife and five children. Following Judge Withey's death, District Judge George R. Sage of the Southern District of Ohio presided over the court for a time.

The First Terms of Court

The statute creating the Western District of Michigan provided that the District and Circuit Courts would hold two joint terms together each year, beginning on the third Mondays in May and October in Grand Rapids. Consequently, Judge Withey opened the first term of the District and Circuit Courts on Monday, May 18, 1863. The boosters of Grand Rapids had intended that court would be held in a new courtroom being constructed in Ball's Building, also known as Ball's Block, a three-story commercial building on the northwest corner of Pearl and Canal (now Monroe) Streets that also housed Daniel Ball's bank and McConnell's hardware store. However, the room was not ready on May 18, so Judge Withey held court during the three days of the first term (May 18–20) across the street at Mills and Clancy's Hall, on Canal Street, between Lyon and Pearl Streets.[32]

After U.S. Marshal Osmund Tower opened court, Judge Withey appointed Lewis Porter to be clerk of both the District and Circuit Courts. After the judge swore Porter in and received his bond, Porter read out loud the judge's own appointment and then swore in Frederick O. Rogers as the district's first U.S. Attorney and Isaac Parrish as a Circuit Court Commissioner. The judge directed Porter to obtain a seal and record books, admitted twenty attorneys to the bar of the court, and adjourned court for the day. On May 19 and 20, Tower again opened the court, but there was no business, and Judge Withey promptly adjourned court on both days.

On July 1 and 2, 1863, coincidentally the first two days of the Battle of Gettysburg, Judge Withey called a special term of court to show off the finally completed courtroom in Ball's Block.[33] The *Grand Rapids Daily Eagle* described it as

[a] large, convenient and well lighted room . . . in splendid style. . . . The walls, doors, window frames, etc., have been painted and grained in the best style of the painter's art. Tasty inside blinds, matching the walls in finish, have been put upon the windows, and a finely finished, elevated bench for His Honor, Judge Withey, has been erected at one end of the hall, with a desk for the Clerk, to match in appearance, in front of it. To make the room complete in appearance and comfort, the floor has been covered with grass or hemp carpeting, and the room is to be provided with arm or office chairs. Altogether, this is one of the most convenient and tasty court

rooms we ever saw, alike creditable to the man who planned the work and the artists who did it.[34]

However, as in May, there was no court business on either day.

The District and Circuit Courts reopened for another two-day special term on September 7 and 8 to deal with two matters. First, Judge Withey appointed three court officers, George W. Dodge as crier as well as Galen A. Graves and Moses B. Hopkins as masters in chancery. Then Withey held his first substantive hearing, a petition for a writ of habeas corpus brought by Herman Champlain of Ionia to have Provost Marshal Norman Bailey produce in court his son, George W. Champlain. George was a deserter from the 21st Michigan Volunteer Infantry Regiment, which had been recruited throughout Michigan's western Lower Peninsula in the summer of 1862. George joined the regiment on August 11, 1862. He was wounded in combat at Perryville, Kentucky, in October, and he was hospitalized in Louisville, from where he deserted and returned home, where Bailey arrested him. The petitioner's attorney, D. W. Jackson, argued that George's enlistment was illegal because he had been only seventeen years old when he joined the regiment without his father's consent. Judge Withey heard the arguments and denied the petition, holding that the father had given implied consent based on his knowledge that George had enlisted and had received a bounty, regular pay, and decorations, and yet his father had not objected until George was arrested.[35] This was Judge Withey's only military habeas corpus case because a week later President Lincoln suspended the writ for soldiers. However, during and after the war a significant portion of Judge Withey's docket involved charges against civilians who had helped soldiers desert.

The new District Court's initial lack of cases was not surprising. Congress had held that all cases pending in the District of Michigan at the time of the split would remain in the eastern district's courts in Detroit. Court activities in Grand Rapids did pick up slightly in the October 1863 term, which ran for thirteen days from October 19 until October 31, and then from November 11 to 17. Court usually was called to order at 10 a.m. and adjourned promptly when there was no more to do, such as on eight of the scheduled court days in October and November. All but two of the seventeen cases considered during that term were criminal, and all but one were filed in the District Court rather than the Circuit Court.

At the beginning of the term, Judge Withey seated a grand jury, which produced fifteen indictments charging postal theft, inciting a soldier to desert, and failure to pay the license fee imposed on nearly everything to pay for the war. Two of the license cases charged lawyers, one of whom was Franklin Muzzy, a former Democratic state senator from Berrien County who was fervently against the war and may have refused to pay the fee as a matter of principle. The first jury trial, *Billings v. Parker*, a Circuit Court case to collect a debt, took place on October 18. After both sides gave their evidence, the jury found for the plaintiff in the amount of $1,181.30.

The Judiciary Act of 1869 and the Creation of Circuit Judges

During the first half of the nineteenth century, the Justices of the U.S. Supreme Court were increasingly overwhelmed by the volume of appeals they were called upon to decide and by their duty to attend Circuit Courts in each of the districts in their assigned judicial circuits. Congress took one step in reducing their circuit-riding in the Judiciary Act of 1844,[36] which reduced the Circuit Justice's duty to attend each of his districts' Circuit Courts from twice each year to just once. Twenty-five years later, in order to further decrease these burdens on the Justices, Congress passed the Judiciary Act of 1869,[37] which added two Justices to the Supreme Court and established a new judicial position, a separate "circuit judge" for each judicial circuit, who was to have the same power and jurisdiction as a Supreme Court Justice had when holding a Circuit Court. Now most Circuit Courts could be held by the circuit judge and the district judge, and the Justices needed to attend only one Circuit Court term every two years in each district in his assigned circuit, instead of one such term annually.

On December 17, 1869, President Ulysses S. Grant nominated Judge Withey to be the first circuit judge for the Sixth Circuit, and the Senate confirmed his appointment on December 22. However, Judge Withey had second thoughts about the time, strain, and discomfort involved in holding multiple Circuit Court terms in Michigan, Ohio, Tennessee, and Kentucky each year. Although the annual salary of a Circuit Judge was twice that of a District Judge ($5,000 instead of $2,500), Withey notified President Grant that he had decided to decline the appointment and remain a district judge instead. On January 10, 1870, Grant nominated instead Detroit attorney Halmer Hull Emmons as Circuit Judge for the Sixth Circuit.[38] The circuit judges assigned to the Western District of Michigan prior to the creation of the U.S. Circuit

Court of Appeals in 1891 were Emmons (1870–1877) and two judges from Tennessee, John Baxter (1877–1886) and Howell E. Jackson (1886–1891).

Judge Withey and Changing the Law

Judge Withey was diligent, hardworking, and not afraid to change his mind if convinced that justice required him to do so. Although he was usually described as conservative, he did not hesitate to reinterpret the law in innovative ways if he felt the need. In a century in which most lawyers saw the common law as a fixed and perfect body of knowledge based on logic, Withey took a more practical approach, consistent with the observation of future Supreme Court Justice Oliver Wendell Holmes, Jr. that: "The life of the law has not been logic; it has been experience." In addressing the graduating class of the University of Michigan Law Department in 1871, Withey warned the graduates that:

> It is well to remember . . . that much of the common law reaches back to times of extremely arbitrary and austere views, both in social life and in government; to those periods in history when the image of justice was rude or but dimly seen. Its rules and maxims are supposed to stand upon reason, but in the light of enlarged common sense and juster views exceptions have been found and many old ideas have been discarded. Statutes and decisions will continue to make changes in the future as in the past; so that it will not do to conclude that all you have learned as law is either absolute perfection or as unchallengeable as the laws of the Medes and the Persians. . . . While we venerate the Common Law, and regard it as eminently the embodiment of human wisdom, and that the law should remain as it ever has, a conservative science, it is nevertheless justly subject to such modifications as are demanded by the altered conditions of the world and of the emancipatory ideas of the age, for then, and then only, can the law be made properly to touch the rights, obligations and relations of persons in social and business affairs.[39]

Two of Judge Withey's groundbreaking decisions show how he acted on this principle.

Federal Eminent Domain on White Lake

Before the Civil War, there was a common assumption among lawyers and judges that, in the absence of a specific statute, the power of eminent domain, the power to take private property for public uses, resided only in the state governments and not in the government of the United States.[40] In *Avery v. Fox*,[41] a case that Withey decided on January 1, 1868, he took an important step in dispelling that assumption.

White Lake in northern Muskegon County is about four miles long and one mile wide. It stretches from its eastern end, where the White River passes the towns of Whitehall and Montague, to a strip of land at its western end, about 250 yards wide, which separates White Lake from Lake Michigan. Today, ships pass from one lake to the other through an artificial channel about four hundred yards long at its western end, but at the time of this case, water from White Lake reached Lake Michigan through its natural narrow channel that ran northwest from the western end of the lake for almost three quarters of a mile, parallel to the Lake Michigan shore, and then turned and ran about two hundred yards west to Lake Michigan, about 3,550 feet north of the current outlet.[42] This channel was at best only four to ten feet deep and was subject to windblown sand that had to be dredged every year, at great cost, which even so kept the channel barely navigable. Various local groups petitioned Congress to create a new, deep entrance across the western end of White Lake in order to provide an excellent harbor for large freight and passenger ships that could not navigate the narrow and shallow natural channel. After studying the matter, Congress decided that maintaining the old channel was not economically viable, and in March 1867 the House and Senate appropriated $57,000 to cut the current direct channel, two hundred feet wide and twelve feet deep, between the lakes.[43]

Avery was a timber merchant who owned seventy acres of land fronting on the old channel. He brought logs from the interior through the White River to White Lake and then through the natural outlet, where he ran a sawmill and had a dock on Lake Michigan for shipping his timber. When he learned of the project to abandon his channel and dig a new one, he sued in the Circuit Court for the Western District seeking an injunction to prevent the defendants, contractors and employees acting for the federal government from constructing the new channel. He claimed that the proposed channel would destroy the value of his property and business and would constitute a taking of the value of his property. He asserted that if a new, shorter channel were opened, water from White Lake would "prefer," by the laws of nature, to flow to Lake Michigan that way. In addition, if the government no longer dredged the old channel, it would silt up entirely. Both consequences would make his land and business valueless. He also made the conventional argument of that time that the defendants could not claim eminent domain as a justification because the federal government had no such power.

On January 21, 1868, Judge Withey, sitting as the Circuit Court justice, alone as usual, heard arguments on Avery's request for an injunction and denied it.[44] In a written opinion, he rejected the argument that the United States lacked the power of eminent domain:

> The United States have a right to make the cut between White Lake and Lake Michigan—the land, where the proposed cut is to be, having first been secured—provided thereby private interests are not seriously impaired or private rights destroyed. It is an incident to the sovereignty of the United States, and a right recognized in the constitution, in that clause which prohibits the taking of private property without just compensation, that it may take private property for public use—of the necessity or expediency of which Congress must judge, but the obligation to make compensation is concomitant with the right.[45]

The key facts to be determined, then, were whether Avery would suffer any compensable loss and, if so, how much. Essentially, would the new channel reduce the future navigability of the old channel once the proposed new channel opened?

Both parties submitted affidavits of experts whose conclusions, naturally, differed totally. Because this was a request for an injunction to stop work ordered by Congress instead of a suit for compensation under the doctrine of eminent domain, Judge Withey emphasized that he had to be cautious. In the end, he denied the injunction request because the fact of loss was questionable. Not only was the effect of the new channel on the old channel unclear, plaintiff might even benefit from the new channel by the likelihood that he could rearrange his production facilities to allow larger ships to load timber from a dock on White Lake.

Judge Withey and the Steamboat Daniel Ball[46]

Sometimes important cases that revolutionize constitutional law emerge from events that are relatively commonplace, as was the case of the steamboat *Daniel Ball*, in which a decision by Judge Withey, affirmed by the U.S. Supreme Court, began the long judicial expansion of the power granted to Congress by Article I, section 8 of the Constitution, "to regulate Commerce . . . among the several States."

The *Daniel Ball* was a side-wheel steamboat owned by three businessmen of Grand Rapids: Jesse Ganoe, Byron Ball, and Demetrius Turner. Launched in 1861, the vessel was 141 feet long and capable of carrying 123 tons of passengers and freight. It was designed and built to traverse the Grand River between Grand Rapids and Lake Michigan at Grand Haven. Because it had a draft of only two feet, the *Daniel Ball* could not navigate on Lake Michigan safely, so the captain had to unload westbound passengers and freight going farther than Grand Haven.

The case began when a steamboat inspector appointed by Judge Withey boarded the *Daniel Ball* and demanded to see her license and safety certificate. Finding that the ship had neither, the inspector imposed mandatory fines of $500 on both the vessel and its owners. The inspector's authority to inspect and to fine came from two federal statutes[47] that established a system for licensing all steamboats carrying passengers and freight "in or upon the bays, lakes, rivers, or other navigable waters of the United States" and for inspection and certification of each boat's hull annually and its steam boilers every six months. These statutes were passed to regulate an industry and a technology that was crucial to commerce across the nation but was also terribly dangerous. From the first steamboat, Fulton's *Clermont*, launched in 1807, their number grew exponentially and became the nation's primary carrier of goods and people. By 1825, steamboats began to transit the Great Lakes and were a key to the great migration of New Englanders to Michigan during the following decade. However, like new technology in other times, steam power had outpaced safety. Poorly designed and manufactured steam boilers exploded at a terrifying rate, often killing every person aboard the ship by scalding or burning. Governments, both state and federal, saw the need for some kind of action, but the young nation's laissez-faire principles made them pause. Finally, in 1838, Congress passed a law for licensing and inspecting most steamboats, although it did not establish safety standards until 1852.[48]

The owners of the *Daniel Ball* did not pay their fine. They apparently relied on an opinion by District Judge Ross Wilkins pronounced in the District of Michigan a decade earlier that vessels that did not cross state lines were engaged in "internal" commerce and subject to state laws only.[49] On April 2, 1868, the U.S. Attorney for the Western District, Augustus D. Griswold,[50] filed an admiralty libel in the U.S. District Court in Grand Rapids seeking to confiscate the vessel and sell it to pay the fines. The owners objected on two grounds: first, that the Grand River was not a "navigable water of the United

States," and, second, that the power given to Congress to regulate commerce between the states did not extend to a vessel operating entirely within a single state. The United States was represented by Ebenezer S. Eggleston, Assistant U.S. Attorney for the Western District. John S. Newberry of Detroit, one of Michigan's preeminent admiralty experts, appeared for the vessel and its owners.

The parties agreed to submit the case to the court on the pleadings and proofs rather than have a trial in open court. On Saturday, July 25, 1868, the District Court's journal noted that Judge Withey had ordered the libel dismissed but that he had also held that the government had probable cause to seize the ship and begin the libel. He later issued a written opinion explaining his decision.[51] In that opinion, he held, first, that the Grand River clearly was, in fact and in law, a navigable water of the United States and second, that the inspection statute was constitutional as it applied to the *Daniel Ball*: "The carriage between Grand Rapids and Grand Haven was internal, but the commodity carried was proceeding to another state, and such other state, as well as Michigan, was interested in the trade and traffic of that commodity from the time it left Grand Rapids. As an article of export from the latter and of import to the former, both states were interested in the traffic, trade or exchange of that commodity; hence it was commerce among the states." Nevertheless, he concluded, he had dismissed the libel as a matter of fairness because the owners had relied on Judge Wilkins's earlier opinion and so had no notice that they were violating the law.

Both parties appealed to the Circuit Court for the Western District, causing Supreme Court Justice Noah Swayne to make one of his rare appearances in the Western District as Circuit Justice. On November 5, 1868, after counsel for the parties argued, the court took the appeal under advisement. The next day, the Circuit Court reversed the judgment below as noted by the clerk in the Circuit Court journal: "[T]he said steamer is greatly of a [*sic*] violation of the laws of the United States as said libel charged whereby the said steamer became and was and still is liable to the United States in the penalty prescribed by law being the sum of five hundred dollars which said sum is a valid lien on the said steamer. . . ."[52] Although Justice Swayne did not explain his reasoning further, the only logical conclusion is that he agreed with Judge Withey's interpretation of the inspection statutes but disagreed with his view on reliance and fairness.

The owners then sought review by the U.S. Supreme Court, which heard the appeal on December 5, 1870, in Washington, D.C. The U.S. Solicitor General, Benjamin H. Bristow, appeared for the government and Andrew T. McReynolds of Grand Rapids for the ship and owners.[53] The Court, in an opinion by Justice Stephen Johnson Field, affirmed the ruling of Justice Swayne in the Circuit Court.[54] Like Withey, the Court had no trouble finding the Grand River to be "navigable" and also agreed with his interpretation of the Commerce Clause. Field acknowledged that "commerce which is carried on entirely within the limits of a State and does not extend to or affect other States" was not subject to federal control. However, he also concluded that, as to the *Daniel Ball*, "So far as she was employed in transporting goods destined for other States, or goods brought from without the limits of Michigan and destined to places within that State, she was engaged in commerce between the States, and however limited that commerce may have been, she was, so far as it went, subject to the legislation of Congress."

The owners paid their fine, but the era of steamboats on the Grand River was ending, with railroads taking their place. The owners moved the *Daniel Ball* to Lake Huron, where, in October 1876, she caught fire while approaching Bay City. All of the passengers and crew were rescued, but the ship sank, a loss to the owners estimated at $15,000.[55]

The 1879 Grand Rapids U.S. Courthouse

Although elegantly laid out, the courtroom in Ball's Block was not a long-term solution for housing the federal court in Grand Rapids. In 1869, the owners of Ball's Block tripled the length of the building and turned it into Sweet's Hotel, effectively evicting the court. Judge Withey moved his operations to the Ramsey Block, 14–16 Pearl Street, at the southwest corner of Pearl and Campau Streets, while he listed as his office his residence, 3 College Avenue, "north from Cherry Street, next east of Prospect."[56] Meanwhile, the post office and the growing number of other federal agencies continued to be housed in other buildings around the city. On December 5, 1872, Michigan's U.S. Senator Thomas White Ferry "asked and, by unanimous consent, obtained leave to bring in a bill (S. 1199) for the construction of a court house, post-office, and other federal government offices at Grand Rapids, Michigan." The bill passed the Senate on January 8, 1873, and the House of Representatives on February 10; it was signed into law by President Ulysses S. Grant on February 21.[57]

The 1879 Grand Rapids U.S. Courthouse, known as the Government Building.

As enacted, the statute authorized the Secretary of the Treasury to purchase in Grand Rapids a "suitable lot of ground" and to erect on it "a building of brick suitable for the accommodation of the court-house, post-office, and other government offices in that city," at a cost, for the land and building not to exceed $200,000. A commission of nine individuals from throughout the Western District, including Judge Withey, was appointed to select a site. These commissioners advertised for proposals and received ten bids from which they selected three, but the Treasury Department rejected them all and sent its own architect to survey the area. The architect recommended three other parcels of land, and in April the Secretary selected a central block in Grand Rapids, bounded by Lyon, Division, Pearl, and Ionia Streets, at a condemnation price of $68,064.85, which, "with attendant legal expenses," brought the total to $70,000, the full amount authorized by Congress for the land.[58] Over the next four years, as construction proceeded slowly, Congress appropriated another $142,000 to complete the building, resulting in an impressively modest overrun on the original budget of just $12,000.[59]

The Government Building and its surroundings, c. 1880.

Excavation for the foundation was difficult because the site was low and swampy, "a singing frog pond," as well as part of a ravine. The site was not ready for raising the structure until the spring of 1876, and the building was not completed until 1879. During construction, Judge Withey continued to hold court in the Ramsey Block. The original designer for what came to be known in Grand Rapids as the Government Building was William Appleton Potter, the Treasury Department's supervising architect from 1874 to 1877. Potter's design was illustrated in a drawing in the July 1876 edition of the *American Architect and Building News*.[60] The drawing shows the exterior of a three-story building in the Gothic Revival style, with a steep hipped roof, Gothic-style ornamentation, windows and entrances with arch surrounds, and two sets of multiple chimneys, one on either side of the central portion of the building. The exterior walls were faced with pressed brick with stone belts and cornices, all on a landscaped lot encircled with a low iron fence that sat on imported stone.

At some point, though, somebody (probably James G. Hill, Potter's successor in 1877) made some changes. The interior layout remained essentially the same: the courtroom and offices for the judge and staff were still on the third floor, the first floor held the post office, and the second floor was occupied by the U.S. Attorney, the U.S. Marshal, the Collector of Internal Revenue, and other government offices.[61] The basement held the furnaces and storage room for eighteen carloads of coal. The basic footprint of the exterior (126 feet by 63 feet) and the basic shape and structure of the exterior also remained the same, but the Gothic ornamentation was replaced and the pitch of the roof was lowered, changes that transformed the Government Building from Gothic Revival to a simpler, more contemporary Italianate style.

The court moved in to its new quarters on September 1, 1879, and Judge Withey held the first session on October 7. The furnishings, desks, tables, chairs, and other furniture were made with the finest oak or walnut. The door trimmings were of solid bronze while the gas fixtures were in ornamental designs made of nickel and copper. The federal District and Circuit Courts continued to be held there until 1908 when the Government Building was demolished to begin construction of its successor.

Succession of Clerks in the District and Circuit Courts, 1863–1912

Lewis Porter was sworn in as the Western District's clerk for both the District and Circuit Courts during the first session in May 1863, but he left two years later in May 1865. He was replaced by attorney Isaac H. Parrish who served both courts for ten years, until December 30, 1875. After Parrish, Judge Withey engaged in some nepotism, which was not unusual in those days. First, in January 1876, he hired one of his wife's brothers, Chester B. Hinsdill, as clerk for both courts. Then, as business grew, a decision was made to have a clerk for each court. In October 1878, Withey kept Chester as the District Court clerk and, with the concurrence of Circuit Judge John Baxter, hired his wife's other brother, Henry M. Hinsdill, two years younger than Chester, as clerk of the Circuit Court. Chester Hinsdill resigned as of January 1, 1886, and Judge Withey entered an order the next day appointing deputy clerk John McQuewan to replace Chester as the District Court clerk. Henry Hinsdill continued as Circuit Court clerk for another year until February 1, 1887, when Withey's successor, District Judge Henry F. Severens, appointed Charles L. Fitch as the new circuit clerk. McQuewan served as District Court clerk until his death on December 18, 1900, when he was replaced by Charles J. Potter. Fitch served as Circuit Court clerk until the dissolution of the Circuit Courts on January 1, 1912.

The Eastern and Western Districts of Michigan, 1878

The Southern and Northern Divisions of the Western District

After the creation of the Western District in 1863, it only took a few years before other interests suggested dividing the district itself in two. On March 22, 1869, Michigan Congressman William L. Stoughton from Sturgis, St. Joseph County, submitted to the House a bill to divide the Western District into Southern and Northern Divisions.[62] The Southern Division would include the counties of St. Joseph, Cass, Kalamazoo, Berrien, Van Buren, and Allegan, "and all that lies to the south and west thereof." A single annual term of the district and Circuit Courts of the Southern Division would be held in Kalamazoo, while a single term of the courts of the Northern Division (including the rest of the Western District) would continue to be held in Grand Rapids. On December 10, 1869, Michigan Congressman Randolph Strickland, from DeWitt, Clinton County, submitted his own bill (H.R. 487) to create a third district, the Northern District of Michigan, that would include all of the Upper Peninsula. The bill also proposed that the northern district would have its own District Judge who would hold two terms of its District and Circuit Court annually in Houghton.[63]

Neither bill passed, but a decade later Congress recognized changes in Michigan's population patterns and adopted part of each. On June 19, 1878, Congress redrew both the external and internal boundaries of the Western District.[64] The portion of the Upper Peninsula previously part of the Eastern District was reassigned to the Western District, so that all of the Upper Peninsula came within one court's jurisdiction. Congress did not go so far as to create a separate northern district but did assign all of the Upper Peninsula to a new Northern Division of the Western District. The counties in the Lower Peninsula assigned to the Western District became the District's Southern Division. District and Circuit Courts in the Southern Division would continue to be held in Grand Rapids, beginning on the first Tuesday of March and October. Courts in the Northern Division would be held, not in Houghton, but in centrally located Marquette, beginning on the first Tuesdays of May and September.

By doubling the number of terms of court to be held in the Western District from two to four, Congress imposed on the district's sole judge the burden of two round trips from Grand Rapids to Marquette each year, though the timing was not bad: the first week of May and September could be pleasant on the shores of Lake Superior. The first session of the District and Circuit Courts in the Northern Division was held on September 3 to 5, 1878, with Judge Withey presiding alone. After a short three-day session in September, Withey returned on May 14, 1879, for a week of hearings and administrative matters. In May 1880, Withey could not attend court in Marquette, but on the order of Circuit Judge Baxter, District Judge Henry Billings Brown of the Eastern District of Michigan filled in.

Succeeding Judge Withey

From 1861 until 1915, only one Democrat served as President of the United States, Grover Cleveland. Likewise, Michigan, although a Democratic stronghold until the 1850s, became and remained a Republican fortress for the rest of the nineteenth century. Thus, the relatively few Democratic attorneys practicing in western Michigan after 1860 had to believe that they had little or no

Judge Henry Franklin Severens

chance of obtaining a federal judgeship or any other federal office. However, that chance seemed to be attainable when Judge Withey died in April 1886 during President Cleveland's first term in office. The question was which of them would get the nomination.

Although Withey's nomination in 1863 had been uncontested, in 1886 several candidates were rumored to be in the running, including Edward F. Uhl[65] and Lyman D. Norris,[66] both of Grand Rapids, John Lewis of Greenville in Montcalm County, and Henry Franklin Severens of Kalamazoo, all four considered superior attorneys.[67] The selection of a judicial candidate to be appointed by the President was usually a gift in the hands of a state's U.S. senator or senators who belonged to the President's political party. Because both of Michigan's U.S. senators at that time were Republicans, the rules of selection were somewhat vague. Norris was supported by two of Michigan's Democratic U.S. congressmen, Charles C. Comstock of Grand Rapids and William C. Maybury of Detroit. However, the others also had champions, including, for Severens, his former law partner in Kalamazoo, Republican Congressman Julius C. Burrows, and Democratic National Committeeman Donald M. Dickinson of Detroit, the President's close friend and early backer.[68] Norris was an early leader, according to the newspapers, but there were whispers that, at the age of sixty-two, he was too near retirement to stay on the bench long. With the strong possibility that Norris's successor would be appointed by a Republican President, the opportunity to cement a Democratic judge, as well as other court officers, for the long term was too good to waste. Uhl's name was "pressed upon the President" next, even though Uhl continued to express his support for Norris. Ultimately, Severens's friends prevailed. Cleveland nominated him on May 14, 1886, just three days after Severens's fifty-first birthday, and he was confirmed by the U.S. Senate on May 24, 1886. The annual salary of the office was $3,500. A Democratic Detroit newspaper hailed the appointment, noting: Mr. Severens is a lawyer of ripe experience, a jurist of high attainments, a man of mature years and physical vigor, and a citizen who possesses the respect and admiration of those who know him."[69]

U.S. District Judge Henry Franklin Severens

Like Judge Withey, Judge Severens was a native Vermonter who came to Michigan as part of the great Yankee exodus. Judge Severens was born in Rockingham, in southeastern Vermont, on May 11, 1835, to Franklin and Elizabeth Stowell (Pulsipher) Severens. Like many children of that time, he attended school only three months of the year and spent the rest of his time working on his parents' farm. Determined to attend college, he worked as a teacher to pay for preparatory studies. He entered Middlebury College in 1854 and graduated in 1857.[70] That same year, he moved to Bellevue, Iowa, where he began a school with a Miss Eliza Chrissy. But the venture was unsuccessful, and after a short time in the classroom he "resigned and entered the [Bellevue] office of Booth and Graham as a student."[71]

In August 1858, Severens was back in Vermont where he married Rhoda Ranney of Westminster, Vermont. He continued to study law, and he was admitted to the Windham County, Vermont bar. In 1860, the couple moved to Three Rivers, St. Joseph County, Michigan, where Severens was admitted to the local bar. He began a law practice, and he was elected to a term as County Prosecutor in 1861.[72] Tragedy struck the family when Rhoda Ranney Severens died in childbirth on August 21, 1862, followed five days later by the death of their newborn son, Franklin C. Severens. Both were buried in Riverside Cemetery in St. Joseph.[73] In December 1863, Severens married, for a second time, to Sarah Clarissa (Whittlesey) Ryan, a widow and a relation of his mother. During their marriage they had two daughters, Catherine and Mabel.

In February 1865, the family moved to Kalamazoo, which promised more opportunities for a young lawyer. Severens resided in Kalamazoo for the rest of his life, even after he was appointed to sit on the federal District Court in Grand Rapids. When he arrived in Kalamazoo, he began to practice law with former U.S. Senator Charles Stuart and had great success for twenty years, including arguing eleven cases in the Michigan Supreme Court and one case before the U.S. Supreme Court.[74] He did, however, suffer periodically from ill health, and he abandoned his practice for several years before returning to the bar. Like many other attorneys then and now, Severens became interested in politics, but he was a Democrat in a solidly Republican state, and he lost races for Congress in 1866, for the state senate in 1868, and for the Michigan Supreme Court in 1877, where he lost to the incumbent, Justice Thomas Cooley.

Severens served on the District Court for almost fourteen years, but he remained anchored in Kalamazoo. When appointed, Severens promised that "My future residence depends upon the necessities which may arise. If there is any inconvenience to the public, I shall make such a change as is demanded to remedy it."[75] Fourteen years later, when Republicans were seeking a successor for Severens, after his appointment to the Sixth Circuit, Grand Rapids attorneys complained that Severens, "in his continued absence from the seat of justice has frequently delayed litigation and in many instances put litigants to added expenses and great inconvenience. Attorneys from distant parts of the district and from other states have come to Grand Rapids to do business in the United States court and have been obliged to carry their business to the home of the judge to have it attended to."[76] Despite such local concerns, Severens was highly regarded among federal judges in the states of the Sixth Circuit, particularly by Circuit Judge William Howard Taft. When President William McKinley appointed Taft to head the Philippine Commission, Taft recommended that Judge Severens be appointed to replace him as circuit judge. Thus, on February 6, 1900, with the recommendation of a Republican circuit judge, a Republican President nominated the Democrat Severens to become a judge of the U.S. Court of Appeals for the Sixth Circuit and of the U.S. Circuit Courts for the Sixth Circuit. The U.S. Senate confirmed those appointments on February 20, 1900. The occasion was marked by the presentation of a portrait of Judge Severens painted by Percy Ives, a well-known Detroit artist. The portrait was a gift of the bar of western Michigan. A second portrait, by Kathryn Leona Wood, hangs in one of the Sixth Circuit's courtrooms in Cincinnati.[77]

Judge Severens served as Circuit Judge until he retired on October 3, 1911, at the age of 76.[78] He lived another twelve years and died on June 8, 1923, in Kalamazoo's New Borgess Hospital, at the age of eighty-eight. He was buried in the city's Mountain Home Cemetery.[79] At a memorial service held by the Michigan Supreme Court, he was warmly remembered:

> As judge of the courts of which he was a member, he occupied an eminent position and his associates in the Court of Appeals regarded his knowledge of the law and his good, clear judgment as of much value, in deciding the many intricate questions which came before that court for determination. His desire to do exact justice to all the parties whose claims were submitted for his decision, his clearly defined reasons for the conclusions which he reached and the confidence which all had in his absolute integrity of purpose in all his judicial actions marked him as one of the leading jurists of his time and he justly secured the reputation which he gained as one of the leaders of the profession of law in the Nation.[80]

Judge Severens and Mail Fraud

Although cases involving the post office have been a regular part of the District Court's docket since the Western District's inception, most of them were relatively mundane charges of theft of mail or stamps or suits to collect on a delinquent postmaster's bond. However, in 1872 Congress passed "An act to revise, consolidate, and amend the Statutes relating to the Post-office Department,"[81] which added criminal penalties for illegal usage of the mail by private citizens. The act specifically defined as illegal the mailing of "any obscene book, pamphlet, picture, print, or other publication of a vulgar or indecent character,"[82] and using the mail for "any fraudulent lottery, so-called gift-concerts or other similar enterprise offering prizes, or concerning schemes devised and intended to deceive and defraud the public for the purpose of obtaining money under false pretenses."[83]

THE CASE OF THE SPIRIT POSTMASTER

One such case brought before Judge Severens in 1890 is an oddity worthy of individual note: the case of "Doctor Walter E. Reid, the Spirit Postmaster."[84] A federal grand jury for the Western District indicted Reid, a resident of

Grand Rapids, for mail fraud based on a confidence scheme he ran. Reid's jury trial began on April 2, 1890, and continued through April 5. At trial, the prosecution, led by U.S. Attorney Lewis G. Palmer, elicited testimony that, over a period of years and describing himself as the Spirit Postmaster, Reid had used the U.S. mail to distribute fraudulent advertisements. In them, he promised that he could obtain advice from peoples' "spirit friends" on the subject of any matter bothering them, be it "financial matters, sickness of any description, family troubles, or are undecided what to do about any special matter." All that the fraud victim—the mark—had to do was to was follow Reid's instructions:

> First. Write the full name or names of your spirit friends on slips of paper. Second. Address them by terms of relationship or friendship. Third. Ask your question. Fourth. Sign your own name in full. When this is done, place your question in an ordinary envelope, and seal it. Write a few lines on another sheet of paper, giving instructions to whom the replies should be sent, and place your sealed letter and note of instructions in a larger one, and address, Dr. W. E. Reid, 28 Canal St., Grand Rapids; 'Personal' in one corner. Dr. Reid has answered several thousand letters during the past two years and has been uniformly successful.

Reid's fee for his service was just one dollar, plus six cents for postage, although he charged five dollars if the letter to the spirit friend was sewed shut or sealed with wax (and thus harder to open surreptitiously). Witnesses also testified that Reid received a large number of responses to his ads with the requested fees, that Reid had made statements "tending to prove the business to be a fraud," and that he had learned the "trick of opening a sealed letter." The increased fee for some envelopes was apparently to discourage his "marks" (victims) from sending any letters sewn shut or sealed with wax.

Reid's defense was simple, that this was not a scheme to defraud because he did indeed have supernatural powers. His counsel proposed to prove his defense through the testimony of marks still convinced of Reid's bona fides and by having Reid "give an exhibition or test of his power in open court." The court refused to admit either type of evidence. In his charge to the jury, Judge Severens admitted that "every man has an absolute right to believe what he will. It is a phase of religious privilege which is guaranteed by the fundamental law of the land to every citizen." However, he warned,

A man may not carry his belief into conduct which is injurious to the public, and contrary to law. . . . The interests of society require that every man's conduct should conform to the law; and while it protects him in his freedom of opinion and belief in all religious or spiritual matters, it will not permit him, under the guise of that belief, to do a thing which the laws of the country condemn. To permit this (to employ the language of the supreme court of the United States in dealing with an analogous question) would be to make the professed doctrines of religious belief superior to the law of the land. . . .

As to Reid's defense of supernatural powers, Severens told the jury that: "No man has a right to embark in a business and insist that the legality of it shall be tested by principles beyond the understanding of others, and not by the apprehension of the courts and juries of the country." On April 5, the jury found Reid guilty as charged. On May 13, Severens and circuit judge Howell Jackson denied Reid's motion for a new trial, and on May 16 Severens sentenced Reid to one year in the Detroit House of Correction at hard labor.[85]

THE CASE OF THE COUNTERFEIT BLUEBERRY PLANTS

Another case of mail fraud involved a defendant who advertised to sell blueberry plants that turned out to be wild huckleberries. This case must have been of special interest to Severens, who had grown up on a farm and still maintained a farm south of Fennville in Allegan County for relief from the stress of his judicial duties. According to one authority, Judge Severens introduced mint farming to that region and in 1896 owned "'the largest peppermint field in the world,' nearly a mile long on the Severens Marsh, reclaimed swamp land."[86]

On October 8, 1890, L. Delos Staples, the defendant in *United States v. Staples*,[87] was indicted for mail fraud for sending through the U.S. mail brochures and circulars advertising to sell superior wheat seeds and berry plants, including blueberries, even though "defendant intended giving no plants of any value for the money received." Instead, according to the indictment, when he received orders and money, he sent no wheat seeds at all. As for the blueberry orders, "defendant shipped the common wild huckleberry, which he gathered in the woods, while his advertisement described what would be understood as a cultivated plant, and it carried the ideas that he was engaged in its culture; that many hundreds of these huckleberry plants were set out and cared for by purchasers, and entirely failed to live."

The trial began on December 11, 1890, and the case went to the jury on December 13. In his instructions, Severens, himself a seller of produce, noted that:

> Now, gentlemen, you are familiar, as the public generally are, with the fact that seedsmen and nurserymen, as well as all other parties who have anything to sell, have the habit of puffing their wares, and we are all familiar with the fact that it is a very prevalent thing in the course of business to exaggerate the merits of goods people have to sell; and within any proper reasonable bounds such a practice is not criminal. It must amount to more substantial deception in order to be subject to cognizance by the courts. A certain degree of praise and commendation of one's goods in business is allowable; but when that is carried to the extent of obtaining the public's money by means of actually fraudulent representations, then it comes under the condemnation of the law. You will consider all of these charges without losing sight of this very prevalent practice, and in reference to this second subject—that is, the sale of these blueberry plants, and the advertising of them—you will see whether this is within the range of an ordinary and legitimate business, or whether it goes beyond those bounds, and is a downright deception.[88]

The jury returned later on December 13, acquitting Mr. Staples as to the wheat, but convicting him on the charge of selling counterfeit blueberry plants and as to a third count in using the mail to defraud newspapers by placing his fraudulent advertisements and then not paying for them. On January 27, after many delays, Judge Severens sentenced Staples to fourteen months, like Reid in the Detroit House of Correction, with no adjustment for time served.

The 1889 Marquette U.S. Post Office and Courthouse

When Congress created the Northern Division of the Western District of Michigan in June 1878, Marquette did not have a federal facility to use as a courtroom. Judge Withey held the Northern Division's first term in Marquette, on September 3 to 5, 1878, and he held it in borrowed space, as the judges did for the next several years. Congress did not authorize a federal

The 1889 Marquette U.S. Post Office and Courthouse, known as the "Marquette Government Building." In this photograph, taken in December 1888, the building is not yet in operation and the window glass has not yet been installed.

The 1889 Marquette Government Building. This photograph was taken in December 1890, six months after the first court sessions.

building and courthouse for Marquette until July 1882, authorizing the Secretary of the Treasury "to purchase a site for, and cause to be erected thereon, a suitable building, with fireproof vaults therein, for the accommodation of the United States courts, post-office, and internal revenue, and other government offices, at the city of Marquette, in the State of Michigan," at a maximum cost for the site and building of $100,000.[89]

On May 9, 1883, the Treasury Department did purchase a suitable site at the corner of West Washington and North Third Streets at a cost of $7,276.60, but as often happened with projects for federal buildings, further progress was slow. By September 30, 1885, construction had not begun and just over $1,000 had been spent on the building.[90] The exterior was complete by December 1888, but the interior was not complete and occupied until July 3, 1889, just under seven years after Congress authorized it and eleven years after the sessions in the Northern Division began. The construction cost $92,273.06 and brought the total cost of the project to $99,549.66, a whisker under the original appropriation limit.[91] The result was a three-story brick building with a five-story tower, all in a mixed Italianate/Romanesque style, designed by the staff of Mifflin E. Bell, supervising architect for the Treasury Department from 1883 to 1886. The first court sessions in what came to be known as Marquette's Government Building opened on July 16, 1889, with District Judges Severens and George R. Sage of the Southern District of Ohio presiding.[92]

The U.S. Circuit Courts of Appeals

On March 3, 1891, Congress passed the Evarts Act, which established the U.S. Circuit Courts of Appeals, nine intermediate appellate courts, one in each circuit, to hear all appeals from decisions of the District Courts.[93] In each circuit, the sitting circuit judge, such as Judge Jackson, was also assigned to the Circuit Court of Appeals and was joined by a newly appointed second circuit judge. Each session of a Circuit Court of Appeals was to be heard by a three-judge panel consisting of the circuit justice and the two circuit judges. Congress did recognize that the Circuit Justices would rarely attend, so the law allowed one of the panelists to be replaced by a District Judge, which turned out to be what usually happened.[94] Henry Billings Brown was the first Circuit Justice of the Circuit Court of Appeals for the Sixth Circuit, and the other seat was filled (very snugly) by U.S. Solicitor General William Howard Taft, the future President and Chief Justice of the United States.

Even though the Evarts Act ended their appellate function, the old Circuit Courts remained in existence. Besides the old problem of having two trial courts in each district, the name of the new appellate courts, the fact that circuit judges sat on both the old Circuit Courts and the new appellate Circuit Courts confused the public and often still confuses historians. The House of Representatives had voted to abolish the Circuit Courts, but the Senate—in a nod to "extremists who still thought of the pioneer days when the Justices were active on circuit and thus, supposedly, kept the common touch,"[95] to Circuit Court clerks who lobbied feverishly to save their jobs, and to District Court clerks who feared that they would be replaced by their Circuit Court colleagues—convinced Congress to retain the old Circuit Courts, which bumbled on, with decreasing dockets, for another twenty years.

The Chinese Exclusion Acts

As originally adopted, the U.S. Constitution did not define who was a citizen of the Unites States but, instead, authorized Congress to establish a uniform rule allowing persons who were citizens of other countries to acquire U.S. citizenship by naturalization.[96] In 1790, Congress passed the first naturalization statute; it established time-of-residence requirements but also limited naturalization to "free white persons" of "good moral character."[97] In the wake of the Civil War, the abolition of slavery, and the Fourteenth Amendment's extension of citizenship to all persons born within the United States,[98] Congress passed the Naturalization Act of 1870, which opened up naturalization to "aliens of African nativity and to persons of African descent."[99] However, persons not white or African were still excluded from citizenship by naturalization.

By contrast to its policy on naturalization, Congress did not limit immigration into the United States by national origin or racial ancestry until later. To the contrary, in 1868 the United States entered into a treaty with China that encouraged Chinese immigration.[100] Seven years later, however, Congress passed the Page Act of 1875, which denied immigration to "undesirable" persons, including "any subject of China, Japan, or any Oriental country" who was subject to a long-term employment contract and so presumably a forced laborer.[101] In 1880, the United States and China renegotiated the treaty to suspend Chinese immigration, and in 1882 Congress passed the first of what were called the Chinese Exclusion Acts, followed by six more through 1902.[102]

Those laws first limited and then barred the immigration and naturalization of Chinese nationals. These laws resulted from an alliance of racial prejudice and a fear on the part of organized labor that the availability of Chinese laborers drove down wage levels for all workers. The acts were not repealed until 1943, during World War II when China was an ally of the United States against Japan. The Magnuson Act[103] allowed Chinese immigration (although only 105 individuals each year) and permitted Chinese nationals already in the United States to become naturalized citizens.

The exclusion acts proved to be a burden on the federal officers tasked with enforcement, especially on customs officers who were assigned to discover and arrest Chinese-looking persons who did not have certificates showing that they were either U.S. citizens by birth or had immigrated legally before 1882. That burden also fell on U.S. Commissioners who held hearings on the acts and issued deportation orders.[104] Between 1882 and 1905, an estimated ten thousand Chinese people appealed to federal judges against negative immigration decisions.[105] However, like cases under the Fugitive Slave Acts, it is difficult or impossible to tell how many Chinese people were deported because most deportation orders issued by commissioners were not appealed and most of the records kept by commissioners have been lost.

One appeal in the Western District that demonstrates the law's summary procedure involved two young Chinese men, named in court records as Sing Lee and Ching Jo,[106] who were arrested in Petoskey, Michigan, on February 7, 1893. After a summary hearing, Commissioner Clay E. Call found them guilty and sentenced them to twenty days of hard labor in the Kent County Jail, followed by deportation.[107] Lee and Jo retained Grand Rapids attorney Daniel E. Corbitt, who petitioned the District Court for a writ of habeas corpus, alleging that the current version of the exclusion act, passed on May 5, 1892, lacked due process because it provided for deportation based solely on a summary hearing by a commissioner rather than a judge, a hearing held without a jury and with a presumption of guilt that placed the burden on the defendants to prove that they were in the country legally. On February 28, 1893, after hearing arguments, Judge Severens affirmed the commissioner's order, finding that there was no constitutional defect in the act and that Congress had acted within its powers. He did question, on his own initiative, whether the statute authorized imprisonment for any period longer than necessary to organize the deportation, but he also noted that the twenty days had passed and so did not rule on that issue.

CHAPTER 4

The Western District Enters
the Twentieth Century, 1900 to 1920

Succeeding Judge Severens

WHEN NEWS SPREAD IN January 1900 that President William McKinley was to appoint Judge Severens to the U.S. Court of Appeals for the Sixth Circuit, Grand Rapids attorney George P. Wanty was endorsed by most of the Grand Rapids bar, as well as by the Justices of the Michigan Supreme Court, to succeed Severens as judge of the District Court. Although he was only forty-four years old, Wanty was recognized as one of the premier trial and appellate attorneys in western Michigan, representing "the greater business and financial interests," and he was a Republican. Besides his ability, experience, and party affiliation, Wanty also satisfied what was viewed among Grand Rapids attorneys as a crucial criterion. He was from Grand Rapids, so there would be no repeat of Judge Severens's habit of holding court in Kalamazoo. The only concern raised against Wanty was his health.

Three weeks later, though, the *Grand Rapids Herald* reported rumors that two other candidates were also under consideration. One, Thomas J. O'Brien, was, like Wanty, a leading Grand Rapids attorney and Republican. He was also a close personal friend of President McKinley. The other new candidate, Clement Smith, was a circuit court judge from Hastings in Barry County, located between Grand Rapids and Kalamazoo.[1] The *Herald* added the next day that "The only thing at present certain about the final result is that none of the candidates has a positive assurance of appointment."[2]

It appears that the selection of a new judge was not about the quality of the candidates but instead about a political fight over who really controlled the Republican party in western Michigan. In Grand Rapids, the party was fractured, and Samuel L. Lemon, the U.S. collector of customs, was ambitious. Lemon thought that his support of Wanty's candidacy would reunite the Republicans and propel Lemon into the governor's seat in a few years. On the other hand, Wanty had opposed the election in 1894 of U.S. Senator Julius C. Burrows, from Kalamazoo, and those Republicans who had supported Burrows argued that a Burrows loyalist should get the appointment. However, the state's senior U.S. Senator, James McMillan of Detroit, was the dominant figure in the party statewide and a supporter of Lemon. After Thomas O'Brien announced that he was not a candidate, McMillan's support of Lemon apparently was enough to swing the appointment to Wanty,[3] although both camps went to Washington and lobbied for their candidate until the day the President announced Wanty's nomination on March 7. The Senate confirmed Judge Wanty on March 13, 1900.

U.S. District Judge George Proctor Wanty

George Proctor Wanty was born in Ann Arbor, Michigan, on March 12, 1856, and thus was the Western District's first District Judge born in Michigan. His parents, Samuel and Elizabeth (Proctor) Wanty, had emigrated from England in 1853. They settled first in Brooklyn, New York, then in Detroit, and finally in Ann Arbor.[4] After graduating from Ann Arbor High School, George worked as a bank clerk in Ann Arbor and as a bookkeeper for an iron manufacturing company in Bay City. He left Bay City to enter the University of Michigan's Law Department where he earned a bachelor of laws degree in 1878. He then moved from Ann Arbor to Grand Rapids where he opened a successful law practice with various partners. In 1883, he partnered with Hiram A. Fletcher to form the law firm of Fletcher & Wanty, the direct ancestor of the current firm known as Wheeler Upham. After Fletcher's death in 1899, Wanty added Loyal E. Knappen, his future successor on the U.S. District Court, to the firm. In 1883 and 1884, Wanty served as president of the Michigan State Bar Association, and over the years he also held several posts with the American Bar Association including as chair of its General Council.

On June 22, 1886, Wanty married Emma M. Nichols; they had a son, Thomas Cooley Wanty, and a daughter, Helen Wanty, later Helen Wanty Albee. Emma Nichols Wanty was a successful and respected physician at a time when female doctors were rare. Born in Cannonsburg, Kent County, she graduated from the Women's Medical College in Chicago and practiced and

Judge George Proctor Wanty

taught medicine in that city until her marriage. She continued her practice in Grand Rapids, including serving as a visiting pediatrician and gynecologist at St. Mark's and Union Benevolent Association hospitals.[5] The Wantys were very popular among the rising generation of young lawyers and professionals in Grand Rapids.

As had been the case with his predecessors, Judge Wanty found himself during most terms alone holding both the District and Circuit Courts. He complained publicly that "there is an appellate court with no appellate judge," and he supported a bill in Congress to merge the District and Circuit Courts and to appoint the current circuit judges as court of appeals judges.[6]

Judge Wanty was tall, with a commanding presence tempered by a warm sociability, but it turned out that the concerns about his health that were used against him during the succession battle were prescient. Although he was able to perform his judicial duties with distinction for more than five years, on January 9, 1906, he suffered what was described as a "hemorrhage of the bowels" while on the bench of the U.S. Circuit Court of Appeals in Cincinnati where he was serving as a visiting judge.[7] He was hospitalized at The Jewish Hospital in that city for a week, and doctors warned him that his condition was life threatening. After returning to Grand Rapids and taking two months' rest, he returned to his bench to clear up pending cases.[8] He continued on the bench until May 29, and he then adjourned court until August so that he, his wife, and his children could make a European tour, "thinking it would benefit him."[9] However, on Friday, July 6, while the family was in England, he suffered another hemorrhage. "One of the best surgeons in London was called to perform an operation, in the hope of saving his life. [On Saturday], he seemed to be improved, but [on Monday, July 9] he suffered another hemorrhage of the bowel and the efforts of the surgeons were in vain."[10] He died at the age of fifty.

Judge Wanty's many friends worked diligently to return his body from London to Grand Rapids by ocean liner and special train. On July 21, a memorial service was held in his courtroom in the 1879 Government Building, presided over by U.S. Supreme Court Justice William R. Day, a fellow graduate of the University of Michigan. After several public memorial services, Judge Wanty was buried in Oak Hill Cemetery in Grand Rapids. Although Emma Wanty was five years her husband's senior, she lived for twenty-five years after his death, dying in 1931 at the age of eighty. She too was buried at Oak Hill as, after long lives, were their children.

Judge Wanty and the Grand Rapids Water Conspiracy

On March 4, 1902, two residents of Grand Rapids appeared before Judge Wanty in his courtroom in the 1879 Government Building to plead guilty to conspiracy to violate the national banking act by embezzling tens of thousands of dollars from the city's Old National Bank. The defendants were Grand Rapids City Attorney Lant King Salsbury and Stilson V. MacLeod, who had been until recently an officer of the bank. The next day, on March 5, the courtroom was packed, with every spectator seat taken and the standing room filled in anticipation of the judge's imposition of sentence. U.S. Attorney George Covell called the defendants forward separately to receive the court's sentence: two years' imprisonment to be served in the Detroit House of Correction. Judge Wanty addressed MacLeod briefly on the seriousness of his offense; as the defendant returned to his seat, his usually ruddy complexion was almost white. Speaking to Salsbury, the judge noted that it grieved him to sentence an attorney, but Salsbury had betrayed his profession and his honor. The charged offenses were serious enough and the defendants prominent enough to merit local interest, but the defendants' involvement in an embezzlement scandal that had embarrassed Grand Rapids for almost a decade ensured that their fate was reported prominently across the country.

The scandal arose from the city's need for clean water to replace its inadequate and polluted system of pumping water from the Grand River. In 1900, soon after it became known that the city would seek proposals for a new system, a conman from New York City came to Grand Rapids and met with Mayor George Perry and the mayor's trusted advisor, attorney Thomas F. McGarry, to discuss his syndicate's proposal to build an aqueduct from Lake Michigan to Grand Rapids. They agreed that for the New Yorkers to be awarded such a contract, it would be necessary to use bribes, and McGarry identified Salsbury as "the man who could secure the franchise if anyone could."

As it happened, Salsbury needed money and was quite willing to spread the bribe money. Salsbury was a well-respected attorney, thirty-three years old, who had been educated at Albion College and the Law Department of the University of Michigan. He was admitted to the bar in 1890, began a prosperous private practice in Grand Rapids, and worked assiduously to become a member of the city's elite. He lived in a beautiful home on the city's exclusive Lawn Court. He joined the Masons, the Elks, the Knights of Pythias, the Foresters, the Maccabees, and the Woodsmen. He entered politics as a Democrat, twice lost races for Kent County Prosecutor, and was appointed to the Democratic Party's state central committee. He became particularly close to George Perry, and when Perry was elected mayor in 1898, the mayor told the Democratic aldermen of the Common Council, who had a majority of eighteen to six, to elect Salsbury to a two-year term as city attorney.

Salsbury was young, popular, and now part of the city's power structure, but he had a dark secret. Besides his law practice and real estate investments, Salsbury liked to gamble on the price fluctuations of company stocks and wheat futures. By December 1899, Salsbury had suffered a string of bad luck and owed $12,000 (about $350,000 today) that he could not pay. In desperation, Salsbury quietly turned to MacLeod, who agreed to cash checks written by Salsbury even though Salsbury had no money on deposit. Trying to recoup and cover the resulting hole in the bank's accounts before it was discovered, Salsbury lost another $10,000. By June 1900, MacLeod was hiding a hole of about $20,000 in the bank's records.

When Salsbury received the funds to pay bribes, he first paid off his own debt to the bank and then proceeded to provide funds to Mayor Perry, lawyer McGarry, fourteen of the city's twenty-four aldermen, the city clerk, a state senator, two state representatives, and the editors of the city's three newspapers. Eventually, the scheme became public when Salsbury tried to get another bribe from a different consortium, which then sued him. A Kent County grand jury indicted Salsbury, and he was convicted in state court.

After he returned from his federal sentence, Salsbury turned state's evidence in state court and identified everybody he had bribed. They were then indicted in turn. Perry and one or two other bribe recipients were acquitted, but the rest either pleaded guilty or were convicted.

Judge Wanty and the Railroad Tax Cases

One of the most important cases decided by Judge Wanty involved a challenge by Michigan's railroads against the method the state used to determine their tax liabilities. Wanty's opinion deciding in favor of the state made him known nationally, especially after the U.S. Supreme Court affirmed Wanty's decision. However, the amount of labor and stress that the case imposed on the judge may well have contributed to his death.

The source of the case was a momentous change in how Michigan levied and calculated state and local taxes on railroad corporations. From 1850 until 1902, railroads and similar businesses were taxed on their annual gross revenue, while other businesses and individuals were taxed on the current value of their assets, known as an ad valorem tax.[11] The people of Michigan who did not own or operate a railroad generally believed that this resulted in the railroads paying less than their fair share of taxes. In 1900, after twenty years of controversy, the legislature determined to abandon this revenue method to tax railroads and similar corporations and to use instead the ad valorem method imposed on other businesses. However, the legislature could not make this change without an amendment to the state constitution.

In 1899 the Michigan Supreme Court had held that an ad valorem tax on telephone and telegraph lines violated the state constitution.[12] Thus, if such a tax were to be applied to railroads, a constitutional amendment was necessary. In October 1900, a special session of the legislature proposed an amendment that authorized ad valorem taxes on railroads and created a state board of assessors to determine the true cash value of businesses subject to the tax. The electorate ratified this proposal in the November 1900 election.[13] In its 1901 session, the legislature passed the law for the assessment of the property of all corporations at their true cash value by a State Board of Assessors, which would then calculate tax rates for state, township, county, school, and municipal taxes.[14]

The result was a doubling of taxes assessed against railroads in 1902, 1903, and 1904.[15] Naturally, railroads objected, and almost all of them paid only the amount that would have been levied under the prior law. In March 1903, the railroad companies filed dozens of separate suits in the Western District's Circuit Court against Perry F. Powers, Michigan's Auditor General from 1901 to 1904, seeking to enjoin Powers from collecting the additional taxes.[16] Judge Wanty appointed Charles L. Fitch, who was not only the clerk of the Circuit Court but also a master in chancery and a U.S. Commissioner, to take testimony in advance of the trial, resulting in some 20,000 folios, which were reduced to an abstract containing 1,300 pages.[17] Wanty reviewed these documents and conducted two weeks of argument[18] before reaching his decision, which, for the most part, vindicated the state's actions.

In a lengthy and comprehensive opinion dated May 19, 1905,[19] Judge Wanty held, first, that federal courts did have jurisdiction over cases in which the plaintiffs allege, in good faith, that a state has acted in ways that have injured plaintiffs and that violate the U.S. Constitution. Once jurisdiction attached, he added, federal courts can retain jurisdiction to deal with "other questions arising on the record," even if the federal issues raised by plaintiffs fail. Having dealt with the state's jurisdictional challenge, he addressed the merits and held for the state. He ruled that neither a state's change in its "system of taxation" nor the creation of different tax "classes" violated the U.S. Constitution's guarantees of equal protection under the law and due process or of the Constitution's prohibition on taking private property without compensation. In April 1906, the U.S. Supreme Court adopted Judge Wanty's reasoning in affirming his decision.[20]

At a memorial session for Judge Wanty in the Michigan Supreme Court on October 16, 1906, Justice Charles A. Blair remembered:

> It was my privilege to appear before Judge Wanty on the hearing of the Railroad Tax Cases. . . . I had known him as an able lawyer; his disposition of that important litigation satisfied me that he was a great judge. The luminous opinion which he handed down speaks for itself and will continue to declare the merit of its author so long as the reports of the exalted tribunal which approved it remain. It must have been a source of just pride to Judge Wanty to learn that he had been deemed equal to the demands

of a great case by those most competent to determine. Said the Supreme Court of the United States: "In view of the exhaustive and well-considered opinion of the trial judge, with the general trend of which we concur, it is unnecessary to further extend this opinion. It is sufficient to refer to that opinion for a consideration of those questions."[21]

Another Competitive Judicial Succession

Judge Wanty's sudden, unanticipated death left western Michigan's power brokers in some confusion. The *Grand Rapids Daily News* reported that the city's legal community strongly favored Arthur Carter Denison, whom the paper described as a native of Grand Rapids and a lifelong Republican who was extremely popular among members of the profession across the state.[22] However, it did not take long for other candidates to emerge, including Michigan Circuit Court Judge Alfred W. Wolcott, George Clapperton, Roger W. Butterfield, Charles B. Blair, and Thomas J. O'Brien, all of Grand Rapids, as well as Dallas Roudeman of Kalamazoo, James O'Harra of St. Joseph, Michigan Circuit Court Judge Orville W. Coolidge of Niles, Michigan Circuit Court Judge Clarence W. Sessions of Muskegon, and Charles F. Button of Marquette.

Under the unwritten rules of federal judicial appointments, selection of the person to succeed Judge Wanty was controlled by Michigan's senior U.S. senator, Julius Caesar Burrows from Kalamazoo. For some reason, Burrows would not select Arthur Denison but instead favored Loyal E. Knappen, Judge Wanty's former law partner in Grand Rapids. Burrows had become familiar with Knappen years earlier when Knappen practiced in Barry County and Burrows was a congressman representing that area, but there was a problem: soon after Judge Wanty died, Knappen publicly endorsed Denison, and Knappen informed Burrows that he felt honor-bound to continue that support. But as time passed without a successor on the bench, and with Burrows still ruling out Denison, Knappen finally agreed to let Burrows recommend him to President Theodore Roosevelt for the nomination.[23] On December 3, 1906, President Roosevelt nominated Knappen to succeed Judge Wanty, and the Senate confirmed the nomination on December 10.

Judge Loyal Edwin Knappen

U.S. District Judge Loyal Edwin Knappen

Loyal E. Knappen was born on January 27, 1854, in Hastings, Barry County, Michigan, the son of Edward and Sarah M. (Nevins) Knappen. His father, a merchant, died of typhoid just a few months later, and Loyal was raised by his mother. He entered the University of Michigan at the age of fifteen and graduated with the degrees of bachelor of arts in 1873 and, after he became an attorney, master of arts in 1876. After earning his BA, he returned to Hastings to work as assistant principal of Hastings High School for six months and then read law with prominent Hastings attorney James A. Sweezy. He joined the bar of Barry County in 1875, and he married Amelia Isabelle Kenyon of Hastings on October 23, 1876; they had three children, Stuart E., Frederick M., and Florence.

Knappen practiced in Hastings with Sweezy from 1875 to 1878, and with his brother Charles, as Knappen & Knappen, from 1878 to 1883, when Charles retired from practice. Knappen then was a partner with Christopher Van Arman, as Knappen & Van Arman, from 1883 to 1888. In 1888 Knappen and Van Arman formed a firm with Knappen's brother-in-law, William J. Stuart of Grand Rapids, to practice in both towns, with Knappen moving to Grand Rapids. After Van Arman's death, the Hastings office was closed and Knappen practiced in

Grand Rapids only with Stuart until 1893 when Stuart was elected to the superior court. From 1893 to 1899, he practiced with Edward Taggart and Arthur Denison as Taggart, Knappen, & Denison. In 1899 he became a partner with George Wanty until the latter's appointment to the U.S. District Court in 1900.

In addition to his private practice, Loyal Knappen was elected twice as Prosecutor for Barry County, serving from 1879 to 1883. After moving to Grand Rapids he was an assistant Kent County Prosecutor, and he served as a federal Circuit Court commissioner for the Western District of Michigan from 1880 to 1888. He was a member of the public school boards of both Hastings and Grand Rapids, and he was a regent of the University of Michigan from 1904 until 1911. At the completion of his service as regent, the university awarded him the honorary degree of doctor of laws. In 1905, he was president of the Grand Rapids Bar Association.

Judge Knappen remained on the District Court bench for only three years before President William Howard Taft, on January 17, 1910, nominated him to a seat on the U.S. Court of Appeals for the Sixth Circuit that had become vacant when Horace Harmon Lurton was elevated to the U.S. Supreme Court. As a member of the Court of Appeals, Knappen was also a member of the U.S. Circuit Courts for the Sixth Circuit until the abolition of the old Circuit Courts on January 1, 1912. He assumed senior status on the Court of Appeals on April 15, 1924. He is the only person from the Western District to have served as a Circuit Court commissioner, U.S. District Judge, U.S. Circuit Judge, and as a judge on the U.S. Court of Appeals for the Sixth Circuit.

Judge Knappen died of heart disease, at his home, 330 Washington Street, SE, in Grand Rapids, on May 14, 1930, at the age of seventy-six. He is buried in Oak Hill Cemetery in Grand Rapids; his wife, Amelia, was buried alongside him when she died just four months after the judge. On the day after Judge Knappen's death, Arthur Denison, his former law partner and his successor on the bench of the U.S. District Court, remembered Judge Knappen as a man who was "always courteous, always kindly, honorable in the highest degree." Denison praised him as "an unusual example of ability to work both thoroughly and rapidly," and noted that after taking senior status he "continued until the last few months hearing cases and writing opinions in Circuit Court of appeals. . . . Outside his family he has had no interest beside his work. Even yesterday he spent some hours at his desk upon the preparation of an opinion. I am sure, if he could have chosen, he would have preferred just the method of taking off that came to him—still working."[24]

Judge Arthur Carter Denison

U.S. District Judge Arthur Carter Denison

Arthur C. Denison was born on November 10, 1861, in Grand Rapids. His parents, Julius Coe and Cornelia (Carter) Denison, were farmers who emigrated from western New York in 1855 and settled in Paris Township, Kent County, Michigan. After schooling in Grand Rapids, Arthur attended the Law Department of the University of Michigan, receiving his bachelor of laws degree in 1883. In 1886, Denison married Susie L. Goodrich with whom he had three sons: John, Donald, and Arthur. Susie Denison died in 1896; in 1898 Denison remarried to Julia Barlow with whom he had a daughter, Ruth.

After receiving his law degree, Denison returned to Grand Rapids and began to practice with Edward Taggert as Taggert & Denison. In 1900, Loyal E. Knappen joined the firm, which became Taggert, Knappen & Denison. Denison was a leader of the bar. In 1904, he became the third president of the recently formed Grand Rapids Bar Association, and in 1906 he served a year as president of the Michigan Bar Association. Denison was named prominently as a candidate for the District Judge position after Judge Wanty's death in 1906, but that position went to his former law partner, Loyal Knappen. Denison then joined in practice with Hugh Wilson.

Denison's opportunity to join the federal bench came just more than three years later when Knappen joined the U.S. Court of Appeals. On January 17, 1910, President William Howard Taft appointed Denison to replace Knappen. On January 31, the Senate confirmed Denison's nomination, and he received his commission. During construction of the new courthouse in Grand Rapids, Denison maintained a small office in the temporary federal office building across North Division Street.

Judge Denison's tenure on the District Court bench was short. Thirteen months later, on February 25, 1911, President Taft appointed him to replace Judge Severens, who had retired, on the U.S. Court of Appeals for the Sixth Circuit and the U.S. Circuit Court for the Sixth Circuit. Denison was confirmed by the Senate and received his commission on March 2, 1911. Denison was the fourth of the first five judges of the Western Michigan District Court to be appointed to the Sixth Circuit and the third to serve.[25] The fifth, Judge Wanty, died before he could be considered. No judge of the Western District has ever been appointed to the U.S. Supreme Court, although there was speculation that President Taft would have elevated his close friend Denison to that position if Taft had served a second presidential term.

As with his tenure on the District Court, Judge Denison's service as a Circuit Court judge was brief, ending on January 1, 1912, when the old Circuit Courts were abolished. It was on the Court of Appeals that he spent almost all of his time as a federal judge, twenty years of hearings and opinions.[26] In 1925, while still on the Sixth Circuit, President Calvin Coolidge appointed Denison to a nonjudicial position on an investigative body known as the Aircraft Board, to study the status of aviation in the United States, a very controversial subject at that time.

Judge Denison qualified for retirement on his seventieth birthday, November 10, 1931, and he resigned effective December 31 of that year to "return to private practice in order to make more adequate provision for his family than his judicial salary permitted."[27] He joined the Cleveland, Ohio firm of Baker, Hostetler, & Patterson, where he continued that practice until he died on May 27, 1942, in Shaker Heights, Ohio, at the age of eighty. His body was returned to Grand Rapids for burial in Oak Hill Cemetery.

The 1909 Grand Rapids U.S. Post Office and Courthouse

By the turn of the twentieth century, it had become clear that the city's 1879 federal Government Building was too cramped to house the ever-growing

The western exterior of the former 1909 Grand Rapids U.S. Post office and Courthouse, known as "Noah's Ark," photograph taken 2016.

The western and southern exteriors of the 1909 Grand Rapids U.S. Post office and Courthouse, photograph dated November 1, 1910.

The southern
entrance to the
former 1909 U.S.
Post office and
Courthouse,
photograph
taken 2016.

federal presence in the city. Besides, there was an opinion in the community that the brick, Italianate style of the 1879 building looked old-fashioned
and did not sufficiently reflect the dignity and aspirations of the people of
Grand Rapids. Now the furniture capital of the nation, the city had 110,000
residents in 1900 and was still growing. As is often the case, though, with
public construction projects, there was a problem: money. The Government
Building had cost $212,000, and Congress was loath to spend more to extend
or replace a building that was less than thirty years old. However, when the
city's leaders noticed that Congress had appropriated $800,000 for a new
building in Richmond, Virginia, they let Michigan's congressional delegation
know that Grand Rapids deserved a federal building that was just as good.

    Luckily, in 1906 Congress embarked on an enormous drive to construct
new federal buildings across the country. The city officers and the local con-

gressman, William Alden Smith, worked persistently to convince Congress to add Grand Rapids to the list of cities to receive one of the new buildings. On June 30, 1906, Congress passed an "Omnibus Public Buildings Act" that increased the maximum cost of certain existing building projects and authorized more than 100 new federal buildings,[28] including one for Grand Rapids. In section 14 of the act, Congress authorized the secretary of the treasury to "dispose of" the Government Building and to "cause to be erected upon the same site there of a suitable building, . . . for the use of the United States post-office, courts, and other governmental offices in said city, at a limit of cost for said building of not to exceed five hundred thousand dollars."[29] In a separate statute passed the same day, Congress appropriated money to begin the construction of many of those buildings, including an appropriation of $10,000 for Grand Rapids.[30]

On March 4, 1907, Congress appropriated $150,000 more "for continuation of building." Because Congress had directed that the new building be on the same site as the old, the Government Building had to be destroyed to start the project, and the occupants had to move elsewhere pending the completion of the new building. So, in the same appropriation, Congress added $16,000 for moving expenses and the rent for "temporary quarters."[31] Suitable quarters for the federal courts to rent were found close by, in a building just across the street to the east, at what was then 116 to 120 North Division Avenue, between Pearl and Lyon Streets.[32] Further appropriations followed from May 1907 to December 1910, both for construction and for rent—a total of the $500,000 authorized for the building and $19,300 for rent.[33]

The new building was designed by the office of James Knox Taylor, the Treasury Department's Supervising Architect from 1897 to 1912. Some design elements were mandated by Congress in the authorizing statute: fireproof vaults, heating and ventilating apparatus, elevators, and approaches. Other elements were left to the architects, including size, although the designated maximum cost indicated that the new building would be much larger than the old. The Government Building took up much less than the full site; the remainder of the site was a park. The architects used practically all of the site to create a massive and imposing new four-story building in the Florentine Renaissance style with Beaux Arts features. Instead of marble or brick for the exterior walls, the architects chose a light-colored granite, which was more durable and better suited to resist the corrosive smoke emanating from the factories of the furniture manufacturing capital. More than three railcar loads of Vermont white granite were used for the building's exterior facing.[34] The building has arched doorways, large pillars, and horizontal bands of stone called string courses. Pyramids crown the windows, and the solid bronze double entrance doors are recessed. The cavernous block-long public corridor on the first floor leads to a spiral staircase up to the second floor, on the west side of which were the two main courtrooms, as large as ballrooms and two stories high, with tall windows overlooking Ionia Avenue. In both courtrooms, the judge's bench was set on a raised stage between two imposing Ionic columns, each eighteen feet tall and three feet around. Scattered throughout the building would eventually be eleven large safes, some the size of small rooms, manufactured by the Herrington-Hall-Marvin Safe Company, of Hamilton, Ohio, and bearing the date 1909. One carried the image of the seal of the United States. There was also a holding cell. In addition to the stairway, the architects provided space for three elevators, which the building contractor ordered from Otis Elevator, two electric elevators for passengers and one hydraulic for freight, to be installed by December 24, 1909.[35]

Although the exterior of the new federal building was dignified and stately, and its interior was much larger than that of its predecessor, concerns developed during and after construction, as is common for many new buildings. In May 1910, even before the construction was complete, Senator Smith complained that the space allocated to the post office was too small and that the city needed a second post office.[36] In February 1911, Judge Denison, while in Washington on other business, met with the Supervising Architect Taylor "to submit to him complaints against the telephone service and other features of the federal building at Grand Rapids." Taylor assured the judge that his staff would "make the needed improvements in the building . . . in order that it will be entirely satisfactory to its occupants."[37] One deficiency that may have been troubling from the beginning but which did not become crucial for four decades was that, large as the building was and while it was built with two courtrooms, it had only one chambers suite for a judge, situated on the southwest corner of the second floor. When Congress authorized a second judge for the District Court in 1954, a local newspaper commented that there was no office space available for the new judge and that he might have to have his chambers in the office of the U.S. Marshal.[38] Ultimately, the second floor was remodeled to create a second set of chambers on the northwest corner.

The laying of the cornerstone for the new building became the subject of a local dispute that had to be resolved in Washington. In anticipation of the event, the Grand Rapids Board of Trade invited the local Masonic order to take charge. The Masons prepared for a gala celebration and asked many dignitaries to attend, including President Theodore Roosevelt. Then some members of the Board of Trade objected to the Masons being entirely in charge, and the board declared that the Masons would merely assist in the ceremony. The Masons refused to proceed under such terms and walked out. The board tried to take up the planning, but "dissension broke out among the members," and on December 29 "it was announced that the attempt to hold the ceremony would be abandoned altogether."[39] Instead, authorities decided to conduct a quiet, private laying of the cornerstone, to take place on December 31, 1908. Just before that ceremony could take place, though, Supervising Architect Taylor sent a telegram from Washington to the contractors directing them to hold the laying in abeyance. Knox gave no explanation in his order, and the *Detroit Free Press* reported on January 1, 1909, that it had learned from a source in Washington that the reason "is carefully guarded here," and that both Knox and Michigan's Senator William Alden Smith declined to comment.[40] Two days later, the *Free Press* identified Senator Smith as the person who vetoed the private ceremony. According to the newspaper, Smith took the issue personally because, as a congressman, he had obtained the appropriation for the building, and he wanted the fruits of his efforts to be recognized with the pomp and ceremony of a public event.[41]

Ultimately, a decision was made by somebody that the laying of the cornerstone would take place in a gala public ceremony, sponsored by the Masons, on February 12, 1909, which was the 100th birth date of President Lincoln, a cherished icon for the people of Grand Rapids who had signed into law the statute creating the Western District of Michigan. It was also the day of the annual nominating convention of the Michigan Republican Party to be held in Grand Rapids. On February 6, the convention announced that among the guests of honor would be Congressman Nicholas Longworth and his wife, Alice Roosevelt Longworth, the popular daughter of President Roosevelt.[42] She was frequently referred to as "Princess Alice," and her twenty-fifth birthday was also February 12. The presence of Mrs. Longworth and of the state Republican Party in Grand Rapids for its nominating convention assured a fine turnout at the cornerstone laying.[43]

The major tenant of the new federal building, as of the old, was the U.S. Post Office, which occupied the entire first floor. In addition to the judicial chambers, the second floor contained two courtrooms on its west side, one designed for the District Court and the other for the old Circuit Court, which expired at the end of 1911. The U.S. Attorney's office was on the northwest corner of the third floor, and the bankruptcy hearing room on the fourth floor. Other tenants included the local congressman, the Federal Bureau of Investigation, the Secret Service, the Railroad Retirement Board, and, a few years later, the Selective Service registrars.

On November 12, 1924, the 1909 federal building avoided a disaster that could have destroyed the entire building and that did level a wooden loading station. In the late afternoon, all of downtown Grand Rapids was shocked by the sound of an enormous blast that shattered windows for blocks around the federal building. An explosion had destroyed the frame loading station which had been attached to the east side of the federal building, fronting on Division Avenue North, for the post office. The city's police and fire departments rushed to the scene and secured the blast site. In the rubble they found two men dead and another dying, as well as seven men with broken bones and several others with minor injuries.[44] The explosion was heard across the city where it broke window panes in some five hundred businesses.

The force of the explosion was so great that it destroyed most of the machinery in the dock and threw a postal truck onto the roof of the federal building. Several automobiles parked nearby were badly damaged, and mail packages and pouches, thrown high in the air, came down in a shower.[45] The only damage to the federal building itself was broken window glass, but a blast of soot through one of the broken panes in the courtroom struck Judge Sessions full in the face, whereupon he immediately recessed the trial he was hearing until the next day. Ella Mae Backus, an Assistant U.S. Attorney and clerk whose office was on the third floor directly above the explosion, found her room and the corridor outside her door full of smoke and the top of her desk completely covered with broken glass.

After inspecting the site, postal inspectors sent from Chicago concluded that the explosion was caused by a break in the natural gas line that ran through the federal building and under the floor of the loading dock. Investigators from the Grand Rapids police and fire departments agreed that gas was likely the cause of the destruction. Explosions caused by leaking gas lines were common in 1924, and workers at the post office had complained about the smell of gas for days before the explosion. The demolition of the loading building and the force required to launch a truck onto the federal building's roof were consistent with the enormous power unleashed by a gas explosion.

The Grand Rapids Gas Lighting Company, which had installed the federal building's gas system and supplied its gas, naturally disagreed and argued that a prematurely detonating mail bomb was a more likely culprit. This theory gathered some support from people who remembered the dozens of bombs sent through the mail, allegedly by radical unionists, to government buildings and officials and to prominent businessmen just after the war. More recently, on the previous March 12, a dynamite bomb planted by racketeers near an illegal bar in Detroit injured thirty people.[46] However, the investigators rejected any bomb theory and pointed out that the amount of dynamite needed to achieve the results, particularly lifting the truck onto the roof, was too large to be practical for a mail bomb.

The District Court continued to meet in the 1909 courthouse until December 29, 1972. In March 1931, Congress authorized the "extension and remodeling" of what was then a twenty-three-year-old building, "under an estimated total cost of $300,000."[47] However, two years later, Congress repealed that appropriation along with those for many other federal building projects.[48] In January, 1973, the District Court and other federal agencies moved to what is now the Gerald R. Ford Federal Building and U.S. Courthouse at 110 Michigan Street NW in Grand Rapids.

In 1974, the vacant 1909 court building was added to the National Register of Historic Places. In 1981, its lower three stories were remodeled to house the Grand Rapids Art Museum, which remained there until 2007 when it moved to the city's Monroe Center. Following the exit of the museum, the building was once again vacant and fell into terrible disrepair. On the top floor, plastic tarps and barrels collected rainwater dropping from holes in the roof. But fortunately, the grand old building was saved once again in 2010 when Ferris State University acquired it. The university renamed the building for its founder, Woodward N. Ferris, and remodeled and restored it in accordance with federal and state preservation standards to provide additional space for the university's Kendall College of Art and Design.

The 1911 Sault Ste. Marie Federal Building and U.S. Courthouse, and the First Sessions of the District Court in Sault Ste. Marie

Sault Ste. Marie, a community, now a city, at the eastern end of Lake Superior, is one of the oldest European settlements west of the Allegheny Mountains.

The northeastern exterior and entrance to the former 1911
Sault Ste. Marie Federal Building and U.S. Courthouse, now the City Hall.
The U.S. courts last used this building in 1941.

It has been part of the United States since 1783, part of the state of Michigan
since 1837, and part of the Western District of Michigan since 1878. But Sault
Ste. Marie did not have a public federal building until 1911, and the Western
District did not hold court there until 1913.

Because it was a border and frontier location, Sault Ste. Marie had had
a U.S. Army military reservation, Fort Brady, since 1822. On July 8, 1886,
Congress ordered that most of the military reservation at Fort Brady be sold
and other land in or near Sault Ste. Marie be purchased to construct a new
Fort Brady.[49] Although the fort was moved to higher ground in 1893 (the
current site of Lake Superior State University), sale of the old fort's land was
slow, and by 1906 there was sufficient land remaining to accommodate a federal building. Early in 1906, Congress undertook a vast project involving the
construction, enlargement, and increases in authorized costs for more than
three hundred federal buildings in towns and cities across the nation at a cost
of more than $25 million.

However, the Sault's community leaders were disappointed that the bill

1911

Eastern District
- Northern Division
- Southern Division

Western District
- Northern Division
- Southern Division

● Place of Holding Court
  (1900) Court added

* Designated as a Place of Holding Court
  for the Northern Division

Marquette ●   Sault Ste. Marie ● (1912)

Bay City ●

Grand Rapids ●   Port Huron ● *

Detroit ●

Eastern and Western Districts of Michigan, 1911

submitted by the House to the Senate did not include a building for their town. Determined not to give up, Mayor Frank Perry and George P. Mc-Callum went to Washington to lobby Congress to include the city in the final version of the bill. At first, Congressman Horace Olin Young, who represented Michigan's Upper Peninsula, seemed to favor Escanaba for a new building, but Senator Julius Caesar Burrows promised his influence for the Sault.[50] So, at the last minute, the Senate Committee on Public Buildings did add Sault Ste. Marie to the list. The final statute, enacted on June 30, 1906, authorized the construction of a "United States post-office" at Sault Ste. Marie, "on ground now owned by the United States," for a maximum cost of $100,000.[51]

The "ground now owned by the United States" was available because on

May 12, 1906, Congress exempted from the sale of old Fort Brady an area "bounded on the north by that part of Water street adjacent to the Government park, on the east by Brady street, on the south by Portage avenue, and on the west by Bingham avenue."[52] On June 30, Congress also appropriated $20,000 to begin construction,[53] and in March 1907 appropriated an additional $60,000 to continue construction.[54] By 1908, Congress became aware that it had underestimated the cost of many of the buildings it had authorized. So, in May 1908, Congress increased the maximum cost allowed for many buildings including raising the maximum cost of Sault Ste. Marie's new building to $150,000,[55] which it covered by appropriations in March 1909 and June 1910.[56]

The result was a building designed under the supervision of James Knox Taylor, the Supervising Architect of the Treasury Department whose office also designed the 1909 Grand Rapids federal building. Located at 225 E. Portage Avenue, it was and still is a handsome three-story building with walls of cut limestone from a Bedford, Indiana quarry. Its style has been described variously as Renaissance Revival, Palladian, and Romano Tuscan. On September 9, 1977, the building was placed on the National Register of Historic Places.

Although the building authorized by Congress was characterized as a "post-office," the architects made sure that the third floor was appropriate for use as a federal court. So, it was not shocking when, on July 9, 1912, Congress directed the District Court[57] of the Western District to hold two terms there annually, in January and July.[58] The court's first term was held from Tuesday to Thursday, January 14–16, 1913.[59] Judge Sessions and other federal officials arrived in Sault Ste. Marie the day before from Marquette and were met with temperature lows between 0 and 4 degrees Fahrenheit.[60] There were three criminal cases on the docket, all charging "white slavery," and bankruptcy cases. After three days, Judge Sessions declared the term over and returned to Grand Rapids.

The court continued to hold terms in Sault Ste. Marie until 1941, although during some years the Sault terms were held instead in Marquette or Grand Rapids. The last term actually held in Sault Ste. Marie began on Tuesday, June 3, 1941. Another term was scheduled for January 1942, but the attack on Pearl Harbor intervened, the canal locks became a high-security area, and the federal courts rarely returned to Sault Ste. Marie. Congress has kept Sault Ste. Marie on the list of approved cities in which to hold the District Court in

Judge Clarence William Sessions

the Northern Division[61] although the city no longer has a federal courthouse or facility. In 1980, the building was sold to a private party, which in turn sold it in 1989 to a nursing home corporation for the company's corporate headquarters and as a home for the River of History Museum. In May 2008, that corporation donated the building to the city of Sault Ste. Marie, which renovated it and has used it as the city hall since June 2011. The museum was moved to another building in the city.

U.S. District Judge Clarence William Sessions

Judge Clarence W. Sessions was born on February 8, 1859, on a farm in North Plains Township, Ionia County, Michigan, the son of William and Julia (Jennison) Sessions. In addition to farming, William Sessions was attracted to politics, and he was elected to the state legislature in 1872 for one term. The family moved to the town of Ionia when Clarence was twelve years old, and he graduated from Ionia High School in 1877. He began attending the University of Michigan in the fall of that year, but left in 1880, near the end of his junior year, due to "eye difficulties." He returned to Ann Arbor and graduated with a bachelor of arts degree in 1881. For a short time after graduating, he worked in the lumber business with his father, but he decided to become a lawyer and read law in Ionia at the firm of Mitchell, Bell & McGarry. In 1882, Sessions married Mary S. Foote, the daughter of a Presbyterian minister, and they had two children, Clarence and Marjorie. He became a member of the bar in Ionia in the spring of 1884, and in August 1885 he moved his practice to Muskegon where he practiced until 1906, first with Lewis M. Miller and then as a partner in Nims, Hoyt, Erwin, Sessions & Vander Werp.

In 1893, Judge Sessions was appointed to a one-year term as Muskegon city attorney and served in that position again from 1897 to 1899 and again in 1902. In 1905, he was elected as a Republican (defeating his former partner, Dan T. Chamberlain) to be judge of Michigan's Fourteenth Circuit Court, serving Muskegon County from 1906 until 1911. When Judge Wanty died, Sessions "announced his candidacy for the federal judgeship."[62] Although he had strong support in Muskegon, the power of the Republican party was in Grand Rapids where he was not considered a serious candidate at that time. Four years later, Sessions was a candidate to become the Chief Judge of the U.S. Court of Customs Appeals.[63] In March 1910, there was a report that President William Howard Taft had chosen Sessions, but a few days later, to his disappointment, President Taft announced that he had nominated Michigan Supreme Court Justice Robert M. Montgomery instead. It seems that Taft had told one of Michigan's U.S. senators that he would appoint Sessions, forgetting that he had already promised Michigan's other senator that he would appoint Montgomery.[64] On February 25, 1911, President Taft made up for this mix-up by nominating Sessions to replace Judge Denison on the District Court for the Western District. The Senate confirmed the appointment, and Sessions received his commission on March 2.

During his twenty-year career on the federal bench, Judge Sessions achieved national notice for several cases and rulings involving the sale and manufacture of alcoholic beverages, electoral spending limits, baseball's reserve clause, and one of the greatest American civilian maritime disasters of all time. He also became well known to litigants appearing before him for his policy of speedy justice, a policy that he based on his attitude that "as long as I have strength there shall be no unnecessary delay in any court in which I preside." Sessions was always "a jurist who has been acclaimed for his speedy justice, who was devoted to public life, and a judge who was unable to relax while there was work to be done."[65] Beginning in 1919, this policy placed him under enormous stress as he struggled to deal with the grossly swollen dockets caused by Prohibition.

Judge Sessions and the Federal League Case[66]

In April 1914, Judge Sessions heard a request for an injunction in a case whose subject matter, baseball's reserve clause, was still controversial seventy years later. His decision in the case is often misunderstood by lawyers and the general public alike as upholding the reserve clause. In fact, in his opinion he expressed his belief that the reserve clause was unenforceable, but he refused to grant relief to the parties challenging the clause based on an ancient rule of judicial discretion that allowed a judge to refuse to rule on the request for an injunction. Thus, Sessions's stated belief that the clause was unenforceable did not constitute a ruling that established legal precedent.

Organized professional baseball began in 1876 with the formation of the National League of Professional Baseball Clubs. During the remainder of the nineteenth century, the National League managed to fight off various other leagues trying to compete with it as a "major" league. Two of the strengths of the National League were an agreement among teams to limit players' salaries and a clause in its standard player contract, the reserve clause, which allowed teams to extend a player's contract indefinitely, thus keeping players from leaving to join other teams while the contract allowed teams to fire players on ten days' notice.

In 1900, one of the numerous minor leagues trying to become major, the Western League, renamed itself the American League of Professional Baseball Clubs and began to compete with the Nationals. The American League placed teams in major cities and raided the National League for star players by offering them contracts with higher salaries, no salary ceiling, and no reserve clause. The National League resisted, but the American League teams were drawing far more fans while many of the National League teams were struggling financially. At the end of the 1902 season, the two leagues entered into a "National Agreement" in which the leagues remained separate but the American League agreed to adopt the reserve clause. Both leagues agreed not to employ any player of another team covered by the reserve clause, not to play against any team that violated the agreement, and not to allow their ballparks to be used by any team that violated the agreement.

The National Agreement helped the National League to improve its finances and kept major league baseball stable for a decade. Then in 1913 another group of would-be major league baseball team owners formed the Federal League of Baseball Clubs with plans to form new teams in competition with the National and American Leagues. Copying the American League's 1900 strategy, the Federal League team owners announced that they would pay players more, with no salary cap, and that they would ignore the reserve clause. Several American and National League stars either signed contracts with Federal teams or used the threat of doing so to negotiate better contracts with their current teams. One of those players was catcher William Killefer, Jr. of the Philadelphia Phillies of the National League.[67]

Killefer was born in Bloomingdale and raised in Paw Paw, both towns in Van Buren County, Michigan, within the jurisdiction of the Western District of Michigan. He played as a catcher in the major leagues from 1909 until 1921, known to the public either as Red or as Reindeer Bill. He joined the Philadelphia Phillies of the National League in 1911 and soon became the favorite catcher of legendary pitcher Grover Cleveland Alexander. Over their careers, Killefer caught 250 major league games with Alexander. Before the 1913 season, Killefer signed a one-year contract to play with the Phillies for $3,000. Although the contract stated that it was just for the 1913 season, it contained the National League's standard reserve clause: "In consideration of the compensation paid to [the player] by [the club], [the player] agrees and obligates himself to contract with and continue in the service of [the club] for the succeeding season at a salary to be determined by the parties to such contract." In other words, the team reserved the right to keep Killefer for as many years as it wished, at a salary to be agreed upon each year.

At the end of the 1913 season, Killefer was approached by the Federal League's new team in Chicago, known initially as the Chi-Feds and later as the Whales. The Chi-Feds were owned by millionaire Charles Weeghman, a former waiter who had become rich by starting and operating a popular chain of lunch counter restaurants in Chicago, and his partner, William M. Walker. On January 8, 1914, after some negotiation, Killefer signed a three-year contract with the ChiFeds for $5,833.33 per year with no reserve clause. Weeghman gave Killefer $500 as a down payment and told him to come back to Chicago to travel with the rest of the team to Louisiana for spring training. Two weeks later, the Phillies, in a panic that the team might lose not only Killefer's own skills but also those of Alexander if he followed his favorite catcher to Chicago, gave Killefer a new, three-year contract for $6,500 per year. According to the contract, Killefer's actual salary was to be $4,875 per year, while the balance, $1,625, was compensation for accepting the reserve clause. This strategy, obtaining a Federal League contract and then returning to the player's original team with a significant raise, was adopted by other players recruited by the Federals and became known in the newspapers as "doing a Killefer."

Killefer tried to return the $500 he had received from the Chi-Feds, but Weeghman refused to accept it. Instead, Weeghman and other Federal League owners decided to use Killefer's switch back to the Phillies as their vehicle to have a federal court issue a ruling that the reserve clause rendered the Nationals' standard contract unenforceable. On March 20, 1914, after months of threatening and posturing among the teams and their leagues, Weeghman and Walker, "co-partners doing business under the firm name and style of Chicago Federal League Base Ball Club," began a lawsuit in the U.S. District Court for the Western District of Michigan seeking temporary and permanent injunctions restraining Killefer from playing for any baseball team or club other than the Chi-Feds. On March 27, the plaintiffs filed their bill of complaint setting out allegations to support their request for equitable relief: that finding a skilled catcher was more difficult than finding a skilled player for any other position and that Killefer was a catcher of "unique and extraordinary skill" whose loss would cause the ChiFeds to suffer "irreparable injury" both because of those skills and because he had been "widely advertised as a drawing card" for the Chi-Feds.[68]

The request for an injunction made this complaint a "libel" in equity, a form of jurisprudence that had been developed in medieval England by the chancellor's courts in parallel with the king's common law courts. During the American colonial period, the courts of the colonies had adopted both the common law and equity in civil (i.e., noncriminal) cases, as later did the courts of the states and the federal government. The distinctive feature of equity is that, while the common law operates under strict and specific laws and rules in deciding whether to grant or deny relief, usually in the form of money damages, equity is based on vaguer concepts of morality, fairness, and discretion, which give its judges, historically known as chancellors, leeway to formulate relief. That relief is usually a court order or injunction requiring the defendant to do something or not to do something. The chancellor has discretion to structure the injunction to fit a specific case. That discretion is tempered by certain "equitable maxims" that shape and limit the scope of the relief available. One important maxim is that the chancellor could not act if the petitioner had an adequate remedy at law, usually meaning money damages. Another maxim states that the chancellor would not force an employee under contract who had left the employer to return to work for that employer. Instead, the available relief is an injunction barring the employee from working for anybody else. A third maxim that became crucial to the Killefer case is the doctrine known as "unclean hands" under which a plaintiff seeking equitable relief must not have acted, with respect to the subject of the case, in a manner that was "unconscientious, inequitable, or characterized by bad faith.... It is not alone fraud or illegality which will prevent a suitor from entering a court of equity; any really unconscientious conduct, connected with the controversy to which he is a party, will repel him from the forum whose very foundation is good conscience."[69]

Why Weeghman's attorneys filed the complaint against Reindeer Bill in the U.S. District Court for the Western District in Grand Rapids is not clear. Their stated reason was that the court had jurisdiction because Reindeer Bill still had his legal residence at his parents' home near Paw Paw, within the Western District of Michigan. In fact, the U.S. Deputy Marshal served the pleadings not by handing them to Bill but by leaving them at the Paw Paw home of William Killefer Sr., Bill's father. The Chi-Feds and the Federal League certainly had an understandable desire to avoid litigating the case in Philadelphia, and while a judge in Chicago might have been more favorable to a local team, he might also have been a fan of the American League's Chicago White Sox, who feared that Weeghman's team was a threat to their business. Still, why the Western District? Maybe it was simply that Grand Rapids was the alternative forum convenient for Weeghman and for the Federal League's general counsel, Edward E. Gates, who lived in Indianapolis. Or it may have been a matter of choosing a district where the petitioners could make a plausible argument for personal jurisdiction over Reindeer Bill, who may have lived in Paw Paw in the offseason. Whatever the reason, neither the court nor the defendants challenged the plaintiffs' choice of the Western District, a choice plaintiffs would come to regret.

The hearing on the Chi-Feds' request for a temporary injunction took place before Judge Sessions, in his second-floor courtroom in Grand Rapids' 1909 federal building, on Saturday, April 4, 1914. The first business was a petition by the Phillies to intervene as defendants, a petition the judge promptly granted. The attorneys of record for the plaintiffs were Stuart E. Knappen of Grand Rapids, the son of U.S. Court of Appeals Judge Loyal Knappen, and Silas H. Strawn of Chicago, a founder of that city's present-day firm Winston & Strawn. Edward Gates was also there for the Federal League, which was not a party to the suit but clearly had an interest in the outcome. The Phillies and Killefer were represented by George Wharton Pepper, founder of the present-day Philadelphia-based firm Pepper Hamilton; Samuel Clement, counsel for the National League and also from Philadelphia; and former Michigan Supreme Court Justice William Carpenter of Detroit.

Edward Gates opened the argument for the plaintiffs by explaining that his clients had acted with a good-faith belief that Killefer's 1913 contract was invalid because the reserve clause in the National League's standard contract was not enforceable. Sessions interrupted Gates frequently, indicating by his questions that he was thinking of a more basic question: should plaintiffs be charged with unclean hands? The judge noted that, even if the National League contract might have been open to challenge had plaintiffs obtained such a court ruling before they entered into a contract with Killefer, that was not what had happened. The evidence established that when the Chi-Feds approached Killefer and signed him, the team knew of his Phillies contract and knew that no court had held it invalid. That being so, Sessions asked, did the plaintiffs have "moral rights" to an injunction?[70] He pointed out that the Chi-Feds were not even parties to the contract they were trying to overturn, that the actual parties, Reindeer Bill and the Phillies, seemed to be satisfied now with the reserve clause, and that the Chi-Feds had caused the breach of that contract by offering Killefer more money. Was it possible that the Chi-Feds had come to court seeking equitable relief with unclean hands?

Pepper, considered to be the most able attorney in Philadelphia, argued for the defendants and wisely focused his comments on the judge's questions, declaiming: "Should the seducer of an employe [*sic*] be entitled to equity in court?" It seemed that the direction of the judge's thinking surprised Gates and Strawn. Gates tried to recover by insisting that if the reserve clause was invalid as a matter of law in 1913, it did not matter whether or not a court had already ruled it so. It was void when the 1913 contract was signed, and, when Killefer had finished the 1913 season with the Phillies, he owed that team no further contractual duties. Both he and the Chi-Feds were legally and morally free to enter into a contract. After hours of argument, the hearing ended late on Saturday afternoon, and Judge Sessions took the matter under advisement.

Six days later, on April 10, Judge Sessions issued his opinion denying the Chi-Feds' injunction request.[71] The opinion's opening paragraph confirmed that Sessions had focused on the issue of unclean hands and not on the legality of the reserve clause:

This record shows that the defendant, Killefer, is a baseball player of unique, exceptional, and extraordinary skill and expertness. Unfortunately, the record also shows that he is a person upon whose pledged word little or no reliance can be placed, and who, for gain to himself, neither scruples nor hesitates to disregard and violate his express engagements and agreements. His repudiation of one contract, for the making of which he had been paid several hundred dollars, and his breach of another contract, entered into after at least a week's consideration and deliberation, give rise to the present controversy. Viewed from the standpoint of common honesty and integrity, his position in this litigation is not an enviable one.

So, Killefer had acted with unclean hands, but he was the defendant. Did his unclean hands mean that the hands of the ChiFeds, which was a plaintiff, were also too dirty to obtain equitable relief?

Before deciding the question of unclean hands, Judge Sessions did address the validity of the reserve clause in Killefer's 1913 contract and stated his belief that it was unenforceable. He reasoned that because the clause did not specify a salary figure for the future seasons, it did not establish a contract for those upcoming seasons but merely an executory contract, "a contract to make a contract." Sessions explained:

> [E]xecutory contracts of this nature can neither be enforced in equity nor form the basis of an action at law to recover damages for their breach. The reasons for the decisions are that such contracts are lacking in the necessary qualities of definiteness, certainty, and mutuality. The 1913 contract between these defendants, relative to the reservation of the defendant Killefer for the season of 1914, is lacking in all of these essential elements. It is wholly uncertain and indefinite with respect to salary and also with respect to terms and conditions of the proposed employment. It is nothing more than a contract to enter into a contract, in the future, if the parties can then agree to contract. Although it is founded upon sufficient consideration, it lacks mutuality, because the Philadelphia Club may terminate it at any time upon 10 days' notice while the other party has no such option and is bound during the entire contract period. A contract exists, but, if broken by either party, the other is remediless, because the courts are helpless either to enforce its performance or to award damages for its breach.

If Sessions had stopped there, he would be remembered as eviscerating the reserve clause. However, Sessions next turned to the question of unclean hands. He ruled that, whatever the problems with the 1913 contract, the Chi-Feds' behavior barred the team from an injunction.

> While it is true that the plaintiffs and Mr. Killefer have entered into a legal and binding contract, for the breach of which the one may be compelled to respond in damages to the other, it is also true that, because both have acted wrongfully and in bad faith, a court of equity will neither adjust their differences nor balance their equities. The motion for an injunction must be denied, not because the executory part of the 1913 contract between the defendants was of superior or any legal force and effect, not because the contract between plaintiffs and defendant, Killefer, is not in itself such a one as the courts will enforce, not because there are any equities in Killefer's favor which excuse or exempt him from the performance of his engagements, and not because the merits of the controversy are with the Philadelphia Club, but solely because the actions and conduct of the plaintiffs in procuring the contract, upon which their right to relief is and must be founded, do not square with one of the vital and fundamental principles of equity which touches to the quick the dignity of a court of conscience and controls its decision regardless of all other considerations.

The legal effect of Sessions's denial to entertain or grant the requested injunction was that his discussions of the reserve clause were merely obiter dicta, lawyerly Latin meaning a comment that is not a part of the decision, not binding on the parties, and not precedent. The plaintiffs immediately appealed to the Sixth Circuit Court of Appeals, which, on June 30, 1914, affirmed Sessions's decision as to unclean hands and also, in passing, expressed agreement with his analysis of the reserve clause issue.[72]

Charles Weeghman lost this case, but he continued to fight the National League. He built a stadium in the north side of Chicago where the Chi-Feds/Whales played in 1914 and 1915. After the 1915 season, the Federal League sued the American and National Leagues in Chicago under the Sherman Antitrust Act. The case never went to trial, but a settlement was reached in which the major league team owners bought out the owners of four struggling Federal teams and two Federal owners bought two struggling National League teams. In the settlement, Weeghman bought Chicago's National League team, the Cubs, and moved the team from the west side to his stadium on the north side where the Cubs still play. Weeghman lost money on various investments and over time sold control of the Cubs to chewing gum magnate William

Wrigley, and Weeghman Park became Wrigley Field. Bill Killefer played for the Phillies in 1916 and 1917, but ironically the Cubs traded with the Phillies to obtain both Reindeer Bill and Grover Alexander for the 1918 season where they played together until 1926.

Despite Judge Sessions's disapproval of baseball's reserve clause, it continued to be used in player contracts. In 1922, in an opinion by Justice Oliver Wendell Holmes, Jr., the U.S. Supreme Court held that the clause did not violate the Sherman Antitrust Act because the essence of baseball, the games, was amusement, not commerce, and so scheduling and playing games, even among teams headquartered in different states, was not interstate commerce.[73] It finally took a 1975 decision in a labor arbitration between two major league players and major league baseball, not antitrust law, to end the reserve clause.[74]

Judge Sessions and the SS Eastland Disaster[75]

Early on the morning of July 24, 1915, the steamship *Eastland*, pride of the St. Joseph–Chicago Steamship Company, floated at her berth on the Chicago River, just west of the Clark Street Bridge. The crew was preparing to board its legal capacity of 2,507 passengers, most of whom that day were employees of the Western Electric Manufacturing Co. and their families, on their way to a company picnic at Washington Park in Michigan City, Indiana. The passengers began boarding at 6:30 a.m., and as the ship filled up, she began to roll slowly toward the dock. The ship's engineer ordered that the ballast be shifted and the list recovered. About an hour later, as the ship reached its limit of passengers, the *Eastland* rolled over away from the dock, coming to rest on her port side at the bottom of the river. Many passengers on the top decks were thrown into the water while those on lower decks found themselves trapped as water poured into the ship's interior spaces. Hundreds of passengers on the upper decks and most of the crew escaped by climbing on the exposed, and now horizontal, starboard side of the hull and walking onto ships that had come to the rescue. Organized and individual rescue efforts began almost immediately including by sailors, police, and firemen, and private individuals, many of whom jumped into the river to rescue floundering passengers. Despite these selfless and heroic efforts, 848 people died (4 crew members and 844 passengers—men, women, and children), either drowned or crushed.

The *Eastland* had been designed and built by a Port Huron, Michigan company, Jenks Ship Building Company, between 1902 and 1903. As it happened, she was the only passenger ship the company ever built. She was meant to operate in the summer and fall between South Haven, Michigan, and Chicago, carrying passengers and cargo, particularly Michigan fruit, to Chicago and vacationers to South Haven and other places on the Lake Michigan shore. She was iron-hulled, 265 feet long and 38 feet wide, with four passenger decks above the waterline. This last dimension, her high freeboard, the distance on a ship between the water level and the highest deck that would let in water, looked good for sailing in high waves, but it gave her a high center of gravity, which, under the principles of marine design customary at that time, would have been matched with a deep keel filled with solid ballast. But the designers and builders of the *Eastland* had to take into consideration the fact that South Haven had a permanent sand bar at the entrance to its harbor, which ruled out a deep keel. As a compromise, the designers provided for a relatively shallow, rounded keel and an unusual ballast system with tanks that could be filled or emptied with water from the lake by pumping it through a pipe below the water line. The chief engineer would fill the tanks to provide ballast when the *Eastland* left Chicago and while it steamed across the lake, but he then would empty the tanks to raise the ship to cross the sand bar in South Haven. The status of the tanks when the ship was docked in Chicago, full or empty, became a major issue after the accident.

Over several days following the accident, the ship was raised to secure the last bodies, which would join the hundreds of other dead laid out in the National Guard Armory, where desperate relatives walked up and down rows of corpses looking for loved ones. Chicago was overcome first with grief and then with a thirst for the blood of whoever was responsible, particularly the captain who was one of the first people to leave the ship when she began to roll. Both local and federal law enforcement agencies began investigations, but U.S. District Judge Kenesaw Mountain Landis of the Northern District of Illinois quickly took over. On September 22, 1915, the federal grand jury indicted eight men, including the president and three other officers of the steamship company, for manslaughter, the ship's captain and engineer for criminal carelessness, and two federal steamship inspectors for criminal negligence.

However, the law agencies faced a problem in bringing some of the defendants to court in Chicago. Six of the defendants were residents of the Western District of Michigan, they were presently located there, and they were very unlikely to travel to Illinois voluntarily.[76] Under the federal rules of jurisdiction in effect at that time, Judge Landis could not directly order their arrest by federal officers. Instead, he had to petition Judge Sessions to order their rendition, meaning an order directing that the U.S. Marshal for the Western District of Michigan arrest them and return them to the custody of the federal court in Chicago.[77] Thus, the six could not be brought to trial in Chicago involuntarily without Judge Sessions's consent.

On January 20, 1916, Judge Sessions began hearing testimony and argument in his courtroom on the second floor of Grand Rapids' 1909 federal building on Judge Landis's petition for rendition of the six. Testimony revealed that this was not the first time that the *Eastland* had warned her captain and crew that she was top-heavy and that she was, as the term was then, cranky. In 1904, while steaming from Grand Haven to Chicago, the ship began to list to port and passengers were ordered to go below decks, but she recovered. In 1906, a shift of upper-deck passengers to see something off the starboard side caused a sharp list that also eventually recovered. On another voyage, in 1912, she listed twenty-five degrees to port, then shifted thirty degrees to starboard, and then recovered.

The government's experts explained that the ship's great height and narrow beam as well as the absence of a normal keel or solid ballast raised the ship's center of gravity and lowered her lateral stability. The main deck, closest to the water's surface, had five gangway doors on each side, which were just above the water's surface when the ship was full of passengers and could dip below the water surface so that, if open, a list of only fifteen degrees could bring water pouring onto the main deck. Other evidence established that recent modifications to the ship had increased her weight on the upper decks tremendously making her much less stable and more likely to roll over. The wooden flooring of the main deck and of the two upper decks had rotted and was replaced before the 1915 season with between thirty and fifty tons of concrete. At the same time, five lifeboats and thirty-seven life rafts, weighing together approximately fifteen tons, were placed on the ship's high hurricane deck, responding to a new federal law that required lifeboats for 75 percent of the ship's maximum number of passengers.[78]

All six defendants attended the hearing in Grand Rapids. Their attorneys included Chicago's most famous defender (and former University of Michigan law student) Clarence Darrow, who represented the engineer, Joseph Erickson. Darrow asserted that the real culprit was the city of Chicago, whose engineers and harbor officials had allowed large concrete blocks to accumulate below the *Eastland*'s mooring location and that the addition of the passengers had caused the bottom of the hull to settle on one of these obstructions and roll. Darrow even had a scale model built to demonstrate his claim and had an expert testify. However, the prosecutors submitted the testimony of a diver that there were no obstructions in that location while another witness testified that at its greatest possible depth the ship's hull was several feet above the river bottom.

On February 18, 1916, Judge Sessions issued his opinion denying rendition.[79] After the weeks of testimony as to what caused the wreck, he chose not to rule on that issue. Instead, he explained that the capsizing had not occurred at sea or on Lake Michigan, but in the Chicago River. For that reason, Judge Landis and his federal court lacked subject matter jurisdiction over the case, which instead was in the jurisdiction of the Chicago or Illinois courts. Having found a lack of jurisdiction, Judge Sessions probably should have stopped his opinion there. As in the *Killefer* case, however, he addressed the merits of the case. He added that there was no evidence of any kind to support a conspiracy and that even if there had been such evidence, "a conspiracy to commit [an] impossible crime is impossible."

Judge Sessions and Campaign Finance[80]

On March 20, 1920, a federal jury sitting in Grand Rapids found U.S. Senator Truman H. Newberry and sixteen other defendants guilty of violating the Federal Corrupt Practices Act of 1910, as amended in 1911. Seventy other defendants were acquitted and ten others had pleaded nolo contendere. Judge Sessions imposed on Senator Newberry the maximum sentence under the act: two years in the U.S. Penitentiary at Leavenworth, Kansas, and a fine of $10,000. The other convicted defendants received fines, and three were sentenced to lesser terms in prison. The trial of Newberry and his codefendants was hailed as the high point of the judge's career, but just over a year later the U.S. Supreme Court reversed the convictions, throwing Judge Sessions into a mental and physical decline from which he never recovered.

Federal legislation limiting monetary contributions to candidates for federal elective offices began with the Tillman Act of 1907,[81] which made it a crime for national banks or other corporations chartered by Congress "to make a money contribution in connection with any election to any political office" and for any corporation of any kind to make such a contribution in connection with "any election at which Presidential and Vice-Presidential electors or a Representative in Congress is to be voted for or any election by any State legislature of a United States Senator."

Three years later, in 1910, Congress passed the Federal Corrupt Practices Act,[82] which established campaign spending limits for political parties in House general elections and required that national committees of political parties file postelection reports regarding their contributions to individual candidates. In 1911, Congress amended the 1910 Act to extend its requirements to U.S. Senate candidates and to apply the spending limits to an aggregate of spending on primary and general elections.[83] The 1911 amendments also required financial disclosure by candidates. House campaign expenditures were held to $5,000 and Senate expenditures to $10,000, or the amount established by state law, whichever was less. In 1913, Michigan passed a law limiting expenditures for a primary election to "25 per centum of one year's compensation."[84] For a Senate primary, this resulted in a limit of $3,750.

The 1918 election to fill one of Michigan's U.S. Senate seats proved to be one of the most bitter and costly contests of that era. In 1912, Woodrow Wilson was elected President, the second Democratic President since 1860, and the Democrats had a solid majority in the Senate and the House of Representatives. But as the 1918 election approached, the Republicans controlled the House, and the Democrats' majority in the Senate was threatened. Looking about for an opportunity to add to that majority, Wilson saw that Michigan's Republican Senator William Alden Smith was retiring. The President contacted industrialist Henry Ford and asked him to enter the primary election to replace Smith. Ford had endorsed Wilson for reelection in 1916 and had contributed $58,800 to Wilson's campaign. With his usual energy, Ford entered both the Republican and Democratic primaries.

Ford won the Democratic primary easily, but the Republican primary went to Truman H. Newberry, another very rich man and a director of the Packard Motor Car Company. Ford had done little campaigning for the primaries, while Newberry used newspaper advertising to attack Ford as a pacifist and anti-Semite and for helping his son, Edsel, avoid military service in World War I. Ford made more of an effort in the general election, while Newberry redoubled his advertising campaign castigating Ford and highlighting his own endorsements by former Presidents Theodore Roosevelt and William Howard Taft.

Newberry narrowly defeated Ford, after a recount, by 7,567 votes out of a total of 432,541, and Newberry was sworn in on May 19, 1919, giving the Republicans a one-vote majority in the upper house. However, charges that Newberry had violated federal and state campaign spending laws threatened his claim to the seat. Ford hired detectives and accountants to discover the amount that Newberry had spent on his primary campaign, which, according to this investigation, amounted to more than $175,000. In October 1919, the U.S. Department of Justice empaneled a grand jury in Grand Rapids, and the Senate began its own investigation of Newberry's campaign.

On November 29, 1919, the grand jury indicted Newberry, his brother John, and 133 other men on six counts, including conspiracy to violate the Federal Corrupt Practices Act. The defense moved to dismiss the indictments, challenging the power of Congress under the Constitution to regulate spending on federal primary elections that were, in a sense, the private activities of each party. Judge Sessions denied the motion with what amounted to contempt for the contention that Congress could not act to defend the "self-protection, self-preservation, and continued existence" of democracy free from "the corruption of the electorate."

Trial began in Sessions's Grand Rapids courtroom on January 26, 1920, and continued for two months. The prosecution presented witness after witness to detail how much money each of them had received from the Newberry campaign as well as at least one instance of bribery and coercion. Newberry did not testify. The jury retired to decide its verdict in the late afternoon of March 18 and returned on March 20. The jurors found seventeen defendants, including Newberry, guilty of conspiracy and seventy defendants not guilty. Ten defendants who had previously pleaded nolo contendere were discharged, and charges against the remaining defendants were dismissed either by the prosecution or by the judge.

Truman Newberry immediately exercised his right to appeal to the U.S. Supreme Court. The Court heard arguments on January 7 and 10, 1921, and on May 2 issued its opinion reversing Judge Sessions's ruling that Congress had power under the Constitution to regulate spending on primary elections.[85] The opinion for the Court by Justice McReynolds held that the U.S. Constitution did not grant the U.S. Congress the authority to regulate political party primaries or nomination processes. As a result, the Court struck down the 1911 amendments to the Federal Corrupt Practices Act to the extent they placed spending limits on candidate and political election committee spending in primaries or other nomination processes for federal office. The decision was based on a strict interpretation of the language of Article I, section 4, which grants Congress power to strike down state rules over the times and manner of holding elections for Congress. The court held that the framers of the Constitution had no knowledge of party primaries. Therefore, the word "elections" in Article I cannot include primaries, which "are in no sense elections for an office but merely methods by which party adherents agree upon candidates whom they intend to offer and support for ultimate choice by all qualified electors. General provisions touching elections in Constitutions or statutes are not necessarily applicable to primaries—the two things are radically different."[86]

This was a five-to-four majority decision. Justices White, Pitney, Clarke, and Brandeis dissented on the constitutionality of the Federal Corrupt Practices Act but would have reversed the conviction and remanded for a new trial because of a perceived error in the jury instructions. The holding and interpretation by the majority remained in effect until 1941.[87]

Meanwhile, the Senate Committee on Privileges and Elections investigated the matter and determined that the large amounts spent on Newberry's behalf were not his own funds but were contributed by relatives and friends without his solicitation or knowledge. Consequently, it recommended that the Michigan senator retain his seat. On January 12, 1922, a narrowly divided Senate affirmed that Newberry had been duly elected, but it nonetheless "severely condemned" his excessive campaign expenditures as "harmful to the honor and dignity of the Senate." In the face of continuing controversy, Newberry resigned from the Senate on November 18, 1922. Newberry's case led Congress in 1925 to enact a new Federal Corrupt Practices Act, but this statute proved ineffective in containing congressional campaign financial irregularities in the decades ahead.[88]

CHAPTER 5

Prohibition, Depression, War, and a Growing Court, 1920 to 1960

A Second Western District Judgeship, Temporarily

I N 1921, WHEN THE U.S. Supreme Court reversed Judge Sessions's decision in the Newberry election spending case, the judge "suffered a break in
health and never regained his old-time physical vigor."[1] He struggled on,
trying to retain his goal of swift justice with a docket swollen by cases based
on Prohibition. By 1924, Judge Sessions was sixty-six years old, exhausted,
and overwhelmed by his docket, yet he was still four years short of qualifying
for a judge's pension. Congressman James C. McLaughlin, an old friend from
Muskegon, introduced a bill to allow Sessions to retire immediately yet still
receive a pension. In addition to an affidavit from the judge's doctor attest-
ing to his fragile health, Supreme Court Chief Justice William Howard Taft
signed a statement that Sessions was suffering from heart trouble, had broken
down under strain of his court duties, and would die if required to continue.[2]
Court of Appeals Judge Arthur Denison also submitted a statement that,
for years, Sessions had suffered critical attacks of some form of heart trouble
and lately had been losing ground. Denison noted that Sessions was tempera-
mentally unable to do anything less than all the work there was in sight, with
intense application, and so he had greatly overtaxed himself.

McLaughlin's bill was approved by the House Judiciary Committee, but
the statute that became law on February 17, 1925, was different.[3] Instead of
allowing, really forcing, Sessions to retire with a pension, Congress created a
second district judgeship for the Western District. As a result of the statute,
Sessions was able to remain an active judge, work as much or as little as he
preferred, and receive his full salary without being responsible for the docket.
The statute also provided that the second judge was to be treated as senior in

commission to Sessions and that, upon Sessions's "death, resignation or retirement," his vacancy would not be filled, reducing the Western District court to just a single District Judge again. On May 8, 1925, President Calvin Coolidge made a recess appointment of Grand Rapids attorney Fred Morton Raymond to the new seat, freeing Judge Sessions from most of his judicial burdens.

After his semi-retirement, Judge Sessions spent most of his time and effort on his six-acre estate near Grandville and devoted himself to his family. Judge Sessions's first wife, Mary, died on December 10, 1925, and two years later Judge Sessions married Mrs. Mary Lovell Higginbotham of Ionia. The judge's health continued to diminish, and he was confined to his bed in December 1930. He died in the early morning of Wednesday, April 1, 1931, age seventy-two, at his home in Grand Rapids.[4]

U.S. District Judge Fred Morton Raymond

Fred M. Raymond was born on March 22, 1876, in Berlin (changed to Marne during the First World War), Ottawa County, Michigan, to Joseph and Elizabeth S. (McLennan) Raymond. His early education was in his birth town, and, after completing high school in Grand Rapids, he entered the University of Michigan and graduated from the Law Department[5] with the degree of bachelor of laws in 1899. He returned to Grand Rapids to begin practicing law with the law firm of Hatch & Wilson. On December 30, 1902, Raymond married Mabel H. Kenworthy; they had two children, Elizabeth and Russell. He was very active in professional, civic, and social organizations, including serving as president of the Grand Rapids Bar Association (1922–1923) and of the Berlin Board of Education.

In 1923, Judge Raymond cofounded the law firm Jewell, Raymond & Face, but he left private practice two years later because of an unexpected offer to become a U.S. District Judge. When the new Western District judgeship became effective in February 1925, Raymond did not offer his name to the list. The choice of appointee had been "hanging fire for some months" because the state's Republican leaders could not agree on a candidate. Initially, the apparent leader was Michigan Attorney General Andrew B. Dougherty, who had been endorsed by Senator James J. Couzens, Governor Groesbeck, and the president of Michigan's Republican organization, Kennedy L. Potter.[6] At the end of March, Dougherty was reported to be in Washington with "the federal judgeship . . . tucked in his pocket,"[7] but a month later Dougherty

Judge Fred Morton Raymond

was out, as was another candidate with strong support among state Republicans, the Western District's U.S. Attorney Edward J. Bowman. Both were too divisive in the party. Instead, newspapers reported, the race was between Raymond and state Circuit Judge Orion S. Cross of Allegan.[8]

Raymond's name was first introduced to consideration when U.S. Attorney General John G. Sargent summoned U.S. Circuit Judge Arthur C. Denison of Grand Rapids into consultation. Raymond had no formal political backing but was acceptable to Congressman Carl E. Mapes and Senator Couzens.[9] On May 8, 1925, President Calvin Coolidge named Raymond to a recess appointment for the new seat. Raymond described himself as an astonished and nonpolitical lawyer who neither sought nor strongly desired to be appointed. Newspapers in Michigan approving Raymond's appointment emphasized that he owed nothing to any political party.[10] As required by law, President Coolidge nominated him again to the same position on December 8, 1925, and he was confirmed by the Senate and received his commission on December 18.[11]

Judge Raymond presided over the District Court for six years with diminishing assistance from Judge Sessions, dealing with the unprecedented caseload arising from Prohibition. During his last fifteen years on the District Court bench, he served alone, through the end of Prohibition, the Great Depression, and the Second World War. An indefatigable worker, he attended court as usual on Monday, February 4, 1946, but he suffered a heart attack the next day and died at home in Grand Rapids on the morning of February 6. He would have been eligible to retire on March 22, at his seventieth birthday, but he had been "vigorous and active until shortly before his death," and it had been considered unlikely that he would decide to retire. At his death, he was praised for "his judicial attitude and the fairness of his rulings on controversial matters." His rulings were seldom reversed by the appellate courts.[12]

Prohibition Swells the Western District's Caseload

Without question, nothing ever had as great an impact on the operations of the District Court for the Western District of Michigan as did the Eighteenth Amendment to the U.S. Constitution and the resulting National Prohibition (Volstead) Act,[13] which put the amendment into effect on January 17, 1920.[14] Over the next dozen years, the enforcement of Prohibition would increase the court's caseload at a rate that it had never grown before and, in terms of percentage of cases, that it has never grown since. In fiscal year 1915, the Western District received 182 new civil and criminal cases including old reliable types of cases such as customs and postal theft prosecutions, as well as cases based on the new federal regulatory acts, and civil cases among private parties. Five years later, in fiscal year 1920, the total was not much higher, 199, but in fiscal year 1921 the total cases filed nearly doubled to 378, in 1922 the total was 503, and in 1932, nearing the end of Prohibition, it was 672.

Although the court continued to receive cases on other matters, both criminal and civil, throughout the Prohibition years, the vast majority of the cases filed during that period involved Prohibition. In the Western District of Michigan, the number of criminal cases filed annually peaked at 498 in 1925, and thereafter declined, but not because of lack of violations of the Volstead Act. Instead, the failure of criminal prosecutions to reduce the flow of illegal liquor led the Justice Department to direct its District Attorneys to change their focus to filing civil complaints against the gangs that controlled the liquor business. Whereas between 1921 and 1925 the United States filed a total of seventy-four civil cases, that number increased to 313 between 1926 and 1930 and to 470 in the final three full years of Prohibition, fiscal years 1931 to 1933. The United States did not abandon criminal cases after 1925. During those last three years it filed 894 criminal cases.

Two Prohibition cases arising and litigated in the Western District's Southern Division did attract the attention of the U.S. Supreme Court. Both cases involved the Fourth Amendment of the U.S. Constitution and warrantless searches of automobiles. In one case, the Supreme Court established a rule and a standard that survive today.

United States v. George Carroll

On December 15, 1921, George Carroll and John Kiro were in Kiro's Oldsmobile roadster, traveling west on Grand River Road, about sixteen miles east of Grand Rapids, when they were stopped by three federal Prohibition agents and a state officer. The agents searched the car and found, in the seat upholstery, sixty-eight bottles labeled whiskey and gin. Carroll offered the agents a bribe, but he and Kiro were arrested. They were taken to Grand Rapids and indicted by the Western District Court's grand jury for using an automobile to transport sixty-eight quarts of "intoxicating spirituous liquor."

Before the trial began before Judge Sessions, defendants moved to exclude evidence of the liquor bottles because the agents had violated defendants' Fourth Amendment rights by searching the Oldsmobile without first obtaining a warrant. With notable chutzpah, Carroll also asked for the return of the whiskey and gin. At a hearing held by a U.S. Commissioner, federal agents Scully and Cronenwett testified that, at the time of the arrest, they and their fellow agents had already twice had dealings with the defendants. In September, Cronenwett and Scully, acting undercover, had tried to buy three cases of whiskey from them. According to the agents, the defendants agreed to sell them the liquor but explained that they had to go get the cases. They left in the same Oldsmobile roadster seized in the present case, but never returned. The agents also testified that a week later, while they were patrolling on Grand River, they saw the defendants in the Oldsmobile heading east. The agents pursued in a high-speed chase, but their car could not overtake the Olds. So when they encountered the defendants in the same car and on the same road, they were sure that defendants were carrying booze. The Commissioner denied both motions, and at trial Sessions admitted as evidence one bottle of whiskey and one of gin. The jury convicted both defendants.

Defendants brought a writ of error to the U.S. Supreme Court, which twice heard argument, in 1923 and 1924. On March 2, 1925, the Court, in a vote of six Justices to two, affirmed defendants' convictions.[15] Chief Justice

Taft, writing for the majority, held that because of the mobility of motor vehicles, the Fourth Amendment does not require that police obtain a warrant before searching automobiles, as would be the case in the search of a residence or other private dwelling. Instead, officers may search on probable cause, which in this case was amply supplied by the prior contacts between the officers and the defendants. This was the first time the Supreme Court recognized the car search exception to the warrant requirement, a position that the Court continues to hold more than ninety years later.

The United States v. Richard Husty

In December 1929, Richard Husty and Charles Laurel were arrested in Grand Rapids for Prohibition violations. Like Carroll and Kiro, they were indicted in the U.S. District Court for transporting and possessing intoxicating liquors. After their trial and conviction in March 1930, Judge Raymond sentenced Husty, who had two prior bootlegging convictions, to five years in the U.S. Penitentiary in Fort Leavenworth, Kansas, and a fine of $3,000. Raymond sentenced Laurel, who had no prior convictions, to eighteen months in a federal penitentiary in Ohio.[16]

The agents had arrested the defendants as they were parked in Husty's car and had searched the car, all without a warrant. They found and seized a load of whiskey, the key to the prosecution's case, which defendants moved before trial to exclude. Their motion was denied, and after the sentencing, Husty's attorney appealed to the Sixth Circuit on several grounds, including the Fourth Amendment, and argued that the officers had not seen Husty doing anything illegal, or even suspicious, and so lacked probable cause to search the car without a warrant.

At the pretrial in limine hearing, agent Scully, the same man as in *Carroll*, testified that Husty was known to him as one of the leading bootleggers in Grand Rapids and that the agent had arrested Husty twice before for bootlegging, both arrests resulting in convictions. In fact, at the time of this arrest, Husty had just been released from Leavenworth on his second conviction. Scully said that on the day of this third arrest of Husty, he had received a tip from a reliable, long-time informant that Husty had two loads of liquor in automobiles of a particular make and description, parked in particular places on named streets. Scully found one of the cars in the location the informant had described. Later, Scully testified, he saw Husty, Laurel, and another man enter the car and start it, and Scully moved in and arrested Husty while Laurel and the other man escaped. Based on his tip, Scully searched the car and found eighteen cases of whiskey.

Husty appealed his conviction and his sentence, but the Sixth Circuit affirmed both the conviction and the sentence summarily, without an opinion. However, the Supreme Court granted Husty's petition for certiorari. On February 24, 1931, the Supreme Court, in an opinion by Justice Stone, affirmed as to the Fourth Amendment issue but questioned the length of Husty's sentence and remanded the case to Judge Raymond on that ground alone.[17] On the search issue, Justice Stone held that: "To show probable cause it is not necessary that the arresting officer should have had before him legal evidence of the suspected illegal act. . . . It is enough if the apparent facts which have come to his attention are sufficient, in the circumstances, to lead a reasonably discreet and prudent man to believe that liquor is illegally possessed in the automobile to be searched." Reviewing the evidence, the Court concluded that it was sufficient to establish probable cause.

Prohibition in the Northern Division

The Western District's Southern Division certainly had its bootleggers and topers of illegal booze, and highway U.S. 12, running through the district's southern counties, was a major route used by the Purple Gang for transporting Canadian whiskey from Detroit to Chicago. However, the Northern Division was the district's true hotbed of bootlegging, the manufacture of illegal alcohol, and its consumption. Judge Sessions, who abhorred the liquor business even before it was illegal, spent many terms of court in Marquette and Sault Ste. Marie presiding over the trial and conviction of bootleggers, regularly shipping enough of them south to the Detroit House of Correction to fill a passenger train car or two. One U.S. Commissioner whose records are available, Henry Hatch of Marquette, recorded that between February 14, 1919, and July 26, 1922, he authorized 206 arrests of which 191 were for violations of the Prohibition laws.[18] Judge Raymond was equally tough on Prohibition law violators, sending some defendants to Leavenworth.[19]

On the other hand, not all of the people who manufactured, sold, or consumed illegal alcohol in the Northern Division were dangerous criminals. Most were honest citizens who wanted a drink, including numerous officers of the law. Many of the immigrants who came to work in the Upper Peninsula's iron and copper mines were from countries in which drinking, at least in moderation, was considered a delight sent to man by God. They believed that strict prohibition, old-fashioned teetotalism, was an intrusion into their harmless private pleasures, and for many of them it was also a threat to their modest incomes. As state and federal Prohibition agents discovered, resistance to their work occurred among otherwise peaceful, upright citizens.

One case of Upper Peninsula resistance was resolved before Judge Sessions had to get involved. That incident in the town of Iron River, a mining community with a strong immigrant population, stands as an example of the cultural clashes caused by Prohibition. For years, one of the town's grocers, John Scalcucci, and his brothers, used the basement of their store to make and sell Chianti-style wine with grapes shipped from California. Miners on their way home from work would stop at Scalcucci's for a glass or bottle of wine. At first, the Volstead Act did not change the rituals of this isolated community. A law-abiding man, John Scalcucci comforted himself with an exception in the act that allowed any person to make "non-intoxicating cider and fruit juice exclusively for home use." Wine, he rationalized, was a kind of fruit juice, his mining customers were barely intoxicated by their after-work refreshment, and the Scalcuccis lived above the store.

However, for the Michigan State Constabulary (precursor to the Michigan State Police), wine was wine, and thus its manufacture and its sale were illegal. On February 14, 1920, they raided the Scalcucci store, seizing four hundred gallons of red wine in barrels. Then the trouble began. Iron County State Attorney Martin McDonough refused to prosecute because the officers had not bothered to obtain a warrant, and he ordered the wine returned to the Scalcuccis. The constables reported the problem to federal Prohibition supervisor Leo J. Grove in Marquette. He ordered another raid to take place on February 19, again without a warrant. Once again, McDonough demanded that Grove return the wine to the Scalcuccis, and he told the vintners that if the federal agents returned, they were free to "open fire on them."

Grove kicked this show of force up his chain of command to Major A. V. Dalrymple, chief Prohibition enforcement officer for the central western states. Dalrymple organized his own eighteen-man raiding party and sped to Iron River to arrest, "for rebellion," McDonough, the Scalcucci brothers, and the Iron River chief of police and his deputies. News of the impending raid and arrests leaked out, was broadcast nationally, and caught the national fancy at a time when Prohibition was new and opposing it seemed innocent fun. Although the Scalcuccis only stocked wine, journalists described the fracas as "a whiskey or rum rebellion," which sounded better. As the raiders neared Iron River, citizens hid thousands of gallons of their own homemade hooch in nearby forests and mine shafts.

When Dalrymple and his posse arrived in Iron River, McDonough greeted them and prepared to serve a warrant for Dalrymple's arrest for "publications of false and malicious stories." The major decided to avoid any confrontation for the moment and retired to the Iron Inn for the evening. The next morning, on February 25, Dalrymple and his men loaded up to raid the basement of a priest's home where, they had determined, McDonough had moved the Scalcucci wine for safekeeping. The federal agents rolled the barrels of wine out into an alley between St. Agnes Church and the local school, broke them open, and dumped the wine onto the snow. The open destruction of the barrels greatly pleased the small army of reporters and cameramen who had flocked to Iron River to take photographs that would show the U.S. government either finally taking Prohibition seriously or, if their editors preferred the other side of the story, destroying the property of the Scalcuccis, honest citizens who were just trying to improve the lives of their neighbors.

The national Prohibition Commissioner in Washington decided to end the matter. He sent Dalrymple a telegram ordering him to compromise with McDonough. The raids had become a public circus that had created a major rift between the Department of Justice and Department of Internal Revenue. Dalrymple returned to Chicago the following day and resigned from his post within the year. Michigan dropped its investigation into what the newspapers and radio named the Iron River Rebellion, and McDonough was hailed a hero. The Scalcuccis, though, had lost their wine.

Judge Raymond and John Dillinger's Ford

In the early 1930s, as the end of Prohibition neared, another crime wave replaced bootlegging in the caseload statistics of the federal courts and in public attention: bank robberies committed in the Midwest by small, violent gangs, some of whose leaders and members became folk heroes of a sort, with colorful names such as John Dillinger, Baby Face Nelson, Pretty Boy Floyd, and Machine Gun Kelly. In a short period of time, though, this wave of bank robberies reached a level that exasperated both the authorities and public alike, leading to a declaration of a national manhunt by the director of the Federal Bureau of Investigation, J. Edgar Hoover.

In the attack on these bank robber gangs, police methods that might have been disapproved previously as unconstitutional were condoned as a necessary response to a public emergency. At least that was the position of Judge Raymond in 1934 when faced with a challenge to a warrantless search for and seizure of a "Ford V-8 sedan" involved with one of the most celebrated outlaws of that period, John Dillinger. His gang had committed at least fourteen bank robberies and were believed to be responsible for eleven murders between June 1933 and Dillinger's death in July 1934 at the hands of Hoover and the FBI.

The tale of the V-8 Ford began in January 1934 when Dillinger and his gang robbed a bank in East Chicago, Indiana, during which they shot and killed a police officer, William O'Malley. Dillinger was arrested in Arizona and returned to the Lake County jail in Crown Point, Indiana, for the murder of O'Malley. On March 3, 1934, Dillinger escaped from the jail using, according to witnesses, either a real pistol smuggled into the jail or a fake gun carved from a potato. He and his associates hid out in Minneapolis until March 31 when Dillinger was wounded in a shoot-out with FBI agents. The gang escaped to the farm of Dillinger's father in Mooresville, Indiana. While Dillinger was recovering, his associates bought a new V-8 Ford sedan, one of two vehicles in which Dillinger, his long-time associate John "Red" Hamilton, and their companions, Mary Evelyn ("Billie") Frechette and Pat Cherrington, drove north into Michigan's Upper Peninsula.[20]

On April 17, they arrived at the home of Hamilton's sister, Mrs. Anna Steve, in Sault Ste. Marie.[21] According to a statement by Mrs. Steve, a thirty-six-year-old mother of six and a former parent–teacher association president, Hamilton had a machine gun wrapped in a blanket, Dillinger had a rifle, and both had a revolver and were wearing bulletproof vests. The fugitives stayed about two and a half hours and then left in one of their cars, leaving behind the new Ford sedan after hiding it in a cow shed "on an adjoining lot." Three days later, the famed FBI Special Agent Melvin Purvis, other FBI special agents, and Chippewa County Sheriff J. W. Welsh went to the Steve house, without a search warrant, to arrest Dillinger and Hamilton. Steve gave them the keys to the Ford and told them where to find it. The officers seized the car and obtained a federal court order confiscating it "against all persons excepting the true owner."

Attorneys for Anna Steve filed a petition in the Western District's Northern Division challenging the order on the grounds that she was the "true owner" of the vehicle, a gift from her brother, and that in any case the seizure without a warrant was illegal and against the Fourth Amendment. At a hearing in the district courtroom in Grand Rapids on July 12, 1934, Judge Raymond rejected Mrs. Steve's claim that she became the owner of the $700 vehicle as a gift or in return for a meal and a few hours' "hospitality." The judge ruled that the story was simply unbelievable, "[a] heavy strain on credulity," particularly because Steve admitted that her brother had told her the car was "hot" and she could not use it until 1935. The judge concluded that "[c]onsidering the entire environment, the more rational conclusion is that the automobile was 'planted' for future use in emergencies likely to ensue from the desperate situation of the outlaws and that the gift, if any, was conditional upon nonexistence of such necessary use."

As to the warrantless search of the cow shed, Judge Raymond admitted that the argument advanced by Steve's attorney "finds support in legal precedents." But, he continued, "such precedents, like all others, are subject to challenge and are entitled to reconsideration in the light of existing conditions":

> The present economic emergency which has affected and confused all departments of government finds its counterpart in an emergency, no less serious, which exists in the conflict between the criminal and the rights of society. In this emergency, precedents in construction and application of statutory, constitutional, and common law must be re-examined and modified, if need be, in the interests of society.
>
> Never must it be overlooked that law finds its origin and fundamental purpose in the protection of the weak against the strong, a principle too frequently forgotten or ignored. So extensive has become the immunity available to criminals through advancement of science and the relative retrogression of processes of apprehension, conviction, and ultimate segregation that drastic changes of methods are imperative for the protection of that portion of society which still believes in government by laws.
>
> Too close adherence to precedents will result in an almost impregnable fortress about the criminal, who already makes effective use of the advantages of the machine gun, bullet-proof clothing, and the armoured car in acts of commission and escape; of the talents and influence of the learned professions in escaping conviction and punishment; and of the influence of politicians and the credulity of board of pardon and parole in minimizing penalties. No sufficient reason exists why precedents, established in the days when the contest between the criminal and his prey afforded some slight chance of successful resistance by the victim, should be adhered to for the protection of the criminal.

Judge Raymond later presided over Anna Steve's criminal case. In June 1934, a month before the judge's decision in the Ford V8 case, a Western District grand jury indicted Anna and her son Charles Campbell for harboring and concealing a fugitive from justice.[22] The defendants both pleaded not guilty, and under normal conditions they would have gone to trial in a few weeks. But because of Anna's health problems, they were not tried before Judge Raymond until a year later when Judge Raymond returned to Sault Ste. Marie. Before the trial began, U.S. Attorney Joseph Donnelly advised Agent Purvis that he was not sure of the outcome. On the evening of June 6, 1935, after several hours of deliberation, the jury convicted Anna but acquitted her son.[23] On June 8, Judge Raymond sentenced Anna to four months in the Grand Traverse County Jail.[24]

Dillinger, Hamilton, Frechette, and Cherrington did not enjoy their freedom long after leaving Sault Ste. Marie. Dillinger himself had only a few months to live. On July 22, 1934, he was shot and killed by FBI agents as he fled Chicago's Biograph Theater to avoid arrest. Red Hamilton was mortally wounded when he was shot by police in Hastings, Minnesota, on April 23, within a week of his visit to the Steve family. The gang took him to Chicago and then to Aurora, Illinois, where he died, probably on April 26. A buried body was found with its face and hands covered with lye to prevent identification, but it was positively identified as Hamilton by his prison dental records.

Billie Frechette was not with Dillinger when he died, as she had been arrested on April 9 and had pleaded guilty to harboring Dillinger at her St. Paul apartment. When she was released in 1936, she toured in vaudeville with the Dillinger family for five years and then returned to her birthplace, the Menominee Indian Reservation in Wisconsin, where she lived until her death in 1969. Pat Cherrington was also convicted in 1934 for harboring Dillinger's gang and spent two years at the Milan Federal Facility in Milan, Michigan. Upon her release, she returned to Chicago where she died in 1949.

Chief Judges of the District Court for the Western District of Michigan

Until well into the twentieth century, few judicial districts had more than one District Judge, so precedence among them was not relevant. Before 1948, in districts that did have more than one judge, the judge with the longest service was informally called the Senior District Judge, a primus inter pares (first among equals) who had some ill-defined administrative duties. As Congress added more judges to existing districts, Congress decided to formalize the position of a leading judge in each District Court. On June 25, 1948, in a statute revising the laws on the District and Circuit Courts, Congress included a provision that in a District Court with more than one District Judge, the judge "senior in commission" would be the chief judge of the District Court. The only duty of the chief judge that the statute specified was to "have precedence and preside at any session which he attends."

Because of the terms of the statute authorizing his appointment, Judge Raymond was the Western District's first Senior District Judge from December 18, 1925, when he received his commission, until Judge Sessions died in office on April 1, 1931. From the latter date, the district once more had only one sitting District Judge until the appointment of W. Wallace Kent as the district's second permanent District Judge in 1954, whereupon Judge Raymond Starr became the first chief judge of the District Court. Because of complaints that the duties of a chief judge were creating too much stress for some elderly judges, in 1958 Congress added the requirement that a chief judge had to be under seventy years of age. In 1982, Congress revised the age requirement by specifying that, regardless of age, the chief judge of a District Court must be replaced after seven years in the position.[25] In whatever manner a chief judge leaves the position, the successor is the court's District Judge with the greatest seniority who has not yet turned sixty-five.

Congress has never made clear the exact duties of a chief judge. The old Senior District Judge "was generally expected to exercise whatever administrative authority or power was necessary, however vaguely it might be defined,"[26] and the 1948 Act was little more specific as to a Chief Judge's duties other than to "have precedence and preside at any session which he attends." In practice, the administrative duties of the chief judge of a District Court have increased steadily so that by the beginning of the twenty-first century the chief judge was sometimes assigned only a partial caseload.

1937 Marquette Post Office and Courthouse

Although the Great Depression remains one of the most painful eras in American memory, during the 1930s the federal government went on a building spree, ordering the building of hundreds of new federal post offices and courthouses across the country to try to kickstart the economy. Among those

The 1937 Marquette U.S. Post office and Courthouse.

The District Court's elaborate courtroom on the second floor of the
1937 Marquette Courthouse. Photograph taken in 2019

buildings were three that are still being used in 2020 by the District Court for the Western District of Michigan. One of them, in Marquette, was built as a courthouse, while the other two, in Kalamazoo and Lansing, did not have court facilities until decades after they were built and will be discussed later.

After resisting calls to provide federal assistance to soften the effects of the Depression, in July 1932 President Herbert Hoover joined with Congress to put together the first ever federal relief act, the Emergency Relief and Construction Act of 1932,[27] to provide support, to jumpstart the economy, and to reduce unemployment by providing funds for businesses. Included in the Act was authority for the Treasury Department and the Postmaster General to spend $100 million for public building projects to be selected from a list of hundreds of candidates, including a new post office and U.S. courthouse in both Marquette and Kalamazoo.[28] However, in March 1933 Congress authorized the President to divert funds from that public buildings appropriation to a different target, unemployment in the forestry and timber industries.[29] As it turned out, the President diverted $93 million. Although the Public Works Administration used $28 million of its own funds on some of the listed public building projects, little got done on other projects on the list until Congress returned $65 million for public buildings in June 1934.[30] As in 1932, the Secretary and the Postmaster were authorized to select projects from a list compiled by Congress of eight hundred proposed buildings, of which 604 had been on the 1932 list. Among the 604 were the projects for Marquette and Kalamazoo, although the maximum allowed cost for each was reduced (Marquette from $225,000 to $207,000; Kalamazoo from $517,500 to $440,000, both maximums to include administrative costs).[31]

The reduction in the amount authorized for Marquette's building created a problem. The authorities had decided that the new building would be constructed on the site of the 1889 courthouse. One of the principles of the 1932 Act was to stimulate local employment by mandating that demolition of any old buildings and construction of the new must be performed by local contractors using local laborers. In Marquette, no eligible contractors wanted to submit a bid to perform both demolition and construction for the reduced maximum cost. Finally, in August 1935 Congress appropriated an additional $56,000 for the project "in order to award the contract therefor to the lowest responsible bidder."[32]

Demolition of the old building began on February 19, 1936. The contractor estimated that construction of the new building would begin a month later and take about a year,[33] and he was right. The courthouse opened on April 10, 1937, and two days later, on April 12, Judge Fred Raymond held the first session of the District Court in the new courtroom.[34]

The design of the new building was the responsibility of the supervising architect for the Treasury Department, Louis A. Simon, who held that office for just six years, from 1933 to 1939, although he had supervised the design work for previous supervising architects since 1915. He was known as a conservative designer, preferring to work in a colonial revival or classical style. However, his Marquette building was up to date, a simplified version of art deco, straight lines with little ornamentation except an art deco eagle over the entrance. The supervising engineer was Neal A. Melick, who collaborated frequently with Simon on federal building projects. Many of those buildings are now listed on the National Register of Historic Places, including the Fort Knox Bullion Depository and numerous post offices across the country. As in many of their designs of combination post offices and courthouses, such as the very similar design for the federal building in Bay City, Michigan, the post office in Marquette is on the main floor, the court facilities on the second, and space for other federal agencies on the third.[35] The use of art deco may have been the result of the government's encouragment of architects on federal projects to use standard plans. Inside the main lobby of the new Marquette federal building was a mural by artist E. Dewey Albinson that was commissioned by the Works Progress Administration and painted soon after the building was opened. Albinson depicted Father Marquette with two French voyageurs and two Indians in a canoe.[36]

World War II and the U.S. Office of Price Administration

After the repeal of the Eighteenth Amendment and the end of Prohibition on December 5, 1933, the caseload of the lone District Judge in the Western District of Michigan decreased quickly from 559 civil and criminal cases in fiscal year 1933 to just 226 cases in fiscal year 1934, and to 165 cases in fiscal year 1935. However, in fiscal 1936 and thereafter, the annual total number of cases filed increased to more than 250 and remained at that level or higher thereafter. During World War II, the Western District did not have many famous cases, such as prosecutions of spy rings, traitorous citizens, or disloyal aliens, all of which occurred in the Eastern District of Michigan. Rather, the Western District's docket involved cases that were important to the war effort but were less dramatic. As had been the case in World War I, prosecutions under the Selective Service Act were numerous early in the war, but they dwindled to just thirty-nine in fiscal year 1945. The largest portion of the court's war-related docket during and after the war involved the enforcement of the rules of the Office of the Price Administrator (OPA), an agency acting on the authority of the Emergency Price Control Act of 1942.[37] The Act provided the OPA with the authority to place ceilings on all prices, except those for farm produce, and to ration consumer purchases of a myriad of items required for the war effort, including rubber, gasoline, fuel oil, meat, coffee, and processed foods. By the end of the war, the OPA controlled the retail price of almost 90 percent of consumer food purchases. A subsidiary of the OPA, the Office of the Housing Expediter (OHE), also controlled rent prices for residential properties.

The 1942 Act authorized the OPA and OHE to file both civil and criminal charges in the U.S. District Courts. In the Western District, the number of OPA enforcement suits on the court's docket were initially small, but the number grew, and in fiscal year 1945 they constituted almost half of all of the civil and criminal cases filed that year, 202 of the 414 new cases. The rules of the OPA and OHE remained in force until June 30, 1947, and those agencies filed 309 such cases in fiscal years 1946 and 1947; even after the rules lapsed, in 1948 and 1949, the U.S. Attorney filed another forty-nine OPA and OHE cases.

The District Court case of *Woods v. Boyle*,[38] filed by the OHE and decided in 1948 by Judge Raymond W. Starr, the successor to Judge Fred Raymond, is a typical example of an OPA or OHE case. In May 1945, Russell L. Boyle and Ann Boyle bought a house on College Avenue, SE, in Grand Rapids. They remodeled the upper floor into a separate apartment, which they rented to Mr. and Mrs. Adelbert Green for $150 per month. The Greens were happy to pay that rent because of the city's housing shortage. Two months after the Greens moved in, the "area rent control office" of the OHE decided that the maximum legal rent for the apartment was just $100 per month. The Boyles agreed to lower the rent and reimburse the Greens, but unknown to the rent control office, Mr. Green also agreed to pay Mr. Boyle the $50 difference each month in cash.

Tighe E. Woods, the OHE's local "housing expediter," found out about the cash payments and filed suit, asking the court to order the Boyles to pay treble damages based on the amount of excess rent the Greens had paid. Judge Starr tried the case without a jury. Mr. Boyle claimed that the $50 monthly

Judge Raymond Wesley Starr

cash payment was to pay off a business-related promissory note that Green had owed Boyle for more than a decade, but Starr did not believe him. At the end of the trial, Judge Starr dismissed the charges against Mrs. Boyle, who had testified without contradiction that she knew nothing of the $50, and ordered Mr. Boyle to repay the Greens $1,050 and to pay the United States $400. Mr. Boyle appealed to the Sixth Circuit, which affirmed Judge Starr in a per curiam opinion.

District Judge Raymond Wesley Starr

Judge Fred Raymond died unexpectedly on February 6, 1946, and, on July 23, Michigan Supreme Court Justice Raymond W. Starr was confirmed as his replacement. Judge Starr was born on August 24, 1888, in Pleasantville Township, Emmet County, Michigan, near the Straits of Mackinac, the son of John Travis and Amanda (Blackman) Starr. Both of his grandfathers were veterans of the Union Army during the Civil War. After graduation from Harbor Springs High School in 1907, Judge Starr spent one year as a student at Ferris Institute in Big Rapids, Michigan, majoring in Latin and geometry. He next attended the Law Department of the University of Michigan from which he received his bachelor of laws degree in 1910. With his law degree in hand, he traveled to Grand Rapids where he began to practice law and also began a family. On June 8, 1912, Starr married Minnie Eseleen Johnson of Grand Rapids, whose family was the prominent owner of factories in one of the city's major industries at that time, cigar manufacturing.[39] They had two children, John and Barbara. Starr first practiced with Hyde, Earle & Thornton, then Wicks, Fuller & Starr, and in 1933 he joined his brother James as Starr & Starr.

Although Starr was successful with his many private clients, he also recognized that there were many people in Kent County who could not obtain legal services for lack of funds. In 1911, he founded the first Legal Aid Bureau in the country, where he would go at night to offer help to the poor of Grand Rapids. In 1935, Starr was elected Attorney General of Michigan for a term running from January 1, 1936, to December 31, 1937.[40] Starr was instrumental in settling sit-down strikes in Flint and Detroit, and he was tenacious in defending the Great Lakes. As Attorney General, he represented Michigan and attorneys general from other states before the U.S. Supreme Court and the U.S. House of Representatives to block Chicago and Illinois from increasing their drainage from Lake Michigan. After his term, Starr returned to private practice in Grand Rapids. In May 1941, Governor Murray D. Van Wagoner appointed Starr to the Michigan Supreme Court to succeed another Grand Rapids attorney, Justice Thomas McAllister, whom President Franklin D. Roosevelt had appointed to the U.S. Court of Appeals for the Sixth Circuit.

Justice Starr won the Supreme Court vacancy election in November 1941, and he served as chief judge in 1945. He was reelected in April 1945 for a term beginning on January 1, 1946. However, when Judge Raymond died, Starr's name was prominent in the search for a successor, as were the names of the U.S. Attorney for the Western District, Joseph F. Deeb, and Congressman Frank E. Hook from Ironwood. On February 26, Michigan's members of the Democratic National Committee formally endorsed Starr, but other leading Democrats objected for political reasons. Powerful U.S. Congressman T. John Lesinski complained of a "sell-out" to the Republicans because Starr was the only Democrat on the Supreme Court and his replacement, who would be appointed by Governor Harry F. Kelly, a Republican, would certainly also be a Republican.[41] Lesinski's prediction proved to be correct,[42] but Starr also had the support of U.S. Attorney General Tom C. Clark who convinced President Harry S. Truman to appoint Starr, on July 3, 1946, to replace Raymond. The appointment was confirmed on July 23, Judge Starr

1954

Eastern District

■ Northern Division

■ Southern Division

Western District

□ Northern Division

■ Southern Division

● Place of Holding Court
(1900) Court added
(1900) Court removed

Marquette

Sault Ste. Marie

Bay City

Grand Rapids

Flint

Port Huron

Lansing
(1961)

Mason
(1954) *(1961)*

Kalamazoo

Detroit

The Eastern and Western Districts of Michigan, 1954

received his commission on July 25, and he moved into Judge Raymond's former chambers on the second story of the 1909 federal building. After Congress authorized a second judgeship for the Western District in 1954, Judge Starr served as the Western District's first Chief Judge until he assumed senior status on August 15, 1961. Although he was inactive for the last year of his life because of illness, he remained a Senior District Judge until his death on November 2, 1968, at home in Grand Rapids. He was survived by his widow, two children, eight grandchildren, and one great grandchild.[43] Judge Starr received honorary law degrees from Detroit College of Law (doctor of laws degree, 1938) and Ferris State College (juris doctor degree, 1945).

During his twenty-two years on the bench of the U.S. District Court, Judge Starr heard more than four thousand cases and was reversed only once.[44] At a memorial service, Michigan Governor G. Mennen Williams, who later also served as a Michigan Supreme Court Justice and whom Starr had hired as an Assistant Attorney General many years earlier, reflected that: "Raymond Starr, with one of his hearty northern Michigan chuckles, said to me one day, 'Mennen, when you go campaigning, remember there's more votes in a bar than in a church.' I don't know whether that is to what I owe my success in terms as Governor or not. But in any event, I owe a great debt to Raymond Starr." In addition to his judicial responsibilities, Starr also served as president of the Children's Aid Society and the D. A. Blodgett Home for Children, director of the Michigan Welfare League, and on the board of directors for the Camp Fire Girls. Despite having attended its predecessor for only one year, he served as the first chairman of the board of control at Ferris State College for many years. Starr was instrumental in appointing Wendell A. Miles, a future federal District Judge, as general counsel for the school.

Judge Starr and Michigan's Anti-Heart Balm Statute

Federal courts, except in rare circumstances, have no jurisdiction to grant or deny a divorce or to otherwise become involved in cases involving marital relations. In 1949, though, Judge Starr found himself mired in just such a case in which he seemed determined to put his stamp on a Michigan law known as the "anti-heart balm" act. The case was brought, on the basis of diversity of citizenship, in the names of "Charles Theodore Russick and Robert Lee Russick, infants four and two years of age" by their father, Theodore Russick, as "next friend." The defendant was Lawrence Hicks, formerly a neighbor and family friend, who had, according to the children's complaint, "enticed and induced their mother to leave and desert them and their family home, and to go to other places where defendant might associate and consort with her; and that as a result of his enticement and inducement, defendant Hicks has caused their mother to continuously remain away from them and their home." After the parents divorced, and a Michigan state court awarded Theodore Russick sole custody of the infants, he moved them to Ohio and filed this case on behalf of the young boys. He sought money damages for the loss of "their rights as infants to the maternal care, attention, support, and affection of their mother, and their right to have their home with their father and mother remain inviolate and undamaged."

If Theodore Russick had filed the case as plaintiff in his own name, it was clear a dismissal would have been the result. In 1935, Michigan's legislature

had abolished the common-law claims for damages for alienation of affec-
tions, criminal conversation, seduction, and breach of a contract to marry.[45]
The abolished claims had been created in common law to compensate women
who had been emotionally injured by a man's betrayal. In the 1920s and 1930s,
such claims for emotional distress were often criticized as outdated, subject to
abuse for blackmail, and seeking mere "heart balm." In 1935, Michigan's legislature joined other states in passing "anti-heart balm" laws abolishing heart
balm claims. Theodore Russick hoped that Judge Starr would let him sneak
into federal court under the guise of a claim by his infant sons.

Hicks's attorneys made the appropriate motion to dismiss and were probably
shocked when Judge Starr allowed the case to continue. Rejecting the defendant's objections to the case, Starr asked whether the children's asserted cause
of action for damages existed at common law. He acknowledged that almost all
American courts, including those of Michigan, had never recognized a child's
claim for damages in this context. The exceptions were a 1947 decision by the
U.S. Court of Appeals for the Seventh Circuit and decisions in Illinois and
Minnesota appellate courts in 1947 and 1949. In the absence of any Michigan
law on the point, he asserted that he had the right to decide the issue himself,
and he ruled for the plaintiffs. As for the anti-heart balm act, he ruled that it did
not apply to the children because, as worded, it did not specifically bar a cause
of action that did not exist until he created it then and there. Clearly, Judge
Starr felt for the children who had lost their mother, but he seemed never to
have considered whether the issue of their loss should have been litigated as part
of the divorce and support proceedings in a state probate court.

A Permanent Second Judgeship and a Larger District

Between 1941 and 1952, the annual average number of new criminal and civil
cases filed in all U.S. District Courts grew from 329 to 413 cases per judge. As
the experience of the Western District shows, though, that comparison hides
case-filing growth in the intervening years. In 1940, the Western District,
with one judge, received 189 new civil and criminal cases, and in 1952 there
were 397 new cases filed. However, because of the Office of Price Administration, the number of such filings was actually higher in 1945 and 1947 than in
1952 when the Administrative Office of the U.S. Courts and the Judicial Conference of the United States urged Congress to authorize a major increase in
district judgeships. On February 10, 1954, Congress reacted by authorizing

Judge William Wallace Kent

three new circuit judgeships and twenty-seven new district judgeships, including a second district judgeship for the Western District of Michigan.[46] At the same time, Congress transferred five counties (Ingham, Branch, Calhoun, Clinton, and Hillsdale) from the Eastern District of Michigan to the Western District. Congress deemed this change necessary to justify the Western District's second judgeship by increasing the Western District's population. According to the 1950 national census, the transfer added about 390,000 residents to the Western District, increasing the Western District's population by 20 percent.[47] The transfer of Ingham County, home of the state capital, Lansing, would have a particularly important impact on the court's docket.

District Judge William Wallace Kent

Several western Michigan attorneys were eager to obtain the President's nomination for the Western District's second judgeship. News reports at the time pointed to W. Wallace Kent of Kalamazoo and Howard Campbell of Cadillac as early candidates even before the second judgeship became law.[48] Later other names were mentioned, such as Cyrus Poppen of Muskegon, Earl

Pugsley of Hart, and Max Hamlin of Manistee.[49] However, the Western District nomination was in the hands of U.S. Senator Charles E. Potter who unwaveringly preferred Kent. On March 31, 1954, Potter recommended him to President Dwight D. Eisenhower who nominated Kent to the new position on May 10. The Senate confirmed his appointment on June 8, and he received his commission on June 10. His investiture took place in his hometown, Kalamazoo, despite the absence of a federal courtroom there at that time.

Judge Kent is the first federal judge in the Western District who was born in the twentieth century. He was born on May 1, 1916, in Galesburg, Kalamazoo County, Michigan, to Harold S. and Alice W. (Budd) Kent. As a young boy, he earned his own money as a caddy and newspaper boy. He graduated from Kalamazoo Central High School in 1933, Western State Teachers College (now Western Michigan University) (BA, 1937) and the University of Michigan Law School (JD, with honors, 1940), where he served as editor of the law review. After receiving his law degree, on July 7, 1940, he married M. LaVerne Fredlund, and the couple returned to Kalamazoo to begin a law practice. He served as assistant prosecutor and friend of the court for Kalamazoo County from 1941 to 1944. He then entered private practice as Mason, Stratton & Kent, but in 1945 he accepted an appointment to serve out an unexpired term as County Prosecutor. He returned to his firm in 1946, and he practiced there, primarily as a trial attorney, until he joined the bench of the Western District court in 1954 at the age of thirty-eight, the youngest federal judge of his time.

On the bench, Judge Kent was a smart, no-nonsense, demanding jurist who was a stickler for following the rules. In 1960, in a case in the Marquette federal courthouse, plaintiffs' attorneys were arguing a motion for Kent to recuse himself on an allegation that he was socially close to the defendants, who were Masons. The judge also was a Mason, and he had recently become the Grand Master of Michigan's 175,000-member Masonic fraternal organization. During the argument, the plaintiffs' attorneys left the courtroom and refused the judge's order to return. Kent had the attorneys arrested, and, after an immediate summary hearing, he adjudged both of them in criminal contempt, jailed them overnight, and sentenced them to further jail time and a fine.[50]

Off the bench, on the other hand, Wally Kent was a congenial family man and member of the community who was easy to get along with. He lived his entire life in the Kalamazoo area, although this meant traveling daily to

Grand Rapids on two-lane country roads, until the Kalamazoo federal courthouse was opened in 1963. He also traveled twice each year to the federal courthouse in Marquette, where he held court and went fishing and hunting, frequently with the District Court's clerk, Howard Ziel. When he was in Grand Rapids, he usually joined the other judges and court staff for lunch at Steketee's department store.

In 1961, when Judge Starr took senior status and was succeeded by Noel P. Fox, Judge Kent became the district's chief judge. He served in that position until January 1971 when he left the District Court and was sworn in as a judge of the U.S. Court of Appeals for the Sixth Circuit. President Richard M. Nixon nominated Kent to the Court of Appeals on December 8, 1970, to a seat vacated by Bertram Thomas Combs. Kent was confirmed by the Senate on December 16, received his commission on December 18, and was sworn in on January 6, 1971.[51]

Two of Kent's cases involving school integration show both sides of his character. While he was still a District Judge, he was assigned a case alleging that the schools of the Benton Harbor school district were segregated as a result of the district's use of a neighborhood plan for school locations (*Berry v. School District of the City of Benton Harbor*). In February 1970, after a bench trial, Judge Kent found against the board on several issues but as to neighborhood school systems, he ruled reluctantly for the school board. He found a definite racial imbalance in the schools, but he explained that he was bound by a 1966 decision by the Sixth Circuit (*Deal v. Cincinnati Board of Education*) requiring proof that the board had created the imbalance deliberately for racial reasons.[52] Kent stated that without that Sixth Circuit decision he would have ruled differently because he believed that a school system based on neighborhoods "results in the denial of equal opportunity for education to the black child who is forced ... to attend a predominantly black school."[53] In 1974, after Judge Kent's death, a panel of the Sixth Circuit ruled on the plaintiffs' appeal in *Berry*, abandoned the ruling in *Deal,* and returned the case to the District Court for further proceedings.[54]

In 1973, two years after Judge Kent was elevated to the Sixth Circuit, the Detroit school desegregation case (*Milliken v. Bradley*) was considered on appeal by the Sixth Circuit en banc. The court affirmed a decision by the presiding District Judge of the Eastern District of Michigan, Stephen J. Roth, compelling integration of the Detroit and suburban schools. Judge Kent authored a dissenting opinion in which he agreed that the Detroit schools were unconstitutionally segregated and must be integrated. However, he also insisted that before ruling on the remedy, the case had to be remanded to the District Court to take evidence on whether the suburban school districts were complicit in the de jure segregation of black students. The following year, the U.S. Supreme Court adopted Judge Kent's position on the suburban school districts.[55]

Unfortunately, Judge Kent served on the court of appeals for less than two and a half years, and thus he did not live to see his views on the law of school segregation cases vindicated. He died on the morning of Monday, May 28, 1973, at Bronson Hospital in Kalamazoo, a few hours after he suffered a heart attack at home. He was fifty-seven years old and was survived by his parents, his wife, and the couple's six children. Fellow appeals court judge Harry Edwards mourned Kent's early death: "He was stricken in full stride—at the very apex of his effectiveness—at a time when under normal contemplation, no matter how worthwhile his long career of public service has already been, his most important work still lay ahead."

United States v. Horace Chandler Davis

In 1954, the Western District's District Court and the U.S. Attorney found themselves enmeshed in a Red Scare case. Although the defendant's conviction comported with the law, and although the penalty imposed on the defendant was not nearly as harsh as that suffered by too many other people, the case is an example of the dark McCarthy era, and it can be seen, in retrospect, to have harmed a young man who, in calmer days, might be said to have done nothing but to stand up to a bully.

On May 10, 1954, a subcommittee of the House Committee on Un-American Activities held a hearing in Lansing chaired by Congressman Kit Clardy, a Republican from Ionia who represented Michigan's sixth congressional district and who was an acolyte of Senator McCarthy. The stated purpose of the hearing was to investigate alleged Communist infiltration of education, and the subcommittee had subpoenaed three professors and two graduate students from the University of Michigan to appear and testify. The professors were Horace Chandler Davis, a twenty-six-year-old mathematics instructor; Mark Nickerson, an associate professor of pharmacology; and Clement Markert, a professor of zoology. Clardy had not chosen Davis or Markert to subpoena out of the blue. Davis's father, Horace B. Davis, was openly a member of the Communist Party of the USA, and Davis himself had been a member of the party for a short time, although in 1954 he described himself as a socialist. Markert had served in the International Brigades in the Spanish Civil War. Horace Chandler Davis was born in August 1926 in Ithaca, New York, and was educated at Harvard where he earned a bachelor of science degree in 1945 and a doctor of philosophy degree in 1950. Later that year, he joined Michigan's faculty.

All five of these witnesses answered some general questions put to them by Clardy, but they also all objected to answering any questions they deemed political. While the other four witnesses based their refusals on the Fifth Amendment's protection against self-incrimination, Davis chose instead to object based only on the First Amendment, asserting that those questions were political in nature and that compelling him to answer violated his right to free speech. He explained to Clardy: "I will not discuss politics with a sword over my head; the First Amendment is intended to keep coercion out of politics."[56]

The professors' refusals to answer quickly became known to the university's administration. On the next day, President Harlan Hatcher suspended all three professors pending a "thorough investigation by the University." On July 23, the U.S. House of Representatives voted to cite Davis (but not the other witnesses subpoenaed by Clardy) and sixteen other individuals across the country for contempt of Congress for refusing to answer such questions. Two weeks later, on August 3, Hatcher recommended to the university's regents that the three professors be dismissed. The regents took Hatcher's advice as to Davis and Nickerson but reinstated Markert because of support for him from the faculty and his department.

On August 25, 1954, a federal grand jury of the U.S. District Court for the Western District of Michigan returned a twenty-six-count indictment against Davis, charging him with contempt of Congress under a 1938 statute,[57] which provides, in relevant part, that: "Every person who having been summoned as a witness by the authority of either House of Congress to give testimony . . . upon any matter under inquiry before either House, . . . or any committee of either House of Congress, . . . who, having appeared, refuses to answer any question pertinent to the question under inquiry, shall be deemed guilty of a misdemeanor, punishable by a fine of not more than $1,000 nor less than $100 and imprisonment in a common jail for not less than one month nor more than twelve months."[58] Davis was arraigned in Grand Rapids on September 14; he pleaded not guilty. The prosecutor was the Western District's U.S. Attorney and a future U.S. District Judge, Wendell A. Miles. Davis was represented by prominent civil liberties attorney Philip Wittenberg.

The case was assigned to Judge Kent who tried it without a jury in Grand Rapids. The pretrial phase of the case proceeded slowly, in part because Davis twice moved to dismiss the indictment, arguing that the questions posed were not germane to the subcommittee's investigation and that he had not been advised of the consequences of refusing to answer. Judge Kent denied both motions, and the trial finally began on November 19, 1956, more than two years after Davis's dismissal and his arraignment. Because the parties had no real dispute as to the facts and there was no jury, the trial was very short and concluded the next day. After a day and a half of testimony and half a day of closing arguments, Judge Kent took the case under advisement for seven months. On June 26, 1957, he submitted his judgment, supported by a written opinion, finding Davis guilty beyond a reasonable doubt. On August 5, Kent sentenced Davis to six months in prison and a fine of $250 and left him free on bail pending appeal.

Davis's appeal was argued in the Sixth Circuit on April 21, 1958, before a panel consisting of Circuit Judges Shackleford Miller, Jr. and Potter Stewart and District Judge Paul J. Jones of the Northern District of Ohio. Because of a case with similar issues pending in the U.S. Supreme Court,[59] the *Davis* panel waited until August 21, 1959, to issue its opinion.[60] By that time, Judge Stewart had been appointed to the U.S. Supreme Court, so the decision, affirming the conviction, was by Judges Miller and Jones only. Writing for the two-person panel, Judge Miller explained: "We agree with appellant's construction of the statute that in such a hearing part of the standard of criminality is the pertinency of the questions propounded to the witness, that the witness is entitled to be apprised of the object of the inquiry so as to show the connective tissue between the questions asked and the claimed power of the committee, and that the witness must be apprised that the committee demands his answer notwithstanding the objections made by the witness to answering the question." The panel determined that the subcommittee had satisfied those standards.

On December 29, 1959, the U.S. Supreme Court denied review, and Professor Davis returned to Michigan in February 1960 to begin his prison sentence. He commented that "Six months is after all not too long a hitch to serve in defense of my country. And I think that's just what this is."[61] During his imprisonment, he worked on a mathematical paper, which, when published, carried the comment: "Research supported in part by the Federal Prison System. Opinions expressed in this paper are the author's and are not necessarily those of the Bureau of Prisons." A few years later, Davis moved to Canada and began teaching at the University of Toronto where, in 2020, he is still teaching, at the age of ninety-two. Davis's principal research investigations involve linear algebra and operator theory in Hilbert space.

CHAPTER 6

The Western District in Era of Growth and New Challenges, 1960 to 1990

U.S. District Judge Noel Peter Fox

O N AUGUST 15, 1961, Judge Raymond Starr became the first District Judge of the Western District to assume senior status, a form of semi-retirement created in 1919 in which judges of a certain age and a certain number of years of service can receive the full salary of a judge yet take a reduced (or no) caseload.[1] When a judge opts for senior status, the judicial slot is considered vacant and a new judge can be appointed. Judge Starr's seat on the court remained vacant for almost a year until July 12, 1962, when President John F. Kennedy appointed Michigan Circuit Court Judge Noel P. Fox to replace Starr.

Judge Fox was born on August 30, 1910, in Kalamazoo, Michigan, the second of eight children of Charles K. and Caroline Margaret Kokx Fox. His mother, the daughter of Dutch immigrants, instilled in him a strong devotion to the Catholic Church that continued for the rest of his life.[2] He received his elementary and secondary education at St. Mary's, a parochial school in Muskegon, Michigan. He was taught the value of hard work in a large family, selling newspapers, cleaning furnaces, sweeping out a drug store, and selling Christmas cards door to door.

In 1929, Judge Fox entered Marquette University, in Milwaukee, Wisconsin, where he received his bachelor of philosophy degree in 1933 and his juris doctor degree, cum laude, in 1935. After he received his law degree, he returned to Muskegon where he engaged in private practice with various partners from 1935 to 1951, supplemented with service as Chief Assistant Prosecutor for Muskegon County from 1937 to 1939 and on the Michigan Labor Mediation Board from 1941 to 1944. He ran unsuccessfully for Congress on

Judge Noel Peter Fox

the Democratic ticket in 1938 and 1940. During World War II, he served in the U.S. Navy as a lieutenant for four years. Fox volunteered for combat duty, but his experience in mediating labor relations caused him to be assigned to war labor boards that settled labor disputes, particularly in the Brooklyn Naval Yard.

After the war, Fox returned to his legal practice and continued to handle labor mediation cases. He helped end a one-hundred-day strike against Chrysler and other strikes at Detroit Edison and the Detroit Street Railway. He was unsuccessful both in a 1948 campaign for the office of Michigan secretary of state and in a 1950 run for Congress, but his persistent electoral efforts on behalf of the Democratic Party and his help in nominating G. Mennen Williams as the Democratic candidate for Michigan governor in 1948 led Governor Williams, in 1951, to appoint Fox as circuit judge for the Fourteenth Judicial Circuit of Michigan in Muskegon. Judge Fox consistently won election and reelection until his appointment to the federal bench. Many years later, Fox said that in retrospect he was glad about his nonjudicial electoral defeats. "I'd have never been able to accept the kind of political contributions you need to keep getting elected."

Fox was an early favorite for the federal nomination to succeed Judge Starr because he was supported by Michigan's two U.S. senators, both Democrats,

Philip Hart and Patrick McNamara. The delay in his appointment seems to have been the result of several factors. He was an activist, liberal Democrat with past service as chairman of the Democratic party in Muskegon County, whereas the Western District was highly conservative and Republican. Fox readily admitted his liberal activist philosophy where the Constitution was involved.

Another objection to Fox's nomination was that he was not from Grand Rapids, where a number of prominent attorneys wanted the nomination. However, after eight years of a Republican administration, President Kennedy wanted to appoint as many liberal Democrats to federal positions as he could. A more serious concern about Judge Fox was that he had suffered two heart attacks in the preceding decade.[3] Because of that concern, he undertook a rigorous medical examination, which he passed.

Judge Fox was confirmed unanimously by the Senate on July 25, 1962, he received his commission on July 31, and he was sworn in on August 9 at a special session of the District Court held in Muskegon. Judge Fox served on the District Court for twenty-four years with only a few absences from the bench for health reasons. During his tenure on the District Court, Judge Fox lived up to his reputation as the court's fearless "liberal voice" while dealing with a stream of controversial cases. Often criticized as soft on crime, he acknowledged that after visiting all of the state's penal institutions during the 1940s, he found that the clanging of prison doors shutting behind him "was a hell of an experience" that did affect his sentencing philosophy. He did not believe in imposing lengthy jail terms except for the most serious crimes. During the 1970s, he angered many white parents and school administrators when he ordered desegregation plans for the Kalamazoo, Lansing, and Benton Harbor school districts.[4] He was denounced as an idiot and as prejudiced by non-Indian sports fishing interests in a case in which he ruled that an 1836 treaty between the federal government and Indian tribes in northern Michigan guaranteed the Indians the right to fish commercially in the Great Lakes free of state regulation.[5]

The religious foundation of Judge Fox's beliefs came through clearly in his writing and speeches. One of his law clerks likened him to a modern-day chancellor in a court of equity, doing what was "right" instead of what some might characterize as technically legal. His views on morality came through strongest where race was concerned. He emphasized that the depressed economic and social conditions of many blacks were "vestiges of slavery," and in his cases involving discrimination in schools he was determined to create integrated schools despite virulent opposition.

Judge Fox served as Chief Judge from January 6, 1971, to December 31, 1979, when he assumed senior status and cut back sharply on trial work. However, he continued to work on some of his cases, including the onerous Indian fishing case over which he presided for a decade, from its inception in 1973 until 1983 when he turned it over to Judge Richard A. Enslen. In January 1985, Judge Fox quietly left the courthouse and his chambers.[6] He was still on the court's roster as a senior judge when he died at the age of seventy-six on June 3, 1987, at the Villa Elizabeth Nursing Home in Grand Rapids where he had lived since February 1986. He is buried in St. Mary's Cemetery in Muskegon, Michigan. Judge Fox married the former Dorothy Ann McCormick on August 1, 1934. They were the parents of a daughter, Maureen, who had two children, Noel and Virginia. Soon after they were born, Maureen found herself divorced, seriously ill, and not able to care for them. She and the children moved in with her parents, who eventually adopted the children.

When Judge Fox left active service in 1985, Judge Douglas Hillman lauded him as "a great humanitarian who was also a great fighter against discrimination — race, religion, sex and age — long before that was popular." Judge Enslen added that "Judge Fox leaves a body of work that is rich in philosophy and a source of insight for his successors. He understood that the Constitution is an anti-majoritarian document, and though sometimes he was the subject of derision, he stood fast."[7]

The 1963 Kalamazoo Court Facility

In October 1963, the Western District of Michigan inaugurated a new District Court facility in Kalamazoo, housed on the first floor of the city's recently remodeled 1939 U.S. Post Office. Chief Judge W. Wallace Kent presided over the Kalamazoo court's first jury trial beginning on Monday, November 3, the culmination of a long campaign by the people of southwestern Michigan to bring a federal court to the area.

The first attempt to provide Kalamazoo with a federal court was the fruitless effort by Congressman William L. Stoughton in March 1869 to divide the six-year-old Western District into Southern and Northern Divisions with Kalamazoo the seat of the Southern Division and Grand Rapids of the Northern Division.[8] Judge Severens often conducted business of the District Court in

Kalamazoo, reportedly at his home and at what was known as the government office, located at the southwest corner of South Burdick Street and West South Street, but there was no official federal courtroom at either location.

In 1932, Kalamazoo became a candidate for a new post office under the Emergency Relief and Construction Act[9] to replace the city's old Romanesque post office. As was the case in Marquette, the money for the construction of such a building in Kalamazoo was delayed by more pressing national relief efforts, and also by a local struggle over where to build the new structure. At the post office's dedication ceremony in 1939, Kalamazoo businessman John H. Burke Sr. complained that "the long delay in [the building's] construction was due in great extent to mercenary persons who wanted the location in a different place than the present site recommended by postal inspectors."[10] The inspectors had determined that a new site was required because the site of the old post office was too small to meet the city's current and future needs. For the new building, the United States purchased land at 410 W. Michigan Avenue, on the northwest corner of West Michigan and North Park Street. In 1937, before construction could begin, the contractor had to demolish two older buildings that were in the way, a chapel of the Park Street Church of Christ and the meeting hall of the local chapter of the Grand Army of the Republic, an organization of veterans of the Union armies of the Civil War.[11]

The supervising architect for Kalamazoo's new post office was Louis A. Simon, who had also designed the Marquette federal building that had been completed a year earlier, and as in Marquette, the supervising engineer was Neal A. Melick. The Kalamazoo building's official plaque, near its eastern entrance, also lists three Michigan men as associate architects, Manuel Newlander and R. A. Leroy of Kalamazoo and George D. Mason of Detroit,[12] although the Federal Judicial Center's website lists Kalamazoo architects Stapert, Pratt, Bulthuns, Sprau & Croth as the building's architects.[13] Whoever was or were the architects(s), the result was a single-story building in a clean, art deco style with a smooth exterior clad in a light brown limestone. The design and exterior cladding were selected to match the 1931 Kalamazoo County Courthouse across Michigan Avenue and a block east. Although the federal building's style is similar to that of the 1937 Marquette post office and courthouse, the buildings are structurally different in one major aspect. Instead of Marquette's three stories, the Kalamazoo building has only one, making it one of the few art deco federal buildings of one story.

The new building's cornerstone was laid in 1938, and the post office began to move in during April 1939. The building's official dedication took place on Armistice Day, Saturday, November 11, 1939. Various organizations marched through the city to celebrate the twenty-first anniversary of the end of the Great War, ending at the post office. The large crowd, including several visiting postmasters, was given a tour of the facilities. Then the official representative of the federal government, fourth assistant postmaster general Smith W. Purdum, dedicated the building, and one of the county's two surviving Civil War veterans raised the American flag. That evening, 150 Kalamazoo citizens feted Purdum at a banquet held in the Park-American Hotel.

Missing from the dedication was any federal judge or a mention of a courthouse. Although the 1932 statute authorizing funding for the building had designated it as a post office and courthouse, Congress did not authorize the Western District to hold court there until 1954,[14] and the building would have no courtroom or judge's chambers for almost a decade.

In the same statute, Congress authorized the Southern Division of the Western District to hold court in Kalamazoo and in Mason, the Ingham County seat, although neither location had a federal court facility. The District Court never sat in Mason, which Congress deleted in 1961 in favor of Lansing. However, neither city would host a federal court soon. As an angry Congressman Kit F. Clardy of Lansing pointed out, Congress may have added cities in which the Western District's judges could hold court, but it did not authorize any money to provide quarters for the court in either city.[15]

According to Congressman August Johansen of Battle Creek, the General Services Administration (GSA) did begin soon after, in 1955, to plan "to remodel Kalamazoo's old post office building to provide quarters for federal agencies and additional federal court facilities for [the] western District of Michigan."[16] The hang-up, according to Johansen, was that a federal statute,[17] 28 U.S.C. 142, repealed in 1982,[18] provided that "Accommodations at places for holding court shall be held only at places where Federal quarters and accommodations are available, or suitable quarters and accommodations are furnished without cost to the United States." Johansen claimed that some parts of the federal government were concerned that plans for GSA to pay for adding the court facility as part of remodeling the post office in a building owned by the U.S. Post Office might violate that law.

Congressman Johansen negotiated with his colleagues for a waiver of sec. 142, although some congressmen, including future President Gerald Ford,

The Kalamazoo Federal Building, Post Office, and Courthouse.

were skeptical. Nevertheless, Johansen prevailed, and on May 19, 1961, Congress passed another omnibus judges act that included a waiver for Kalamazoo: "The limitations and restrictions contained in section 142 of title 28, United States Code, shall be waived with respect to the holding of court at Kalamazoo, Michigan, by the United States District Court for the Western District of Michigan."[19]

The remodeling of the post office proceeded apace, and in October 1963 the new court facility, including a courtroom and judge's chambers located on the first floor of what was now renamed officially the Kalamazoo Federal Building, Post Office, and Courthouse, was ready for action.[20]

Under a new local court rule, the Kalamazoo court was responsible for all cases arising in nine counties (Berrien, Van Buren, Cass, Kalamazoo, Allegan, Calhoun, Branch, St. Joseph, and Hillsdale), three of which were part of the 1954 county switch. Judge Kent, at that time the District Court's Chief Judge, was, like Judge Severens, a resident of Kalamazoo, and he gladly accepted the assignment to preside in the new court, a welcome change from his former daily commute to Grand Rapids. The courtroom's first trial, a jury trial,

The 1938 cornerstone for the Kalamazoo Federal Building, Post Office, and Courthouse.

The southern entrance to the Kalamazoo Federal Building, Post Office, and Courthouse.

opened on Monday, November 4, 1963. In that case, Benton Harbor Malleable Industries sued the United Automobile Workers, asking for $2.5 million in damages for what were claimed to have been strikes in 1952 and 1953 that violated the no-strike provision of the parties' contract. On November 22, the trial was still proceeding when Judge Kent was advised on the bench that President Kennedy had been shot; he immediately adjourned the trial.[21] Court resumed on December 2, and on December 5 the jury returned a verdict of $1,210,000 against the international union but only $115,000 against the local union, which had carried out the strikes. Judge Kent granted the plaintiff's motion for a new trial, but in March 1966, some fourteen years after the strikes at issue and just before the retrial was to begin, the unions agreed to settle the case by paying Malleable Industries $350,000.[22]

Judge Kent kept his chambers and held court in the Kalamazoo facility until he was appointed to the U.S. Court of Appeals for the Sixth Circuit in 1970, and he still kept a local office there until his sudden death in 1973. No other District Judge took up residence in the Kalamazoo court facility until 1980 when newly appointed Judge Richard Enslen, another native of Kalamazoo, moved in. After Judge Enslen took senior status in 2005, he kept his chambers in Kalamazoo until he stopped hearing cases in 2009. In 2007, District Judge Paul Maloney became the resident judge in Kalamazoo and continues there as of this writing. The three judges of the district's U.S. Bankruptcy Court also use the Kalamazoo facility for trials, pretrial conferences, and motion hearings, as did U.S. Magistrate Judge Doyle Rowland from 1984 to 2000, when he was killed in a car accident.

The District Judges Appointed during the 1970s

From 1863 to 1971, Presidents of the United States appointed just ten District Judges to the U.S. District Court for the Western District of Michigan. During the 1970s, two Presidents, Richard Nixon and Jimmy Carter, added five more District Judges to that roster. President Nixon appointed Albert J. Engel, Jr. in 1971, and Wendell A. Miles in 1974. Judge Engel replaced Judge Kent whom Nixon appointed to the Sixth Circuit, and Judge Miles replaced Judge Engel when Nixon also appointed him to the Sixth Circuit. President Carter appointed three judges, all in the last quarter of 1979: Douglas W. Hillman, Benjamin J. Gibson, and Richard A. Enslen. Judge Enslen replaced Judge Fox, who assumed senior status, and Judges Hillman and Gibson were

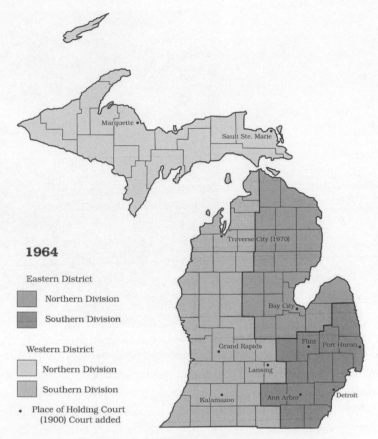

1964

Eastern District

Northern Division

Southern Division

Western District

Northern Division

Southern Division

• Place of Holding Court
   (1900) Court added

The Eastern and Western Districts of Michigan, 1964

appointed to new seats on the court, which Congress created in October 1978, giving the court four district judgeships.[23]

U.S. District Judge Albert Joseph Engel, Jr.

Albert J. Engel, Jr. was born on March 21, 1924, the son of Albert J. Engel and Bertha (Bielby) Engel, in Lake City, Missaukee County, Michigan, where his father was a lawyer. The family later moved to Muskegon, Michigan, and then to Washington, D.C., when Albert Sr. was elected to Congress in 1934. After Albert, Jr. graduated from high school in 1941, he entered the University of Maryland, but he left after his first year to enroll at the University of Michigan. Because of his father, he was present in the House gallery on December 8, 1941, when President Roosevelt gave his "day that will live in

Judge Albert Joseph Engel, Jr.

infamy" speech in which he asked Congress to declare war against the Empire of Japan. In February 1943, after a term at Michigan, Engel left Ann Arbor to join the U.S. Army, initially as a private but later as an officer commanding an ordnance disposal unit that disarmed live aerial bombs and other explosive devices for two years in England, France, Belgium, and Germany.

After he was discharged in April 1946, as a captain with five battle stars, he returned to the University of Michigan and earned a bachelor of arts degree in 1948 and a bachelor of laws degree in 1950. After one year in Washington, D.C., as an administrative assistant to Congresswoman Ruth Thompson, Engel returned to Michigan to practice law in Muskegon in the law firm of Engle and Engel until he joined the state's judiciary.

In 1966, Albert, Jr. was elected a judge in Michigan's Fourteenth Circuit Court in Muskegon County, serving on that bench from January 1967 until December 1970 when he became a U.S. District Judge. President Richard M. Nixon appointed Engel on December 15, 1970, to succeed Judge Kent. Engel's appointment was confirmed on December 17, and he received his commission on December 18.

Judge Engel left the District Court three years later, on January 4, 1974, when President Nixon appointed him to the Sixth Circuit, succeeding once more Judge Kent, who had died of a heart attack. Nixon nominated Engel for the appellate court on December 5, 1973, he was confirmed by the Senate on December 13, and he received his commission on December 19. Both of Engel's federal court nominations came at the recommendation of Michigan's U.S. Senator Robert P. Griffin. Engel served as Chief Judge of the Sixth Circuit from 1988 until October 1, 1989, when he assumed senior status. He closed his chambers on December 31, 2002, ending a thirty-one-year career in the federal judiciary. Judge Engel died in Grand Rapids on April 5, 2013, at the age of eighty-nine, from complications of lung cancer. He was survived by his wife of sixty-one years, the former Eloise Ruth Bull of Muskegon. Despite Engel's dumping Eloise into the water from a sailboat on their first date, they married in 1952. Together they had four children, Albert J. Engel III, Katherine Ann, James R., and Mary Elizabeth. His favorite hobbies included travel, bridge, music, and many outdoor activities, especially canoeing, fly fishing in Colorado, and scuba diving in the Cayman Islands. A branch of the Sixth Circuit's law library, located in Grand Rapids' Gerald R. Ford Federal Building, is named in honor of Judge Engel.

U.S. District Judge Wendell Alverson Miles

Wendell A. Miles was born on April 17, 1916, in Holland, Michigan, the third of four children of Fred Thomas Miles and Dena Del (Alverson) Miles. Both of his parents were teachers when they met, and his father subsequently became a lawyer.[24] In 1930, Fred Miles was elected Circuit Court Judge for Michigan's Twentieth Judicial Circuit Court, serving Ottawa and Allegan counties, a post he held until 1947. Wendell Miles went to Holland public schools and then attended Hope College in Holland. He performed as a drummer in both schools. At Hope College, he received a bachelor of arts degree in philosophy in 1938, then he entered the University of Wyoming where he obtained a master of arts degree in 1939. He returned to Michigan where he earned his law degree from the University of Michigan Law School (JD, 1942). While in law school, Miles was strongly against American involvement in the war in Europe, but Pearl Harbor changed his mind. He was able to persuade his draft board, which had just reclassified him 1-A at Christmas 1941, to allow him to finish law school the following June by which time he had already passed the Michigan bar examination, which had been moved up because of the war. In the fall of 1942, he reported for duty at Fort Riley, Kansas, as a private in the U.S. Army.

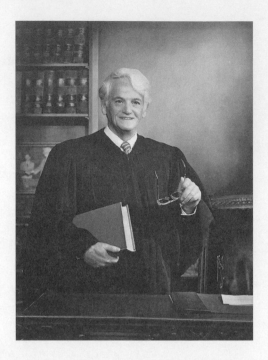

Judge Wendell Alverson Miles

His request for officer's training was denied at first because he was only 5'5" tall, but his law degree enabled him to receive a commission as an officer. He served in a variety of roles in the European theater, including as captain in the 493rd Military Police Escort Guard, which was involved in transporting German prisoners of war to prison camps in Texas. He also served in General Patton's Third Army, interrogating German prisoners during Patton's drive through Europe. After the war, Miles remained in Europe and tried black marketeering cases as an officer of the Judge Advocate General's Corps in Marseilles and then Strasbourg, France. In Strasbourg, he met and married Mariette Bruchert, a French woman who worked for him as a translator. After another transfer to Heidelberg, Germany, the couple had their first of three children, a daughter.

The family returned to the United States on Christmas Day, 1947, and then went on to Michigan where they settled in Holland. Fred Miles resigned from the bench in order to practice law with Wendell as Miles & Miles in Holland. In addition to his private practice, Wendell was elected Ottawa County Prosecutor in 1948; he was reelected twice, serving in that position until 1953. He also began teaching history at Hope College and joined the Holland public school board.

As it is today, the appointment of the U.S. Attorney for any judicial district was political, determined by the state's U.S. senators belonging to the party of the President. After Republican President Eisenhower won election in 1952, after twenty years of Democrats in the White House, it was a given that the incumbent U.S. Attorney for the Western District of Michigan, Joseph Deeb, would leave office. Although many Republican attorneys in the Western District campaigned to replace Deeb, Wendell Miles had become a favorite of Michigan's most powerful Republican politician, Arthur Summerfield, chair of the Republican National Committee and Eisenhower's nominee as Postmaster General. Summerfield recommended Miles to the President to succeed Deeb, and the President concurred. When the former Supreme Allied Commander in Europe met the former captain in the White House, Ike called Wendell "one of my boys." On June 16, 1953, during a dinner in Holland's Warm Friend Tavern celebrating his appointment, Wendell Miles was sworn in by his father as the Western District's new U.S. Attorney.[25]

Just as Joseph Deeb's term as U.S. attorney ended when President Eisenhower was inaugurated, Miles's term ended with the inauguration of President John F. Kennedy in 1961. Anticipating the end of his career as U.S. Attorney, Miles had campaigned as a Republican for Michigan Attorney General in the 1960 election, but he was not successful. He returned to private practice, this time in Grand Rapids, with the law firm of Miles, Mika, Meyers, Beckett and Jones where he practiced until 1970. He became one of the most prominent and successful trial lawyers in the state, often fighting for utility companies with the same energy and intelligence he had brought to prosecuting criminal defendants for the United States.

In 1968, he ran for circuit judge on the circuit court where his father had served for seventeen years, Michigan's Twentieth Judicial Circuit Court, but he lost the election to Chester A. Ray. However, when Judge Ray died in April 1970, Michigan Governor William Milliken appointed Miles to finish Ray's term. He remained on that court until March 1974, when President Richard M. Nixon chose him to take over Judge Engel's judgeship on the federal District Court.

According to press reports, Michigan's U.S. Senator Robert Griffin, who was unofficially in control of federal patronage in the state, and who had been instrumental in elevating Judge Engel to the appellate court, considered fifteen candidates, including seven circuit judges, one probate judge, and the current U.S. Attorney for the Western District, all of whom were campaigning for the position.[26] However, Judge Miles had the support of both Senator Griffin, whom he had supported in his race for Congress, and Vice President Gerald R. Ford. A few days later, Griffin announced that he had recommended Judge Miles to the President for the open judgeship. Miles was nominated by President Nixon on March 29, 1974, the Senate confirmed his appointment on April 10, he received his commission on April 17, and he was sworn in on May 4.

In 1974, the Western District had only two district judgeships, and the court would not have more than two judge slots until 1979. When Judge Miles took the bench, his sole colleague, whose office was at the opposite end of the hall, was Judge Fox whose seniority made him the district's Chief Judge. Although relations among District Judges in the Western District have been convivial during most of the years in which the court has had more than one judge, Judges Fox and Miles disliked each other thoroughly. It was not just that one was a Democrat and one a Republican, or that they had different views on the rule of law and a judge's role in the system of justice. Their enmity was personal.

In his 2004 interview for his oral history, Judge Miles emphatically recounted a case in which he represented the City of Grand Rapids against an African American man who alleged that he had been denied the transfer of a liquor license because of racial prejudice. Miles stated that Judge Fox insulted his clients and witnesses for three weeks and wrote an opinion "attacking the integrity of people I knew were fair, able, and dedicated and had been very poorly served."[27] Judge Fox ruled for the plaintiff on the claim of racial prejudice,[28] but the Sixth Circuit reversed his decision three years later, finding that there was no evidentiary proof to support Judge Fox.[29] According to Judge Miles, this incident made him a "marked man" for Judge Fox. In his oral history, Miles also complained that "When I was appointed, I was assigned as a second, third-rate [sic], subordinate to Judge Fox, who at first made sure we didn't have any more help, and enjoyed Florida in the winter and his cottage on Lake Michigan in the summer. . . . Judge Fox wasn't working, so we were slipping behind worse than the general problem all over."[30]

Another conflict between Judges Fox and Miles involved the assignment of cases between them. When there was only one District Judge, that was not an issue. Today, all federal courts have multiple judges, and assignment of cases by a blind draw among the judges of a district or division is mandatory. However, when multiple judges were a relatively new phenomenon, other procedures were adopted. In the Western District, beginning on April 23, 1974, all cases were assigned initially, by Western District Local Rule 1(a), to the Chief Judge who then decided which cases to reassign to the other judge. Judge Miles, as the second judge, would have none of it. He refused to accept cases reassigned to him from Chief Judge Fox and insisted that assignments be controlled by a blind draw. After some disputes between the judges, the court eventually did adopt a blind draw system for all cases.

There is no doubt that Judge Fox had his own view of those incidents, particularly the claim that he did not work and that he made sure that he and Miles received no help with their swollen docket. One of Judge Fox's law clerks from 1976 to 1978 remembers that Fox went to Washington several times to beg for another judgeship for the Western District, that the judge spent just a week in Florida each winter, and that though he did live during the summers at his cottage on White Lake in Muskegon County, he held hearings at the Whitehall City Hall and jury trials at the Oceana Circuit Court. Another former law clerk remembered Judge Fox holding hearings on the porch of his cottage. Fox also arranged for District Judges from other districts to visit the Western District during the summer and help clear out the overloaded docket. Despite his dislike of Judge Miles, Judge Fox never publicly expressed his feelings in that regard but kept them to himself.

After Judge Fox assumed senior status at the end of 1979 and was replaced by Judge Enslen, Judge Miles served as the District Court's Chief Judge from January 1, 1980, until he himself assumed senior status on May 6, 1986. While he was on senior status Judge Miles was appointed by Supreme Court Chief Justice William H. Rehnquist to a seven-year term on the secretive U.S. Foreign Intelligence Surveillance Court (1989–1996). All of the work on this court had to be performed in soundproof facilities in Washington, D.C. Judge Miles resigned from all judicial activities on December 31, 2008. Mariette Miles died in 2009, and Judge Miles died on July 30, 2013, in Grand Rapids, at the age of ninety-seven. Both were survived by their three children, Lorraine, Michele, and Thomas.

Judge Miles was a bundle of enormous energy, and he brought this energy to everything he did. Even after he retired from the bench, he could be seen in the courthouse, often working on the court's history. In April 2011, he had a successful pacemaker implanted after court security officers noted that he was having difficulty getting into the building. Miles tried to brush them off, saying "Just take me to my office, I will be fine." They overruled him and called for an ambulance instead. At the judge's memorial service, U.S. Magistrate Judge Hugh W. Brenneman, Jr., described the judge who "was who he was because he chose to be. This is the point. He was sometimes an observer ... but he was usually a doer who participated." Brenneman added that: "Wendell never lived his life timidly, but embraced it vigorously. His was a life marked by passion, whether it was for his children and grandchildren whom he loved so dearly, the wife he worshiped, or the father he idolized. When he worked, he worked hard, putting in long hours. When he played, he played hard. He was very competitive. When he had to fight, he fought hard and without apology."

U.S. District Judge Douglas Woodruff Hillman

Douglas W. Hillman was born on February 15, 1922, in Grand Rapids, Michigan, to Lemuel S. Hillman, a graduate of Cornell and a banker at Old Kent Bank in Grand Rapids, and Dorothy (Woodruff) Hillman, a graduate of Smith College. In February 1930, when Judge Hillman was eight years old, his father was hit and killed by an automobile, and his mother had to raise their four children alone. Judge Hillman graduated from Grand Rapids Central High School in 1940, and that September he entered the University of Michigan. As a freshman, the diminutive but always competitive Hillman tried out for the varsity hockey team and was the last person to make the cut. Although the team lost eleven out of twelve games, because six Canadians on the team dropped out of the university to join in the war, Hillman played in enough games to earn his varsity M.

In 1942, Hillman joined the U.S. Army Air Corps. While training in Stockton, California, to fly bombers, he met and fell in love with Sally Jones, a college student. He was assigned to the European Theater and flew forty-eight combat missions over Europe commanding a B-24 Liberator bomber from bases in Italy. A number of missions took him over the German-controlled oil fields at Ploesti in German-occupied Romania, as well as over Regensburg and Munich in Germany. On his last mission, over Ploesti, his plane was hit by anti-aircraft fire and he lost power in one of the four engines. He ordered his crew to bail out, but after three of the crew jumped, he managed to regain power and returned to base where he and the remaining crew parachuted to

Judge Douglas Woodruff Hillman

safety before the aircraft fell into the sea. Hillman and his crew, including the three who initially bailed out, survived the war.

Judge Hillman was awarded the Distinguished Flying Cross and the Air Medal. When his combat tour was over, he was assigned back to Stockton to train new pilots. There he and Sally married in September 1944, and they eventually became the parents of two children. Hillman's combat service and medals entitled him to be discharged before the end of the war in the Pacific, so he and Sally returned to the University of Michigan where he entered the law school despite having only one year as an undergraduate. He earned two degrees, a bachelor of arts in 1946 and a bachelor of laws in 1948. He then returned to Grand Rapids and began the private practice of law. The bulk of his practice was insurance defense involving automobile accidents and product liability. This gradually evolved into defending medical malpractice claims. In 1965, Hillman became president of the Grand Rapids Bar Association, and in 1970, the Grand Rapids branch of the American Civil Liberties Union awarded Hillman its Annual Civil Liberties Award, just one of the many awards he received during his career of intensive involvement in civic and professional issues.

In October 1978, Congress created two new district judgeships for the

Western District of Michigan, the court's third and fourth judgeships.[31] U.S. Senator Donald Riegle recommended Hillman to President Jimmy Carter to fill one of those seats, and President Carter did nominate Hillman on July 12, 1979. The Senate confirmed Hillman's appointment on September 25, 1979, and he received his commission the next day. Judge Hillman served as the District Court's Chief Judge from April 1986 to February 1991, when he assumed senior status. He suffered a stroke in 2000, and he retired on October 1, 2002. Judge Hillman died on February 1, 2007, at a hospice in Muskegon, Michigan, at the age of eighty-four. Mrs. Hillman died on January 13, 2013, in Montague, Michigan.

One of Judge Hillman's most important and enduring services to the bench and bar was the creation of what is now called the Hillman Advocacy Program. While observing young attorneys trying cases before him, Judge Hillman, a skilled trial attorney, observed that many of them lacked basic knowledge and skills of how to conduct a trial. He and Judge Miles, an equally accomplished trial advocate, decided to set up a workshop, in conjunction with the district's branch of the Federal Bar Association, to teach the missing knowledge and skills using federal courtrooms, live witnesses, experienced attorneys who donated their time, and video equipment. Now an annual three-day seminar, the program probably was unique in the country at its inception in using federal courtroom facilities. The workshop has continued to provide high-quality, professional courtroom training to hundreds of trial lawyers for forty years.

U.S. District Judge Benjamin F. Gibson

Benjamin F. Gibson was the Western District court's first and, to date only, African American District Judge and later Chief Judge. He was born on July 13, 1931, in Safford, Dallas County, Alabama, the son of Eddie and Pearl Gibson. The family moved to Detroit where his father was a production worker for Ford Motor Company. Judge Gibson graduated from Detroit's Miller High School in 1948, then served in the U.S. Army for two years, from 1948 to 1950. Returning to Detroit, he attended Wayne University (now Wayne State University) where he received a bachelor of science degree in business administration in 1955. He worked as an accountant for the City of Detroit and then was the first African American hired as a professional by the Detroit Edison Company, all while attending the Detroit College of Law (now Michigan State University College of Law) at night. In 1961, after graduating

Judge Benjamin F. Gibson

from DCL (JD, with distinction, 1960, fifth in a class of one hundred), he left Edison to join the staff of the Michigan Attorney General as an Assistant Attorney General assigned to the Michigan Public Service Commission, while doing post-graduate work toward a master of laws degree in labor law at Wayne State University Law School. In 1963 he became the first African American Assistant Prosecutor for Ingham County, and in 1964 he founded a private practice in Lansing with Stuart Dunnings. He remained in private practice until 1978. In 1979, he became the first African American law professor at the Thomas M. Cooley Law School in Lansing.

President Jimmy Carter nominated Gibson on July 12, 1979, to the new fourth District Judge seat on the court that had been authorized by Congress in October 1978.[32] Both he and Judge Hillman had been among forty-three applicants considered by a merit selection panel appointed by Senator Donald Riegle to fill the two new judgeships. The Senate confirmed Gibson's nomination on September 25, and he received his commission the next day. His investiture ceremony was held at Cooley Law School on October 2, 1979. Judge Gibson served as the district's Chief Judge from February 14, 1991, until April 30, 1995. He assumed senior status on July 13, 1996, his sixty-fifth birthday, and he retired from the bench on January 31, 1999, at the age of sixty-seven. Judge Gibson married Lucille Nelson of Memphis, Tennessee, on June 23, 1951; they are the parents of six children.

Off the bench, Judge Gibson, like many of his colleagues, was active in the community, serving on such boards as the Thomas M. Cooley Law School, Butterworth Hospital, the Grand Rapids Foundation, and United Way, and he garnered numerous awards for his service to the community, including the Champions of Justice Award from the State Bar of Michigan in 1993. Notwithstanding his accomplishments, Gibson was not inclined to dwell on the fact that he was in several instances the first black person to achieve them. To the contrary, he said, "I hate these firsts. You always have a tendency to say, 'this person is the first this or the first that.' Sometimes, there may be a tendency to emphasize the racial part, and I think the accomplishment gets lost in the shuffle."

But these accomplishments had not come without pain. Gibson pointed out that when he was hired by the Detroit Edison Company as an accountant, he was the first black person to be hired by that company as a professional: when he later tried to join the company's legal department he was turned down. He said he was told that race was the reason. Thus, of particular concern to the first black judge on the court was opening doors to other members of the black middle class who were willing and able to contribute to their community. "In Lansing," Gibson observed, "blacks were an integral part of the community." But he said that when he came to Grand Rapids in 1979 to join the court, the situation in Grand Rapids was not the same. "Blacks were the invisible man." In 1988, he began cochairing with Meijer Inc. Chairman Fred Meijer a program called "Project Blueprint" to recruit and train minorities who wanted to serve on the boards of community agencies. "Here's a group of people not on welfare, who are homeowners, who pay taxes. They're saying, 'We are here. We want to make a greater contribution.'" Sponsored by United Way and the Kellogg Foundation, Project Blueprint offered courses, workshops and seminars for both potential volunteers and the agencies, with the goal of having local boards reflect the ethnic diversity of the community. In three years, 150 minorities were recruited and placed on the boards of seventy nonprofit agencies and organizations. Gibson remarked at the time, "We're not there yet, but we're getting there."[33] By 2010, the number of graduates of the program reached 750.[34]

On the bench, Gibson, like his counterparts, found that many of his cases touched on high profile issues. In one such instance, a Kalamazoo state judge refused to rule on whether a mentally impaired thirteen-year-old girl should have an abortion. Gibson said that her guardian had approved the procedure, and the attending doctor said it had to be performed that week: "But because of his own personal reasons, the [state] judge wouldn't decide the case, so it was brought to federal court." Gibson promptly entered an order directing the state court judge to rule on the matter. The state judge denied the abortion, and the teenager had the baby, which was later placed in a foster home because she couldn't care for it. Another case touched on workplace employment issues. The city fired a police officer because he left his wife and chose to live with another woman. When the police officer brought suit in federal court over the propriety of the discharge, Judge Gibson ordered that he be reinstated.[35] In 1982, a public outcry arose in Grand Rapids when a touring company brought the musical comedy, "Oh! Calcutta!" to the new DeVos Hall auditorium. The show featured twenty-two minutes of eight actors performing in the nude. Persons objecting claimed that this was a violation of the local obscenity law. But Judge Gibson ruled that the police could not arrest the actors because the city's obscenity law was not specific enough to prevent the show. *Grand Rapids Press* theater reviewer David Nicolette wryly observed that the show "went off without a hitch, and much of the time without a stitch." Judge Gibson thought that his most controversial ruling may have been when he precluded a public school from hanging on a wall a picture of Jesus Christ. "I caught a lot of flak on that," Gibson said.[36]

Regardless of the issue, Gibson was noted for his high regard for counsel appearing before him. He was considered very methodical and thorough, and conveyed a feeling of receptiveness. Grand Haven attorney Philip R. Sielski said that he was impressed by the general feeling of openness he received in Judge Gibson's court. "It's real hard to explain, but I felt that even though he ruled against us, he gave us our day in court. In my experience, sometimes a judge doesn't come across that way." These thoughts paralleled those of Grand Rapids attorney David Dodge, who defended numerous criminal defendants in Judge Gibson's court. Dodge observed that "He just doesn't overreact. Some judges don't have a temperament for it. He has a judicial temperament that I think is like a model for judges."[37]

Judge Richard Alan Enslen

U.S. District Judge Richard Alan Enslen

Judge Richard A. Enslen was born on May 28, 1931, in Kalamazoo, Michigan. His father, Ehrman T. Enslen, was a photo engraver who moved to Kalamazoo from Alabama. His mother, Pauline (Dragoo) Enslen, from Fremont, Michigan, came to Kalamazoo to work for Gibson Guitar.[38] Judge Enslen graduated from Kalamazoo Central High School in 1949 and entered Kalamazoo College that fall with a scholarship, but in 1951, during the Korean War, he left school to enlist in the U.S. Air Force. He was stationed at Mountain Home Air Force Base in Boise, Idaho, where he met and married his first wife, Joan, the mother of his first six children. At the end of his service in 1954, he enrolled in Western Michigan University instead of Kalamazoo College because tuition was lower at Western. During his senior year, he transferred to the law school at Wayne University in Detroit (now Wayne State University Law School) where he graduated in 1958 with a bachelor of laws degree and passed the examination to join the Michigan bar.

After graduation, he and his growing family returned to Kalamazoo to find a job, law related or not. He worked briefly as an assistant trust officer for the First National Bank & Trust Company, but he found trust work boring and soon entered the private practice of law with Stratton & Wise. Judge Enslen left that firm after two years when the partners told him that he could not bring in an African American client. As early as high school, he had become passionately interested in the status of African Americans in America, and the partners' refusal to allow him to represent a black man convinced him to leave the firm. From 1960 to 1964, he practiced law successfully with lawyers Ed Ryan and Jack Bauckham as Bauckham & Enslen. He also worked for Senator John F. Kennedy during his 1960 presidential election campaign. In the summer of 1964, Enslen's strong convictions against racial injustice convinced him to join the National Lawyers Guild and other lawyers on a voter registration drive in Mississippi. During his months in the South, Enslen faced death threats and had the unique experience of being asked by the local prosecutor to try a criminal jury trial against a white man for assaulting a black student.

When he returned to Kalamazoo that fall, Enslen began a solo practice and also began giving speeches throughout the Midwest about racial equality, but he was ready for something new. In the fall of 1965, after meeting Sargent Shriver, the driving force behind the creation of the Peace Corps, Enslen accepted an appointment as Peace Corps country director for Costa Rica, where he lived with his wife and six children for two years.

While in Costa Rica, Enslen learned about new openings for judges in the Kalamazoo Municipal Court. With the help of friends back home, he ran a campaign in absentia from Costa Rica and was elected to a two-year term as judge. Soon after the election, the municipal courts were abolished, and he was promoted to become a judge of a state district court in Kalamazoo County. After two years on that bench, he resigned to return to private practice, possibly because he wanted to speak out against the Vietnam War. He continued to be active in politics, and in 1970 Enslen was the Democratic candidate for the U.S. House of Representatives in the race for Michigan's third congressional district seat. He lost in the general election and returned to private practice with the firm Howard and Howard. In 1976, he formed a new firm, Enslen & Schma, which he maintained until he became a U.S. District Judge. Among the most important of his cases during this tour of private practice was representing the Metropolitan Kalamazoo Branch of the NAACP in the suit that led to the use of busing to desegregate Kalamazoo's public schools.

On November 30, 1979, based on the recommendation of Senator Donald W. Riegle, Jr., President Jimmy Carter nominated Enslen to become a judge of the Western District, filling a seat vacated when Judge Fox took senior status.[39] The Senate confirmed Enslen's appointment on December 20, and he received his commission on December 21. He opened his chambers in the court's Kalamazoo facility, which had been initiated by Judge Kent in 1963. His confirmation, the last of the three new judges, came none too soon as the court had a backlog of 2,400 pending cases.

In 1985, Judge Enslen married Pamela G. Chapman; they had one child. In 1986, he completed the requirements for an advanced law degree at the University of Virginia and received a master of laws degree. In December 1999, the *Kalamazoo Gazette* named him its person of the century for law and the courts. Judge Enslen served as the court's Chief Judge from 1995 until 2001. He assumed senior status on September 1, 2005, and he took inactive status. He died on February 17, 2015, at his home on Gull Lake, near Kalamazoo. He was eighty-three and had been in failing health for a few years before his death.

Grand Rapids' Gerald R. Ford Federal Building and Courthouse

Even before it was completed, there were complaints that Grand Rapids' 1909 federal building was too small, particularly for its post office operations. In the 1930s, Congress authorized a stand-alone post office building near the old Union Railroad station, but Congress failed to appropriate any funds for the project. Finally, in 1962, Grand Rapids inaugurated a new post office building.[40] But even with the vacated space, the 1909 building, long derided as Noah's Ark for its impressive and stately exterior and its cramped interior, was still too small. So in 1966, the city and federal governments decided on a new, larger federal building and courthouse.[41] Judge Fox, tongue in cheek, gave one of the reasons for the need of a new courthouse: "We needed better restrooms for jurors." Judge Fox explained that, in long, drawn-out modern cases, the lack of special relief stations for jurors locked in deliberation was a hindrance to justice.

Rather than tear down the historically and architecturally significant Ark, it was decided to build a new federal building as part of the urban renewal project in Vandenberg Plaza, which had been created in the mid-1960s. Begun in the 1950s, urban renewal involved the wholesale demolition of the northern part of the city's downtown, including the old city hall, police headquarters, and the county building, and the replacement of those municipal buildings with several modern, much taller structures as well as a controver-

The Grand Rapids Gerald R. Ford Federal Building and U.S. Courthouse.

sial work of art. In 1969, the project added a bright orange, forty-two-ton, fifty-four-foot-long, forty-three-foot-tall, free-form metal sculpture by artist Alexander Calder that was fabricated in Tours, France. The work is a type of sculpture that the artist called a "stabile" to differentiate it from his moving "mobile" works. Named La Grande Vitesse (meaning "the great speed or swiftness," or possibly "grand rapids"), it was at first criticized, but it became so popular that the development area, officially Vandenberg Center Plaza, became commonly known as Calder Plaza. The sculpture became an emblem for the city and is included in the city's official logo. The Calder was the first civic sculpture in the nation financed by both federal and private funds.

In 1970, city residents could see the digging and laying of the footings for the new federal building at the northern end of the plaza, on Michigan Street between Ottawa and Monroe Avenues. Designed by a local architectural firm, Daverman & Associates, and built by a local construction company, Owens-Ames-Kimball, the new building is in the modernist style and has seven stories of offices and courtrooms above ground, although a shortage of funds precluded completion of all of the outside trim except the customary eagle above the main entrance. The new federal building's striking appearance fits in with the modern steel and glass towers that also surround the plaza. Its modernist design also belies the fact that it was built during a time of strict federal economy that required some corner cutting. For example, in order to save money in construction, the building was not properly insulated, so that it was very expensive to heat and cool. Also, the insulation that was provided for pipes and ducts was composed of asbestos and now requires costly and difficult removal. So, at more than forty-five years old, it is showing its age.

As with its two federal building predecessors, the new building's purpose was to consolidate all of the federal entities in Grand Rapids at one location. When the avocado green and white structure opened, it housed two federal district courtrooms and judges' chambers on the fourth floor, a magistrate's courtroom and chambers on the sixth floor, two bankruptcy courtrooms and chambers on the seventh floor, and offices for the U.S. Attorney and staff on the fifth floor. The building also housed the offices of the referees in bankruptcy, the U.S. Marshal's office, the U.S. probation service, the Internal Revenue Service, the Federal Bureau of Investigation, the Bureau of Alcohol, Tobacco, and Firearms, the U.S. Secret Service, the Social Security Administration, members of Congress, the General Services Administration, a major office of the U.S. Department of Defense, a branch of Michigan State University's cooperative extension service, and other agencies.

As was also the case for its predecessors, though, the requirements of its tenants soon outgrew the available space. The first big problem was the addition in 1979 of more district courtrooms, with their auxiliary offices, to accommodate two additional district judgeships. Because the new courtrooms, like the originals, are two stories high, they displaced not only most of the office space on the sixth floor but on the seventh floor as well. A courtroom and chambers for a new magistrate was also added.[42] Another problem was the continuing need for more space for other tenants as their personnel increased. For example, in the mid-1970s the U.S. Attorney had only four Assistant U.S. Attorneys, while in 1995 when the U.S. Attorney's office moved out of the federal building, the number of Assistant U.S. Attorneys had increased to more than ten, and by 2016 they numbered in the thirties. Similarly, most of the other tenants of the federal building that are not part of the District Court have relocated to other space in Grand Rapids, including the U.S. Bankruptcy Court, which moved out in 2005.

When it came time for the federal court and the other agencies to leave the 1909 federal building, Judge Fox, a navy veteran, insisted on holding a decommissioning ceremony, as would be done for a retiring naval vessel. The ceremony took place on December 29, 1972, in the 1909 building's main courtroom, with Judges Fox and Engel presiding and with several speakers. The first court business in the new building took place a few days later, on the morning of January 3, 1973, when Judge Engel heard a case involving the interstate transportation of a stolen motor home. That afternoon, Judge Fox presided in his courtroom in the new building for the first time to accept a guilty plea.

Gerald R. Ford was a U. S. Representative from January 1949 until December 1973, representing Michigan's fifth district, which included Grand Rapids and surrounding areas. In December 1973, several members of Michigan's congressional delegation advised Ford, who had become Vice President of the United States on December 6, succeeding Spiro Agnew who had resigned, that a bill would be introduced in the House of Representatives, at their behest, to name the new federal building in Grand Rapids the Gerald R. Ford Federal Office Building. On December 11, 1973, U.S. Representative Kenneth J. Gray (D. Ill.) introduced the bill, H.R. 11897. In December 1974, after Ford had become President, succeeding Richard Nixon, who also had resigned, the bill passed in the House of Representatives and in the Senate, and it was presented to President Ford for his signature. Instead, the President vetoed the bill on January 4, 1975, and he issued a memorandum of disapproval, published in the Congressional Record on January 5, advising Congress that he rejected the idea of a federal building named for a sitting President.[43] After President Ford left the White House at the end of his term, the House and the Senate passed new bills, sponsored by Senator Robert Griffin and by Representative Harold S. Sawyer, that designated the building officially as the Gerald R. Ford Building.[44] President Jimmy Carter, who had defeated Ford in the 1976 presidential election, signed the new bill into law on May 4, 1977. The building's present signage identifies it as the Gerald R. Ford Federal Building and U.S. Courthouse.

Judge Hillman and the House of Judah: U.S. v. Lewis

On November 21, 1985, a federal grand jury in the Western District of Michigan returned a two-count indictment against William A. Lewis and seven alleged accomplices. The indictment accused the defendants of conspiracy to hold five children in involuntary servitude in violation of federal law,[45] and that as a result of the conspiracy one of the children, twelve-year-old John Yarbrough, died. The indictment also alleged that those events occurred at a residential camp, commonly referred to as the House of Judah, located near Grand Junction in Allegan County, Michigan. The case was assigned to Judge Hillman, who tried it without a jury[46] over twenty trial days beginning on August 8, 1986. At the close of the evidence and the parties' arguments, Hillman found that "the alleged masters, as evidenced through their improper acts, [intended] to totally subjugate the will of the victims for the purpose, at least in part, of obtaining their labor" and so were guilty of violating the federal statutes enacted to enforce the Thirteenth Amendment's abolition of slavery."[47]

The House of Judah was a small religious sect founded by defendant William A. Lewis, a charismatic leader known to his flock as "My Lord Prophet David Israel." Lewis preached that members of the cult were the only chosen people and that all nonmembers were sinful and unworthy. These are not unusual beliefs in many religions, but the House of Judah distinguished itself by the ferocity and brutality with which the Prophet and his accomplices punished members, including children, who did not live up to his commandments.

The sect began in Chicago, grew to about one hundred members, and moved to a remote, rural area, about twenty miles from the city of Allegan. According to trial testimony, initially the camp environment was warm, cooperative, and friendly. By 1981, though, the Prophet perceived backsliding and rule breaking. In March 1982, the Prophet required that adult members sign a document in which they agreed to accept punishment for "sins against God and my Lord and also for my children." Punishment was specified in the document to include death, banishment, confiscation of material goods, imprisonment, beating, burning, hanging, or stoning of both the adult member and that member's children. The Prophet then began a punitive regimen including whipping followers at a whipping block with up to eighty "licks" using a thick axe handle called Big Mac. Witnesses at trial also described the Prophet ordering the burning of a seven-year-old on the face with a hot iron, the burning of another member by placing red-hot coals in his mouth and in each of his hands, and constant beatings of adults and children.

One frequent target of the Prophet's punishments was John Yarbrough. On June 29, 1983, John did not go to work, and the Prophet ordered him to

be beaten once more. Two or three of the other defendants took turns beating and otherwise torturing the twelve-year-old boy. He died five days later.
Witnesses testified that John's beatings and beatings of other men, women,
and children were carried out before the entire congregation, who cheered in
support of the beatings. Evidence also established that, like other cult leaders,
the Prophet isolated his followers from family, friends, and the general public,
while submitting them to a regimen of fear that kept them from leaving or
even objecting to their subjugation.

Horrific as the Prophet's treatment of his followers was, Judge Hillman
acknowledged that he was not judging the House of Judah's religious beliefs.
"First of all, this unusual case involves, to some extent at least, the religious
beliefs and practices of a small, black religious sect whose beliefs are highly
unorthodox and far from the mainstream of traditional, religious concepts in
this country. It should be obvious to all that those facts alone have no bearing
on the guilt or innocence of the accused. This country thrives on diversity.
First Amendment rights are sacred." Nor did the court have jurisdiction to
punish defendants for murder, manslaughter, or child abuse. It was perhaps
for these reasons that the court imposed a relatively lenient sentence. "Those
proceedings were properly left to state law enforcement officials. Although
beatings and other brutal conduct are relevant to this case, as will be demonstrated later, one must nevertheless be careful to keep in mind that the charges
in this federal prosecution are related exclusively to the Thirteenth Amendment; that is, slavery."

Reviewing the evidence, the judge had no problem finding the defendants
guilty as charged in the indictment. He conceded that, under the law, parents
could not be held liable for subjugating their own children and that he could
find no precedent holding third parties liable where the children were living
with their parents at the time. However, he refused to interpret the Thirteenth Amendment to require that the prosecution prove that the defendants
had subjugated the will of the children's parents as well. On December 19,
1986, the judge sentenced the Prophet and three other defendants to three
years' incarceration and three others to two years in jail. All also received long
probation periods.[48] Defendants appealed, but the Sixth Circuit affirmed
Judge Hillman's analysis and conclusion, and the U.S. Supreme Court refused
further review.[49]

William A. Lewis, the Prophet, served his sentence and upon release set
up a new House of Judah in Wetumpka, Alabama, with many of his former

congregation including John Yarbrough's mother. Lewis died in 2004 at the age of eighty-four.

Alternative Dispute Resolution in the Western District

Alternative dispute resolution (ADR) is a term used by lawyers, courts, and legal scholars to describe methods designed to encourage the consensual settlement and resolution of a civil case and avoid prolonged and expensive pretrial and trial events. Since the early 1980s, ADR has been an important part of civil litigation in U.S. District Courts. The Western District of Michigan has been a pioneer in, and a strong advocate of, ADR as a tool for assisting District Judges to deal with heavy civil caseloads, to decrease the time taken for civil cases to process through the court, and to reduce the costs of civil litigation imposed on the court and litigants alike. While there was some sentiment in the federal judiciary across the country in the 1980s that the focus of trial judges should be on trying cases rather than settling them, many judges, frequently experienced litigators, welcomed ADR because it sped up the docket and brought clients down to earth. "Litigants hear about somebody who fell off a bike and got $300,000, but they don't know anything about the circumstances," observed Judge Hillman. "They just drift on toward their trial. ADR brings some reality to these cases; it brings them to a workable, manageable level. It's easier on the litigants. It's not a terrible all or nothing decision."

In both federal and state courts, the emphasis on settlement through ADR is far different from what was the norm just a few decades ago. Settlements and other pretrial matters, such as discovery, were in the hands of the parties. Unless a party filed a motion to compel discovery or a motion to dismiss or for summary judgment, the court might not become involved in the case, indeed might not know anything about the case, until days before the date scheduled for trial. Then, on the trial date, the judge would meet with the parties' attorneys and unrepresented parties in chambers with the represented parties waiting in the courtroom. The judge would try, sometimes perfunctorily, to effectuate a settlement that would preclude the need to proceed with the trial. Many cases did settle on the day of trial, but only after the parties had incurred large attorney fees as well as the costs of the discovery process, obtaining and paying expert witnesses, and other trial preparation.

The Development of ADR in the Western District—An Overview

Historically, managing civil cases ab initio in federal District Courts in order to resolve them early in the process was not a high priority for federal judges. Except in wartime or during Prohibition, their court dockets were not overwhelming, and the judges preferred to leave civil case management to the attorneys. In the late 1960s and early 1970s, there was an increasing recognition by some in the judiciary of the need for enhancing docket control and actively encouraging settlement conferences. Judge Noel P. Fox was one such herald of these developments in the Western District.[50] Beginning in the mid-1970s, a wave of new civil and criminal cases, largely cases based on new federal statutes, greatly increased federal court dockets.[51] Because Congress mandated that District Courts give criminal cases priority, a backlog of unresolved civil cases developed. Despite Congress adding new judgeships, the time for a civil case to proceed from filing to trial increased in most District Courts, in some courts to three years or more. In the Western District of Michigan, for example, between 1975 and 1978 the median time for a civil case to proceed from filing to trial was more than four years.[52]

In March 1990, Judge Enslen, who was one of the Western District's earliest advocates of ADR after he joined the court in December 1979, appeared by invitation before the U.S. Senate's Judiciary Committee to discuss prospective methods intended to reduce delays in civil cases. In his statement, he remembered the state of the court's docket a decade earlier: "It was a joke in my district just before I came on the bench, and that was that if you never wanted to see a case again, it should be filed in the Federal District Court for the Western District of Michigan. There were 2,500 cases, two judges, both older people, and we never saw the light of day when we were either removing a case for defense reasons or filing a case for the plaintiff, and that was a sad situation."[53] Although in 1979 Congress granted two new district judgeships to the Western District, and Judge Fox's election of senior status resulted in Enslen's appointment, reducing the caseload for each judge, the court's civil backlog continued to increase, as it did in District Courts across the country.

Observing the state of civil litigation from his courthouse in Kalamazoo a few months after he took the bench, it was clear to Judge Enslen that leaving the management of civil cases before trial to the parties and their attorneys would not bring the dockets to a manageable level. After talking to other judges and attorneys and looking into experiments being conducted across the country, he decided that ADR and other forms of active case management, which held an increasing appeal in a great many federal District Courts, would be a reasonable solution for his court. He began investigating how to introduce ADR to the court as well as what ADR programs might work best. He attended conferences and discussed these issues with other judges and attorneys involved in creating and developing this new tool. In the time he could spare from performing his duties as a District Judge, Judge Enslen undertook postgraduate study of the judicial process at the University of Virginia School of Law. In May 1986, he became one of the first judges in the nation to earn a master of laws degree specializing in the judicial process. His thesis was titled "ADR: Another Acronym, or a Valuable Alternative to the High Cost of Litigation and Crowded Court Dockets?" By the time he addressed the Senate Judiciary Committee in 1990, Judge Enslen was a nationally recognized speaker and a prolific writer on innovative ADR techniques.[54]

In January 1983, years before he spoke before Congress or received his master of laws degree, Judge Enslen's enthusiasm, knowledge, and study convinced the other judges of the Western District to adopt a series of local rules authorizing and setting the procedures for three ADR programs. Those early programs were summary jury trials, mediation (now known as case evaluation), and mini-hearings, all of which will be discussed shortly. Before their adoption, the court held a one-day meeting with about three hundred members of the federal bar to acquaint them with the ADR methodology and to make sure that they understood and were comfortable with the new rules. In January 1985, the court joined nine other districts in a federal pilot arbitration program.

By March 1990, when Judge Enslen addressed the Senate Judiciary Committee, the Western District had added rules for two more ADR programs, a classic voluntary mediation program, known as voluntary facilitative mediation, and early neutral evaluation. The judge was able to tell the senators that, largely as a result of the adoption of this comprehensive set of ADR programs, between 1984 and 1989 the median time required in the Western District to move a civil case from the filing of the defendant's answer to the complaint until the beginning of trial had decreased by about one third, from eighteen months to twelve months, despite an influx of complex environmental and criminal cases that took time and resources away from other civil cases.[55]

Settlement Conferences

Traditionally, the most common method of ADR in the Western District has been settlement conferences conducted by a District Judge or a Magistrate Judge, although in the Western District normally not by the judge who will preside at trial. Settlement conferences are held in most civil cases, even cases in which some other type of ADR has been utilized unsuccessfully.[56] These conferences occur in most cases shortly before trial, although the parties may voluntarily ask the court for an earlier settlement conference to preclude unnecessary pretrial costs. Thus, statistically, in the Western District more cases are referred to settlement conferences than to any other form of ADR. For example, between 2008 and 2016, of the 4,600 civil cases referred to some form of ADR, 2,600 of those cases were referred to settlement conferences (55 percent).

Many people do not think of settlement conferences occurring just before trial to be anything new or part of a court's *alternative* dispute resolution program. Such conferences have been a standard part of court procedure for a century or more, and in the Western District most cases eligible for ADR have been assigned voluntarily to another ADR program earlier in the pretrial process. However, no matter their characterization, settlement conferences result in the resolution of many cases, and many of the keys and spirit of settlement conferences have been adapted to newer ADR techniques. For example, a party with binding settlement authority is required to be present in the courthouse at the time of the conference, and being available by telephone is not sufficient, since putting someone off by phone is too easy. In addition, facing the time and effort of traveling to the courthouse, for example to Marquette in February, makes parties devote time and attention to the conference, to focus on that case. When a corporation is a party, a corporate officer with binding authority is required to be present. Nor has it been sufficient to say that the party's attorney has "binding" authority, since it is the party and not the attorney who has to buy into any agreement forged during the heat of negotiation. As Magistrate Judge Hugh W. Brenneman, Jr., has explained, it is unfair to place an attorney in a position of having to look over his or her shoulder when returning to advise a client that the settlement reached was not as favorable as the party had anticipated.[57]

Summary Jury Trials

This was the first ADR program that Judge Enslen investigated and brought to the Western District,[58] and it was likely the spur to the whole ADR process in the Western District. This founding program was invented in 1980 by U.S. District Judge Thomas Demetrious Lambros of the Northern District of Ohio. He created the first rules for such trials specifically in order to resolve two long-pending personal injury cases in which the parties adamantly refused to discuss settlement. Judge Lambros required the parties to conduct a half-day, nonbinding jury trial before a six-person jury who were not told that they were involved in a nonbinding exercise.[59] Because of the success of this procedure, Judge Lambros conducted dozens of summary jury trials. Intrigued by the results obtained using this procedure, Judge Enslen invited Judge Lambros to Kalamazoo to help him conduct a summary jury trial of a Western District case in his courtroom.[60] Then Judge Enslen conducted a summary trial with each of the Western District's other District Judges to introduce them to the concept. All of those cases settled, so impressing the other judges that when the court first added an ADR local rule, summary jury trial was one of the three programs included.

The Western District's local rule on summary jury trials is succinct: they are "an abbreviated proceeding during which the parties' attorneys summarize their case before a six-person jury. Unless the parties stipulate otherwise, the verdict is advisory only."[61] Although Judge Lambros limited his procedure to tort cases, Judge Enslen saw it as a flexible process that could be molded by the court and by the parties for use in just about any type of civil case that might be properly filed in a federal District Court.

Between the inception of the rule and 1984, Judge Enslen took one step further to save the time of the District Judge. He assigned some thirty summary jury trials, the most in the United States at that time, to Magistrate Judge Hugh W. Brenneman, Jr., thus removing the District Judge from the process altogether. Of those thirty cases, twenty-seven settled. In 1984, Enslen and Brenneman made a video about the procedure for the Federal Judicial Center for distribution to other courts. In an interview in October 1984, after he had tried about twenty summary jury trials himself, Judge Enslen explained how he and recently appointed Magistrate Judge Doyle Rowland ran summary jury trials in Kalamazoo.[62] It was the same procedure used by Brenneman in Grand Rapids.[63]

First, the court required that the parties, as well as their attorneys, be present. In a two-party case, ten prospective jurors were summoned from a list that is separate from the regular jury list. Judge Enslen did not tell them that their verdict was not binding, but only that the attorneys had agreed to present their proofs in a compact, summary fashion that would let the case be finished in one day, after which the jurors were allowed to leave. Each side received two peremptory challenges, leaving a panel of six jurors.

The jury seated, the judge allowed the lawyers an hour or two to present their claims or defenses in any way they wanted. They could allow their clients and experts to testify briefly live, or they could read to the jury from depositions and interrogatory answers, or the attorneys could tell the jurors their client's "story" themselves so long as there was evidentiary or discovery support for what they said. Usually the rules of evidence were ignored, and the attorneys were told not to raise objections. Once the presentation was over, the judge would instruct the jury quickly, taking just ten or fifteen minutes, and then he would give the jurors a verdict form and tell them that he wanted them to agree on a verdict unanimously. Depending on the facts and issues in the case, he might bifurcate the trial between liability and damages. When the jurors reached a unanimous verdict by secret ballot, they returned to the courtroom. The judge would then explain to the jurors that the verdict was not binding, but that nevertheless they had been very helpful in the adjudicatory process. Enslen felt that if the jurors believed the verdict was really in their hands, they would give it the attention it deserved. He would ask the jurors to stay, if they wished, to explain to the lawyers and parties how and why they had reached their verdict and to answer any other questions. After the jurors left, the judge would hold a settlement conference with all of the parties and attorneys who now had a better idea of what jurors might think of both sides of the case.

During the first seven years of ADR in the Western District, the court conducted sixty to seventy summary jury trials, of which all but two cases settled before the real trial. By giving litigants "their day in court," where they could tell their story to a jury, this cathartic procedure often eliminated emotional barriers to settlement. However, in the twenty-first century, the program has fallen out of use because it proved to be labor intensive and too costly, particularly for the court, compared to the other forms of ADR. In 2017, summary jury trials remain an ADR option, but during the decade from 2008 to 2017, it was chosen in just one case, in 2009.

Voluntary Facilitative Mediation

This is a traditional form of mediation in which a mediator, an experienced attorney mutually selected by the parties from a list of experienced attorneys maintained by the clerk's office, acts as a counselor and go-between to resolve the case.[64] The mediator may discuss settlement with all of the parties at once or individually, shuttling back and forth. Because the parties pay the mediators their hourly rate, the mediators can afford to spend the time necessary to reach a resolution or to conclude that mediation will not resolve the case. The court provides formal training for the attorneys to be added to the list and continues to meet with all on the list regularly.

In an early and dramatic use of this type of mediation, Judge Enslen combined pretrial litigation with mediation to settle the remaining issues in a long-running and complex Indian fishing rights case, which the court had transferred to him in 1983 at the request of Judge Fox. Facing seemingly intractable and bitter disagreements among the parties in the decade-old case, in September 1984 Judge Enslen appointed a "special master" to combine the judicial duties of a magistrate, to prepare the case for trial, with the negotiating and advising tasks of a mediator to reach a settlement. Together, Judge Enslen and the special master, Francis E. McGovern, were able to achieve an agreement among the parties on a consent decree in May 1985.

Early Mediation, Now Known as Case Evaluation

As used in the District Court's first ADR court rule, the term mediation referred to one of the three original discretionary ADR tools available to the judges of the Western District. That tool was adopted from a procedure in a Michigan state court rule, which was also named mediation.[65] As Judge Enslen commented about this program in 1984, "It's quite different from conventional mediation."[66] In conventional mediation, such as voluntary facilitative mediation, a single mediator works with opposing parties, possibly over hours, days, or weeks, to achieve a settlement. But here, three knowledgeable attorneys act more like evaluators. They review written arguments; they hold a short, informal meeting of attorneys and unrepresented parties, usually lasting less than an hour; and then they issue a nonbinding evaluation, in dollars, of the amount they think a jury might award.[67] The Michigan Supreme Court subsequently changed the name from mediation to case evaluation, and the Western District did the same both to reflect the true nature of the proceeding and to avoid confusion with the Western District's newer ADR tool, voluntary facilitative mediation. Under either title, the rule provides that the parties must accept or reject the evaluation within a fixed number of days and without knowing if the opposing party is accepting or rejecting. If both parties accept, the court enters a judgment in the case. If any party rejects, the case continues toward trial. In Michigan state courts, case evaluation is scheduled for early in the pretrial process, but in the Western District, this proceeding is conducted shortly before trial, and after discovery has been completed so that all of the facts claimed by the parties are known and can be weighed.[68]

In Michigan's state courts, a major component driving settlements in cases using case evaluation is the possibility that a party rejecting an evaluation must pay an opponent's actual costs, including "a reasonable attorney fee . . . for services necessitated by the rejection of the case evaluation."[69] That monetary liability arises if the action proceeds to a verdict and the rejecting party does not "improve" its case evaluation position by more than ten percent.[70] In 1988, the U.S. Court of Appeals for the Sixth Circuit, in a case appealed from the Western District, held that no federal court can shift attorney fees to a party under this ADR process because such an award of fees was not authorized by Congress and so would violate the common-law "American" rule that each party pay its own attorney fees.[71] The Western District still includes the attorney fee provision in its local rules for cases where Michigan law provides the rule of decision or where the parties have consented to the possibility of sanctions.[72]

Mini-Hearings

Mini-hearings were another abbreviated proceeding adopted in 1983, in which attorneys for corporate parties present their positions to the parties' senior officials, that is, persons outranking those individuals whose decisions or behavior led to the litigation in question, in an attempt to settle the dispute, dispassionately as a business matter, essentially a "wise man" procedure. The rules for mini-hearings allowed the parties to fashion the procedure of the hearing as they felt appropriate.[73] The mini-hearing program was never popular, and it disappeared from the rules before 1990, although it was used on occasion thereafter.

Court-Annexed Arbitration

In January 1985, the court joined nine other districts in a federal pilot program and added court-annexed arbitration to its ADR repertoire.[74] Court-annexed arbitration was an ADR project supported by the highest administrative levels of the federal courts and by Congress. The name was meant to distinguish it from the usual private, consensual, and binding form of arbitration. It began as a pilot program in the U.S. District Court for the Eastern District of Pennsylvania in Philadelphia. In 1978, the Judicial Conference of the United States established a test arbitration program in three District Courts, the Eastern District of Pennsylvania, the District of Massachusetts, and the Northern District of California. Results in two of those districts seemed favorable, and Congress authorized those two courts and eight others, including the Western District of Michigan because of its prominence in ADR, to became part of a group of ten experimental arbitration courts.[75] Once more, the overall results were good, and in November 1988, Congress gave formal statutory authorization to those courts and ten additional District Courts to offer arbitration. Eventually that authority was granted to all District Courts.

The statute left the practice rules for arbitration to each court. Under the Western District's local rule, cases valued at less than $100,000 were automatically referred to the experimental program and given 120 days for discovery. Briefs and exhibits were prepared for an arbitrator chosen by the parties from a court-approved list of attorneys with at least five years' trial experience. The arbitrator held a short hearing and could take testimony on disputed issues. The task of the arbitrator was to give a nonbinding ruling on the merits of the litigation, preferably on the spot. However, because the proceedings were not binding and the parties retained their right to a trial, they were urged to adopt the Golden Rule of ADR: "Let opposing parties present their case freely so that, having been heard completely, they will be persuaded by the outcome."

The parties were free to speak their minds, and the proceedings, like mediation, were sealed to avoid predisposing the presiding judge by the outcome. Magistrate Brenneman, the court's early ADR coordinator, reported monthly to monitors of the experimental program at the Federal Judicial Center. At the end of the first year, 61 percent of the cases submitted to the new arbitration had been disposed of without trial, and by the end of 1989, the Western District had placed 1,376 cases in arbitration.[76] However, despite all of the early enthusiasm for court-annexed arbitration, the bar of the Western District lost interest in this program, partly because the court already had case evaluation, which was cheaper and easier to conduct. From 2008 to 2011, parties opted for court-annexed arbitration only once. In 2012, the court struck the procedure from the local rules.

Early Neutral Evaluation

This is a flexible, nonbinding ADR process in which an experienced neutral attorney meets with the parties early in the case primarily to evaluate its strengths and weaknesses and to estimate the value it may have.[77] The parties select the evaluator unless they cannot agree, in which case the court's ADR administrator selects an evaluator. In theory, early neutral evaluation offers a way to resolve a case before the parties have the expenses of pretrial litigation. The procedure might require more than one session, at each of which ADR rules mandate the presence of individual parties, representatives of corporate or government parties, and representatives of any insurance companies, all with ultimate settlement authority, plus the attorneys expected to be primarily responsible for handling the trial. This program is still available to litigants in the court's local rules, but it was chosen just fourteen times between 2008 and 2017.

ADR Other than Settlement Conferences, 2008–2017

During the decade from 2008 to 2017, the most popular ADR program in the Western District, other than settlement conferences, has consistently been mediation. During that decade, parties accepted voluntary facilitative mediation in 1,569 cases (about 78 percent of the two thousand cases referred in that decade to ADR programs other than settlement conferences). The second most popular program over that period has been case evaluation, used in 415 cases (about 21 percent of referred cases), while all of the other ADR tools in the local rules were used in only sixteen cases, about 1 percent.

U.S. District Judge Robert Holmes Bell

Just one District Judge joined the District Court for the Western District during the 1980s, Ingham County Circuit Judge Robert Holmes Bell. Judge Bell was born on April 19, 1944, in Lansing, Michigan, the son of Preston C. and Eileen (Holmes) Bell. He grew up in nearby Williamston and graduated from Okemos High School in 1962. Losing his father to war-related illness at

Judge Robert Holmes Bell

the age of eight, Bell tried to become the "man in the family" and voluntarily assumed many of the chores around the home. This led to traits of orderliness and diligent work. At Wheaton College, in Wheaton, Illinois, he was a track star and graduated in 1966 with a bachelor of arts degree. That fall he entered Wayne State University Law School in Detroit. In 1968, while a law student, he married Helen Mortensen; they have three children, Robert Holmes Bell, Jr., Ruth (Bell) Olsson, and Jonathan Bell. The absence of a father growing up made Bell a dedicated family man at home and often a counselor to young people who appeared before him in his courtroom.

Judge Bell received his juris doctor degree from Wayne State in 1969 and, shortly after, he began working as an Assistant Prosecutor for Ingham County. In 1972, only twenty-eight years old, he ran against a sitting judge, something seldom done successfully, and he was elected judge of Michigan's Fifty-Fifth Judicial District Court in Ingham County by a nearly two-to-one margin for a term beginning on January 1, 1973. In 1978, he was elected a judge of Ingham County Circuit Court where he served from January 1, 1979, until he became a U.S. District Judge. Like Judge Kent, Judge Bell was known for running a no-nonsense courtroom where propriety was important, rules were to be followed, and attorneys were to be prepared.

President Ronald Reagan nominated Judge Bell on March 11, 1987, to the

Western District seat, which became vacant when Judge Miles assumed senior status. Judge Bell was recommended to the President by the U.S. Justice Department and by a panel of Republican congressmen from western Michigan, led by Paul Henry of Grand Rapids. East Lansing's Democratic congressman Robert Carr praised Bell as "eminently qualified for the federal bench, . . . an exceptional judge."[78] Bell has described himself as a conservative, sympathetic to the social views of President Ronald Reagan. On June 30, 1987, three months after his nomination but before he was confirmed, he unexpectedly found himself in the news dealing with abortion. Another state circuit judge disqualified himself from a case challenging the effective date of a recent Michigan law banning payment for late-term abortions for women eligible for Medicaid.[79] On July 1, Judge Bell ruled that under state law the ban was required to take immediate effect.[80] By coincidence, on that same day, the Senate confirmed his appointment, and he received his commission the following day.

Judge Bell served as the Western District's Chief Judge from 2001 until 2008, and Supreme Court Chief Justice John Roberts appointed him chair of the criminal law committee of the U.S. Judicial Conference. In 2002, the State Bar of Michigan named him one of the bar's Champions of Justice, praising him as "a just, compassionate, and giving individual." The State Bar of Michigan again honored Judge Bell with the Frank J. Kelley Distinguished Award for his forty-seven years of exemplary service. Judge Bell taught at Thomas M. Cooley Law School, lectured for the Federal Judicial Center, and served on several non-profit boards during his long career. In January 2017, Judge Bell decided to elect inactive status and to close his chambers, effective February 1, 2017.

The 1988 Lansing Court Facility

Lansing acquired a new federal building and post office during the Great Depression, which, like the federal building in Kalamazoo, did not have a court facility and, decades later, was altered to provide one. In May 1926, during the period of national prosperity and economic growth that followed the end of World War I and preceded the Great Depression, Congress used a revenue surplus to impress constituents and improve the national infrastructure by passing a law directing the secretary of the treasury to embark upon a program to build new "accommodations" for the federal government in the

The Lansing Charles E. Chamberlain Federal Building and U.S. Post Office.

District of Columbia as well as an enormous number of "courthouses, post offices, immigration stations, customhouses, marine hospitals, quarantine stations, and other public buildings of the classes under the control of the Treasury Department in the States, Territories, and possessions of the United States."[81] The 1926 Act authorized, but did not appropriate, a total of $150 million for land acquisition and construction but limited annual spending from that authorization to $25 million. Five years later, in March 1931, in the depths of the Depression, Lansing was among the cities selected for a new post office. Congress, in its annual deficiency appropriation, provided funds for more than three hundred building projects under the 1926 Act, including "Lansing, Michigan, post office, and so forth: For acquisition of site and construction of a building, under an estimated total cost of $850,000."[82]

Although the people of Lansing were, on the whole, happy to receive this gift, there were some critics who pointed out that the city already had a "commodious and beautiful" federal building and post office, a Romanesque jewel on Capitol Avenue, across the street, to the east, from the capitol.[83] In actuality, that post office, no matter how beautiful, was no longer large enough for its purposes, and Lansing did need a new federal building. As is often the case in the construction of large projects, progress on Lansing's new post office was slow. The usual disputes over site selection dragged on until the treasury chose a large lot at 315 W. Allegan Street, directly south of the capitol. The Treasury Department could not begin construction until it entered into a contract in November 1932 with H. G. Christman–Lansing Co., a subsidiary of a large building firm in South Bend, Indiana. The contract provided that Christman would complete the work within 480 calendar days (sixteen months).[84] Six months later, in May 1933, former U.S. Representative Grant M. Hudson laid the building's cornerstone,[85] and the building was completed in 1936.

Although most state capitals do have a federal courthouse, the lack of a court facility in the 1933 Lansing federal building was not surprising. Lansing is only about seventy miles from Grand Rapids and ninety miles from Detroit, less than a two-hour train trip or drive either way, even before the three cities were joined by interstate highway I-96. For that reason or some other, Congress had not yet added Lansing to the list of locations where the judges of the Western District could hold court. With the recent death of Judge Clarence Sessions, the District Court was back to just one authorized judgeship, held by Judge Fred Raymond, and its one authorized venue in the Southern Division, Grand Rapids, seemed to be adequate to handle any cases that might arise in the Lansing area.

As we have seen, in 1954, as part of a compromise among members of Congress from Michigan, Congress voted to authorize the Western District court to sit in Kalamazoo as well as in Mason, which, although it is small and in a largely rural and agricultural area, was nevertheless the county seat of Ingham County, closer to the center of the county, and more convenient than Lansing to people living in the south-central part of the district.[86] Lansing, although the center of the state government, was then a small city in the corner of the county and had a population of just 90,000, less than half of the county's population. Mason also had a large county courthouse that might be used by the federal court. However, it appears that the courts of the Western District never sat in Mason.

During the late 1950s, local and federal leaders in Lansing began campaigning to switch the Mason authorization to Lansing. Leading this effort was Republican Congressman Charles Ernest Chamberlain, a veteran of World War II who represented Michigan's sixth congressional district from 1957 until 1974. A lawyer and former Ingham County Prosecutor, Chamberlain was a strong proponent for a federal court presence in Lansing. Chamberlain first submitted a bill to accomplish the switch in 1957, and in 1961 his perseverance paid off in part when Congress removed Mason from the list and added Lansing.[87] The next step was a federal court facility, but in that effort Chamberlain was not successful, although he continued his efforts during his nine terms in Congress. It was not until after he left Congress that his successor, Democrat Bob Carr, and a bipartisan coalition were able to get the General Services Administration to agree to spend $2 million to renovate a large space on the western end of the post office, part of the mail-sorting department, into a federal court facility. Their campaign included a 1983 resolution by the District Court calling for a federal courthouse in Lansing and an endorsement of the resolution in January 1984 by the Western District's chapter of the Federal Bar Association led by the chapter's president-elect, John L. Coté.

On June 23, 1986, the Federal and Ingham County Bar Associations hosted a ceremony to commemorate the beginning of construction on the new courtroom; Chief Judge Douglas Hillman presided. Because there was no hole to dig, the dignitaries smashed a hole in a wall instead. In November 1987, Congress recognized former Congressman Chamberlain by officially designating the entire Lansing federal building as the Charles E. Chamberlain Federal Building and U.S. Post Office.[88] The Lansing court facility was completed and ready to go into operation on April 18, 1988, when the facility and a metal plaque commemorating the building's new name were dedicated in a ceremony presided over by Judge Albert Engel, the former U.S. District Judge who was then on the bench of the Sixth Circuit.[89] A few days before the dedication, on April 14, the *Lansing State Journal* described the facility's decor as "bold, classy, massive—and strictly reflective of the late 1980s."[90] The facility included a large courtroom with a state-of-the-art sound system, judicial chambers, a smaller courtroom for other matters including the Bankruptcy Court and Magistrate Judges, a jury assembly room, a law library, offices for the rest of the court staff, and two jail cells. New signage for the building was celebrated on December 17, 2001, at a ceremony and reception hosted by the Federal Bar Association.

When Judge Robert Holmes Bell was appointed to the U.S. District Court for the Western District of Michigan in March 1987, many people expected that he would become the resident judge in the Lansing court facility when it was completed.[91] Initially, Judge Bell worked in a spare chambers and courtroom in the Grand Rapids Gerald R. Ford Federal Building and Courthouse. He commuted about an hour each way from Okemos, where he had lived since law school. When the Lansing court facility was finally completed, Judge Bell moved his chambers there. He held court there until the fall of 1990 when events caused him to move back to Grand Rapids. With Judge Bell sitting in Lansing and Judge Enslen sitting in Kalamazoo, Judges Gibson and Hillman were the only district judges not on senior status in Grand Rapids. They both announced at nearly the same time in 1990 that they planned to assume senior status soon, which would have left Grand Rapids without a full-time nonsenior district judge. In order to avoid that situation, Judge Bell returned his chambers in the Ford courthouse and moved to the Grand Rapids area.

The Lansing facility did not have a resident district judge or staff again until 1992 when President George W. Bush appointed David W. McKeague, a Lansing attorney, to the District Court for the Western District. Judge Mc‑Keague opened chambers in the Chamberlain Building and held court there from 1992 to 2005 when President George H. W. Bush appointed him to the Sixth Circuit. Since 2005, the Lansing court facility has had no resident District Judge, and in 2007 the court entered an administrative order temporarily suspending the Lansing jury wheel.[92] Consequently, since that administrative order, the District Court in Lansing has had no source of jurors, and no jury trials, civil or criminal, have been held there. The court's 2013 Juror Selection Plan indicates that the suspension is likely to remain in effect until there is a permanent judge in residence in Lansing.[93]

Despite the absence of a resident District Judge, the Chamberlain Federal Building does have a human federal court presence. Senior Circuit Judge McKeague maintains an office on the second floor of the building, as does Senior Circuit Judge Richard F. Suhrheinrich. The U.S. Bankruptcy Court does use the smaller courtroom for hearings each month, and occasionally District Court judges, Magistrate Judges, and federal administrative law judges use one of the courtrooms for trials and hearings. In addition, the Chamberlain Federal Building continues to house an office of the District Court clerk staffed with several deputy clerks.

The Western District's Indian Casino Cases

There are 326 Indian reservations in the United States. The largest is the Navajo Nation Reservation in Arizona and New Mexico, which covers 27,425 square miles, but many reservations are a great deal smaller, including those in Michigan. Historically, they all had a problem with poverty caused by the lack of jobs. However, in 1976, the U.S. Supreme Court ruled that states had no power to regulate Indian activity on Indian land.[94] That ruling opened the way for a possible solution to Indian poverty: gambling casinos on Indian land, which would be free of state laws and rules governing gambling. Beginning with a bingo hall operated by the Seminole Tribe of Florida, Indian casinos sprang up across the nation, despite continuing efforts by state and federal governments to close them down or at least to impose tough state oversight. Because eleven of the twelve recognized Michigan tribes are located in counties that are allocated to the federal western judicial district, that district's court became the arena for many cases involving Indian gambling and Indian casinos.

U.S. v. Dakota

In September 1984, the United States and the state of Michigan filed a civil suit in the Northern Division of the Western District of Michigan against two individuals, Frederick and Sybil Dakota, and the Keweenaw Bay Indian Community. The federal and state governments sought an injunction barring the individuals from operating a commercial gambling casino on tribal land and enjoining the tribe from issuing licenses allowing commercial gambling on its reservation. Chief District Judge Wendell Miles dismissed the claims of the state government because the doctrine of Indian sovereignty protects Indian tribes from assertion of state authority, although the state and two other Indian communities were allowed to appear in the case as amici curiae.

Defendant Keweenaw Bay Indian Community (KBIC) exercised control over the L'Anse Reservation, which includes two noncontiguous sections on both sides of Lake Superior's Keweenaw Bay in the western Upper Peninsula. Defendants Frederick and Sybil Dakota were members of KBIC who, in 1984, received a license from KBIC's Tribal Council to operate gambling for profit on approximately 1.16 acres of land on the L'Anse Reservation. On July 4, 1984, the Dakotas opened a resort and casino named the Pines where guests, Indian or not, could play blackjack, craps, poker, and pull tabs.

The parties filed cross motions for summary judgment and submitted three volumes of exhibits totaling 1,378 pages. In March 1985, Judge Miles held a hearing on the motions at L'Anse, and on June 28 of that year he entered the requested injunction and a declaratory judgment holding that commercial gambling did violate federal organized crime laws as well as the federal

Assimilative Crimes Act, which transforms violations of state criminal laws committed on federal land into a federal crime.[95] On July 18, 1986, a panel of the Sixth Circuit affirmed Judge Miles's decision.[96]

U.S. v. Bay Mills Indian Community

In November 1985, while the *Dakota* appeal was pending, the United States filed another suit in the District Court's Northern Division at Marquette against the Keweenaw Bay tribe and four other Indian communities, all located in northern Michigan: the Bay Mills Indian Community, the Sault Ste. Marie Tribe of Chippewa Indians, the Grand Traverse Band of Ottawa and Chippewa Indians, and the Hannahville Indian Community. As in the earlier case, the government sought an injunction barring the defendants from operating gambling casinos on tribal land based on the Assimilative Crimes Act and the federal Organized Crime Act. Both sides moved for summary judgment and filed numerous, extensive briefs. On December 2, 1987, Judge Hillman, who had succeeded Judge Miles as the court's Chief Judge, heard all of the parties' motions for summary judgment and took them under advisement. On August 11, 1988, Judge Hillman rendered his decision dismissing the case based on a well-established doctrine, which none of the parties had raised in that case or in the *Dakota* case, that a court should not enter an injunction barring a defendant from committing a crime.[97] Instead, prosecution of the defendants under the criminal law provided the government with an adequate remedy at law, absent showing that tribes' operations constituted a public nuisance.

Chief Judge Hillman explained: "The rule is based on two concerns: First, criminal prosecution generally provides an adequate remedy at law so that equitable relief [i.e., an injunction] is unnecessary, and, second, injunctive relief may deny a defendant the procedural rights otherwise available in a criminal prosecution." As for the injunction in *Dakota* affirmed by the Sixth Circuit, he pointed out that this issue had never been raised or addressed in that case in either the district or appeals court. The judge also noted, as reasons for his decision, that the injunction requested by the government would impose a substantial financial and social burden on the defendant tribes and that the denial of an injunction would not unduly harm the federal government, whose other departments and agencies seemed to support and encourage Indian gaming.

State of Michigan v. Bay Mills Indian Community

Even after the decision by Judge Hillman, disputes among the federal government, state governments, and Indian tribes over the control of commercial gambling casinos on reservations continued to fester. Then, in November 1988, Congress passed the Indian Gaming Regulatory Act (IGRA)[98] to establish a structure for federal regulation of gaming on "Indian land" while also protecting Indian sovereignty and allowing state governments to have some oversight. One of the Act's provisions requires tribes operating "class 3" gambling on land under tribal jurisdiction to ask the relevant state to negotiate in good faith a "Tribal-State compact" to establish the relationship between the parties in various areas, including law enforcement.

The Bay Mills Indian Community entered into a compact with the state of Michigan that authorized the tribe to conduct class III gaming activities (i.e., to operate a casino) on Indian lands located within the state's borders, but prohibited it from doing so outside those borders. Bay Mills opened a casino on its reservation near Sault Ste. Marie in the Upper Peninsula. In 2010, the tribe opened a second casino on land that it had purchased through a congressionally established land trust. The second casino is in the village of Vanderbilt, Michigan, in the Lower Peninsula, 125 miles from the Bay Mills Reservation and, crucially, on Interstate Highway 75, the state's most-traveled north-south tourist corridor. Legislation transferring the Vanderbilt land to the tribe stated that it should be treated as an Indian land. Bay Mills interpreted this to mean "Indian land" as used in the IGRA, which would allow Bay Mills to operate a casino there based on the community's existing compact with the state.

Another tribe, the Little Traverse Bay Bands of Odawa Indians, which owned a much larger casino near its headquarters in Petoskey, Michigan, thirty miles northwest of Vanderbilt, sued the Bay Mills tribe in the District Court for the Western District, seeking an injunction to close the Vanderbilt casino on the basis that it was illegal and had hurt the Petoskey casino's business. The state of Michigan filed a similar suit, also arguing that the Vanderbilt casino was illegal and that it breached the Tribe-State compact between the state and the Bay Mills tribe. Other tribes with casinos, calling themselves a Coalition of Tribes Opposed to Off-Reservation Gaming, also supported the Odawa suit.

The Bay Mills case was assigned to Chief District Judge Paul Maloney who consolidated the two suits. After a hearing on the Odawa tribe's motion for a preliminary injunction, on March 29, 2011, the judge granted the motion and entered a preliminary injunction directing the closure of the Vanderbilt casino pending a final decision in the case. Bay Mills filed an interlocutory appeal to the Sixth Circuit, seeking to overturn the injunction on the grounds that the District Court had no jurisdiction and that Bay Mills' Vanderbilt property was Indian land under the IGRA.

The Sixth Circuit heard argument on the interlocutory appeal on May 12, 2012, and on August 15 reversed Judge Maloney's decision.[99] The court of appeals held that, although both plaintiffs had standing to sue, the District Court lacked jurisdiction because of a catch-22 in the IGRA. The statute gave U.S. District Courts jurisdiction over disputes involving casinos on Indian land, defined as "all lands within the limits of any Indian reservation; and . . . any lands title to which is either held in trust by the United States for the benefit of any Indian tribe or individual or held by any Indian tribe or individual subject to restriction by the United States against alienation and over which an Indian tribe exercises governmental power."[100] If, as plaintiffs argued, the Vanderbilt casino was not on Indian land, then there was no federal issue involved, and the District Court had no jurisdiction to decide anything about it. On the other hand, if, as the defendant asserted, the Vanderbilt casino was indeed on Indian land, then it was legal. Either way, the District Court should have dismissed the consolidated cases.

The appellate court added that the state's common-law claims for an injunction failed because of the same dilemma but for a different reason. In the compact, the tribe had abrogated its sovereign immunity over gaming disputes occurring on Indian land, but not its general sovereign immunity from suits by the state. So, if the Vanderbilt casino was on Indian land, it was legal, and, if it was not, sovereign immunity barred plaintiffs' suits against Bay Mills. The state sought review by the U.S. Supreme Court of the Sixth Circuit's reversal of Judge Maloney's ruling. The Supreme Court granted certiorari and heard arguments on the consolidated cases on December 2, 2013. On May 27, 2014, the Supreme Court affirmed the Sixth Circuit's decision on a vote of five justices to four.[101]

Writing for the majority, Justice Kagan noted Michigan's assertion that: "Whatever words Congress may have used in IGRA, it could not have intended that senseless outcome." Senseless it might be, "But this Court does not revise legislation, as Michigan proposes, just because the text as written creates an apparent anomaly as to some subject it does not address. Truth be told, such anomalies often arise from statutes, if for no other reason than that Congress typically legislates by parts—addressing one thing without examining all others that might merit comparable treatment." The real problem was that Congress was so focused on the current problem, unregulated Indian casinos on reservations, that it did not, or could not, consider a logically likely future problem, Indian casinos on land owned by a tribe but outside its reservation.

CHAPTER 7

The District Court in the Modern Age, 1990 to 2020

U.S. District Judges Appointed during the 1990s

TWO NEW DISTRICT JUDGES joined the bench of the Western District during the 1990s, both in 1992, during the last year of the presidency of George H. W. Bush. President Bush appointed David W. McKeague to replace Judge Hillman, who assumed senior status, and appointed Gordon J. Quist to a new, and initially "temporary," judgeship created by Congress with the proviso that it would become permanent when Judge Gibson died, assumed senior status, or left the bench for some other reason. Judge Gibson elected senior status in 1996.

U.S. District Judge David William McKeague

David W. McKeague was born on November 5, 1946, in Pittsburgh, Pennsylvania, the son of Herbert and Phyllis McKeague. He was raised in East Lansing, Michigan, and he graduated from East Lansing High School in 1964. He received his undergraduate and law degrees from the University of Michigan (BA, 1968; JD, 1971). He served in the U.S. Army Reserves from 1969 to 1975. After law school, he returned to Lansing and entered into private practice for twenty-one years at the firm of Foster, Swift, Collins, and Smith, where he handled a broad variety of commercial law matters. McKeague was also active in Republican politics and was a delegate from Michigan to the Republican National Convention in 1988. He is married to Nancy Palmer McKeague, and they have six children together.

On September 11, 1991, President George H. W. Bush nominated McKeague to the Western District bench to replace Judge Douglas Hillman, who had assumed senior status on February 13, 1991. The Senate confirmed Judge McKeague on February 6, 1992, and he received his commission four days

Judge David William McKeague

later. In addition to his other duties, Judge McKeague has taught federal jurisdiction at the Michigan State University College of Law and at the University
of Michigan Law School since 1998, and he has lectured frequently for other
educational programs. He is the coauthor of a chapter on removal jurisdiction in the third and fourth editions of *Business and Commercial Litigation
in Federal Courts*.[1] He currently serves on the board of trustees for Michigan
State University College of Law and the Pine Rest Christian Mental Health
Hospital in Grand Rapids. He is a founding master and past President of the
American Inns of Court Chapter at Michigan State University College of
Law and a past President of the Wharton Center Advisory Council

On November 8, 2001, Judge McKeague was nominated by President
George W. Bush to a seat on the U.S. Court of Appeals for the Sixth Circuit
vacated by Judge Richard Fred Suhrheinrich, who had taken senior status
the previous summer. The Senate did not confirm Judge McKeague's first
nomination to the Sixth Circuit, and he was renominated by President Bush
in 2003 and in 2005. He was finally confirmed on June 9, 2005, when the Senate voted 96–0 to confirm him.[2] Judge McKeague was the fifth nomination
to the Sixth Circuit by the younger President Bush to be confirmed by the

Judge Gordon Jay Quist

Senate. Judge McKeague assumed senior status on November 1, 2017, and in 2020 he continues to hear cases.

During his federal court career, Judge McKeague has been appointed by the Chief Justice of the United States to serve on four committees of the Judicial Conference: Chair of the District Judge Education Committee (1998–2003); Defender Services Committee (2000–2005); Budget Committee (2005–2013); and Judicial Security Committee (2015–the present), as the chair since 2018.

U.S. District Judge Gordon Jay Quist

Gordon J. Quist was born in 1937 in Grand Rapids, Michigan. He graduated from Grand Rapids Christian High School in 1955, and he attended Calvin College for two years, after which he transferred to Michigan State University where he graduated in 1959 with a bachelor of arts degree. He entered George Washington University Law School in Washington, D.C., and he graduated in 1962 with a juris doctor degree with honors. He worked as an associate in Washington (1962–1964) and in Chicago (1964–1967) before returning to Grand Rapids to join the firm of Miller, Johnson, Snell & Cummiskey as a civil litigator, particularly in the area of business litigation. He remained at the firm for twenty-five years and became a partner and then the firm's managing partner in 1986. He is married to Martha Jane Quist, and they have five children.

On March 20, 1992, President George H. W. Bush nominated Quist to the new District Court seat on the Western District bench authorized by Congress on December 1, 1990.[3] The Senate confirmed his appointment on June 26, 1992, and he received his commission on June 30. When Congress created this judgeship,[4] it designated the judgeship as "temporary," but this designation was not precise, because it did not mean that this new judgeship necessarily faced vacation. The statutory text explained that the first of any one of the court's five district judgeships faced being abolished if vacated at least five years after the statute's effective date (i.e., after December 1, 1990): "The first vacancy in the office of district judge . . . occurring five years or more after the effective date of this title, shall not be filled." That first such vacancy occurred on July 13, 1996, when Judge Benjamin Gibson assumed senior status. Gibson's seat (established October 20, 1983) was not filled and was effectively abolished, returning the Western District to four district judgeships.[5]

In 2000, Judge Quist was appointed to the Judicial Conference Committee on the Code of Conduct, and he was chair of that committee for two years. Judge Quist assumed senior status on January 1, 2006, and in 2019 he "went off the draw." He continues to hear cases in 2020.

U.S. District Judges Appointed between 2000 and 2010

President William Clinton did not have the opportunity to appoint any District Judges to the Western District of Michigan during his two terms in office (January 1993–January 2001), but his successor, President George W. Bush, made three appointments to the District Court during his two terms (January 2001–January 2009). In June 2005, the delayed confirmation of President Bush's appointment of Judge McKeague to the Sixth Circuit created a vacancy in McKeague's seat on the Western District's District Court. Two other vacancies opened up because of District Judges assuming senior status, Judge Enslen on September 1, 2005, and Judge Quist on January 1, 2006. On June 28, 2006, President Bush appointed two Michigan judges and one private practitioner to fill those vacancies, Paul L. Maloney, Robert J. Jonker, and Janet T. Neff. However, because Congress had become more contentious politically toward judicial appointments, the Western District's three District Court nominees had to endure a long wait before they were confirmed, although not as long as Judge McKeague's wait to join the Sixth Circuit.

The constitutional right to select nominees to the federal judiciary belongs to the President, although it had long been a custom that the President accepted the nomination advice of any U.S. senators belonging to the President's political party who represent the state in which a district court was located or the state to which a seat on a court of appeals was traditionally allocated. If there was no such senator, the President considered advice from other officials of his party from that state, such as senior congressmen or other leaders of the state party. A judicial seat was so important that a President very rarely appointed a nominee who was not a supporter of the President's party.

The President's constitutional power to nominate candidates is balanced by the Senate's constitutional power to advise the President and to vote whether to confirm nominations. In decades past, and with a few notable exceptions, the Senate accepted most presidential nominations unquestioned no matter which party had a majority of senators. By 2001, however, if the majority in the Senate was not of the President's party, every nomination was contested, and nominees might wait years to find out if they would be confirmed. On the same day in November 2001 that President George W. Bush nominated District Judge David McKeague to a traditionally Michigan seat on the Sixth Circuit, President Bush also nominated two other Michigan Republicans, Henry Saad and Susan Bieke Neilson, to two other traditionally Michigan seats on the appellate court. In June 2002, President Bush also nominated Richard Allen Griffin to a fourth traditionally Michigan seat on the Sixth Circuit.

At the time of all of those nominations, the Democrats held a slight majority in the Senate. Because Republicans, when they had earlier had a majority, had blocked many judicial nominations by President Clinton, including two nominees from Michigan to the Sixth Circuit, Helene White and Kathleen McCree Lewis, the Senate Judiciary Committee, under the chairmanship of Senator Patrick Leahy (D. VT), blocked all Bush nominations including the four Michigan nominations to the Sixth Circuit. In the 2002 midterm congressional elections, the Republicans regained control of the Senate, and the new Senate Judiciary Committee, chaired by Senator Orin Hatch (R. UT), began to process the Michigan Sixth Circuit nominations.

In March 2003, Michigan's two U.S. senators, Democrats Carl Levin and
Debbie Stabenow, announced that they would block hearings before the Senate Judiciary Committee on all of President Bush's judicial nominees from
Michigan because President Bush refused to renominate White[6] or Lewis.
Nevertheless, the Republican majority on the Judiciary Committee held confirmation hearings for Saad, McKeague, and Griffin,[7] and the committee sent
all three to the full Senate. Levin and Stabenow convinced the Democratic
caucus to filibuster the three in order to prevent them from being confirmed.
By 2005, Democrats were filibustering the confirmation of ten Bush nominees to various courts of appeals, including Saad, McKeague, and Griffin. The
Republicans threatened to invoke the "nuclear option," a rarely used procedure in which the Senate can change its rules to cut off filibustering on the
confirmation of executive or judicial appointees by lowering the vote threshold to end debate to a simple majority rather than by the sixty votes required
for other matters. Trying to bring peace, fourteen moderate Republican and
Democratic senators joined to forge a deal by which some of the filibustered
nominations would receive a confirmation vote, although specifically not
Saad's nomination. Both Levin and Stabenow ultimately voted in favor of
McKeague, who was confirmed unanimously and took his seat in the Sixth
Circuit in June 2005. The senators also voted to confirm Griffin.

In 2006, the Western District's three District Judge nominees also found
their confirmations delayed by a renewal of the Senate's toxic political environment. In September 2006, Senators Levin and Stabenow announced
that they would support all three nominees, and the Judiciary Committee
approved them. This was the result of a compromise because nominee Janet
Neff was a choice of Michigan's two Democratic senators. However, the Senate did not act on their nominations because a single U.S. senator, Samuel
Brownback, Republican of Kansas, objected to Janet Neff's confirmation.
Brownback stated that his objection was based on the fact that Neff had
attended a same-sex commitment ceremony for the daughter of her long-
time neighbors. Rather than block just Neff's appointment, though, Senator
Brownback blocked confirmation votes for a dozen of President Bush's judicial nominees, including Neff, Maloney, and Jonker. After their nominations
expired at the end of 2006, the President nominated them again in March
2007, and they were confirmed that summer.[8]

Judge Paul Lewis Maloney

U.S. District Judge Paul Lewis Maloney

Judge Paul L. Maloney was born in 1949, in Cleveland, Ohio. He received his undergraduate education at Lehigh University, in Bethlehem, Pennsylvania (BA, 1972) and his law degree (JD, 1975) from the University of Detroit Law School, now the University of Detroit Mercy School of Law. He is married to Marie Maloney, and they have three children. After law school, he moved to Berrien County, Michigan, the county seat of which is St. Joseph. He served as assistant until he was appointed Chief Assistant Prosecutor in October 1981. In 1989, he became a Deputy Assistant U.S. Attorney General in the criminal division of the U.S. Department of Justice. In 1993, he was hired as a special assistant to the Director of the Michigan Department of Corrections. In 1995, Michigan Governor John M. Engler appointed him judge of Michigan's Fifth District Court in Berrien County. In 1996, the Michigan Supreme Court consolidated Berrien County's district, circuit, and probate courts into one Berrien County Trial Court. Governor Engler appointed Judge Maloney a circuit judge. Maloney was assigned to the new court's criminal division, and in 1999 the Michigan Supreme Court appointed him Chief Judge of the consolidated court, a position that he held until the U.S. Senate confirmed his appointment as U.S. District Judge.

On March 19, 2007, President George W. Bush made his second nomination of Judge Maloney to a seat on the Western District bench vacated by Judge Enslen, who assumed senior status in September 2005. Judge Maloney's appointment was confirmed on July 9, 2007, and he received his commission

Judge Robert James Jonker

on July 13. As planned, Judge Maloney also took over Judge Enslen's chambers and courtroom in the Kalamazoo federal building, although Judge Enslen also maintained an office in that building. He served as the U.S. District Court's Chief Judge from 2008 to 2015 after waiting a mandatory period of one year following his appointment to the court.

U.S. District Judge Robert James Jonker

Judge Robert J. Jonker was born on March 9, 1960, in Holland, Michigan, to Jerry and Delia (Roels) Jonker. He graduated from Holland Christian High School (1978), Calvin College (BA, 1982), and the University of Michigan Law School (JD, 1985, summa cum laude). After two years as law clerk to Judge John F. Feikens of the U.S. District Court for the Eastern District of Michigan, he returned to Grand Rapids to practice commercial and environmental litigation with the firm of Warner, Norcross & Judd until 2007. On June 28, 2006, President George W. Bush nominated Jonker to be a judge on the U.S. District Court for the Western District of Michigan, replacing Judge Gordon Quist who had assumed senior status the previous January. After Jonker's nomination lapsed at the end of 2006 and President Bush nominated him again on March 19, 2007, the Senate confirmed his appointment on July

Judge Janet Theresa Neff

9. Judge Jonker received his commission on July 16. In 2015, Judge Jonker became the court's Chief Judge. He is married to Nancy, and they have two children.

U.S. District Judge Janet Theresa Neff

Judge Janet T. Neff is the first woman to be appointed as a U.S. District Judge for the Western District of Michigan. She was born Janet Theresa Nebiolo, the daughter of Pauline J. and Lino Nebiolo, on April 8, 1945, in Wilkinsburg, Pennsylvania, near Pittsburgh. She graduated from the University of Pittsburgh (BA, cum laude, 1967) and Wayne State University Law School (JD, 1970). She is married to attorney David Neff, and they have two daughters.

Following law school, Judge Neff served as an estate and gift tax examiner for the Internal Revenue Service (1970), as a law clerk for the Michigan Court of Appeals (1970–1971), and as an assistant city attorney for Grand Rapids (1971–1973). After five years of private practice as an associate and partner with a Grand Rapids law firm, VanderVeen, Freihofer & Cook, she was appointed a Commissioner of the Michigan Supreme Court (1978–1980) and briefly as an Assistant U.S. Attorney for the Western District of Michigan (1980). Following another period in private practice in Grand Rapids with William J. Reamon, PC (1980–1988), she was elected as a judge of the Michigan Court of Appeals where she served for more than eighteen years (1989–2007). Like Judges Maloney and Jonker, her first nomination by President George W. Bush in 2005 expired without a vote, and President Bush nominated her again on March 19, 2007. The Senate confirmed her second appointment on July 9, 2007, and she received her commission on August 6, 2007.

Judge Neff was a member of the Board of Commissioners of the State Bar of Michigan (1980–1984), an officer of the Grand Rapids Bar Association (1985–1990), including serving a term (1989–1990) as the association's first woman president in its eighty-eight-year history, and a faculty member of the Hillman Advocacy Program (1988–1991). She received the 1998 Law Enforcement award presented by the Order of the Sons of Italy, and in 2006 she was named the Outstanding Member by the Women Lawyers Association for Western Michigan.

Senior U.S. District Judge Robert Allan Edgar

Another District Judge joined the Western District in 2005, but by transfer rather than by a new appointment. Congress created the Western District's Northern Division in June 1878. Judge Withey held the Division's first court session in Marquette the following September, and the District Court has held terms and sessions there ever since and in Sault Ste. Marie until 1941. But the Northern Division never had its own resident District Judge until 2011. Instead, the District Judges whose regular chambers were in the courthouses in the Southern Division traveled north a few times each year to hold court and then return south as soon as their northern business was finished. In the early years, the duty to travel north was a hardship for some judges while others embraced it with a love for outdoor activities and for the different kinds of cases available in the Upper Peninsula. For all of them, though, trips north interfered with their busy dockets in the Southern Division.

In 2005, a senior District Judge from Tennessee, a native of the Upper Peninsula, began handling the Northern Division's docket part-time, and in 2011, he moved to the Upper Peninsula full time. Senior District Judge Robert Allan Edgar was born in Munising, Michigan, on the shores of Lake Superior, in 1940, the son of Robert Richard Edgar and Jean (Hansen) Edgar. The family

Judge Robert Allan Edgar

lived in Marquette, Michigan, until Judge Edgar was twelve years old and his family moved to Athens, Tennessee. Judge Edgar graduated from Athens's McMinn County High School, from Davidson College in North Carolina (B.A., 1962), and from Duke University School of Law (LL.B., 1965). Following law school, he served in the U.S. Army from 1965 to 1967, including a tour as an intelligence officer in Vietnam, where he was awarded a Bronze Star Medal for "meritorious achievement in ground operations against hostile forces." After leaving the army, he began a private practice of law in Chattanooga, Tennessee, which he continued until his appointment to the federal bench in 1985. During his time in private practice, he was elected to one term (1970–1972) in the House of Representatives of the Tennessee General Assembly, and from 1980 to 1985 he served on the Tennessee Wildlife Resources Commission.

On September 11, 1984, President Ronald Reagan nominated Edgar to become a District Judge on the U.S. District Court for the Eastern District of Tennessee, replacing Judge Herbert Theodore Milburn, whom Reagan had appointed to the Sixth Circuit. However, the Senate did not vote on confirming Edgar's appointment, so President Reagan nominated him again on February 26, 1985. The Senate confirmed his second nomination on April

198   A LINCOLN LEGACY

15, 1985, and he received his commission the next day. Judge Edgar served as Chief Judge of the District Court from 1998 to 2005. He assumed senior status on October 7, 2005.

Judge Edgar is the only U.S. District Judge to have been born in the Upper Peninsula, as was his wife, Gail Martin Edgar. They maintained warm memories and close ties with that region, and in the late 1980s, while he was still an active District Judge in the Eastern District of Tennessee, Judge Edgar began serving by designation in the Northern Division of the Western District of Michigan. On May 2, 2011, he closed his chambers in Tennessee and established chambers in the federal courthouse at Marquette to serve as a senior judge for the Western District of Michigan. On June 30, 2016, after five years as the first resident District Judge in the Northern Division, Judge Edgar assumed the status of inactive Senior District Judge. His cases were reassigned to District Judges Quist, Maloney, and Bell, all of whom retained their chambers and resided in the Southern Division.

Redrawing Michigan's Congressional Districts

The number of representatives in the U.S. House of Representatives is fixed by statute at 435. How many congressional districts a state has, and thus the number of its representatives, is adjusted after each decennial census based on the proportion the state's population bears to the national population. According to the results of the 1990 census, Michigan's population increased from 1980 to 1990 by 33,219 residents, but the state fell behind the national population's increase to the extent that Michigan's congressional districts decreased from eighteen to sixteen.

When the number of a state's congressional districts changes, district boundaries must be redrawn (called reapportionment or redistricting), a function that is initially a matter for the state's legislature to consider. Federal courts become involved in the process, and judicial relief becomes appropriate, "only when a legislature fails to reapportion according to federal constitutional requisites in a timely fashion after having had an adequate opportunity to do so."[9] Michigan's congressional redistricting ended up in the federal courts after the 1970 and 1980 decennial censuses, in each case after the state legislature failed to produce any plan at all, much less one that satisfied federal law. By the summer of 1991, it was clear that, once more, the legislature had not only failed to come up with a valid plan reflecting the 1990 decennial census, it was no longer even trying to do so. It appeared that, as before, the legislature preferred to remain deadlocked and to leave the task of reapportionment to the federal judiciary.

The judicial process began on July 30, 1991, when a group of individuals representing the interests of the state Democratic Party, known as the *Good* plaintiffs, filed suit in the Flint courthouse of the U.S. District Court for the Eastern District of Michigan. The sole resident District Judge in Flint was Judge Stewart Newblatt, known to have been a Democrat before his appointment to the federal bench by Democratic President Jimmy Carter. The suit asked Newblatt to set a deadline for the legislature to formulate a plan and requested that if that did not happen, Judge Newblatt undertake to develop and impose a plan himself.[10] A week later, other individuals representing the interests of the Republican Party, known as the *Van Straten* plaintiffs, filed a similar suit in the Western District's Marquette courthouse.[11] Although there was no resident District Judge in Marquette, the *Van Straten* plaintiffs hoped, correctly as it turned out, that the case would be assigned to District Judge Robert Holmes Bell who, by Western District court rule, drew the largest percentage of all cases filed in Marquette. Bell had no record in partisan politics, but he had been appointed to the federal court by Republican President Ronald Reagan, and Bell was, in his own words, "not a Democrat."

A federal statute requires that "when an action is filed challenging the constitutionality of the apportionment of congressional districts . . ." the Chief Judge of the relevant U.S. Circuit Court of Appeals must convene a panel of three federal judges in which one judge must be a Circuit Court judge.[12] Consequently, on August 30, 1991, the Chief Judge of the Sixth Circuit, Gilbert Merritt (himself appointed to the Court of Appeals by President Carter), consolidated the two cases and appointed Sixth Circuit Court Judge James Ryan to join District Judges Newblatt and Bell. Judge Ryan had been appointed to the Michigan Supreme Court in 1975 by Governor William Milliken, a moderate Republican, and to the Sixth Circuit by President Reagan. Although the media made much of the presumed party preferences of the judges, in fact they agreed on most issues and had no trouble working together cooperatively.

After waiting another month in the fond hope that the Michigan legislature might yet produce a plan, the federal three-judge panel decided that it would be their responsibility to produce a valid plan well before the congressional elections in November 1992. The panel ordered the *Good* and *Van*

Straten plaintiffs to submit just one proposed plan for each case's plaintiffs by January 31, 1992. The court also announced that it had retained its own expert to help analyze the parties' plans and, if necessary, to assist the court in drafting a plan of its own. Both plaintiff groups filed their proposed redistricting plans on time, and the trial of the consolidated case began on March 9, 1992, in the district courtroom in Lansing's Charles E. Chamberlain Federal Building and U.S. Post Office. The panel heard the testimony of two congressmen, the drafters of the parties' respective plans, and various expert and nonexpert witnesses. In addition, the court admitted the deposition testimony of two congressmen. At the completion of the testimony and the parties' arguments on March 13, the panel took the case under advisement.

Over many years and in many decisions, the U.S. Supreme Court has explained the constitutional and statutory criteria for a valid congressional redistricting plan. The "first and foremost" criterion is a constitutionally mandated standard described as "one person, one vote." Under that standard, "nearly as is practicable one man's vote in a congressional election is to be worth as much as another's."[13] The Supreme Court has interpreted "nearly as practicable" to mean a good faith attempt to achieve precise mathematical equality of population in each district in a state.[14] The proponents of a plan containing any differences in population must prove that the differences are "unavoidable."[15] Given the results of the 1990 census, the parties and the panel agreed that precise mathematical equality required that Michigan be divided into fifteen congressional districts of 580,956 residents each, and one district with 580,957 residents.[16]

The second criterion for a valid plan is compliance with the landmark Voting Rights Act of 1965,[17] which prohibits racial discrimination in voting and redistricting plans that dilute the votes of racial minority groups resulting in "a retrogression in the position of racial minorities with respect to their effective exercise of the electoral franchise."[18] In other words, the Act forbade gerrymandering based on race that would decrease the number of districts that "have an adequate but not excessive majority of minority voters to assure them a reasonable opportunity to elect their representatives of choice."[19] Therefore, a redistricting plan must retain at least the same number of such "minority districts" as there are under the current plan. Under the 1980 redistricting plan, Michigan had two congressional districts with a majority African American population, both of them in Detroit. Although Michigan's decreasing percentage of the national population required a reduction by two in its number of congressional districts, thus also requiring changes in the boundaries of new districts in order to satisfy the equality criterion, the Voting Rights Act also required that a valid 1990 redistricting plan have at least two minority districts.

Even if a proposed redistricting plan complies with the first two criteria, the plan must also balance "a wide array of secondary and equitable criteria including compactness, contiguity, preservation of the integrity of county and municipal boundaries, maintenance of the cores of existing districts, preservation of cultural, social, and economic communities of interest, political fairness, and racial fairness."[20] Criteria such as compactness and contiguity are intended to avoid gerrymandering, the age-old technique of drawing contorted, often elongated, electoral districts in order to create artificial majorities for one race, party, or other factor. Others are a nod to continuity and relating the politics of congressional districts to the politics of local government. Some, especially political fairness, are ambiguous and harder to judge.

On March 23, 1992, the court announced its decision to reject both parties' plans and to adopt the court's own plan, which the court presented to the parties.[21] The court gave the parties until April 1 to show cause why the court's plan should not be incorporated in a final judgment. The *Van Straten* plaintiffs and one congressman filed responses to the show cause order, but they expressed no objections to the court's plan. The *Good* plaintiffs and other intervenors did not respond to the order to show cause. On April 6, the court issued its final judgment.[22]

The court explained its decision in two opinions, a shorter opinion issued on May 23, with the court's decision, including its own plan, and a second opinion on May 20, 1992, which expanded on the court's explanation of its ruling. The court held, as all parties had stipulated, that Michigan's 1980s congressional redistricting plan was no longer constitutional because of the reduction in the number of districts and in geographical population changes within the state. The court also held that both plans proposed by the parties satisfied the "one person, one vote" principle, by providing for fifteen districts with 580,956 residents according to the 1990 census and one district with 580,957 residents, as well as the Voting Rights Act, by retaining the two districts with a substantial majority of black residents and voters. However, the panel concluded that it had to reject both proposed plans because neither properly balanced the equitable and secondary criteria.

The panel noted that, at trial, the expert witnesses for both plaintiff groups focused on the criterion of political fairness, and both group's experts opined that the plan proposed by the other group failed to satisfy that criterion. The expert testifying for the *Good* plaintiffs asserted that the *Van Straten* plan amounted to gerrymandering to the detriment of both the Democratic Party and current Democratic incumbent congressmen because the plan took four 1980s districts held by Democrats and amalgamated them into two 1990s districts with Democratic incumbents, so that two Democratic incumbents, and no Republican incumbents, would necessarily lose their seats. That expert contrasted that result with the result of the *Good* plan, which amalgamated two districts with Republican incumbents and also two districts with Democratic incumbents, so that incumbent losses would affect both political parties equally.

The expert testifying for the *Van Straten* plaintiffs analyzed the political fairness criterion in a different way. He applied historical data regarding voting patterns across the state to what he termed a "partisan symmetry"[23] test, which, he testified, evaluates a redistricting plan to determine whether it will allow each party to translate the same percentage of overall votes from the entire state into the same number of congressional seats. Thus, according to this expert, if both parties have the capacity to translate votes into seats in the same proportion, the plan achieves partisan symmetry and is politically fair. He concluded that the *Van Straten* plan passed that test while the *Good* plan did not.

In its opinions, the panel explained that it had rejected the testimony of both experts, not because their conclusions were incorrect, but rather because the tests they had chosen were inherently faulty, "excessively partisan," and "designed to advantage the political parties on whose behalf they were drafted and submitted. They are manifestly designed to advantage their partisan proponents in the next and in ensuing congressional elections. Both plans, to some degree, gerrymander district lines not only to achieve partisan advantage but, in a number of instances, to accommodate and advantage incumbent congressmen." Neither plaintiff groups appealed the panel's decision to use its own plan or the details of that plan.

The Crooked Lake Cases, Constitutional Litigation in the Ottawa National Forest

Since the 1980s, the Western District's docket in the Northern Division has had a very high number of cases arising from the presence in the Upper Peninsula of Native American reservations, several state prisons, and large national forests, including the Ottawa National Forest. That national forest covers 993,000 acres in the west of the Upper Peninsula, including most of Gogebic and Ontonagon counties as well as parts of Iron, Houghton, Baraga, and Marquette counties. Within the national forest are thirty-four small, irregularly shaped lakes set in old-growth forests. One of those lakes is Crooked Lake in Gogebic County, near the Michigan–Wisconsin border, three miles long and connected by a series of meandering channels and bays. About 95 percent of the lake's shoreline is located in the Sylvania Wilderness Area, a part of the national forest that the U.S. Department of Agriculture's Forest Service manages as part of the congressionally created National Wilderness Preservation System. The other 5 percent, the northern shore of the lake's northernmost bay, is owned by private citizens, many of whom operate fishing lodges. The Wilderness Act of 1964, which created the concept of federal wilderness areas, provides that:

> Except as specifically provided for in this Act, *and subject to existing private rights*, there shall be no commercial enterprise and no permanent road within any wilderness area designated by this Act and, except as necessary to meet minimum requirements for the administration of the area for the purpose of this Act (including measures required in emergencies involving the health and safety of persons within the area), there shall be no temporary road, no use of motor vehicles, motorized equipment or motorboats, no landing of aircraft, no other form of mechanical transport, and no structure or installation within any such area.

In 1992, the Forest Service promulgated a regulation, known as Amendment 1, which banned houseboats and sailboats from the lake and which also discouraged the use on the lake of electronic depth-finders as well as boom boxes and other electronic equipment. Several months later, the owners of two of Crooked Lake's private lakeshore parcels, the Stupak-Thrall parcel and the Gajewski parcel, sued the United States and the Secretary of Agriculture in the U.S. District Court in Marquette to challenge the legality of Amendment 1. Plaintiffs were represented by attorneys from the Upper Peninsula and Milwaukee, and by the Mountain States Legal Foundation from Denver. In their complaints, plaintiffs asserted that because Michigan law grants the owners of all property touching a lake riparian rights over the entire lake, applying Amendment 1 to them constituted a taking, without just compensation, of their existing private riparian rights over the entire lake, violating both the Wilderness Act and the taking clause of the Fifth Amendment to the U.S. Constitution. The defendants, represented by the Office of the Western District's U.S. Attorney, Michael Hayes Dettmer, conceded that Amendment 1 did not apply to plaintiffs' riparian rights on the bay directly adjacent to plaintiffs' property, but the defendants insisted that Amendment 1 did apply to plaintiffs on the rest of Crooked Lake, particularly all of the waters of the lake located within the wilderness area.

Plaintiffs' cases were consolidated and assigned to District Judge Quist, who held a hearing in the court's Marquette courtroom to determine whether Amendment 1 unlawfully infringed on plaintiffs' riparian rights and whether the amendment exceeded the constitutional authority of Congress. On January 25, 1994, Judge Quist issued a ruling in favor of the government on both issues.[24] Judge Quist easily rejected the government's argument that the rights which the statute excepted from the Wilderness Act were only mineral rights. However, he rejected plaintiffs' assertion that their riparian rights were absolute and that "all management decisions that interfere with any recognized riparian right are barred." Judge Quist noted that Michigan law allows local governments to regulate riparian rights and that the property clause of Article IV of the U.S. Constitution[25] grants Congress the power to regulate property owned by the federal government. As an owner of Crooked Lake, in common with the owners of private properties such as the plaintiffs, the United States had the constitutional power to regulate the waters of Crooked Lake as it had done in Amendment 1.

Plaintiffs appealed, and on November 29, 1995, a panel of the Sixth Circuit affirmed Judge Quist's decision,[26] but the Sixth Circuit subsequently vacated its appellate decision and granted plaintiffs a rehearing en banc (i.e., a new hearing before all of the appellate court's judges except its senior judges). On July 23, 1996, the court announced that it was equally divided, seven judges voting to affirm Judge Quist's decision and seven to reverse. Therefore, Judge Quist's judgment was affirmed.[27] In 1997, the U.S. Supreme Court denied plaintiffs' petition for further review of the case.

That denial ended the Amendment 1 litigation but not the same plaintiffs' attempts to assert their riparian rights over the entire lake against a different amendment adopted by the Forest Service on May 31, 1995. Amendment 5 restricts motorboat usage within the Sylvania Wilderness to those motorboats equipped with electric motors up to a maximum size of twenty-four volts or forty-eight pounds of thrust, and it also limits such boats, speeds to a slow, no-wake speed of about five miles per hour. After losing in administrative proceedings, plaintiffs Stupak and Gajewski sued the secretary of agriculture and other federal officers on several grounds, including the argument used in *Stupak-Thrall v. U.S.*, that Amendment 5 was a taking of their property without compensation in violation of the Fifth Amendment.

The case was assigned to Judge Bell, who heard arguments on the parties' cross motions for summary judgment. In his decision entered in December 1997, Judge Bell struck down the regulation as it applied to plaintiffs. He rejected the government's argument that Judge Quist's decision in the previous case barred plaintiffs from raising the same issues again. He noted that the tie in the decision affirming Judge Quist meant that his decision created no "circuit law" or precedent. He also noted that the earlier case did not involve either motor boating or Amendment 5 and that it was based in considerable part on the reasonableness of Amendment 1 under the facts of the case. Those facts included Judge Quist's finding that there was no history of the use of house boats or sailboats on the lake. In the Amendment 5 case, on the other hand, the regulation would ban plaintiffs' "long standing pre-existing use of the lake, a use that is central to Plaintiffs' livelihood and enjoyment of Crooked Lake." Judge Bell found that Amendment 5 would constitute a taking from these plaintiffs, and it was beyond the scope of the authority granted to the Forest Service, and so was invalid as applied to plaintiffs.[28] Judge Bell "emphasize[d] that this is a narrow ruling. . . . It applies only to one lake in the Sylvania Wilderness and to the few private riparian landowners who have historically used their private establishments for fishing and boating on Crooked Lake." Because of that narrow effect, the defendants did not appeal that decision.

In 2014, a Mr. and Mrs. Herr, who also owned property on the north shore of Crooked Lake, sued to invalidate a 2006 amendment that continued and criminalized the motor boat ban. The case was assigned to Judge Edgar, who initially granted the government's motion to dismiss on statute of limitations grounds, but the Sixth Circuit reversed and returned the case to the District Court.[29] In June 2016, on remand, Judge Edgar upheld the regulation as to any remaining property owners including these plaintiffs.[30] Plaintiffs appealed again, and on July 26, 2017, the Sixth Circuit reversed again and held that the regulation violated owners' existing littoral rights under Michigan law.[31]

Judge McKeague and the Grand Rapids Hospital Merger[32]

In the early 1990s, Grand Rapids had four general acute care hospitals, each nonprofit and operating independently from the others: Butterworth Hospital, Blodgett Memorial Health Center, St. Mary's Hospital, and Metropolitan Hospital. Butterworth Hospital was the largest, followed closely by Blodgett. The other two hospitals were considerably smaller.

At that time, the directors of Blodgett Memorial decided that their current hospital building needed either major renovations or a new facility at a different location. The hospital was located on a fifteen-acre site in a well-established residential community, but it had no land at that site on which to grow. It also was two miles from major freeways so that access for emergency vehicles, delivery vehicles, and patients was difficult, and it had inadequate parking. After considering their options, the directors decided to build a new hospital campus, at an estimated cost of $186 million, on a site along the city's major freeway, I-96, that would provide the necessary modern hospital services and room for future growth as well giving easy access and plentiful parking.

The announcement of the Blodgett Memorial plan led the leaders of the many interests and communities in Kent County to create the Kent County Area Health Care Facilities Study Commission. This organization, known as the "Hillman Commission" because its chair was Senior U.S. District Judge Douglas W. Hillman, had the purpose of studying the needs of Kent County for hospitals and health care and to make recommendations for future hospital planning. In May 1994, the commission issued its final report, which, among other findings, recommended that Blodgett not build a new facility. In response to the report and to other factors, including concerns about constantly rising operating and capital costs and duplication of hospital services, the governing bodies of Butterworth and Blodgett met and decided to merge their hospitals. The hospitals signed a letter of intent to merge in November 1994, and they notified the Federal Trade Commission (FTC) of the merger in early 1995.

The FTC and the Antitrust Division of the U.S. Department of Justice have the responsibility for enforcement of the federal antitrust laws, including the Clayton Antitrust Act,[33] which seeks to prevent anticompetitive practices involving, among other activities, mergers that may substantially lessen competition. The two agencies divide the civil branch of this enforcement based on the type of industry involved in the merger, while the antitrust division has sole responsibility for enforcing the criminal aspects of the Clayton Act. The agencies have allocated to the FTC the investigation and enforcement of civil cases arising from the hospital and medical industry. After receiving notice, the FTC analyzed the proposed Butterworth–Blodgett merger, and the agency performed its standard antitrust analysis, which focuses on how the merger may further concentrate the merger partners' share of the relevant market share. The FTC concluded that it had to oppose the merger because the merged hospitals would likely occupy a very large part of the market for hospital services in the Grand Rapids area, giving the merged hospitals the power to depress, limit, or even destroy competition in that product market. It was not surprising to scholars and attorneys familiar with antitrust law that the FTC looked at the proposed merger with great concern. In its role as champion of competition, the agency tends to equate the concentration of sellers in a market with the ability of any seller to act anticompetitively, to the detriment of the public and of other entities in the market.

In its analysis of concentration, the agency uses a widely recognized formula, the Herfindahl-Hirschman Index (HHI). While presiding over the suit brought by the FTC to block the merger, U.S. District Judge McKeague explained how the HHI works:

> The HHI is the most prominent method of measuring market concentration, commonly used by the Justice Department, the FTC and the courts in evaluating proposed mergers. . . . Under the FTC Merger Guidelines, a post-merger HHI above 1800 is deemed to reflect a highly concentrated market, and a merger producing an increase in the HHI of more than 100 points is deemed likely to create or enhance market power or facilitate its exercise.[34]

The FTC's HHI preliminary calculation for this merger resulted in a post-merger HHI and increase in HHI that was so far in excess of those levels that the FTC felt compelled to block the merger by seeking an injunction, with complete confidence in victory.

On January 23, 1996, the FTC sued Butterworth and Blodgett, under the Clayton Act, in the U.S. District Court for the Western District of Michigan; the case was assigned to Judge McKeague. The FTC filed a motion requesting that the judge enter a preliminary injunction barring the merger. After three months of discovery, Judge McKeague held a five-day hearing in the U.S. Courthouse in Lansing, from April 22 to 26, 1996. On September 26, Judge McKeague issued a lengthy opinion denying the FTC's motion and granting a final judgment in favor of the hospitals.[35]

In his opinion, the judge accepted, for purposes of the motion, that the relevant product markets were general acute care inpatient hospital services and primary care inpatient services, and that the appropriate geographical market was "the immediate Grand Rapids area."[36] The court noted the HHI calculations by the FTC's expert witness, which the defendants did not dispute:

> Dr. Leffler estimated Butterworth and Blodgett would control 47 to 65% of the market for general acute care inpatient hospital services in greater Kent County, depending on whether market share is measured by licensed beds, discharges or inpatient revenues. He estimated that the post-merger HHI would range from 2767 to 4521, reflecting an increase of between 1064 and 1889 points. With respect to the primary care inpatient hospital market, Dr. Leffler estimated the merged entity would control between 65 and 70% of the market. The post-merger HHI would rise to a number between 4506 and 5079, reflecting an increase of from 1675 to 2001 points. Dr. Leffler's statistical calculations thus demonstrate that both relevant markets would be highly concentrated after the proposed merger.

Thus, the FTC was "facially justified in challenging" the proposed merger, and there was a presumption that the merger would be illegal, a presumption that the defendants had the burden to rebut.

However, Judge McKeague also concluded that the defendants had successfully rebutted the presumption: "Based on the unique facts and circumstances that have come to light in these proceedings the Court is firmly convinced that the health care consuming public in both the immediate Grand Rapids area and greater Kent County, and in West Michigan as a whole, and indeed, the public interest in general, are best served by allowing defendants the freedom to pursue the proposed merger." The defendants presented evidence supporting several theories,[37] but the court was most impressed by an agreement entered into between the hospitals, known as the Community Commitment. The hospitals promised to freeze prices for consumers and for managed care plans, to limit operating margins, to provide services in underserved and medically needy communities, as well as other commitments involving governance of the merged entity requiring transparency and involvement of local businesses and the community.

Judge McKeague was also impressed by the testimony of the leaders of the hospitals and of the community demonstrating the depth and breadth of the collaborative community spirit supporting the merger. As the judge later explained: "Committed to my discretion under the law was the question whether, for the sake of public welfare in West Michigan, the force of the federal government should intervene to halt the merger; or whether, on the other hand, the public welfare would be best served by allowing the merger to proceed, trusting that community leaders responsible for overseeing administration of the merged entity would not take harmful advantage of their increased market power and reduction in competition."

In entering a judgment in favor of the merger, Judge McKeague required the defendants "to sign and submit for approval a proposed consent decree incorporating the terms of the Community Commitment and expressing defendants' agreement to be bound thereby during the pendency of any appeal from this Court's order or during the pendency of any administrative proceedings, to the extent actions in furtherance of the merger and implicating the assurances of the Community Commitment are undertaken."

The FTC appealed this decision to the Sixth Circuit, which in July 1997 unanimously affirmed Judge McKeague's decision denying the FTC's motion for a preliminary injunction.[38] The hospitals finalized their merger on September 19, 1997, creating a merged entity named Spectrum Health. Looking at the vital medical industry in Kent County fifteen years later, Judge McKeague was confident that he made the correct decision in 1996. He pointed to what is known as the Medical Mile, a collection of medical-related facilities, most of them located along both sides of Michigan Street from the top of a hill overlooking the city, that includes Spectrum Health's Butterworth Hospital complex, the Van Andel Institute Medical Research Center, the Calkins Science Center, the Cook-DeVos Center for Health Sciences, Michigan State University's Secchia Center Medical School, and Grand Valley State University's facilities for training medical support personnel.

United States v. Marvin C. Gabrion II

The trial of the murder case against Marvin Charles Gabrion II, conducted before Chief Judge Robert Holmes Bell in February and March 2002, gained national attention for many reasons. The alleged crime was brutal and sadistic, and the victim was a pretty, nineteen-year-old, single mother preparing to testify in a state criminal trial that Gabrion had raped her. Furthermore, Gabrion was and is widely believed to have killed the victim's infant daughter as well as Wayne Davis, a friend of Rachel who could have testified against Gabrion in the state rape trial; Jonathon Weeks, who may have been an accomplice; and Robert Allan, whose Social Security checks Gabrion was cashing. Finally, Gabrion's murder trial resulted in the first death sentence imposed in any court, federal or state, in Michigan since 1938.

Michigan was a territory from 1805 until 1837. During that period, although the territorial penalty for murder was death by hanging, and although there was no shortage of killings, the territory carried out few executions, and the state carried out none during its first decade of existence. In 1846, the state legislature passed a law, effective in 1847, that abolished capital punishment as the penalty for murder, replacing hanging with a sentence of imprisonment for life with no possibility for parole.[39] More than a century later, in 1963, a provision in Michigan's new constitution gave added weight to the state's ban on capital punishment for murder. However, neither Michigan's statute nor its constitution could prevent the federal government from executing criminals convicted of crimes for which a federal law allows a death sentence.

One such federal law, the National Bank Robbery Act, enacted in 1934 in the wake of an epidemic of bank robberies, authorized imposing a death sentence for murders committed in the course of a robbery of a federal bank. Thus, in 1937, when Anthony Chebatoris was convicted by a federal jury in Bay City for having shot and killed a bystander while fleeing a botched robbery of a federally chartered bank in Midland, U.S. District Judge Alfred J. Tuttle of the Eastern District of Michigan had the legal authority to sentence Chebatoris to death by hanging, and he did so. Chebatoris was hanged in the federal prison at Milan, Michigan, on July 8, 1938, despite pleas from many people, including Michigan Governor Frank Murphy, that the United States hold the execution in another state. Over the years, Congress has added substantially to the types of crimes over which the federal government can assert either exclusive jurisdiction or shared jurisdiction with a state. In the case of Marvin Gabrion, though, federal jurisdiction arose from one of its oldest bases, a murder committed "within the special maritime and territorial jurisdiction of the United States."[40]

The crime for which Marvin Gabrion was tried, convicted, and sentenced to death took place in Michigan's Newaygo County, a lightly populated region of forests, streams, and lakes lying on the western side of Michigan's Lower Peninsula. Newaygo County also includes within its borders part of the Manistee National Forest, undisputedly land within the special maritime and territorial jurisdiction of the United States.[41] In August 1996, Rachel Timmerman was eighteen years old, tall, blonde, and living with her family in Newaygo County. She had given birth six months earlier to a daughter, Shannon. On August 7, Rachel reported to the Newaygo County sheriff that, on the night before, she had been raped repeatedly by Gabrion, one of the men with whom she had been playing cards and drinking at the home of one of her friends. She explained that after the card games finished, she and a family friend, Wayne Davis, had accepted Gabrion's offer to drive them to their homes in his convertible. Gabrion and Rachel were in the front seat while Davis and Gabrion's nephew were in back. After driving a distance on back roads, Gabrion ordered his nephew and Davis out of the car. Rachel asserted that Gabrion then drove down a track in the woods with Rachel, stopped the convertible, and assaulted Rachel, who fought back but was nevertheless raped.

Trial on the rape charge would have started soon thereafter in Newaygo County Circuit Court, but for two complications. Gabrion disappeared for months and was not arrested until January 20, 1997. His trial was set to begin on June 5, 1997. The witnesses would include Rachel and Wayne Davis. But after Gabrion's arrest, a friend posted bond for him on February 3, 1997 Gabrion was released, and disappeared again. Meanwhile, Rachel was caught violating her parole on a marijuana conviction and was in jail herself from January 11 to May 15, 1997.

On June 3, Rachel told her family that she was going on a dinner date, and the man had asked her to bring Shannon along as well. She and her child did not return home on that night or ever after. There is a question about this man's identity. The Timmerman family remembers Rachel saying he was named Ian and worked with her, likely Ian Decker. There was also evidence that George Weeks admitted to his girlfriend that he picked up Rachel and Shannon as a favor for Gabrion. Both Decker and Weeks disappeared.[42]

A few days later, her father received a letter in her handwriting saying that she and Shannon were in Texas and that she intended to marry a man named Delbert. At about the same time, the prosecutor and the judge received letters in her handwriting stating that she had made up the rape story against Gabrion. Given Rachel's absence, her apparent recanting, and Gabrion's insistence that any sex had been consensual, the prosecutor believed that there was no case, and he dismissed the rape charge on June 25.

Ten days later, on July 5, 1997, two fishermen discovered a sickening sight floating among the weeds on Newago County's Oxford Lake. They called the sheriff, who discovered a dead female in the lake weighted down with two cinder blocks, which were attached to her body with chains and padlocks. Her face was covered with duct tape, and her arms were handcuffed behind her back. On July 10, the sheriff informed Rachel's father that the body was Rachel. The Army Corps of Engineers installed a cofferdam where Michigan State Police cadaver dogs indicated that there were human remains, to try to find out if eleven-month-old Shannon was also in the lake, but Oxford Lake, like many in the county, consists of a very few feet of water covering up to ninety feet of muck. A toddler's small body, weighed down like her mother's, likely would sink deep into the muck. Shannon's body was never found.

Once he heard the full story of Rachel's "date," the sheriff was sure that Gabrion was the prime suspect in Rachel's murder and in Shannon's disappearance. As the investigation developed, the sheriff discovered that Ian Decker had also disappeared on the night of June 4 and that Wayne Davis had disappeared a few days after Rachel's body was found. Gabrion himself was on the run again and would not be found for months. However, he finally made one mistake, cashing the Social Security disability checks of an alcoholic street person named Robert Allen, whom Gabrion had lived with briefly in Grand Rapids and who was now also among the missing.

After months of searching, the Federal Bureau of Investigation found that somebody had changed Allen's mailing address for his checks to a post office box in Sherman, New York, a small town on the shore of Lake Erie. On October 14, 1997, the FBI staked out the Sherman post office and captured Gabrion as he signed for Allen's check. He was carrying a Virginia driver's license in the name of Ronald Stevens at the time. Gabrion was taken to the U.S. District Court for the Western District of New York in Buffalo where, ten days later, he was ordered transferred to the Western District of Michigan for trial on Social Security fraud.

The fraud case was assigned to U.S. Magistrate Judge Hugh W. Brenneman,

Jr. for arraignment and preliminary matters and to District Judge McKeague for a jury trial that took place from March 3 to 5, 1998. The jury found Gabrion guilty, and on July 6, 1998, Judge McKeague sentenced him to sixty months in federal prison, followed by three years of supervised release, a fine of $1,000, and restitution of $13,945.54, payable to either Robert Allen or the Social Security Administration.[43]

With Gabrion in federal custody, attention turned back to the killing of Rachel Timmerman including the issue of which court would try Gabrion. The available evidence indicated that Rachel's killer had made mistakes in killing her that qualified him to be tried for first-degree murder in the U.S. District Court in Grand Rapids, under federal law, with the possibility of being sentenced to death—instead of in Newaygo County Circuit Court, under Michigan law, with the maximum sentence of life in prison with no possibility of parole.

First, the coroner determined that Rachel was alive when she was thrown into Oxford Lake and that she had then drowned. Second, Oxford Lake has virtually no current, so the place she was found was almost certainly where she was dumped and where she died. Third, a survey revealed that her place of death was 223 feet inside Manistee National Forest,[44] and so within federal jurisdiction.

On June 3, 1999, the U.S. Attorney for the Western District of Michigan, Michael H. Dettmer, filed a federal grand jury indictment charging Gabrion with the first-degree murder of Rachel Timmerman; the case was assigned to Chief Judge Bell. On July 2, Magistrate Judge Joseph G. Scoville arraigned Gabrion, who pleaded not guilty. In April 2000, Gabrion submitted to a psychological examination, and on July 7 Judge Bell held a hearing on Gabrion's competence to stand trial and determined that he was competent.

The federal statute laying out the procedure in murder trials requires the prosecution, if it intends to seek the death penalty, to notify the defendant "a reasonable time before trial or before acceptance by the court of a plea of guilty."[45] The U.S. Attorney General is responsible for the decision whether to seek the death penalty following a recommendation by the U.S. Attorney. Gabrion was indicted during the Clinton administration, which, as a matter of policy, did not routinely seek the death penalty and never did so for crimes arising in states that did not have the death penalty. Following that policy, the U.S. Attorney did not intend to seek the death penalty against Gabrion, and no such notice was sent. When President George W. Bush was inaugurated in

January 2001 and John Ashcroft became U.S. Attorney General on February 2, 2001, the policy of the Justice Department changed and many more death penalty notices were filed in cases throughout the United States, including cases in federal courts in states like Michigan with no death penalty available in state courts. Accordingly, on February 26, 2001, the interim U.S. Attorney for the Western District, Phillip J. Green, had the death penalty notice served on Gabrion.[46] In October 2001, Margaret M. Chiara was confirmed as U.S. Attorney for the Western District, and Phillip Green was appointed First Assistant U.S. Attorney.

Since the prosecution of Anthony Chebatoris in 1937, the procedure for trying capital cases in federal District Courts had become more complex in order to satisfy constitutional dictates from the U.S. Supreme Court. In Chebatoris's trial, the role of the jury was to find the defendant guilty or not guilty. If the verdict was guilty, sentencing was reserved for the judge who had the duty to decide whether or not to impose the death penalty. Under the present federal procedure in capital cases, the jury first hears evidence regarding the question of the defendant's guilt during the "liability phase." At the end of that phase, the jury hears arguments by the attorneys, is instructed by the judge, and withdraws into the jury room. If the jury can reach a unanimous verdict of guilty or not guilty, it returns to the courtroom and advises the judge of its verdict. If, after lengthy discussions and review of the evidence, the jury cannot reach a unanimous verdict, it so advises the court. If the jury's verdict is not guilty, the defendant is adjudged acquitted, and the trial is over. If the jury cannot reach a unanimous verdict, the defendant is subject to a new trial and likely will remain in custody. If the unanimous verdict is guilty, the "penalty phase" begins, before the same jury, which hears additional evidence and then must recommend the sentence to the District Judge.

The liability phase of Gabrion's murder trial began on February 12, 2002, in the Gerald R. Ford Federal Courthouse in Grand Rapids, before Judge Bell. The prosecution was conducted by veteran Assistant U.S. Attorneys Donald A. Davis and Timothy P. VerHey. The first day involved voir dire, the examination of prospective jurors to determine each individual's suitability to decide this case. Actual testimony began on Monday, February 25, 2002. Following opening statements, the government began presenting its case with the testimony of Rachel's father, "Tim" Timmerman; then witnesses testified about the discovery of Rachel's body in Oxford Lake; and then Michigan State Police Sergeant Richard Miller described the police investigation and what had been discovered. During the next three days of trial, the prosecution presented expert forensic testimony as well as local witnesses who placed Gabrion near Oxford Lake on the day that Rachel and Shannon disappeared.

Although the prosecutors had no witness who saw Gabrion kill Rachel, they did have a strong circumstantial case, starting with the timing of Rachel's disappearance and Gabrion's motive for keeping her from testifying about the rape. Investigators searched Gabrion's home and found several items, including keys that fit the locks used on the chains attached to Rachel as well as concrete blocks that looked like those weighing Rachel down and that were stained with orange paint and tar that, when tested, were indistinguishable from stains found on the blocks holding down Rachel's body. Investigators also received information that Gabrion had a campsite on a lake near Oxford Lake. There they found bolt cutters, chain, duct tape, a woman's hair clip, and nipples for a baby bottle. Two witnesses testified that they had seen Gabrion with a woman at his campsite on the night Rachel disappeared, and another swore that on the next morning Gabrion told him that he had killed his "girlfriend."

The prosecution rested on Thursday, February 28, and the defense began presenting its case on Friday, March 1, with Gabrion himself. The defense completed its evidence on Monday, March 4, and following closing arguments the judge instructed the jury, which returned to the jury room and began deliberating. The jury resumed its deliberations on Tuesday, March 5, and at about 10 a.m. returned with a verdict finding Gabrion guilty of the first-degree murder of Rachel Timmerman. Judge Bell then adjourned the trial until Monday, March 11, when the penalty phase would begin.

The relevant federal murder statute provides that a person convicted of an intentional killing "shall be sentenced to death if, after consideration of the [mitigating and aggravating factors] . . . it is determined that imposition of a sentence of death is justified." During the penalty phase of a federal murder trial, the jury hears evidence on the relevant mitigating and aggravating factors to determine "whether a sentence of death is to be imposed on a defendant."[47] Mitigating factors might include impaired capacity, duress, and the lack of a prior criminal record. The statute lists sixteen aggravating factors in a case of homicide, including a killing during the commission of another crime; a previous conviction for a violent felony involving a firearm; the "heinous, cruel, or depraved manner" of committing the present offense; and the vulnerability of the victim.

The court was called into session again on March 11. As the penalty phase began and the prosecution presented testimony on the aggravating factors, Gabrion appeared to lose control of himself. He began punching his attorney, David Stebbins, and four Marshals were required to subdue him. It was not clear whether Gabrion actually lost control, was deliberately disrupting the proceedings, or was trying to show that he could not control his temper. Stebbins made three motions: (1) for a mistrial on the ground his client's outburst had prejudiced him with the jury, (2) for leave to withdraw as Gabrion's attorney, and (3) for a new psychological examination of Gabrion. Judge Bell denied all three motions.

From Tuesday, March 12, to Friday, March 15, the prosecution and defense continued presenting testimony on the existence of any mitigating or aggravating factors. On Wednesday, the jury also heard victim impact statements from Rachel Timmerman's family and friends. On Friday, both sides rested, the attorneys gave their closing arguments, Judge Bell instructed the jury, and the jury retired to deliberate Gabrion's penalty. On March 16, during a special Saturday session, the jury returned a unanimous penalty verdict of death. On April 11, Judge Bell entered an order officially sentencing Gabrion to death. Gabrion was the first person in the United States to receive the federal death penalty for a crime committed in a non–death penalty state since the federal death penalty was reinstated in 1988.

Despite that verdict and sentence, the case was far from over. Gabrion appealed to the Sixth Circuit which, in April 2006, remanded the case to Judge Bell to reconsider the issue of the District Court's subject matter jurisdiction over crimes committed in a national forest. In a lengthy opinion issued on August 25, 2006, Judge Bell concluded that the state's 1939 transfer of lands, including Oxford Lake to the United States, and the conduct of both governments afterward did create concurrent criminal jurisdiction. The Sixth Circuit affirmed Bell's opinion, and in April 2009 the Supreme Court denied further review.[48] With the question of jurisdiction decided, the Sixth Circuit turned to issues of guilt and punishment. On August 3, 2011, a majority of a three-judge panel of the Sixth Circuit affirmed the jury verdict as to guilt but reversed the penalty verdict and vacated the death sentence.[49] The majority held that Judge Bell should have instructed the jury that it could consider Michigan's lack of a death penalty as a mitigating factor and that the aggravating factors must outweigh the mitigating factors beyond a reasonable doubt for the jury to choose a sentence of death. The prosecution sought an en banc review of this decision, which the Sixth Circuit granted. In May 2013, the full court, minus its senior judges as required by the law, affirmed Gabrion's death sentence, holding that Michigan's lack of a death penalty was not mitigating evidence of the defendant's background or the circumstances of the crime and that the beyond-a-reasonable-doubt standard was not required for weighing the aggravating and mitigating factors.[50] Finally, on April 28, 2014, the U.S. Supreme Court denied Gabrion's petition for certiorari.[51] In 2016, Gabrion filed a habeas petition under 28 U.S.C. 2255.

At this writing, almost two decades after the murder of Rachel Timmerman, Gabrion is incarcerated in the Special Confinement Unit of the U.S. Penitentiary in Terre Haute, Indiana, where he awaits his execution. The body of Rachel's friend Wayne Davis was found in July 2002 in another lake in the Manistee National Forest that is adjacent to the house of Gabrion's parents. Rachel's daughter Shannon, Robert Allen, and Ian Decker/John Weeks are still missing. Many people believe that Gabrion killed some or all of them.

The Ashcroft Justice Department's death penalty policy did not work out in other federal murder prosecutions in Michigan. In 2001, two brothers, Michael and Robert Ostrander, were indicted in the Western District of Michigan for several federal crimes including the capital offense of causing a death (the murder of a fellow drug dealer) with a firearm during and in relation to a drug trafficking crime. The decision to pursue the death penalty was made by Attorney General Ashcroft. In 2003, juries found both brothers guilty but could not reach a unanimous verdict on the death penalty as to either defendant. Instead, the jurors recommended that both be sentenced to life in prison without the possibility of release, and Judge Bell sentenced them accordingly. In a federal case in the Eastern District of Michigan, Ashcroft ordered federal prosecutors to seek the death penalty against John Bass, a brutal drug kingpin indicted on murder and drug charges. Bass was tried and convicted in August 2003, but the jury returned a penalty verdict of life in prison without the possibility of release, the same sentence Bass was already serving on a state court conviction.

Judge Neff and Sexual Harassment and Hostile Work Environment, Waldo v. Consumers Energy Co.

In 2006, Theresa Waldo sued her employer, Consumers Energy Company, in the Western District in Grand Rapids alleging that she was subjected to gender discrimination, sexual harassment, a hostile work environment, and retaliation, all in violation of both federal and state laws. According to her complaint, the alleged mistreatment arose from her transfer into Consumers' transmission lines department in 2001 and her entry into Consumers' four-year, four-step Line Apprentice Training Program in 2002.

The plaintiff alleged that she was virtually the only female utility worker in the transmission lines department and that her supervisors and coworkers made it clear that she was one female too many. She also alleged that, from 2001 to 2005, she was the recipient of vile, degrading sexual harassment in words and deeds, and that Consumers retaliated against her by dismissing her from the apprenticeship program, denying her a journeyman card, and transferring her to another department with lower pay where she was to begin another four-year apprenticeship program.

The case was assigned to District Judge Janet Neff. In August and September 2009, Judge Neff presided over a nine-day jury trial of the plaintiff's claims of gender discrimination, sexual harassment, hostile work environment, and retaliation, under Title VII of the Civil Rights Act of 1964.[52] Despite graphic testimony in support of Ms. Waldo's claims, at the close of the proofs, the jury returned a verdict in favor of Consumers. Ms. Waldo moved for a new trial on all of her claims. In June 2010, Judge Neff denied Waldo's motion as to the retaliation claim, but the judge granted the motion as to Waldo's claim of a hostile work environment. Judge Neff held that the jury's verdict on the latter claim was against the weight of the evidence to such an extent that the verdict for Consumers was seriously erroneous.

Summarizing the trial evidence, Judge Neff found that during the plaintiff's time in the Line Apprentice Training Program,

[f]oul, sexually offensive language was routine in the work environment, especially ongoing, derogatory, sexually-offensive references to Plaintiff as a female, including the men calling her "cunt," "bitch," "wench," "fucking stupid idiot," etc. Plaintiff testified in detail about other specific instances of this ongoing conduct. For instance, she was told by her supervisor, Jim McDonald, on more than one occasion that he would "wash" her out of the line apprentice program. She was locked in a regularly used port-a-potty on a hot 90-degree day. She was told to clean up tobacco spit of the male workers, and when she refused, the men locked her in the trailer so that she could not leave.

Plaintiff worked in remote areas with no provisions for the necessities of feminine hygiene; plaintiff was told that she could use the woods for bathroom purposes, the same as the men, and when she did, she had no means of disposing of used feminine hygiene products. She was told that no purses were allowed in the crew trucks, because it was too "girlie girl" for the man's world, and when she did carry a purse (for instance, to carry feminine hygiene products), the purse was thrown from the truck into the dirt by male co-workers, and when she then carried a smaller purse-wallet, she was labeled a "lesbian," and/or "dike."' She was told to urinate like the men by opening the bin door of the truck and relieving herself on the steps.

Plaintiff testified that she had to endure sexually explicit materials in the workplace/trucks, including pornographic magazines. Further, male workers generally ignored or shunned her to the extent that she was denied help and learning opportunities. In this regard, Plaintiff testified that her instructor at a training facility pointed a red laser light at her head and said "right there with a .22 shell." The above are only notable examples of the conduct that were testified to at trial.[53]

The retrial took place before a new jury, once more taking nine days, in September and October 2010. This time, the jury returned a verdict in favor of Ms. Waldo and awarded her $400,000 in compensatory damages and $7,500,000 in punitive damages. Consumers moved to have Judge Neff throw out that verdict and instead enter judgment in its favor, or at least to grant remittitur (i.e., that the court reduce the amount of the verdict to just $16,000). Judge Neff denied the motion to vacate the second verdict for the same reasons she cited for granting Waldo's motion for a new trial. On the re-mittitur motion, she held that the relevant federal statute did limit compensatory and punitive damages in this kind of case to $300,000, but she rejected any further reduction of the jury's verdict. On the other hand, Judge Neff pointed out, the same statute allows the court to award a successful plaintiff attorney fees and costs. In March 2012, Judge Neff awarded Waldo in excess of $700,000 in fees, commenting that: "As aptly stated by another court in this district, 'This is a classic case of the obdurate defendant who digs in its heels while litigating the merits of an action, loses, and then cries "foul" when asked to pay the resulting attorneys' fees and costs.'" Consumers appealed to the Sixth Circuit, challenging all of Judge Neff's rulings. On August 9, 2013, a 2–1 majority of the assigned appeals panel affirmed those rulings on all grounds.[54]

Solicitation of Charitable Donations and the First Amendment

The First Amendment of the U.S. Constitution bars Congress, and, through the due process clause of the Fourteenth Amendment, all other American governments and their agencies, from "abridging the freedom of speech, or of the press." However, it is well established that not every utterance or activity that might be characterized as speech under the First Amendment is entitled to the same level of protection. In particular, content-based regulations of protected speech must satisfy strict scrutiny to survive,[55] while "regulations that are unrelated to the content of speech are subject to an intermediate level of scrutiny."[56] The question of the appropriate level of scrutiny for any utterance or activity that comes within the First Amendment remains a common subject of litigation in federal courts. Two recent cases in the U.S. District Court for the Western District of Michigan addressed that question with respect to charitable solicitations in the public.

Planet Aid v. City of St. Johns

One such case was assigned to District Judge Neff. The plaintiff, Planet Aid, is a nonprofit charitable organization that receives donations of used clothing and shoes from the public in unattended, outdoor bins. In February 2014, Planet Aid sued the City of St. Johns, located in Michigan's Clinton County, north of Lansing. In its complaint, Planet Aid sought a declaratory judgment and an injunction to stop the city from enforcing an ordinance that banned unattended donation boxes. Planet Aid asserted that its bins, which included the charity's name and requests for donations, were the equivalent of speech protected by the First Amendment and that the city's ordinance was thus unconstitutional.

In order to support its various charitable purposes and activities, Planet Aid solicits donations of clothing and shoes through its unattended, outdoor donation bins. Planet Aid distributes the items collected from the bins to organizations in other countries. In December 2012, Planet Aid placed bins on the property of two businesses in St. Johns with the consent of the property owners. Although at that time the city did not have an ordinance regulating charitable donation bins, in January 2013 the city sent Planet Aid a letter claiming that "clothing donation containers have been found to create a nuisance as people leave boxes and other refuse around the containers." The letter directed Planet Aid to remove its bins by January 23 or the city would remove them. When Planet Aid did not comply by that date, the city did remove and store the bins, although it did also allow Planet Aid to recover them.

In January 2014, a year later, the city council belatedly voted to adopt an ordinance (Ordinance #618) to prohibit charitable donation bins, in order "to protect the health, safety and welfare of the citizens of the city by preventing blight, protecting property values and neighborhood integrity, avoiding the creation and maintenance of nuisances and ensuring the safe and sanitary maintenance of properties. Unattended donation boxes in the city may become an attractive nuisance for minors and/or criminal activity. It is also the intent of this section to preserve the aesthetics and character of the community by prohibiting the placement of donation boxes." However, the ordinance included an exemption for any "donation box that exists on the effective date of this ordinance," thus grandfathering in a recycling center established by a local branch of the Lions Club. As it had done to protect its activities from similar laws in many other towns and cities, Planet Aid asked the court to vacate Ordinance #618.

On April 29, 2014, Judge Neff conducted a hearing on Planet Aid's motion for a preliminary injunction. The city admitted that the bins and the language on them were speech regarding charitable giving and were entitled to some level of protection under the First Amendment, but the city denied that the ordinance was a content-based restriction subject to strict scrutiny. Instead, the city argued, Planet Aid's bins were like commercial outdoor advertising signs, and that courts have held consistently that such advertising signs are content-neutral and not subject to strict scrutiny. The city asked the court to hold that, like laws regulating commercial signs, Ordinance #618 is a restriction that is neutral regarding content, time, place, and the manner of restriction and that it is, therefore, constitutional.

After the hearing, Judge Neff granted Planet Aid's motion for a preliminary injunction. The judge concluded: "Planet Aid's operation of donation bins to solicit and collect charitable donations qualifies as protected speech under the First Amendment" and that Ordinance #618 was subject to strict scrutiny, holding that: "Plaintiff, in arguing that the ordinance fails strict scrutiny because it implements an overly broad, prophylactic ban on all bins so the City can avoid dealing with hypothetical nuisances or other issues that may arise with certain bins in the future, has borne its burden of proving a substantial likelihood of succeeding on the merits of its free speech claim."[57]

The city appealed, but in April 2015 the Sixth Circuit affirmed Judge Neff's decision.[58]

Speet v. Schuette

While the Planet Aid case involved just a few collection bins on private property that the public can choose to use or to ignore, a case assigned to District Judge Jonker a few years earlier dealt with a form of contribution request that many people find much harder to deal with, begging by individuals walking up to pedestrians or cars on public streets. The issue presented to Judge Jonker was whether an individual approaching people to ask for money or work is a request for a charitable donation worthy of strict scrutiny under the First Amendment.

Begging by the down-and-out has existed on city streets around the world since well before the ratification of the Bill of Rights. Some cultures treat such beggars as holy, but for most other cultures, beggars, often called panhandlers in the United States, are often subjected to bans on the grounds that they are unsightly, invaders of privacy, and a potential danger to society or even to civilization itself. Michigan law has long taken the latter side of the argument and has tried to find a legal cure for begging through arrest, jailing, and fines. In 2012, Judge Jonker presided over a constitutional challenge to one such Michigan criminal statute, dating from 1929 or earlier, that treated a "disorderly person" as any person caught begging in a public place. Violation of the statute was a misdemeanor bringing, upon conviction, a penalty of not more than ninety days' in jail, or a fine of not more than $500, or both.

The Grand Rapids Police Department frequently ticketed or even arrested panhandlers under the begging statute. Between 2008 and 2011, the department arrested or cited 399 people for begging. Among those arrested were James Speet and Ernest Sims, residents of Grand Rapids who routinely begged on the city's streets either by holding up signs or by asking passers-by for a small contribution money. Mr. Speet, who was homeless, received food stamps, and also collected bottles, cans, and scrap metal. He also often sought and found odd jobs by holding up a sign in public that read "Need Job, God Bless." He was prosecuted many times under the state law before he was arrested in Grand Rapids in July 2011 for holding up the job sign. Mr. Sims, a disabled veteran of the U.S. Air Force and a student at Grand Rapids Community College, relied on a $260 disability assistance check and food stamps for survival. When unable to afford his expenses, he asked people for "spare change to help a veteran" on the public streets of Grand Rapids. On July 4, 2011, a Grand Rapids police officer arrested Sims, who was asking for change for bus fare. Sims pleaded guilty and was sentenced to a fine of $100 or two days in jail.

In September 2011, Speet and Sims, represented by the American Civil Liberties Union Fund of Michigan, filed suit in the U.S. District Court for the Western District of Michigan against the Attorney General of Michigan, the city of Grand Rapids, the city's chief of police, and a police officer. The plaintiffs alleged that the begging statute, on its face, violated their rights to free speech under the First Amendment and to the equal protection of the law under the Fourteenth Amendment. Plaintiffs asked Judge Robert J. Jonker, who was assigned to the case, to declare that the state's anti-begging law was unconstitutional, to enter a permanent injunction barring the law's enforcement, and to award them damages.

Both plaintiffs and defendants moved for summary judgment. Plaintiffs relied on numerous judicial decisions in other jurisdictions striking down anti-begging laws on the basis that begging for money or a job for oneself is no different from solicitation of money or goods by charities on behalf of others. Both activities are forms of speech clearly protected by the First Amendment and any limitation on them is subject to strict scrutiny analysis. The defendants, represented by attorneys from the office of Michigan's Attorney General, argued that the anti-begging statute was constitutional because begging "can include conduct elements, such as fraudulent statements; confrontational interaction; trespassing on private property; or other disagreeable behavior that has the potential to interfere with businesses serving the public."

On August 24, 2012, Judge Jonker issued an opinion finding Michigan's anti-begging law unconstitutional on its face.

> Michigan's ban on begging is a content-based restriction on protected speech that applies to traditional public forums; therefore, the strictest scrutiny applies. The government must demonstrate that the statute is narrowly tailored to achieve a compelling state interest. . . . The government describes its interest in the statute as linked to the government's "important regulatory interest in safety, regulating the flow of pedestrian and vehicular traffic, protecting businesses and tourism, and protecting against the risk of duress and fraud associated with the solicitation of funds. . . ." Even if these

concerns amount to compelling state interests, the Court is not persuaded that the total prohibition on begging in public places is narrowly tailored to achieve these ends. Less restrictive means of furthering these interests exist. Nothing prohibits the government from regulating directly the conduct the government identifies as problematic. The government can and does prohibit fraud, assault, and trespass. But what the government cannot do without violating the First Amendment is categorically prohibit the speech and expressive elements that may sometimes be associated with the harmful conduct; it must protect the speech and expression, and focus narrowly and directly on the conduct it seeks to prohibit. That the statute does not restrict charitable solicitation, which involves the same kinds of risks the government associates with begging, further calls into question the necessity of the total prohibition on begging. Content-neutral regulations could accomplish the goals the government describes.[59]

The defendants appealed to the Sixth Circuit, which heard arguments on June 13, 2013. A month later, on August 14, the appellate court affirmed Judge Jonker's decision. The panel agreed that "begging is a form of solicitation that the First Amendment protects." The panel also agreed with Judge Jonker that "the statute violates—on its face—the First Amendment.... Michigan's anti-begging statute cannot withstand facial attack because it prohibits a substantial amount of solicitation, an activity that the First Amendment protects, but allows other solicitation based on content."[60]

CHAPTER 8

U.S. Commissioners, U.S. Magistrates, and U.S. Magistrate Judges

OVER MORE THAN TWO centuries, Congress has constantly expanded the duties of the federal court officers who were originally, in the late eighteenth century, called Circuit Court commissioners and who, after many changes in title and responsibilities, are today, in the early twenty-first century, officially titled United States Magistrate Judges. While the first statute creating commissioners limited their power to setting bail, Magistrate Judges have become a crucial second tier of federal judges within the U.S. District Courts. Whatever their title, these officers are not Article III judges with the full jurisdiction of District Judges, but the scope of duties Congress has allowed them within the limitations of the Constitution is very broad, allowing Magistrate Judges to assist District Judges in keeping the District Courts operating. Some District Courts have not made full use of Magistrate Judges, but that is not the case with the U.S. District Court for the Western District of Michigan, which includes its Magistrate Judges in every activity allowed by Congress and by the Constitution.

In criminal matters, the Western District's Magistrate Judges take full charge of federal misdemeanors as well as the initial proceedings in federal felony cases. They issue search and arrest warrants, review criminal complaints, handle initial appearances and arraignments of defendants, conduct initial pretrial conferences, conduct preliminary hearings and bond hearings, appoint defense counsel, set bail, and empanel the court's grand juries and receive indictments returned by the grand juries. In criminal cases involving Class A misdemeanors (those carrying a possible sentence in excess of six months), Magistrate Judges are authorized to preside over the entire case from inception through trial and sentencing if the parties consent. Consent is not required for petty offenses. In civil matters, parties may consent to a Magistrate Judge handling a case in its entirety. If the parties do not consent, Magistrate Judges may still preside over settlement conferences, and all pretrial aspects of the case, such as nondispositive motions and discovery disputes; they can be responsible for all activity associated with a civil case except dispositive motions and trials. Even with dispositive motions in cases where the parties have not consented, Magistrate Judges frequently hear and consider such motions and then report and recommend a result to the District Judge.

Magistrate Judges also have the authority to advise District Judges in resolving two types of civil cases that numerically represent almost a half of the court's docket. One set includes cases filed by state and federal prisoners challenging the constitutionality of their convictions as well as civil rights actions by prisoners in federal and state prisons and county jails complaining about the conditions of their incarceration. The other set of cases involves appeals from administrative denials of Social Security disability benefits. In both sets of cases, the Magistrate Judge makes a report and recommendation of the disposition to the District Judge assigned to the case. The parties may, and frequently do, consent to the Magistrate Judges handling those cases entirely. In the Western District, Magistrate Judges are also involved in the District Court's programs for alternative dispute resolution, in foreign extradition proceedings, and in bar admission and naturalization ceremonies, as well as participating with District Judges on the court's administrative committees.

From Circuit Court Commissioners to Magistrate Judges

Circuit Court Commissioners

Magistrate Judges and their authority have evolved from the brief provision in the U.S. Judiciary Act of 1793, discussed in chapter two, allowing District Courts to appoint "discreet persons learned in the law" to set bail in cases involving federal crimes. This was due basically to the difficulties of travel in late eighteenth-century America, especially on the frontiers. Since 1898, Congress has constantly added to the duties that District Courts could direct to be performed by those judicial assistants, to whom the 1793 judicial act initially gave no title, who were soon thereafter called Circuit Court commissioners or simply commissioners, then U.S. Commissioners, then most recently U.S. Magistrates and U.S. Magistrate Judges. In the beginning of federal courts, Circuit Court commissioners were few, but, inevitably, as their duties increased, so did their number. Congress allowed each judicial district's old Circuit Court to appoint as many commissioners as the circuit judges deemed necessary, and so their numbers naturally grew over time. In 1878, for example, there were nearly two thousand commissioners nationally, all of them part-time.[1]

During his twenty-three years on the bench, Judge Withey and the district's circuit judges appointed more than seventy Circuit Court commissioners. Just during the first two years of the Western District of Michigan, 1863 and 1864, they appointed nineteen Circuit Court commissioners, who lived in thirteen locations in the western Lower Peninsula.[2] The total number of appointees grew to twenty-two by 1872, including one at Escanaba, the first commissioner in the Upper Peninsula.[3] When Congress reallocated all of the Upper Peninsula to the Western District in June 1878, Judge Withey recognized the growing population of the Upper Peninsula and appointed Circuit Court commissioners in Marquette, Sault Ste. Marie, Ironwood, Houghton, and Newberry. Withey's successor, Judge Severens, appointed about twenty Circuit Court commissioners from the beginning of his tenure in May 1886 through the end of the Circuit Court commissioner system in May 1896. In all, the available records of the Western District identify almost one hundred Circuit Court commissioners who were appointed between 1863 and 1895, spread throughout the Western District from St. Joseph to Marquette and from Ironwood to Sault Ste. Marie.[4]

During the years the Circuit Court commissioner system was in effect, from 1793 to 1896, commissioners were compensated by fees calculated on what specific act the commissioner performed. The fees were paid in civil cases by the litigants and in criminal matters by the United States, based on rates established by the laws of the state in which the commissioner was appointed, rather than by a single federal law. From those fees, commissioners had to pay all of their expenses related to their work as commissioner, so it is not surprising that some commissioners inflated the fees they charged. While private litigants might be expected to keep track of the fees they were charged, apparently the United States did not always do so. As one author has noted, "Being compensated on a fee basis, many commissioners were prone to issue complaints and hold preliminary examinations at the slightest real, imagined, or contrived violation of a federal law. . . . Apparently, it was a common practice for commissioners, Deputy Marshals, and informer-witnesses to act in collusion in order to submit the highest possible fee bills."[5]

Another criticism of the Circuit Court commissioner system was that many commissioners lacked legal training. Apparently, the appointing judges did not equate "discreet persons learned in the law" with attorneys or with membership in the bar. Although some commissioners were attorneys, either in private practice or officers of federal or state governments, most were not. This became a growing problem as Congress slowly increased their duties to include enforcing the Fugitive Slave Act before the Civil War, enforcing the 1866 Civil Rights Act after the war, adjusting seamen's wage disputes, conducting extradition hearings under the Chinese Exclusion Acts, and enforcing other federal laws such as internal revenue laws, federal wildlife and game laws, and migratory bird treaties.[6]

In the Western District, as throughout the system, Circuit Court commissioners usually included the clerks of the U.S. District and Circuit Courts as well as clerks of state or local courts. Clerks of the District and Circuit Courts of the Western District, who also served as Circuit Court commissioners, included Isaac H. Parrish, Chester B. Hinsdill, Henry M. Hinsdill, and Charles L. Fitch. Judge Withey appointed Isaac Parrish in 1863 as one of the Western District's first Circuit Court commissioners, and in 1865, when Withey appointed Parrish as the clerk of both the District and Circuit Courts for the Western District, Parrish kept his commissioner appointment as well. From 1875 to 1878, Chester B. Hinsdill, Judge Withey's brother-in-law, who had been a senior commissary officer in General Sherman's army, also served as clerk for both the District Court and the Circuit Court. When the clerkships were separated in 1878, the judge appointed Chester Hinsdill to be the clerk of the District Court and Chester's brother Henry Hinsdill to be the clerk of the Circuit Court. Withey also appointed both men Circuit Court commissioners. Other prominent Circuit Court commissioners included John W. Stone of Allegan County, who later served in Congress and as a justice of the Michigan Supreme Court, and Loyal E. Knappen of Hastings in Barry County, who would be appointed to the bench of the U.S. District Court in 1906 and to the bench of the Sixth Circuit Court of Appeals in 1910.

U.S. Commissioners

Throughout the existence of the Circuit Court commissioner system, critics alleged that the sheer number of circuit commissioners, their lack of legal qualifications and knowledge, and the unregulated fee system were an invitation to fraud and injustice.[7] Responding to this criticism, in May 1896, Congress added a provision in that year's appropriations for the Justice Department that abolished the office of circuit commissioner: "The terms of office of all commissioners of the Circuit Courts heretofore appointed shall expire on the thirtieth day of June, eighteen hundred and ninety-seven; and such office shall on that day cease to exist."[8]

In the place of Circuit Court commissioners, Congress ordered each District Court—not the Circuit Court—"to appoint such number of persons, to be known as United States commissioners, at such places in the district as may be designated by the District Court, which United States commissioners shall have the same powers and perform the same duties as are now imposed upon commissioners of the Circuit Courts." Congress also specified that U.S. Commissioners were to be appointed for a term of four years, albeit a tenure terminable by the District Court at any time. Congress also prohibited federal employees from holding the position of U.S. Commissioner,[9] with the exception of court clerks and deputy clerks who had obtained the approval of the U.S. Attorney General. Despite concerns about Circuit Court commissioners who were not attorneys, Congress did not require that U.S. Commissioners be licensed attorneys but just that they be "learned in the law." A great many of the U.S. Commissioners appointed in the system's early years were not licensed attorneys.

Like Circuit Court commissioners, U.S. Commissioners were compensated through fees paid by the United States in criminal cases and by litigants in civil cases. However, the rate chargeable for each type of act or service performed by a commissioner was no longer set by each state but was established in a congressionally approved, uniform fee schedule. Because Congress did not raise the amount of the fees for fifty years, many U.S. Commissioners, the vast majority of whom were nonattorney part-timers in smaller locations, struggled financially. On the other hand, during Prohibition, this schedule temporarily provided a very few busy U.S. Commissioners in big cities with income far exceeding that of District Judges. In response, Congress, which was not yet ready to pay U.S. Commissioners a salary, instead imposed on them an income ceiling. The low fees and income ceiling did allow Congress to achieve one of its goals, reducing the total number of U.S. Commissioners nationwide as many of them resigned to pursue better sources of income. In the Western District, the number of commissioners declined from forty-six

Circuit Court commissioners in office in 1891, to seventeen U.S. Commissioners in office in 1902, and eleven U.S. Commissioners in office in 1917.[10]

The reforms of 1896 made some improvements in keeping the system honest and frugal, but they did not really improve what was supposed to be the commissioners' main goal, assisting the Article III judges in carrying out their judicial duties. Toward the middle of the twentieth century, District Judges complained that the duties to be performed by U.S. Commissioners, acting independently at great distances from the seat of the District Court, might have been necessary when travel was slow and difficult, but modern transportation and the telephone and telegraph made those concerns no longer relevant. In 1942, the Administrative Office of the U.S. Courts produced a study of the U.S. Commissioner system that noted that the fixed fee rates, established in 1896 and not raised since, deterred able candidates, particularly successful attorneys, leaving the courts with a corps of U.S. Commissioners who were not lawyers and who, with the best intentions, lacked the knowledge and skills to perform the increasingly complex tasks that would assist the District Courts. Still, Congress was not ready to install a salary system for U.S. Commissioners, although, in 1946, Congress did raise the fees in the schedule.

The question of whether and how to reform the U.S. Commissioner system percolated for another two decades, but by 1966 Congress could no longer ignore that the system's critics were correct and had to concede that too many U.S. Commissioners were not capable of providing the assistance that the District Judges needed. Of the 701 U.S. Commissioners in office that year, 180 were not practicing attorneys, 17 were clerks or deputy clerks, and only 16 were either full-time or listed no other profession. Most of those U.S. Commissioners were underworked, so that only seventy-two of them had earned more than $3,000 in fees (about $23,000 in 2017 dollars) in each of the three previous years. On the other hand, because Congress had capped their annual fee income at $10,500, commissioners in some busy districts were overworked and underpaid.[11] There were no nationwide criteria or procedures for their appointment, and their restricted authority limited their ability to reduce District Judges' caseloads. The judges of some Article III courts resisted any more piecemeal changes to the system because their experience with commissioners had been so bad that the District Judges had preferred to perform the commissioners' duties themselves. The District Judges of the Eastern District of Michigan had experienced so many problems with its U.S. Commissioners, including conspiring with criminal defense attorneys in setting bail, that the court had fired all of its commissioners in 1946 and instituted a plan for releasing most arraigned criminal defendants on their own recognizance. At congressional hearings on changing the commissioner system again, the Eastern District's Chief District Judge, Theodore Levin, begged Congress to send him more District Judges instead.

U.S. Magistrates and U.S. Magistrate Judges

Congress finally did act to "reform the first echelon of the Federal judiciary" by starting from scratch once more with the Federal Magistrates Act of 1968, subtitled "An Act to abolish the office of United States commissioner, to establish in place thereof within the judicial branch of the Government the office of United States magistrate, and for other purposes."[12] As the subtitle indicates, the 1968 Act abolished the U.S. Commissioner system and fired all U.S. Commissioners as of July 1, 1971, although many were reappointed as U.S. Magistrates. Unlike U.S. Commissioners, U.S. Magistrates were required to be attorneys with at least five years' experience and to be members of their state bar. They were also to be paid a salary.

Other major changes contained in the 1968 Act dealt with the appointment of U.S. Magistrates. Unlike previous laws that allowed each Circuit or District Court to decide how many commissioners to appoint, Congress gave the Judicial Conference of the United States[13] the authority to set the number of magistrate positions in each district based on studies of need conducted for the judicial conference. In 1970, the conference authorized 82 full-time and 449 part-time positions nationally. Once the judicial conference has allocated to a district its authorized number of magistrates, the district's active District Judges (i.e., excluding senior judges) appoint magistrates, by a majority vote, from a list of candidates vetted by a committee composed of both attorneys and lay people. Under the 1968 Act, full-time magistrates serve terms of eight years, while part-time magistrates serve a four-year term. Both full-time and part-time appointments can be renewed. Over the years, part-time appointments have been phased out except where needed, such as in a national park where a small docket does not justify a full-time salary. By 2014, the judicial conference had reversed the balance of part- and full-time positions to 531 full-time and 40 part-time magistrates.

Most districts courts, including the District Court for the Western District of Michigan, were happy for the assistance of magistrates and allowed them to exercise the full powers granted to them by Congress. Those powers included, in addition to the powers previously assigned to U.S. Commissioners, the authority to conduct pretrial and discovery proceedings, review habeas corpus petitions, and act as special masters. In 1976 and 1979, Congress expanded the magistrates' authority further to include trying misdemeanor criminal cases and civil cases with the consent of the parties.

Predictably, judges in a few districts, including the Eastern District of Michigan, were still leery of the U.S. Magistrates. Some of the Eastern District's judges treated the magistrates as lowly employees and denied them every aspect of judicial status, such as wearing robes, calling their office their chambers, or even using the judges' elevator in the Detroit federal courthouse. This was the very opposite of the treatment received by magistrates in the Western District. In 1990, after years of debate, Congress decided to emphasize the importance of the magistrates' judicial role by officially changing their title from U.S. Magistrate to U.S. Magistrate Judge.

One aspect of the 1968 Act raised a serious constitutional question. The Act provided that a majority of a district's judges could assign to magistrates "additional duties as are not inconsistent with the Constitution and laws of the United States." Federal courts differed as to just what those "additional duties" could be without violating Article III of the Constitution. Amid general confusion on this issue, Congress amended the Magistrates' Act in 1976[14] and 1979[15] to specify that a District Court could designate magistrates to preside over civil trials if the parties consented.

Some Cases of a U.S. Magistrate Judge

Hugh W. Brenneman, Jr. was a U.S. Magistrate Judge for the Western District of Michigan from 1980 until he retired in July 2015. Examples of his involvement in a variety of cases show the breadth of duties that can be assigned to a Magistrate Judge.

Writs of Habeas Corpus

LARRY PAT SOUTER V. KURT JONES, WARDEN

Absent some attachment to a federal context, murders are prosecuted in state courts under state law. However, a murder case can come before a U.S. District Court via a petition for a writ of habeas corpus, known as "the great writ," filed by a person in the custody of a federal, state, or local government to challenge the legality of his or her detention. The most common type of petition for a writ is one filed by a convicted criminal, serving a sentence in a state prison, who asks the District Court to throw out a judgment of guilty as violating the U.S. Constitution. The one thing all prisoners have is time, and many of them use that time to file one or more petitions for habeas corpus. The federal courts seldom grant such a writ, and most petitions are rejected, usually because today most state courts are well able to try a criminal case without violating a defendant's federal constitutional rights. However, the importance of a District Court's reviewing all petitions seriously cannot be overstated, as one petition in particular proves.

Ms. Kristy Ringler was killed on August 25, 1979. At 3 a.m., she was found lying in the middle of a rural road in Newaygo County, which is north of Grand Rapids, with a gash on her head. She died later that morning from her injuries. The last person known to have seen Kristy alive was Larry Pat Souter, whom she had met at a bar earlier in the evening, and with whom she had partied afterward at a trailer. Larry told the county sheriff's investigators that he had last seen Kristy when she began walking home by herself. Her body was found only nine hundred feet from the trailer. A forensic pathologist retained by the sheriff who examined Kristy's body stated his belief that Kristy's injuries were consistent with a vehicle collision rather than a homicide. The state police crime laboratory reported that glass particles found in and around the wound and the body were inconsistent with automobile headlight glass. Nor were they brown, the color of the pint-sized Canadian Club whiskey bottle that Larry told the investigators he was carrying that night and which they recovered nearby. On the bottle, investigators did find a trace of type A blood, Kristy's type, but it was also Larry's type and the type of 43 percent of Americans. Larry showed the police a cut on his hand and explained that it had been caused by a jagged doorknob earlier in the evening. During the investigation, the sheriff inadvertently cut his own hand on the same doorknob. Larry had no other blood on his clothes or boots, and, significantly, the sheriff reported that at that time police noted that Kristy also did not have much blood on her. With little evidence to continue, the police put the file away, Kristy's family grieved and buried her, and there the matter stood for four years.

In 1983, a detective suggested to the county medical examiner (not the forensic examiner who had examined the body) that the cut on Kristy's head could have been caused by a sharp-edged bottom of the whiskey bottle. Even though experts had ruled out the brown bottle as a source of the glass because

of the glass color, the examiner agreed with the detective, but the County Prosecutor declined to charge Larry. The police made no further investigation until 1991, twelve years after Kristy's death, when a newly elected sheriff, who had
committed his office to reviewing unsolved homicides, revived the case. The
sheriff had no new evidence, but he convinced the county medical examiner
to issue a second, stronger report, which concluded that Kristy's injuries had
indeed been caused by the sharp edge of Larry's whiskey bottle. Larry was arrested, tried, and, on March 13, 1992, convicted of second-degree murder. The
trial judge sentenced him to a term of twenty to sixty years' imprisonment.

While Larry was in prison, he and his appellate attorney, John Smietanka,
unsuccessfully exhausted his state court appellate remedies.[16] Then, on January 20, 2002, ten years after Larry's conviction, Smietanka filed, on Larry's
behalf, a petition in the U.S. District Court for the Western District of Michigan, asking that the court issue to the warden of the prison a writ of habeas
corpus. Under the court's customary procedures, Magistrate Judges review
habeas petitions and make recommendations to the District Judge assigned
to the case. Larry's petition went to Magistrate Judge Hugh W. Brenneman,
Jr. for review.

The state of Michigan, representing the warden, moved for summary judgment on the basis that Larry's petition was barred by the federal one-year
statute of limitations applicable to habeas actions. In his report and recommendation to the District Judge, Brenneman held that, although Larry had
failed to file his petition on time, he had demonstrated credible new evidence
of his actual innocence that was sufficient for the purpose of the rarely used
doctrine of equitable tolling. Tolling allows a judge to avoid the bar of a limitations period that has already expired in the interests of justice and to allow
the court to reach the merits of the claim. Larry's new evidence included the
facts that the whiskey bottle did not have any sharp edges and that, contrary
to the prosecutor's claim at trial that Kristy had no meaningful amount of
blood on her when found, in fact Kristy's body was covered with blood while
Larry had no blood on him that night. Also, several of the prosecution's scientific witnesses at trial submitted affidavits to the federal court in which they
backtracked on their testimony. Judge Brenneman specifically found that Larry's new evidence "chip[s] away at the rather slim circumstantial evidence
upon which the petitioner was convicted."

Although the District Judge rejected Brenneman's recommendation to
grant equitable tolling, the persistent Smietanka appealed the District Court's

decision. On January 18, 2005, almost thirteen years after Larry went to prison, the Sixth Circuit Court of Appeals adopted that recommendation and reversed the District Court's decision.[17] The Sixth Circuit found Larry's case to be that rare, if not unique, case where the possible showing of actual innocence was sufficient to justify equitable tolling. The appellate court remanded the case to the District Court to decide the legal merits of Larry's petition, which could have resulted in granting him a new trial.

Then a most fortuitous thing happened. After *The Grand Rapids Press* ran an article about the Sixth Circuit's groundbreaking decision, a woman came forward to say that she thought that her father might have hit Kristy with the side mirror of his mobile home on the road on that night a quarter of a century earlier. She also said that she had told the Newaygo County authorities her information at the time of Kristy's death. Investigators for Larry tracked down an identical old vehicle in a Florida junk yard, and they discovered that its side mirror was at the exact height to cause Kristy's head wound. Furthermore, Freedom of Information Act requests to Newaygo County turned up evidence that had been withheld from Larry's attorney before trial as well as instances of bad evidence-handling procedures. Larry's conviction was ultimately set aside, and he was released from prison in 2005. The county's liability insurer, after mediation, agreed to pay Larry substantial damages. The avenue of relief provided by the federal courts had well served both Larry and the ends of truth and justice.

BERGHUIS, WARDEN V. SMITH

Sometimes a much less dramatic case can take a Magistrate Judge's work to the U.S. Supreme Court. In 2010, the Supreme Court reversed a decision by the Sixth Circuit and confirmed Judge Brenneman's interpretation of a controversial provision in a federal statute. That provision of the Antiterrorism and Effective Death Penalty Act of 1996[18] prohibits a federal court from granting habeas relief to a state prisoner unless the state court's adjudication "resulted in a decision that was contrary to, or involved an unreasonable application of, clearly established Federal law, as determined by the Supreme Court of the United States." In this case, Judge Brenneman had to recommend to the District Judge whether to grant a writ of habeas corpus involving a claim that Michigan courts had violated a petitioner's Sixth Amendment right to an impartial jury drawn by a fair cross section of the community under criteria determined by the Supreme Court in 1975 and 1979.[19]

The petitioner, Diapolis Smith, was an African American man who was convicted in 1993 of second-degree murder and felony firearms possession by an all-white jury in Kent County Circuit Court; the judge sentenced him to life in prison with the possibility of parole. At that time, African Americans constituted 7.8 percent of Kent County's jury-eligible population and 6 percent of the pool from which potential jurors were drawn. Of the venire panel of sixty to one hundred persons, "at most" three of them were African American. Smith's attorneys raised the Sixth Amendment issue unsuccessfully in the circuit court. The attorneys argued that the county's policy for filling the juror requirements for its circuit court and its twelve district courts, sending prospective jurors to the district courts first and only after that to the circuit court, "siphoned" African American jurors from the circuit court's venire panels. The trial court considered two statistical tools, absolute disparity and comparative disparity, as well as expert testimony, and concluded that African Americans were indeed underrepresented in Kent County venires.[20] However, the court denied Smith's objection because there was insufficient evidence that the jury procedure systematically excluded African Americans. The Michigan Court of Appeals held that the county's juror allocation system at Smith's trial did result in underrepresenting African American jurors and reversed the trial court's decision. The Michigan Supreme Court reversed the court of appeals and held that Smith had not established a prima facie violation of the Sixth Amendment.[21]

In 2003, Smith petitioned the U.S. District Court for the Western District of Michigan for a writ of habeas corpus, raising twelve issues including the violation of his Sixth Amendment right. The petition was assigned to Judge Brenneman, who prepared a lengthy report and recommendation concluding that some issues were procedurally defective and, therefore, not subject to federal habeas review and that the remaining issues were without merit. As to the Sixth Amendment issue, Judge Brenneman concluded that the decision of the Michigan Supreme Court, that Smith had not satisfied the criteria established by the U.S. Supreme Court in *Duren*,[22] was not unreasonable and that, therefore, the federal courts could not grant Smith habeas relief.

District Judge Quist accepted Judge Brenneman's recommendation on that issue and on the other eleven issues, and denied Smith's petition.[23] On appeal, the Sixth Circuit reversed Quist's decision, remanded the case, and directed the District Court to "order Smith's release from state custody unless the state of Michigan commences a new trial within 180 days of this order."

The Sixth Circuit ruled that Smith satisfied the prima facie case test of *Duren* because the evidence did establish that the underrepresentation of African Americans was unfair and unreasonable and that he did establish systematic exclusion of African Americans by the district-court-first rule.

The U.S. Supreme Court granted certiorari and unanimously reversed the decision of the Sixth Circuit, vindicating Judge Quist's reliance on the analysis by Judge Brenneman. In an opinion by Justice Ginsburg, the Court held that "[t]he Sixth Circuit erred in ruling that the Michigan Supreme Court's decision 'involv[ed] an unreasonable application o[f] clearly established federal law.'"[24]

International Judicial Assistance

In a 1989 case, Magistrate Judge Brenneman, then still titled a U.S. Magistrate, found himself delving in the area of international comity.[25] The case involved a request from a court in the Federal Republic of Germany, the former West Germany, for "judicial assistance" in obtaining a blood sample from a Rick Brunke, a resident of the Western District of Michigan, for use in a paternity case pending in the Local Court of Pforzheim, a city in the West German state of Baden-Wurttemberg. Brunke had received notice of the paternity action and request for a blood sample in 1985, but he had managed to avoid providing the sample for more than three years. Finally, the German authorities asked via a "letter rogatory," for help from the U.S. government. In March 1989, the United States petitioned the District Court for the Western District of Michigan for an order directing the putative father to submit to the extraction of a blood sample for use in the paternity action. The petition was assigned to District Judge Gibson who appointed Magistrate Judge Brenneman a "commissioner" to render judicial assistance. Brunke delayed proceedings again, and it was not until November 1989 that he appeared for a hearing on the request. The only issues in question were whether Brenneman had discretion to grant or deny the petition (the United States argued that he was required to grant it), and whether the court should decline to enter the order because of its lack of power to enforce such an order by contempt. Brenneman held that the undisputed discretionary power of the District Court, the language of the court order appointing him as commissioner, and his status as a judicial officer of the court meant that he had discretion to either grant or deny the petition. Furthermore, he noted: "The appropriateness of a particular type of sanction . . . is not determinative of whether the order should issue." The court granted the relief requested by the German authorities.

The Magistrates and Magistrate Judges of the Western District

The Western District of Michigan has had a total of thirteen magistrates and Magistrate Judges under the 1968 Act. In July 1971, Chief Judge Fox and Judge Engel appointed two of the Western District's veteran U.S. Commissioners as the court's first two part-time U.S. Magistrates, Stephen W. Karr in Grand Rapids and Lloyd R. C. Fayling in Kalamazoo. In 1972, the same District Judges appointed two additional part-time magistrates, John R. Weber in Marquette and Stuart D. Hubbell in Traverse City. Magistrates Fayling, Weber, and Hubbell served the court for many years, but because of their location, the small amount of work in their assigned areas, and their part-time status, they remained useful but peripheral to the District Court's operations. The role of the magistrates in those operations was covered, for the most part, by the court's appointment of full-time U.S. Magistrates.

On October 2, 1973, Magistrate Karr was reappointed as the Western District's first full-time U.S. Magistrate, based in Grand Rapids. On April 1, 1980, the District Court appointed Hugh W. Brenneman, Jr. as the district's second full-time magistrate, also based in Grand Rapids. Doyle A. Rowland was appointed as a part-time magistrate for Kalamazoo on July 23, 1984, and he was reappointed as a full-time magistrate on January 16, 1985; he was then reappointed for another eight-year term in 1993. Magistrate Karr retired before the name change to Magistrate Judge, but both Brenneman and Rowland became Magistrate Judges in 1990. Rowland died in February 2000 in an automobile accident, and in October 2000 he was replaced by Ellen S. Carmody, the court's first female Magistrate Judge. Carmody retired in November 2019 and she was succeeded by Sally J. Berens. On January 11, 1988, Timothy P. Greeley succeeded Magistrate Weber in Marquette, the last appointment of a part-time magistrate in the Western District. Magistrate Greeley received a full-time appointment in December 1989 and became a Magistrate Judge in 1990. Greeley retired in March 2019, and he was succeeded by Maarten Vermaat. Two weeks after Greeley's first appointment, on January 28, 1988, the District Court appointed Joseph G. Scoville as a full-time magistrate assigned to Grand Rapids. Magistrate Scoville also became a Magistrate Judge in 1990. He retired in July 2014, after twenty-six years with the court, and he was succeeded by Phillip J. Green. Magistrate Judge Brenneman retired a year later, on July 31, 2015, after thirty-five years of service, and was succeeded by Magistrate Judge Ray Kent. In 2020, the Western District of Michigan has four Magistrate Judges. Three of them, Judges Green, Kent, and Berens, have their chambers in the Gerald R. Ford Federal Building and Courthouse in Grand Rapids. Judge Vermaat has his chambers in the U.S. Post Office and Courthouse in Marquette.

U.S. Magistrate Stephen W. Karr

On July 20, 1971, Stephen W. Karr became the first U.S. Magistrate appointed to the District Court for the Western District of Michigan. He had earlier also been the District Court's first law clerk. As a magistrate, he demonstrated the intelligence and the leadership qualities that were a hallmark of his life. Born on the Greek island of Samos on June 20, 1919, Judge Karr emigrated to the United States with his parents, William and Angeline Karr, in 1920. He won a Regents Scholarship to the University of Michigan, graduated from the literary college in 1941, and then entered the law school. World War II interrupted his education. He initially trained as an artillery officer, but he was recruited by the Office of Strategic Services (OSS) to join guerillas in Greece. However, the British intelligence services claimed a monopoly on running guerillas in occupied Greece, and Judge Karr was sent instead to run an OSS training base in Ceylon (now Sri Lanka) where he trained Asian volunteers to conduct espionage, intelligence, and sabotage missions in their occupied homelands. He rose to the rank of major, and he was awarded the Santimala (Peace) Medal by the King of Siam (Thailand) for his service. After the war, he returned to Ann Arbor and law school, graduating in 1947. He ultimately became a full colonel in the U.S. Army Reserves where he served as a military judge.

After graduation, Judge Karr was hired by District Judge Raymond Starr of the Western District in Grand Rapids to be the district's first law clerk. The position of law clerk in the federal courts began in 1882 when Horace Gray became a Justice of the U.S. Supreme Court and hired young lawyers to spend a year or two doing legal research, writing draft opinions, and any other legal or administrative tasks requested. Gray paid his law clerks himself, but the other Justices soon saw the value of a law clerk. In 1919 Congress agreed to pay for one clerk for each Justice, and, in 1930 and 1936, Congress extended the position to the judges of the Courts of Appeal and District Courts as well. However, the legislators did not for some years appropriate money to pay district court law clerks, so the Western District (meaning its sole judge) could not hire a law clerk until it hired Karr in 1947. Judge Starr and law clerk Karr proved to be a strong team, and during Karr's two and a half years as law clerk, he and Judge Starr were never reversed by the Sixth Circuit.

In 1950, Karr finished his clerkship and began a private practice in Grand Rapids specializing in corporate, bankruptcy, and estate law. He also served as a U.S. Commissioner from 1950 until 1971 when the Sixth Circuit finally authorized the Western District of Michigan to appoint the district's first two U.S. Magistrates, both part-time. On July 20, 1971, the District Court appointed Karr to be its first U.S. Magistrate, and on July 26 the court named Lloyd Fayling of Kalamazoo to be its second U.S. Magistrate. In 1973, the Western District was authorized to appoint a full-time U.S. Magistrate, and on October 2, 1973, the District Court appointed Karr to that full-time position, which he held until he retired on December 31, 1987.

Upon his retirement, Judge Karr was given the Service to the Profession Award by the Western Michigan Chapter of the Federal Bar Association for his service in the improvement of the administration of justice in the federal courts. As a pioneer magistrate, Judge Karr was instrumental in establishing the status of magistrates in the District Court for the Western District of Michigan and beyond. As Magistrate Judge Hugh W. Brenneman, Jr., the district's second full-time magistrate, remembered, "Questions about a Magistrate Judge's duties, not to mention whether a Magistrate Judge should be accorded the indicia of his or her office, have never been serious issues in the Western District of Michigan. This was primarily due to one man. Steve's prudent and deliberate approach to asserting the jurisdiction of his office, coupled with his advice and good counsel to the court, allowed the role of the Magistrate Judge in Western Michigan to become firmly rooted and evolve over time."[26] As another author wrote: "[Steve Karr] always had an extraordinary reputation with the judges and attorneys within the district as an extremely knowledgeable, fair, and competent judicial officer. . . . He developed such a reputation for expertise . . . that magistrates in other districts mentioned his name as someone who was able to give advice to new magistrates throughout the circuit. In fact, because of the reputation he earned both magistrates and judges . . . sought his advice on how to . . . handle legal matters."[27] Judge Karr's reputation spread to other districts as well, helping to set standards for efficient and amicable relationships between district judges and their magistrates.

Magistrate Karr died on September 28, 2007, at the age of eighty-eight, survived by his wife of fifty-seven years, Bette L. Karr.

U.S. Magistrate Judge Hugh Warren Brenneman, Jr.

U.S. Magistrate Judge Hugh Warren Brenneman, Jr. retired on July 31, 2015, after thirty-five years of service to the District Court, the longest serving Magistrate Judge in the District Court for the Western District of Michigan. Judge Brenneman was born on July 4, 1945, in Lansing, Michigan, the son of Hugh and June (Redman) Brenneman. He grew up in East Lansing where he attended high school. He graduated from Alma College (BA, 1967) and from the University of Michigan Law School (JD, 1970). While in law school, he obtained a commission as an officer in the U.S. Army through the Reserve Officers Training Corps. After being admitted to the State Bar of Michigan, he worked as a law clerk for the Hon. Marvin J. Salmon in Michigan's Thirtieth Judicial Circuit Court in Lansing.

In 1971, Brenneman was called to active duty and served nearly four years as a captain in the Army's Judge Advocate General's Corps. After attending military law school at the University of Virginia, he was stationed at Aberdeen Proving Grounds, Maryland, where he variously served as a legal assistance officer, defense counsel, and prosecutor, before being promoted to Chief, Military Justice. He later transferred to the Army's Legal Services Agency in Fall's Church, Virginia, where he was an appellate attorney handling appeals from courts-martial before the military appellate courts. Brenneman's later appointment to the federal bench marked the last time all of the sitting full-time judges in the Western District—circuit, district, magistrate, and bankruptcy—had served on active duty in the U.S. military.

After his discharge in 1974, Brenneman became one of four Assistant U.S. Attorneys in the U.S. Attorney's Office in the Western District of Michigan in Grand Rapids. In an office that had only four assistants represent the United States throughout Michigan's western Lower Peninsula and its entire Upper Peninsula, the duties of each assistant ran the gamut from prosecuting federal crimes, to defending the United States in civil actions, to appearing in Bankruptcy Court.

Brenneman left the office in 1977 to enter private practice with the law firm of Bergstrom, Slykhouse & Shaw PC, in Grand Rapids, where he stayed for three years in a civil litigation and criminal defense practice. In August 1978, he led the way in creating a chapter of the Federal Bar Association in west

Michigan. As discussed in chapter 11, the new organization was designed to provide a vehicle for communication between the expanding federal court and the attorneys who would be practicing in it. Brenneman chaired the organizing committee and later became the first president of the chapter. In order to give the chapter credibility as a new entity, it was formed under the auspices of the Federal Bar Association, an organization that was at that time composed largely of attorneys employed by the federal government in Washington, D.C.

In 1980, the Western District received a second full-time position for a U.S. Magistrate. Congress added that position because it had also created the two new district judgeships for the district. Using for the first time the merit selection process envisioned by the Federal Magistrate Act, the District Court selected Brenneman from a large number of attorneys. The procedure required a panel of private attorneys from within the district to pare down the list of applicants and to send a manageable number to the court for personal interviews. On April 1, 1980, Brenneman entered the position of full-time U.S. Magistrate. In 1990, Congress changed the title of the position, and Brenneman became one of the Western District's first U.S. Magistrate Judges. Although he has retired from his magisterial duties, Judge Brenneman has remained very active as the inaugural president and trustee of the court's historical society and as the court historian. Brenneman is also a founding master and past president of the Gerald R. Ford Chapter of the American Inns of Court in Grand Rapids.

U.S. Magistrate Judge Doyle A. Rowland

Doyle A. Rowland was born in Northville, Michigan. He graduated from Eastern Michigan University in 1964 with a bachelor of science degree and from the Detroit College of Law in 1967. From 1976 through 1980, he served as Midland County Prosecuting Attorney. He also served as Asst. City Attorney for Midland, and he served a term as president of the Midland County Bar Association. On July 23, 1984, he was appointed as a part-time magistrate for the U.S. District Court for the Western District of Michigan. On January 16, 1985, he was appointed a full-time magistrate assigned to the federal courthouse in Kalamazoo. In 1990, Congress changed the magistrates' title, and Rowland and the other magistrates became Magistrate Judges.

The lack of a resident federal prosecutor and of adequate detention or court facilities in the Kalamazoo courthouse made it difficult for Rowland to handle criminal cases, so he focused instead on undertaking a variety of civil matters. District Judge Richard Enslen, who presided in Kalamazoo, welcomed Rowland and made him his right-hand man, granting Rowland the autonomy and responsibility to monitor aspects of Enslen's Kalamazoo civil docket so that Rowland could efficiently process civil litigation before trial. He also gave Rowland authority to act in an area that was one of the judge's great interests, alternative dispute resolution in the civil cases pending in Kalamazoo. Rowland's successful involvement in ADR and in case management, motion practice, and traditional settlement proceedings served as an example that other District Judges of the Western District adopted, changing significantly how the court used Magistrate Judges in managing their own dockets.

Judge Rowland died in a tragic two-car automobile accident on February 29, 2000, when his car was broadsided and he was ejected through the front windshield. He was pronounced dead at the scene. He was survived by his wife, Carol Rowland, and their children, Matt and Andrew.

U.S. Magistrate Judge Timothy P. Greeley

Timothy P. Greeley was born on March 13, 1954, in Battle Creek, Michigan, and he grew up in Kalamazoo. He graduated from Kalamazoo Central High School in 1972, Western Michigan University in 1976, and Wayne State University Law School, magna cum laude, in 1980. After graduation from law school, he served for two years as a law clerk for District Judge Philip Pratt of the U.S. District Court for the Eastern District of Michigan. He then joined the Lansing law firm of Foster, Swift, Collins and Coey in Lansing.

In the mid-1980s, the District Court for the Western District, led by then Chief Judge Hillman, concluded that the court needed to have a greater federal judicial presence in the Northern Division. Until then, there had never been a resident District Judge in either of the federal courthouses in the Upper Peninsula. Judges traveled from the Lower Peninsula to hold terms of court and then returned home. Accordingly, the position for a part-time magistrate was created in 1987, and in January 1988 Timothy P. Greeley was appointed a part-time U.S. Magistrate for the court's Northern Division in Marquette. As a practical matter, Greeley was doing the job of a full-time magistrate when the position finally became full-time in December 1989. As with the other magistrates serving in 1990, Greeley's title was changed to U.S. Magistrate Judge. He continued in that position until March 15, 2019, when he retired and was succeeded in the Northern Division by new U.S. Magistrate Judge Maarten Vermaat.

The civil docket in the Northern Division is heavily weighted toward prisoner civil rights cases and habeas corpus cases and is well suited for a resident Magistrate Judge. In 1988, there was no U.S. Attorney's office in the Northern Division. Since then, three Assistant U.S. Attorneys and an Assistant Federal Public Defender have been stationed in Marquette. The criminal docket of the Northern Division is primarily made up of controlled substance cases, felony firearm cases, and cases originating within Indian country. Unlike most federal District Courts, the Northern Division has a large number of domestic violence and sexual assault cases in the Upper Peninsula's extensive Indian country. The presence of federal law enforcement in the Upper Peninsula has grown significantly since 1988. The Magistrate Judge in the Northern Division performs a substantial amount of civil case management and handles much of the criminal docket up through guilty-plea proceedings or final pretrial conferences.

U.S. Magistrate Judge Joseph G. Scoville

Joseph G. Scoville was born in Chicago, Illinois, on July 4, 1949, the first of three children of Joseph and Gloria (Silvestri) Scoville. His father was a lawyer who usually worked as a sole practitioner for small clients and who was a veteran of four years in the Pacific theater during the Second World War. Judge Scoville grew up in a very close family including his grandparents who had emigrated from Italy. He attended Catholic schools and graduated from Chicago's St. Patrick High School. After graduation, he decided to go east for college and was admitted to Michigan State University where he majored in pre-law. At MSU, he also met his future wife, Margaret, who was from Detroit. He graduated from MSU in 1971 with high honors and Phi Beta Kappa. He was accepted at the University of Michigan Law School and received a partial scholarship. He joined the Michigan Law Review, but he decided to drop it, which upset his father. He graduated in 1974 with the juris doctor degree, magna cum laude, and he moved back to Chicago with his wife to practice law at the law firm McDermott, Will & Emery. After two years, they decided to leave Chicago because Mrs. Scoville did not like living there, so in 1976 they moved to Grand Rapids where Judge Scoville had an offer to join one of the city's premier law firms, Warner, Norcross & Judd. He practiced in that firm as an associate and a partner for twelve years as a litigator. Among his many cases of public importance, he successfully argued an appeal to the

U.S. Supreme Court on an issue of federal preemption in which he obtained a unanimous reversal.[28]

In January 1988, Judge Scoville was appointed a U.S. Magistrate for the Western District. Like the court's other full-time magistrates, his title became Magistrate Judge in 1990. He thinks that he won the appointment as U.S. Magistrate through his contacts with the federal courts, his efforts as a member of the board and past president of the local chapter of the Federal Bar Association, and his work on Judge Hillman's advocacy education classes. He applied for the position at the suggestion of Magistrate Brenneman when Magistrate Karr retired at the age of sixty-eight. There were ninety-five applicants to replace Karr, and Scoville was chosen for the final list of ten candidates by a nominating committee independent of the District Court, and the District Court chose him from that list. He believes that his candidacy was helped by the fact that he was not political and was not viewed as a Republican or a Democrat.

On his first day of work as a Magistrate, January 27, 1988, he took over Magistrate Karr's chambers, which were tiny and meant for the old commissioners. He did not get any training for his position until the summer of 1988 when he attended the magistrates' "baby judge school" in Washington, D.C. Nevertheless, he loved his job and continued to love it during his twenty-six years on the court. Many Magistrates dislike dealing with the hundreds of prisoner cases that are filed each year, but Scoville found them interesting because the issues in those cases involved constitutional law. He was also heavily involved in court management, drafting court rules, supervising the court's pool of pro se law clerks, and managing the court's docket when three of the district judgeships were vacant. Magistrate Judge Scoville retired from the court on July 31, 2014, after more than twenty-five years of service with the court, during which he earned a reputation as a fair, intelligent, and practical judge whose no-nonsense approach to the administration of justice helped successfully resolve thousands of criminal and civil cases.

U.S. Magistrate Judge Ellen Stephenson Carmody

Ellen S. Carmody was born on June 19, 1952, in Philadelphia, Pennsylvania, the daughter of William and Mary (Finley) Stephenson. She grew up in Ambler, Pennsylvania, then a small town and now a suburb of Philadelphia. In 1970, she graduated from an all-girl Catholic high school in Gwynedd

Valley, Pennsylvania. After high school, she entered Grand Valley State College (now Grand Valley State University) in Grand Rapids, Michigan, from which she graduated in 1974 with a bachelor of arts degree. For the next five years, she worked as a special education teacher for the Grand Rapids Public Schools, teaching students with severe emotional impairment. In 1980, she entered the University of Michigan Law School, graduating with a juris doctor degree, magna cum laude. In 1983, District Judge Hillman hired Carmody to be his law clerk for two years. During her term as law clerk, among her other experiences, she assisted Judge Hillman in resolving and closing the marathon Benton Harbor school desegregation case. She also worked extensively with Judge Enslen on a case that spanned more than two decades, which involved the governance of Michigan's prisons. After her clerkship, she joined the firm of Law, Weathers, & Richardson, as an associate and partner, and she specialized in commercial and employment litigation. In October 2000 she was appointed a U.S. Magistrate Judge, replacing the late Magistrate Judge Doyle A. Rowland. Judge Carmody was instrumental in developing the court's fledgling Accelerated Community Entry (ACE) program, which is designed to reduce the high rate of recidivism of serious drug offenders after long periods of incarceration. She has also been an adjunct professor at Grand Valley State University and the law school at Michigan State University. Judge Carmody is married to Robert Rosenberg, MD, and she has a daughter, Caitlin.

As another example of the span of cases that a Magistrate Judge might experience in the Western District, Judge Carmody, with the consent of the parties, tried to conclusion a very lively and heavily contested patent case involving a machine that measured the speed at which a baseball travels after encountering a hitter's bat. That simple description belies the technical complexity of the patent claims, of the evidence presented, and of Judge Carmody's lengthy opinion.[29]

U.S. Magistrate Judge Phillip J. Green

U.S. Magistrate Judge Phillip J. Green was born in Denver, Colorado, on August 27, 1956, to Omer and Ruth Jean (Coad) Green, the fourth of eight children. He grew up in southern Illinois, close to St. Louis, Missouri, where he attended Catholic schools through high school. He entered the U.S. Navy at age seventeen, one week after graduating from high school in 1974. He served on active duty for two years and in the active reserves for another four, including a one-year stint as a chaplain's assistant at Fort Knox, Kentucky, with the U.S. Army.

Judge Green studied at Southern Illinois University–Edwardsville from September 1976 until January 1979, when he entered the Benedictine seminary at St. Meinrad College in southern Indiana. He received his bachelor of arts degree from St. Meinrad College in 1982, with a major in philosophy and a minor in the classics. Judge Green spent a year with the Trappist monks at St. Joseph's Abbey in Spencer, Massachusetts. He also studied for a year at Kenrick Seminary School of Theology in St. Louis, Missouri. Following the seminary, Judge Green taught in a Catholic parochial school for four years. Realizing there was little market for philosophers, Judge Green attended St. Louis University School of Law, earning his juris doctor degree, magna cum laude, in 1990. In his third year of law school, Judge Green served as editor-in-chief of the *St. Louis University Law Journal*.

Following law school, Judge Green served for a year as a law clerk to the Hon. Theodore McMillian of the U.S. Court of Appeals for the Eighth Circuit. In 1991, Judge Green received an appointment through the Attorney General's Honors Program to the U.S. Department of Justice, Civil Division, Federal Programs Branch. He represented the United States and federal agencies in litigation involving constitutional and administrative challenges to federal statutes and programs, national security issues, and employment discrimination. Judge Green left the Department of Justice in 1994 to join the firm Bryan Cave, LLP, in St. Louis, where he represented clients before federal and state courts, the National Labor Relations Board, and the Equal Employment Opportunity Commission. After a year, he returned to the Department of Justice, Civil Division, where he continued his work as a trial attorney.

In October 1998, Judge Green joined the U.S. Attorney's Office in Grand Rapids, Michigan, where he worked as a federal prosecutor for sixteen years. He served in various positions, including Deputy Criminal Chief, First Assistant U.S. Attorney, and Senior Litigation Counsel. The Attorney General appointed him as interim United States Attorney on January 8, 2001, and he served in that capacity until October 29, 2001, when the Senate confirmed his presidentially appointed replacement. Judge Green tried more than thirty felony jury trials, including cases involving murder, kidnapping, bank robbery, sexual assault, drug offenses, and firearms offenses. He prosecuted the first criminal RICO case in the Western District of Michigan, convicting thirty-one members of the Holland Latin Kings gang.

Judge Green was appointed as Magistrate Judge for the Western District of Michigan on August 1, 2014. Judge Green married Ann Marie Keeley on May 25, 1985. They have five children.

U.S. Magistrate Judge Raymond S. Kent

U.S. Magistrate Judge Raymond Kent was born on March 23, 1956, in Grosse Pointe, Michigan. He grew up in Mt. Clemens, Michigan, and he graduated from Mt. Clemens High School in 1974. He entered and graduated from Michigan State University (BA in communications, 1981) and Wayne State University Law School (JD, 1987). He then worked for five years for the Chicago law firm of Sidley & Austin. In 1992, he joined the Grand Rapids law firm of Buchanan & Bos, and in 1995 he formed his own practice in Grand Rapids, the Law Offices of Ray Kent, PC. In 2005, he was appointed the Federal Public Defender for the Western District of Michigan, and in August 2015 he was appointed a U.S. Magistrate Judge in that district, succeeding Hugh W. Brenneman, Jr. Like former Magistrate Judges Brenneman and Scoville, Judge Kent is a past President of the Western Michigan Chapter of the Federal Bar Association.

U.S. Magistrate Judge Maarten Vermaat

On January 9, 2019, Chief Judge Robert J. Jonker announced the appointment of Maarten Vermaat as a U.S. Magistrate Judge. Effective on March 15, 2019, the appointment is based in Marquette, where Vermaat filled the position opened by the retirement of Magistrate Judge Timothy P. Greeley, who retired after thirty years' service as the resident Magistrate Judge for the Northern Division. Judge Vermaat was born on June 22, 1962, in Beloit, Wisconsin, the son of first-generation Dutch immigrants. In 1984, he graduated from the U.S. Naval Academy in Annapolis, Maryland, and was commissioned as a second lieutenant in the U.S. Marine Corps. Judge Vermaat rose to the rank of major during his more than twelve years of active service in aviation, earning the Air Medal for distinguished combat service. After more than twelve additional years with the U.S. Marine Corps Reserve, Judge Vermaat retired from military service in 2009 with the rank of colonel.

After completing his active military service, in 1996, Judge Vermaat entered Yale Law School from which he graduated in 1999 with a juris doctor degree. He began his legal career as a law clerk for Chief Judge Robert G. Coats of the Alaska court of appeals. He then served as an Assistant District

Attorney in Anchorage, Alaska, where he later joined the law firm of Dorsey & Whitney. In 2003, Mr. Vermaat moved to Michigan and joined the U.S. Attorney's office in Grand Rapids as an Assistant U.S. Attorney. A year later, he moved to the U.S. Attorney's office in Marquette where he was the Assistant U.S. Attorney for the district's Northern Division until his appointment as a U.S. Magistrate Judge. He is active in the Federal Bar Association. He lives with his wife and their two sons in Marquette.

U.S. Magistrate Judge Sally J. Berens

In September 2019, Chief Judge Robert J. Jonker announced the appointment of Sally J. Berens as a U.S. Magistrate Judge, effective on November 2, 2019. The appointment is based in Grand Rapids where Judge Berens filled the position opened by the retirement of Magistrate Judge Ellen S. Carmody, who retired after almost two decades of distinguished service on the court.

Judge Berens grew up in Allegan County, Michigan, and graduated from Hamilton High School. She attended Harvard University, graduating in 1998 with a bachelor of arts degree in linguistics, magna cum laude, and a master of arts degree in comparative literature. She graduated from the University of Chicago Law School with honors in 2001. Ms. Berens next served as a law clerk for Circuit Judge Andrew Kleinfeld of the U.S. Court of Appeals for the Ninth Circuit, and then she joined the law firm of Gibson, Dunn & Crutcher in Palo Alto, California, for ten years. In 2012, Ms. Berens returned to western Michigan when she accepted a position as an Assistant U.S. Attorney in the Western District of Michigan.

CHAPTER 9

Bankruptcy Administration in the
Western District of Michigan

D ELEGATES TO THE ORIGINAL Constitutional Convention who
were lawyers or businessmen, were aware of the concept of bankruptcy from both British statutes and British common law. Great
Britain had been administering the problems of insolvent debtors since the
Statute of Bankrupts passed in Parliament in 1542. The American delegates
relied on the British example to include among the specific powers granted
to Congress the power to enact "uniform laws on the subject of bankruptcies
throughout the United States."[1] Early on, decisions of the federal courts established that the "uniform laws" to which the drafters referred were intended
to preclude states from enacting their own bankruptcy laws and to provide
Congress with the sole power to legislate rules for a national bankruptcy
system.[2]

Having excluded the possibility of state bankruptcy laws, however, the
drafters did not mandate that Congress actually create a federal bankruptcy
law system. Instead, they left that decision to the discretion of Congress, and
during most of the next century and beyond, Congress rarely decided to exercise those powers. Between 1788, when the Constitution was ratified, and
1898, when bankruptcy finally became a permanent fixture of American law,
bankruptcy laws existed for a total of only fifteen years. The three bankruptcy
laws Congress passed before 1898, in 1800, 1841, and 1867, were unpopular
with both creditors and debtors, all triggered by severe financial crashes, and
abolished as soon as the economy recovered, thus leaving creditors and debtors to the mercy of differing state laws for debt collection.[3]

The Bankruptcy Acts of 1800 and 1841

Congress first attempted a national bankruptcy law in April 1800, during one of the nation's first recessions. The 1800 Bankruptcy Act[4] was the product of a Congress controlled by banker-friendly Federalists. It applied only to "merchant" debtors,[5] and was essentially a device that only creditors, not debtors, could invoke. The 1800 Act was administered directly by U.S. District Judges, assisted by commissioners whom the judges appointed for each case, who were authorized to seize and sell the bankrupt's property and to imprison a reluctant bankrupt. The 1800 Act's only advantage for debtors was the possibility of a discharge of their debts upon completion of the case, but only with the consent of two-thirds of the bankrupt merchant's creditors.[6] The 1800 Act was supposed to last five years, but both the creditors and the debtors were unhappy about the costs of administration and the small returns achieved, and the economy improved sooner than expected. By December 1803, populist President Thomas Jefferson and a Congress controlled by his Democratic-Republican Party repealed the 1800 Act.[7]

In 1837, the Great Panic hit the United States, causing a complete reversal of power in the federal government, and winning the Whig Party the presidency as well as majorities in both the House of Representatives and the Senate. One of the consequences of this financial collapse was that Congress attempted, in August 1841, to draft another bankruptcy law. The Whigs' 1841 Bankruptcy Act[8] opened bankruptcy relief to "[a]ll persons, whatsoever, owing debts." The 1841 Act's main purpose was not debt collection but, instead, relief for the mass of insolvent debtors victimized by the financial collapse. The 1841 Act allowed debtors to file voluntary petitions and to receive a discharge of their debts without the consent of their creditors. As with the 1800 Act, the District Courts had exclusive jurisdiction over bankruptcy cases as well as the burden of the 1841 Act's administration, although the judges were authorized, as in the 1800 Act, to appoint commissioners to assist them. During the 1841 Act's short lifetime, petitioners filed 685 cases in the District of Michigan, each petition requiring District Judge Ross Wilkins to appoint a commissioner to receive proof of debts and to carry out other administrative duties. Nevertheless, substantive orders and jury trials on disputed facts remained Judge Wilkins' responsibility.

Nationally, 33,000 individual debtors sought bankruptcy relief in the District Courts under the 1841 Act, but, as with its predecessor, the 1841 Act proved to be highly inefficient, with high administrative costs resulting in low returns to creditors, and it came too late to be useful. By 1843, the economy had improved significantly so that the benefits of the law seemed to the public and to Congress to no longer be worth its defects. The 1841 bankruptcy law was repealed in March 1843, just fourteen months after it went into effect.[9]

The Bankruptcy Act of 1867

In 1867, Congress enacted its third bankruptcy law, which was the first bankruptcy legislation to occur during the life of the U.S. District Court for the Western District of Michigan. Two years after the end of the Civil War in 1865, Congress was again induced to regulate insolvency owing to the lingering effects of the prewar Panic of 1857 as well as the tattered economies of the former Confederate states and the stressed economies of the rest of the states. The Bankruptcy Act of 1867[10] allowed bankruptcy petitions by both debtors ("voluntary petitions") and creditors ("involuntary petitions"). During the 1867 Act's first four years, more than 100,000 petitions for relief were filed nationally. The burden of the administration of those petitions fell, once again, on the District Courts, designated as courts of bankruptcy acting under the "general superintendence" of each district's old Circuit Court. The 1867 Act required the District Court to be "always open for business . . . as well as in vacation as in term time" meaning in chambers as in open court, and at any location within the district.

Registers in Bankruptcy

One innovation of the 1867 Act was the creation of a new category of court officer, the register in bankruptcy, who replaced commissioners in assisting the hardworking district judges. Unlike a commissioner, who was appointed to assist the District Court in a specific bankruptcy case, and who had many other duties outside bankruptcy, a register in bankruptcy was appointed for two-year terms and did not have responsibilities outside of bankruptcy. Also, unlike commissioners, registers were required to be attorneys who were "counsellors" of the District Court or of a court of record in their state of residence. The registers, so named because they kept a register or list of bankrupt debtors, performed most of the day-to-day administration of the bankruptcy system. However, the 1867 Act did not grant registers any jurisdiction over judicial matters, which left much for the district judges to do. Registers conducted their bankruptcy duties in their own offices and were responsible for paying all expenses related to their bankruptcy work. Those expenses and the register's other compensation were not paid directly by the federal government but instead were paid solely by fees collected from the participants in the bankruptcy cases.

The Registers in Bankruptcy of the Western District of Michigan

The 1867 Act directed each District Court to appoint at least one register in each congressional district within the District Court's jurisdiction. In order to minimize the possibility of District Court judges using register appointments as gifts to friends and allies, the Act specified that District Courts could make register appointments only from a list of candidates recommended by the Chief Justice of the U.S. Supreme Court.[11] In 1867, Michigan had six congressional districts, of which two, centered in Grand Rapids and Kalamazoo, were within what were then the boundaries of the Western District. Unlike some districts courts that appointed multiple registers in each congressional district, the courts of both the Western and Eastern Districts of Michigan appointed the minimum, just one register per congressional district. In 1867, Judge Withey appointed two attorneys from the Chief Justice's list to be registers for the Western District, Henry E. Thompson of Grand Rapids for the Fourth Congressional District and James Davidson Burns of Kalamazoo for the Second Congressional District.

Henry E. Thompson was a Civil War veteran, an officer in the 6th Michigan Volunteer Cavalry Regiment, and part of General George Armstrong Custer's Michigan Cavalry Brigade. Thompson was wounded during the Gettysburg campaign in July 1863, and discharged due to disability in 1864 as a colonel. He returned to Grand Rapids where he read law and was admitted to the bar. He practiced law and served as register until about 1884. In 1901, he moved to California, where he died in 1913.

James Davidson Burns attended the Law Department of the University of Michigan in 1860–1861. After graduating, he practiced law in Kalamazoo. Burns continued as register into the 1890s, and died in Kalamazoo in April 1910.

James Edward Dalliba, an attorney practicing in Marquette, was appointed the register for the Upper Peninsula in 1867, even though Michigan's Upper Peninsula was split between the Eastern and Western Districts of Michigan.

When Congress reallocated all of the Upper Peninsula to the Western District in June 1878, Dalliba continued in his position as register. Dalliba was born in Troy, New York, on December 8, 1821. He graduated from Hamilton College in 1841, read law, and was admitted to the bar in New York in 1843. He practiced in Utica, New York, and Chicago until 1860 when President Lincoln appointed him U.S. Attorney for Colorado. In 1865 he moved to Marquette where he practiced law and was appointed register in 1867.

Like its predecessors, the 1867 Act proved to be inefficient, resulting in high fees, small dividends to creditors, and long delays. Congress repealed the 1867 Act in June 1878, effective September 1.[12] Despite the repeal, Thompson, Burns, and Dalliba continued to be listed as registers in various official and unofficial directories of the era. Thompson is listed as a register in bankruptcy for the Western District through 1883, Burns through 1895, and Dalliba until he died in 1894. Thompson, Burns, and Dalliba, like registers in other districts, remained in office after the 1878 repeal probably in order to complete and close pending bankruptcy cases and to be paid. The 1878 Repeal Act provided "[t]hat such repeal shall in no manner invalidate or affect any case in bankruptcy instituted and pending in any court prior to the day when this act shall take effect; but as to all such pending cases and all future proceedings therein, and . . . the acts hereby repealed shall continue in full force and effect until the same shall be fully disposed of, in the same manner as if said acts had not been repealed." Because the registers were not compensated from the District Court's budget, the district judges had no compelling reason to speed up the closing of the pending cases or to terminate a register, no matter how little bankruptcy work he was performing. Consequently, the court kept some cases open for decades after the 1867 Act's repeal.

The Bankruptcy Act of 1898

During the last decades of the nineteenth century, American commerce changed from agricultural and local to industrial and national, while the cyclical nature of the economy went from boom to bust and bust to boom. In that environment, businessmen acted as both creditors and debtors in their turn, engaging in interstate trade under both guises. Vacillating between both roles, businessmen realized they needed protection from the inequality of laws and courts in other states, as well as a chance for their foundering businesses to get a second chance. Two severe financial panics, in 1893 and 1896, demonstrated both the continued volatility of the national economy and the inability of state laws to deal with widespread financial crises.

During the 1870s and 1880s, the United States experienced economic growth and expansion driven by the international sale of commodities such as wheat, corn, and beef at prices well below those charged in Europe and other international markets. In 1893, however, foreign wheat prices crashed, erasing the American advantage and affecting not only American farmers but also railroads and banks, the core of the American financial structure. As a result of the panic, stock prices plunged, five hundred banks closed, fifteen thousand businesses failed, and thousands of farms ceased operation. Michigan had one of the highest unemployment rates in the country at 43 percent, and in Detroit soup kitchens were opened to help feed the destitute. Facing starvation, people chopped wood, broke rocks, and sewed in exchange for food.

Despite these financial woes, Congress was divided as to whether it should enact a new bankruptcy act. Most Republicans were in favor of a new act in order to provide relief for fragile businesses large and small. While Democrats might have been expected to feel the same, they opposed a law that they saw as a trap for farmers and individual consumers who would be encouraged to take ill-advised financial chances. Finally, in 1898, as the economy improved, the Republican majority in both houses of Congress managed to unite and enact the nation's first modern bankruptcy legislation, the Bankruptcy Act of 1898, sometimes called the Nelson Act.[13]

Like earlier bankruptcy statutes, the 1898 Act placed original jurisdiction over bankruptcy cases in the hands of the U.S. District Courts, as courts of bankruptcy. The 1898 Act did away with the office of register in bankruptcy and replaced it with a similar position, the referee in bankruptcy,[14] which would have more responsibility than registers in the day-to-day administration of bankruptcy cases. In addition to the duties of the registers, the 1898 Act gave referees the responsibility for most of the judicial work in bankruptcy cases. The duties of referees included the consideration of bankruptcy petitions, the examination of property schedules and the lists of creditors filed by bankrupts, administering oaths, maintaining records in bankruptcy proceedings, and distributing the property of bankrupts in cases where the District Court judge was absent. Referees' decisions on substantive matters were subject to review by the District Court.

Each District Court was required to appoint, for two-year terms, a sufficient number of referees so that at least one of them was available in each county in the district needing their services. Unlike the 1867 Act, the 1898 Act gave the District Court discretion to decide what number was sufficient for each county and to choose referees without prior approval of the Chief Justice of the Supreme Court. The qualifications required to be appointed a referee were simple: the court could appoint any person, attorney or not, who was competent to perform the duties of the office, so long as that person did not hold any other U.S. office and was not related "by consanguinity or affinity within the third degree" with any Article III judge. Although the District Court's almost complete discretion to appoint referees might sound like an invitation to appoint too freely, the 1903 *Annual Report of the Attorney General of the United States* expressed concern that many districts did not appoint enough referees and that those who were appointed were not in locations that were within easy access of a large proportion of a district's residents. The same report did acknowledge the high standard of the current corps of referees, adding that "When it is remembered that the fees of these officers are reduced to a minimum, and only in rare instances at all compensatory for the loss of other practice, it is surprising that this high standard has been maintained."[15] Under the 1898 Act, referees in bankruptcy were expected to perform their bankruptcy duties part-time, in addition to carrying on private business practice outside of bankruptcy law. The two-year appointments were usually renewed, providing an experienced corps of referees.

Under the 1898 Act, referees, like registers, were court officers but not salaried employees of the federal government. Like registers, they usually operated out of their own law offices and were not compensated directly by the federal government. Instead, they were compensated by, and paid expenses from, the bankruptcy estates they administered. The first draft of the 1898 Act submitted to Congress had provided for referees to receive salaries, but the final law provided instead that: "Referees shall receive as full compensation for their services, payable after they are rendered, a fee of ten dollars deposited with the clerk at the time the petition is filed in each case, except when a fee is not required from a voluntary bankrupt, and from estates which have been administered before them one per centum commissions on sums to be paid as dividends and commissions, or one half of one per centum on the amount to be paid to creditors upon the confirmation of a composition."[16] From those fees and commissions, referees paid all of the costs of the operation of the Bankruptcy Courts, hopefully leaving the referee a profit. This compensation scheme remained in effect for the next fifty years.

The Referees of the Western District of Michigan, 1898–1925

Some District Courts began administration under the 1898 Act by appointing large numbers of referees, but Judge Severens initially appointed just three, each with jurisdiction over a region. For most of the life of the 1898 Act, one referee was located in each of Grand Rapids, Kalamazoo, and Marquette. The referee in Grand Rapids was responsible for cases in Kent, Ottawa, Ionia, Montcalm, Mecosta, Muskegon, Osceola, Lake, Newaygo, and Oceana Counties (a total of 351,326 residents in 1900); the Kalamazoo referee covered Benzie, Calhoun, Cass, Barry, St. Joseph, Eaton, Allegan, Van Buren, and Kalamazoo Counties (238,984 residents in 1900); and the Marquette referee handled cases arising in the entire Upper Peninsula (261,362 residents in 1900).[17] That division of work proved effective, and the number of referees in the Western District remained small, even sinking to two referees after 1929 when the Kalamazoo position was left vacant.

REFEREES IN THE GRAND RAPIDS REGION, 1898–1925

Charles Benton Blair   Charles B. Blair was born on January 3, 1858, in Grand Rapids. He was educated in the Grand Rapids public schools until he was fourteen years old. He then attended private schools in New York state before entering Harvard College in 1876 from which he graduated in literature in 1880. He returned to Grand Rapids for a short time to study law with his father. From 1881 to 1882, he studied at the Law Department of the University of Michigan.[18] He then transferred to Harvard Law School, which he attended in 1883. He returned to Grand Rapids, and was admitted to the bar in August 1883. In October 1898, Judge Severens appointed his fellow Democrat as referee in bankruptcy, but Blair's tenure was just three years. On October 10, 1901, Blair resigned his position because, he explained, he was about to leave for California for business, and he planned to be absent from Michigan for several months. He eventually did return to Grand Rapids and resumed practicing law, but he did not immediately resume his duties as referee.[19]

Alfred Hatch Hunt   On the day that he accepted Charles Blair's resignation, October 10, 1901, Judge Wanty appointed a thirty-year-old Grand Rapids native and attorney to a two-year term as referee in Blair's place. Alfred H. Hunt was born in Grand Rapids on April 18, 1871. After he graduated from the University of Michigan with both a bachelor's degree (1895) and a law degree (1896), Hunt returned to his native city to practice law. The small compensation referees could achieve led Hunt to resign from that position at the end of his term in October 1903. Hunt died at home unexpectedly on April 30, 1911, at the age of forty.

Kirk Edward Wicks Sr.   Kirk E. Wicks Sr., the son of John H. and Mary Wicks, was born on September 19, 1869, in Watson Township in Allegan County, Michigan, east of Allegan City. After graduating from high school, he taught school for a year and then decided to become an attorney. He graduated from the Law Department of the University of Michigan (bachelor of laws, 1892) and moved to Grand Rapids where he joined the firm in which Charles Blair and Willard Kingsley were partners. He later practiced by himself. In August 1903, Judge Wanty appointed him to be referee in place of Alfred Hunt who had completed his two-year term. Wicks resigned as referee thirteen years later, on June 5, 1916. He then entered into a partnership with future U.S. District Judge Raymond Starr. When Wicks died in Grand Rapids on December 16, 1949, aged eighty, speakers at his memorial service praised him for his long, successful career. One speaker focused on "his careful, methodical and impartial administration of the often complicated duties of that office [of referee]."

Benn M. Corwin   Benn Corwin was born on September 20, 1865, in Georgetown Township in Ottawa County, Michigan, southwest of Grand Rapids. He graduated from Grand Rapids Business College in 1888, began studying law in 1890, and was admitted to the Grand Rapids bar in 1894. He joined George Norcross to practice as Corwin and Norcross. On June 5, 1916, the day that Kirk Wicks resigned as referee, Judge Sessions appointed Corwin as Wicks's successor. However, Corwin, who was principally interested in real estate investing, left Michigan in 1925 to join in the land boom in Florida. Unfortunately, the boom was deflating as he arrived, and Corwin eventually returned to Grand Rapids to resume his law practice but not his referee position. Benn Corwin died in 1957 at the age of ninety-one.

REFEREES IN THE KALAMAZOO REGION, 1898–1925

Henry C. Briggs   Henry C. Briggs was born on June 29, 1831, in West Haven, Rutland County, Vermont. In 1836, his parents, Noah and Sarah (Kenyon), moved the family to Allegan County, Michigan. He attended Kalamazoo College and then transferred to the University of Michigan. In 1856, he was elected Allegan County Clerk, and in 1861 he was elected to a term as state senator from Allegan. He served one regular session and one special session and then resigned. After studying law and being admitted to the bar, he moved to Kalamazoo. He served four years as a Kalamazoo County prosecutor followed by eight years (1868–1876) as a Kalamazoo County probate judge. He was sixty-seven years old when Judge Severens appointed him to be the Kalamazoo region's first referee in October 1898. He served until 1912 when he resigned at the age of eighty.

Willard Johnson Banyon   Willard Banyon was born on July 20, 1876, in Chicago, Illinois. When he was about ten years old, his family moved to Benton Harbor, on Lake Michigan. After graduating from Benton Harbor High School, he worked for several years at various jobs, including as Benton Harbor's City Clerk (1893–1894), to earn enough money to attend the University of Michigan Law School. He graduated in 1910, at the age of thirty-four, and returned to Benton Harbor to practice law. Just two years later, when referee Henry Briggs retired, Judge Sessions appointed Banyon as his replacement. Banyon conducted his day-to-day activities as referee from his law office in St. Joseph, Michigan, across the St. Joseph River from his home in Benton Harbor, but he also held hearings in Kalamazoo. In addition to his duties as referee and his law practice, Banyon served as chair of Michigan's first State Crime Commission and of the Benton Harbor Board of Education. He also had interests in manufacturing companies, and he was President the *News-Palladium* newspaper company. Willard Banyon resigned from his referee position in February 1925 to focus entirely on his busy law practice. He died on August 5, 1938, in Benton Harbor.

REFEREES IN THE NORTHERN DIVISION, 1898–1938

Benjamin O. Pearl   Benjamin O. Pearl was born on February 16, 1862, in Springfield, Ohio, where he grew up and where he graduated from high school in 1878. After a few years working in the offices of a steel mill, he entered the Northern Illinois Normal School and Dixon Business College, located in Dixon, Illinois. After graduation (BA, 1883), Pearl moved first to Chicago, then in 1884, he moved to Marquette to pursue a career in law. He worked as a clerk and read law in the chambers of prominent attorney O. F. Clark. Pearl was admitted to the bar in 1890 and joined with Clark to make the law partnership of Clark & Pearl. In 1893, Pearl was elected to Marquette's city council where the other members appointed him President. In 1898, Judge Severens appointed Pearl to be the part-time referee in bankruptcy for the Western District's Northern Division, with responsibility for all bankruptcy cases in the Upper Peninsula. He held that office until he resigned in 1910. Pearl died in Pentland, Luce County, Michigan, on February 20, 1915, after a long illness.[20]

Richard T. Looney   Benjamin Pearl was succeeded as referee for the Northern Division by Richard T. Looney of Houghton, Copper County. Looney was born in April 1862 in Dundas, Canada. His family moved to Hancock, Michigan, in the Upper Peninsula, where he grew up. He was admitted to the bar in 1890, and practiced law in Houghton. After his appointment as referee in 1910, he conducted his duties in both Houghton and Marquette for twenty-eight years. He was still the Northern Division's register when he died on September 19, 1938, at the age of seventy-six.

THE RETURN OF CHARLES B. BLAIR

In 1924, Judge Sessions decided to have only one referee for the entire Southern Division by merging the Grand Rapids and Kalamazoo regions. In 1925, referees Willard Banyon and Benn Corwin both resigned, and in their stead Judges Clarence Sessions and Fred Raymond convinced Charles B. Blair, who had been a part-time referee from 1898 to 1901 and who was now in his late sixties but still active in his practice, to accept a full-time referee appointment with responsibility for the entire Southern Division.[21] Blair served as referee for another fifteen years, retiring in 1939 at the age of eighty-three. He died in August 1949, at ninety-three years old, in Grand Rapids.

The Changing Status of Referees

Two amendments to the 1898 Act, passed by Congress in 1938 and 1946, changed the responsibilities and operations of referees. The Chandler Act of 1938[22] increased the referees' judicial functions, granting them the authority to adjudicate petitions, including administering oaths and examining witnesses. In the same Act, Congress transferred many of the referees' administrative duties to bankruptcy trustees or to clerks of court. The second important change was the 1946 Referees' Salary Act,[23] which finally gave referees the security of an assured income and longer tenure in office. The first half-century of the 1898 Act was difficult financially for referees in many districts across the nation, especially those in districts with small populations, including the Western District of Michigan. Smaller populations, particularly those that were heavily rural, meant fewer petitions in bankruptcy and modest bankruptcy estates, the two criteria that determined the amount of a referee's compensation under the 1898 Act. That compensation system was popular with referees with large dockets and with legislators who did not want to add another item to the federal budget. However, referees with small caseloads found it hard to make a reasonable profit, and the system involved obvious conflicts of interest when referees had to decide what assets to include in the distribution to creditors.

In the Western District, the 1898 Act's first year and a half, ending June 30, 1899,[24] produced just sixty-one petitions. The number of petitions increased to ninety-eight in fiscal 1900, but it decreased to forty-eight during the next year. It is not surprising that Charles Blair, the first referee for the Grand Rapids region, resigned in 1901 and went looking for a more profitable business in California, or that his young successor in Grand Rapids also resigned after one term. The number of filings in the Western District remained stagnant until 1921 when Prohibition began to affect all aspects of the District Court's business. Bankruptcy petition filings increased from 66 in 1920 to 147 in 1922, and then to 229 in 1925. From 1929 through 1939, the Western District's referees received an average of more than four hundred petitions. The increase in petitions nationwide kept the long debate in Congress and the bankruptcy community about changing referee compensation in the background. However, that debate came to the forefront when the economic boom after World War II resulted in the fewest number of filings nationally since 1899. For example, in fiscal year 1946, the Western District's referees received only seventy new cases, the fewest since 1904. As some referees resigned and others laid off employees, both houses of Congress finally decided that the time for referee reform had arrived. The result was the Referees' Salary Act of 1946, an amendment to the 1898 Bankruptcy Act.[25]

The Salary Act was not as innovative as the title suggests. It was true that, from the Act's effective date in 1947, each referee was entitled to be paid a monthly salary that was fixed each year. However, the "fixed" salary was not uniform among referees. Instead, the amount of each referee's salary was based on a complicated set of rules that, in the end, still depended on the number of petitions handled by that referee and the amount of money that referee distributed to creditors. Congress established a maximum annual salary ($10,000 for full-time, $5,000 for part-time), but not a minimum salary. Moreover, those salaries and the expenses incurred by referees were still not paid from the national budget. Instead, referees contributed the fees and other money paid to them by litigants into two funds, a referee's salary fund and a referee's expense fund that was administered by the United States Treasury. In addition to its salary provisions, the Salary Act also improved the attractiveness of the post by increasing the duration of appointments from two years to six, and limiting the circumstances under which they could be removed from office to acts of incompetence, misconduct, or neglect of duty.

Southern Division Referees, 1938–1978

CHESTER CARL WOOLRIDGE

When Charles Blair returned to the referee position in 1924, he insisted that he would do so only if he could have as an assistant a young attorney from his firm, Chester C. Woolridge. During their ten years together, Woolridge learned bankruptcy law and procedure as he acted as Blair's law clerk, researcher, and bailiff. In January 1939, after Blair retired, Judge Raymond naturally appointed Woolridge to take over as referee for the entire Southern Division of the Western District.

Chester Woolridge was born in Libertyville, Illinois, in December 1896, but his family soon moved to Pierport, Manistee County, Michigan, where his father was a carpenter and farmer and his mother taught school. He graduated from nearby Arcadia High School, passed a teaching preparatory course, and taught in country schools for five years. An attorney customer of his family's dairy farm encouraged Woolridge to try law as a career, and he began reading law with the firm of Corwin and Norcross in Grand Rapids. He was admitted to the bar in 1924.

Woolridge was a witness to the changes in referee service and status affected by the Chandler Act and the Referee Salary Act. Although these statutes were great improvements for referees overall, they carried unanticipated problems as well. In 1947, Woolridge had to leave his comfortable office suite in the Michigan Trust Building. Years later, he remembered that the District Court

> [G]ave us the storage rooms on the fourth floor of the old [1909] Federal Building for our offices and courtroom. We had a main office where the public would file cases, a clerk's office, and one judge's office. When Judge Nims joined us [in 1955], there was no office for him; so they cleaned out another small room with no windows under the eaves. We attempted to have air-conditioning installed, but they told us we didn't have enough air circulation to accommodate it. You can imagine how hot it got up there in the summer months. The courtroom had a huge post right in the middle of it, and when it was time to hold court, I would have to ask the court reporter if anyone was present because I could not see around the post. Every time it rained, we had to put some pots down to catch the leaks, and it was a distressing situation. . . . [I]in the courtroom we had a table and chairs for the plaintiff and defendant, so forth. They were just "pickup" facilities until I invested my own money and had prepared a nice table and chairs for counsel, and one for the reporter too. . . . We did not have calendar clerks, audit clerks, or law clerks to help us.[26]

Chester Woolridge retired from his referee position on December 31, 1960, and was succeeded by Edward H. Benson. After retiring, Woolridge became "of counsel" to the Grand Rapids law firm Schmidt, Howlett, Van't Hoff, Snell, & Vana. He died on July 1, 1992, at the age of ninety-five. Speakers at a memorial service, held in the Gerald R. Ford Federal Building five days after Woolridge's death, praised his profound knowledge of bankruptcy law and procedure, as well as his eagerness to pass on that knowledge to a new generation of bankruptcy referees and practitioners. Perhaps his greatest gifts to the court and the people who appeared before him were his warm, even temperament and his civility, attributes which have become a tradition of the Western District's referees, Bankruptcy Judges, and bankruptcy attorneys, some with whom he worked and others who followed in his footsteps.

DAVID EDWARD NIMS, JR.

Chester Woolridge's time at the Bankruptcy Court as a referee also saw momentous changes in the bankruptcy caseload. In 1939, the year Woolridge became referee, the number of new cases decreased from the peak of the Depression at 608 to 398. New case filings decreased even further during and after World War II, bottoming out at just 70 new cases in 1946. However, just as the Referee Salary Act went into effect, the number of filings began to increase once more, from 111 in 1947, to 280 in 1950, and to 655 in 1954. This increasing caseload convinced the court to reinstate the second referee position in the Southern Division. On April 15, 1955, the court appointed Kalamazoo attorney and U.S. Commissioner David E. Nims, Jr. to the second referee position. In 1986, Nims went on to become one of the Western District's first U.S. Bankruptcy Judges under the new Bankruptcy Code. His life and career will be recounted below in the context of that statute.

EDWARD HARVEY BENSON

Edward Benson was born on September 9, 1906, in Grand Rapids. He graduated from Grand Rapids Union High School, Grand Rapids Junior College, and the University of Michigan. He was admitted to the bar in Grand Rapids in 1931 and opened a law office in the Michigan Trust Building. There he conducted a private practice that lasted thirty years until January 1961, when he succeeded Chester Woolridge as one of two full-time referees in the Southern Division. The increase in the caseload that prompted the addition of the second referee in 1955 had continued unabated during the rest of the 1950s, reaching 1,585 new cases in 1961, the year Benson joined David Nims as referee. The bankruptcy docket in the Western District continued to grow until 1967 when it reached 2,053 new cases filed. That number decreased somewhat over the next few years, to a low of 1,471 in 1972, but then increased again to 2,234 during 1975, Benson's last year as referee before he retired at age sixty-eight. He died, after a long illness, on September 24, 1986, in East Grand Rapids, survived by his wife and three children.

LAURENCE EDWARD HOWARD

On January 14, 1976, Laurence E. Howard succeeded Edward H. Benson as a referee for the Southern Division. Shortly thereafter Howard was appointed as a Bankruptcy Judge, and his life and career are discussed below in the context of that judgeship.

Northern Division Referees, 1938–1978

GEORGE CAMPBELL QUINNELL

George C. Quinnell was born on September 16, 1890, in Michigan. He attended the Ferris Institute in 1913 and graduated from Michigan State Normal College—now Eastern Michigan University—(B.Phil. degree, 1914) and from the University of Michigan (B.A., 1920). He then entered the University of Michigan Law School from which he graduated in 1922. His first legal experience was in New York City where he worked for the American Sugar Refining Company, then he moved to Detroit with several law firms. In 1927, he and his wife Evelyn (Pace) Quinnell, moved to Marquette where he began a private law practice. In September 1938, District Judge Raymond appointed Quinnell referee in bankruptcy for the Northern Division, succeeding Richard T. Looney who had died in office. George Quinnell served as the sole referee in the Upper Peninsula until he retired in July 1972. He died in July 1985 in Marquette at the age of ninety-four.

EDWARD ARTHUR QUINNELL

Edward A. Quinnell, the son of referee George C. Quinnell, was born in Marquette, Michigan, on April 27, 1933. He graduated from Julia Graveraet High School in Marquette, from the University of Michigan, and the University of Michigan Law School (JD, 1956). He then returned to Marquette to practice law with his father. In 1960, he was appointed Marquette County Prosecutor, a part-time office, and he served in that position until 1971. In July 1972, Chief Judge Fox appointed Edward Quinnell to replace his father as the part-time referee for the Northern Division. Quinnell served a two-year term, but he resigned in November 1974 after he was elected judge of the Marquette County Circuit Court. He remained on the circuit bench until 1998 when he retired as the county's longest-serving circuit judge. He practiced law with his son until 2005, and he died on June 23, 2013, at the age of eighty.

MARVIN LEE HEITMAN

On November 8, 1974, Marvin L. Heitman, another member in the Quinnell & Quinnell law firm in Marquette, replaced Edward Quinnell as the part-time referee in the Northern Division. Like David Nims, Heitman went on to become one of the Western District's first Bankruptcy Judges under the bankruptcy code. His life and career are discussed below in the context of that judgeship.

The Bankruptcy Reform Act of 1978: The Bankruptcy Code

For a bankruptcy law, the 1898 Act was remarkably long-lived, surviving eighty years of economic ups and downs, including two World Wars and the Great Depression. However, during the decades after World War II, the number of bankruptcy filings exploded, placing ever greater stress on the system and particularly on the referees who had responsibility for both the administrative and substantive aspects of the 1898 Act. By 1960, the need for a new system was clear, but a dispute over a single issue delayed action for almost two decades. Should jurisdiction over bankruptcy cases remain with the District Courts, or should there be a new, separate Bankruptcy Court in each district with their own Article III judges, appointed by the President and confirmed by the Senate? The existing Article III justices and judges were, for the most part, vehemently opposed to creating Article III Bankruptcy Judges, and they lobbied ceaselessly to defeat any legislation that might result in the creation of a Bankruptcy Court totally independent of the District Courts and with judges appointed under Article III. This opposition retarded the passage of bankruptcy reform legislation for almost 20 years, until November 1978 when Congress enacted the Bankruptcy Reform Act of 1978.[27] This act, which created a new U.S. Code Title 11, also known and referred to commonly as the United States Bankruptcy Code. The Code became effective generally on October 1, 1979.

The Code created a Bankruptcy Court whose judges operate largely independent of the District Court yet who are not Article III judges. Nevertheless, many Article III judges attacked even that limited reform law as unconstitutional. The Code established, in each U.S. District Court, "a Bankruptcy Court which shall be a court of record known as the United States Bankruptcy Court for the district." The Bankruptcy Court was an adjunct of the District Court, not a separate court, and the new court had a new set of federal judicial officers, U.S. Bankruptcy Judges. Some original provisions in the Code evidenced the attempts to create Article III Bankruptcy Judges. For example, the original Code provided that, like Article III judges, Bankruptcy Judges were to be appointed by the President with the advice and consent of the U.S. Senate, but unlike Article III, the Code also required that, in each nomination, "the President shall give due consideration to the recommended nominee or nominees of the Judicial Council of the Circuit within which an appointment is to be made." In 2005, after two decades of experience with presidential appointments, Congress changed the responsibility for the appointment of Bankruptcy Judges to "the court of appeals of the United States for the circuit in which such district is located."

Clear proof that even initially, Congress intended that Bankruptcy Court judges not be Article III judges with the provision of the 1978 Code stipulating that instead of holding their offices for life absent impeachment and conviction by Congress for extremely serious misbehavior, the Bankruptcy Judges were appointed to serve a renewable term of office of fourteen years. Additionally, they could be removed before the end of their term of office, but "only for incompetency, misconduct, neglect of duty, or physical or mental disability." The Code also provides that the number of bankruptcy judgeships in each district is determined by Congress with periodic advice from the Judicial Conference of the United States on the need for additional judges. As of September 2012, there were 316 bankruptcy judgeships, plus 34 temporary judgeships authorized for the districts.

Disagreements over the relationship, on the one hand, between Article III's allocation of bankruptcy matters exclusively to the District Courts, and thus to their Article III district judges, and, on the other hand, the Code's provisions allowing Article I Bankruptcy Judges to control and rule in bankruptcy cases continued to fester and resulted in major changes to the Code. In 1982, in *Northern Pipeline Construction Co. v. Marathon Pipe Line Co.*,[28] the Supreme Court decided that it was unconstitutional for Congress to grant bankruptcy jurisdiction to independent courts composed of judges who did not have the protections of Article III, but the Court postponed the application of its judgment so that Congress could enact legislation to restructure the Bankruptcy Courts.

In 1984, Congress did pass an amending act[29] that addressed that issue and many others. The 1984 Act declared that a U.S. Bankruptcy Judge is "a judicial officer of the District Court, may exercise the authority conferred under this chapter with respect to any action, suit, or proceeding and may preside alone and hold a regular or special session of the court, except as otherwise provided by law or by rule or order of the District Court." To deal with the constitutional issue raised by the Supreme Court in *Marathon Pipe Line*, Congress provided in the amending act that the District Courts retained their original and exclusive jurisdiction over all bankruptcy cases. However, each District Court may "refer" bankruptcy matters to its Bankruptcy Court. In practice, most District Courts have entered a "standing order of reference" that refers all bankruptcy cases to the Bankruptcy Court with a proviso that under some circumstances the District Court may withdraw the reference and take a case back. Absent such a withdrawal of reference, the Code relieves the District Court judges of most involvement with the overwhelming majority of all proceedings in bankruptcy except for appeals from decisions of the Bankruptcy Courts. At the same time, the Code relieves the Bankruptcy Judges of the administrative duties of the referee system and established a system of trustees or creditors' committees to assume these responsibilities.

In 2005, Congress distanced the appointment of Bankruptcy Judges further from the Article III schema by moving the appointment power from the President and Senate to the U.S. Courts of Appeals while also authorizing the Judicial Conference of the United States to establish qualifications for Bankruptcy Judges and the judicial councils of the Circuit Courts to establish merit selection committees to recommend nominees for bankruptcy judgeships.

Types of Bankruptcy Under the Code

As enacted in 1978, the Bankruptcy Code divided bankruptcies into different types, each referred to by a different chapter, the most common being Chapter 7, Chapter 11, and Chapter 13.

About three quarters of all petitions filed in the Bankruptcy Courts are cases under Chapter 7, essentially the "straight bankruptcy" familiar from the pre-code bankruptcy laws. Chapter 7 governs petitions for liquidation of the debtor's assets, available to both corporate businesses (such as corporations and limited liability corporations) and to individuals. A Chapter 7 case begins when a debtor files a petition in the district within which an individual resides or, if the debtor is a business, where it conducts its business. From the moment a petition is filed, an automatic stay is imposed on all property in which the debtor has an interest. This includes not only tangible assets, but also intangible assets such as causes of action for the collection of debts, enforcement of liens, or setting off of claims. For individual debtors, the goal of a Chapter 7 bankruptcy petition is to obtain a discharge of all debts existing at the time the petition is filed, with some exceptions such as student loans, fraud claims, domestic support obligations, and drunk driving penalties. In exchange, while everything is stayed, a trustee theoretically gathers up the debtor's assets into what is called a bankruptcy estate, liquidates the assets not exempted under federal or state law, and distributes the proceeds to the debtor's creditors. Creditors holding debts secured by collateral usually have priority of payment over creditors whose debts are not secured. Of course, a secured creditor can also look to its collateral when collecting its debts if it is granted a motion for relief from the automatic stay or once the bankruptcy case is over or the bankruptcy trustee abandons the property. A business Chapter 7 case also involves the liquidation of assets and the distribution of proceeds, but there is no exempt property and no discharge. The business debtor's operations cease when the petition under Chapter 7 is filed, and the business's assets are turned over to a trustee to liquidate.

Most Chapter 11 cases involve the reorganization of businesses, whether created as corporations, partnerships, or sole proprietorships, but an individual who meets a certain threshold of debt can also file bankruptcy under Chapter 11. Cases under Chapter 11 represent only about 1 percent of all bankruptcy cases, but they take up a highly disproportionate share of the time and efforts of the Bankruptcy Court because many of them are very complicated and continue for years. After a business files a petition under Chapter 11, the company's managers draft and present to the court a reorganization plan that must be approved by the Bankruptcy Court and by a majority of the creditors. The management continues the business as the "debtor in possession" under supervision, usually by a creditors committee, but sometimes under the watchful eye of a Chapter 11 trustee. In order to give the debtor some breathing space, Chapter 11, as with bankruptcies filed under any chapter, imposes an automatic stay of most litigation or debt collection against the debtor in both federal and state courts. The court can also terminate the debtor's long-term contracts and authorize the sale of assets free and clear of anyone else's interests, whether the business is a going concern or whether it is liquidating.

Chapter 13 allows individual debtors with regular income to enter into a reorganization plan in which the debtor agrees to use a portion of that income to pay all or part of the debtor's debts over a period of three to five years under the supervision of a trustee, creditors, and the court. While the case is continuing, the debtor's assets are again protected by an automatic stay. When the plan is completed successfully, the debtor receives a discharge. Chapter 13 cases are usually about 20 percent of the caseload of a Bankruptcy Court.

In October 1986, Congress passed a bankruptcy statute[30] that, among other provisions, added to the Code a Chapter 12 that provides special reorganization rights and procedures available only to "family farmers" or "family fishermen" with "regular annual income." Chapter 12, which went into effect on November 26, 1986, is a reorganization provision similar to Chapters 11 and 13, designed specifically for these specific types of businesses because they have a unique set of operating requirements and challenges and have a harder time complying with the complexities of corporate reorganization under Chapter 11, Because of their land, machinery, barns, and other assets, farmers in particular usually have far more debt than the maximum allowed for "wage earners" who file under Chapter 13. Congress intended Chapter 12 to provide emergency and temporary relief against the tightening of agricultural credit in the midst of many bank failures. Chapter 12 originally had an expiration date of October 1, 1993, however, Congress extended the chapter's life several times until Congress made it permanent by the Bankruptcy Abuse Prevention and Consumer Protection Act of 2005.[31]

In the Western District's Bankruptcy Court, petitioners filed 104 Chapter 12 cases during its first two years (1987 and 1988). However, there were only 301 such cases filed from 1989 to 2016, an average of just 11 per year. The number of Chapter 12 cases filed in any year varies with the changing conditions of the economy, so that only thirty-two cases were filed from 2001 to 2008, while the economic downturn in 2007 led to the filing of forty-six new petitions in the following three years, 2009–2011. Although the number of Chapter 12 filings is always a small fraction of the Bankruptcy Court's caseload, Chapter 12 provides significant and necessary assistance to farmers who face a specific set of concerns, like the weather, that other industries do not.

The U.S. Trustee Program

Among the provisions of the original Code was the establishment of a pilot project for the creation of a new class of bankruptcy officials, the United States Trustee.[32] In the Code, Congress directed the U.S. Attorney General to appoint ten persons to serve as U.S. Trustees in seventeen districts (five single districts and five groups of districts).[33] The Act also authorized the U.S. Trustee to appoint one or more Assistant U.S. Trustees. The U.S. Trustees and Assistants had several duties, including to establish, maintain, and supervise a panel of private trustees for Chapter 7 cases; to act as trustee in Chapter 11 cases where necessary; and to supervise the administration of all bankruptcy cases and trustees. The pilot project was a success, and in the 1986 Act, Congress expanded the U.S. Trustee Program by creating twenty-one regions covering all judicial districts except Alabama and North Carolina.[34]

U.S. Trustees are officers of the Department of Justice charged with enforcing civil bankruptcy laws in the United States. The U.S. Attorney General appoints a separate U.S. Trustee to a five-year term of office for each of the twenty-one regions. The U.S. Trustee Program serves as "a watchdog"[35] over the bankruptcy process, promoting the efficiency and protecting the integrity of the bankruptcy system, by monitoring the conduct of bankruptcy parties and private estate trustees, overseeing related administrative functions, acting to ensure compliance with applicable laws and procedures, and identifying bankruptcy fraud and abuse. The program is funded by the U.S. Trustee System Fund, which consists primarily of fees paid by parties and businesses invoking federal bankruptcy protection. The U.S. Trustees are answerable directly to the Attorney General, but the program is administered overall by the Executive Office for U.S. Trustees, located in Washington, D.C., and by ninety-five field offices.

The involvement of the U.S. Trustee in a bankruptcy case depends on the Code chapter asserted in the petition. In each Chapter 7 case, the U.S. Trustee appoints at random an interim trustee from the district's panel of Chapter 7 trustees. In Chapter 11 cases, the U.S. Trustee's office conducts the first meeting of creditors, but most Chapter 11 cases do not require a trustee. In cases without a trustee, the U.S. Trustee cooperates with the creditors' committees to ensure compliance with the Bankruptcy Code. In Chapter 11 cases with a trustee,[36] the U.S. Trustee oversees the appointed trustee's handling of the case and can seek the removal or replacement of the trustee. Because Chapter 12 cases are relatively few, most districts do not have a Chapter 12 panel of trustees, and in those cases, the U.S. Trustee appoints trustees as needed. Each judicial district has one or more standing Chapter 13 trustees who are responsible for the administration of all Chapter 13 cases filed in their district under the supervision of the U.S. Trustee.

The Western District of Michigan and other judicial districts in Michigan and Ohio are part of U.S. Trustee Program Region 9 whose office is in the U.S. Courthouse in Cleveland, Ohio. The office of the Assistant U.S. Trustee for the Western District, currently Matthew W. Cheney, is in the Ledyard Building in Grand Rapids. The Western District office maintains panels of Chapter 7, Chapter 12, and Chapter 13 trustees across the district. Each U.S. Trustee's office employs a staff that includes accounting staffers who review all debtor filings and monitor trustee and attorney fees in all cases. Attorneys employed by the U.S. Trustee represent the office in U.S. Bankruptcy Court and can pursue civil sanctions for some egregious violations of the law in Chapter 7, 12, and 13 cases.[37]

BANKRUPTCY APPELLATE PANELS

Before 1978, all appeals from decisions of bankruptcy referees and judges were heard by the U.S. District Courts, increasing the heavy caseload of the district judges. In order to promote uniform interpretation and execution of bankruptcy law within a federal judicial circuit, as well as minimizing the cost and delay of a bankruptcy appeal, the 1978 Bankruptcy Code authorized a different appellate path. 28 U.S.C. §158(1) allows, but does not require, U.S. Circuit Courts of Appeal to establish Bankruptcy Appellate Panels (known as BAP) made up of bankruptcy judges from the different states within the circuits. The BAP hears appeals from decisions of the Bankruptcy Courts that would otherwise be heard by district judges. The submission of an appeal to a BAP requires (1) the creation of a BAP system by the Circuit Court, (2) a majority of the district judges for the district in which the appeal arises authorizing parties to use the BAP, and (3) the consent of all parties in the case. The BAP typically sits on an appeal as a three-judge panel composed of bankruptcy judges appointed from the circuit's districts, although no judge may participate in an appeal arising from his own district. All appeals from the BAP go up to the court of appeals for that circuit.

Under the 1978 version of §158(b)(1), circuits were free to opt out of establishing a BAP and to continue to have bankruptcy appeals heard solely by the District Courts. In 1994, Congress enacted the Bankruptcy Reform Act of 1994, which included an amendment of §158(b)(1) that required all Circuit Courts to establish a BAP unless the judicial council of a circuit found either that there were insufficient judicial resources in the circuit to do so, or that the establishment of a BAP would result in undue delay or increased costs to parties in bankruptcy cases.[38] As of 2017, only five of the eleven circuits have convened a BAP: the First, Sixth, Eighth, Ninth, and Tenth. The Sixth Circuit BAP began in 1997, and the District Courts all use the BAP except the Eastern District of Michigan, the Western District of Kentucky, and the Eastern District of Tennessee. The Sixth Circuit's BAP hears about 60 percent of the total bankruptcy appeals from the districts that have elected to use it, approximately 150 appeals each year. The panel consists of six bankruptcy judges who are appointed for staggered three-year terms and may be reappointed. The fact that a District Court has declined to use the BAP does not preclude bankruptcy judges from that district from serving on the BAP.

The Bankruptcy Abuse Prevention and Consumer Protection Act of 2005

On April 20, 2005, Congress enacted the Bankruptcy Abuse Prevention and Consumer Protection Act,[39] known colloquially as BAP/CPA, which made such significant changes to the Code that it has also been called the New Bankruptcy Law. According to one of the sponsors of the Senate bill, Congress included in BAP/CPA many provisions "intended to make it more difficult for people to file bankruptcy."[40] Supporters of the Act in Congress as well as most banks and other consumer lenders believed that too many consumers were deliberately running up debts they could not repay and relying on Chapter 7 to bail them out. Opponents of BAP/CPA argued that the law's supporters were grossly exaggerating the number of debtors who were misusing Chapter 7 and that the changes brought on by BAP/CPA would harm more honest but unfortunate debtors than reduce any real abuse. Among the changes included in BAP/CPA were many intended to influence individuals to refrain from or delay filing Chapter 7 bankruptcy, to limit the number of Chapter 7 cases filed, and to steer individuals into filing Chapter 13 instead so that most creditors would receive some distribution from the debtor.

THE CASELOAD AND OPERATIONS OF THE BANKRUPTCY COURT UNDER THE CODE AND THE BAP/CPA

From the effective date of the Code until the effective date of the BAP/CPA, October 17, 2005, the Bankruptcy Court for the Western District received 215,000 bankruptcy cases filed under Chapters 7, 11, and 13. The vast majority, 75 percent, were liquidation cases filed under Chapter 7, while another 20 percent were wage-earner reorganization cases filed under Chapter 13. During the last full fiscal year under the 1978 Act, ending June 30, 1979, there were 2,147 petitions filed. This was above the average of the previous ten years, but not by much. In fiscal year 1981, under the Code, there were 5,182 petitions filed, 3,000 more than in 1979. Part of that increase was due to a flood of 2,400 Chapter 13 filings, probably resulting from the recession that struck the nation in January 1980, at that time the most significant retreat of the economy since the Great Depression. The causes of that recession included large increases in the price of oil and the Federal Reserve's efforts to tame the high level of inflation rampant during the late 1970s. In 1983, during a robust economic recovery, the number of Chapter 13 filings decreased to 1,550 in 1983 and did not surpass 2,000 again until 1996. The largest number of Chapter 13 filings occurred during fiscal years 1997 to 2004, averaging 3,200 per year, but the number decreased steadily after that to 1,455 in 2016.

Filings of Chapter 7 cases also increased with the enactment of the 1978 Code, from 1,700 in 1980 to 2,400 in 1982 and to 5,468 in fiscal year 1991. The number of Chapter 7 filings then nearly doubled between 1994 (4,904 filings) and 2001 (9,687 filings). In fiscal year 2005, just before the effective date of the BAP/CPA, the Western District's Bankruptcy Court received slightly more than 15,000 new Chapter 7 cases. The increase of both Chapter 7 and Chapter 13 filings under the Code before 2005 was related to at least two factors. The first was a general change, beginning in the 1970s, in the buying habits of the public. Consumers embraced the use of credit cards for purchases instead of paying with cash. The vertiginous growth of consumer debt has the complementary effect of a greater need for consumer relief.

The second is the effect of historical and political events that occurred during those decades, including the shock to a wide swath of the economy caused by the events of September 11, 2001. At the same time, consumers and their attorneys were aware for many years that Congress was working on bankruptcy reforms that were likely to restrict eligibility for Chapter 7 bankruptcies. This factor was emphasized during the six months in 2005 (April to October) between the enactment of BAP/CPA and its effective date during which consumers' became aware of the Act's confusing drafting and its more favorable provisions for lenders and banks. The result was a spike in people trying to file Chapter 7 bankruptcies before BAP/CPA took effect.

During the first couple of years after the BAP/CPA became law, a decrease in the number of bankruptcy filings in the Western District seemed to indicate that it was achieving its purpose. There were almost 28,000 Chapter 7 filings in fiscal years 2004 and 2005, there were only 17,300 in fiscal years 2007 and 2008. However, filings under both Chapter 7 and Chapter 13 returned to pre-BAP/CPA levels in fiscal years 2009 and 2010 because of the great recession and the collapse of the housing bubble. Since 2010, the number of filings under both chapters has declined consistently so that there were only 5,700 Chapter 7 filings and 1,500 Chapter 13 filings in fiscal year 2016. The reason for this decrease is not clear, but it may be that people who might have filed a few years before had either adjusted to their changed circumstances, gone on welfare, or found jobs so that, at least temporarily, they did not need relief.

Nevertheless, as was the case nationally, Chapter 11 filings were in most years about 1 percent of the total. During the first decade after the beginning of the Code, from 1982 through 1994, there were more than one hundred Chapter 11 cases filed each year, but the number of filings then decreased to twenty-four in 2016. However, the number of Chapter 11 cases does not tell the whole story of the amount of time and effort those cases impose on the Bankruptcy Court or how much of the court's Chapter 11 work mirrored the economy and industry changes of the particular place or era. For example, during the 1980s, the court was busy in the Upper Peninsula with large Chapter 11 cases related to the decline of the area's mining, oil (Ellingsen MacLean Oil Co., Inc.), and shipbuilding (Upper Peninsula Shipbuilding Co.) industries. In Traverse City, also during the 1980s, the docket addressed the rise and fall of oil on the ridges (e.g., Reef Oil et al.), and the hospitality industry during the 1990s (e.g., Perry Hotel and Grand Traverse Resort). The Kalamazoo docket in the 1980s was filled with hearings related to the decline of auto parts manufacturing and the paper industry in the 1990s, and, in the 2000s, and the metal recycling business. In Grand Rapids throughout these periods, the court was occupied with the demise of major retailers and chains headquartered there (e.g., Gantos, Witmark, Quality Farm & Fleet, House of Flavors, Bill Knapp's, and Family Christian Stores), marine operators (e.g., Dry Land Marina, Cary Marine, and Grand Valley Marine), and heavy industry (e.g., Bofors Nobel Inc.).[41]

The Judges of the U.S. Bankruptcy Court for the Western District of Michigan, 1980–2018

U.S. Bankruptcy Judge David Erwin Nims, Jr.

Judge David E. Nims was born on July 15, 1912, in Grand Rapids, to David E. Nims Sr. and Elizabeth Henrietta (Dietrich) Nims. The family moved around the country following his father's jobs, but they eventually returned to Michigan and settled in Muskegon. Judge Nims graduated from Muskegon High School in 1929. He studied for two years at Muskegon Junior College and then transferred to Wayne (now Wayne State) University where he earned his bachelor degree. In 1933, he entered the University of Michigan Law School from which he graduated in 1936 with a juris doctor degree. From 1936 to 1941, he practiced with a firm in Kalamazoo doing insurance defense trials, but this work was interrupted by World War II.

In April 1941, he was called into active service with the U.S. Army. After training, he was stationed in Reykjavik, Iceland, where he litigated criminal trials. In July 1943, the army apparently decided it needed infantry officers more than lawyers and returned him to Fort Leonard Wood, in the Ozark Mountains of Missouri, for more training. There he married Sybil Spencer whom he had met in Ann Arbor. In September of 1944, he was shipped to Europe where he took part in the Battle of the Bulge. Later, in Germany, after crossing the Rhine, he was wounded by enemy artillery. He received the Purple Heart. After recovering, he transferred to the Judge Advocate General Corps. After the war, he continued as a military judge as a member of the Army Reserves until his retirement in 1968 as a colonel.

When he returned home, Judge Nims resumed his law practice in Kalamazoo. Over the next decade, he served as President of the Kalamazoo Bar Association, chairman of the Family Law Committee of the Michigan State Bar, and for five years the U.S. Commissioner in the Kalamazoo federal court. He was also elected to the Kalamazoo Board of Education and served as chairman of the Kalamazoo Democratic Party. When a second full-time bankruptcy referee position for the Western District was created, Judge Starr appointed Nims to join the incumbent referee, Chester Woolridge, in Grand Rapids. Although the appointment required Nims to move with his family from Kalamazoo to Grand Rapids, he accepted. When Congress created the U.S. Bankruptcy Courts in 1978, Nims was one of the three sitting referees for the Western District. The Bankruptcy Code set a transition period within which sitting bankruptcy referees appointed under the 1898 Bankruptcy Act would continue in office as U.S. Bankruptcy Judges under the code until a successor took office or March 31, 1984.

Judge Nims was appointed as a Bankruptcy Judge under the Code and continued to serve for thirteen years. When, in June 1986, his term as a Bankruptcy Judge expired, he still wanted to work, but he was almost seventy-five years old, and the judges of the Sixth Circuit were reluctant because of his age to give him a new full 14-year term. He retired reluctantly, but because of the district's swollen bankruptcy docket, more than sixteen thousand new cases filed in the previous three years, the Sixth Circuit recalled him for a "relief appointment" renewable annually. He finally retired for good in 1992 because of failing health. Counting his years as a referee, Judge Nims served the court for thirty-seven years, one of the longest-serving Bankruptcy Judges ever. He died on February 28, 2003, in Grand Rapids, at the age of ninety.

Judge Nims was a great scholar of bankruptcy law and a great teacher both to attorneys practicing in his court and others around the country. He also had a great love of people as well as compassion for the debtors he saw from the bench, based in part on his family's experience with bankruptcy when they lost their Muskegon filling station just before the crash in 1929. Attorneys appearing before Judge Nims recognized him as gentle, with a patient disposition, always in good humor, and with a friendly demeanor in court where he created a comfortable atmosphere for all people who came before him. He was also exceedingly punctual. It was important to him that every person before him understood their rights. He treated his staff no differently, and greeted every court employee each morning while walking through the Clerk's office. He loved his work and once commented that he was sometimes ashamed he was being paid.[42]

U.S. Bankruptcy Judge Laurence Edward Howard

Laurence E. Howard was born on February 15, 1934, in Ionia, Michigan, to Leo E. and Marian (Burtch) Howard. After graduation from SS. Peter and Paul Catholic School in Ionia, Judge Howard served in the U.S. Army during the Korean War. During his service, he was stationed in Chicago and attended Northwestern University. After his discharge, he attended Notre Dame University where he received his undergraduate degree (BA, 1958) and his law degree (JD, 1961). After law school, he and his wife, Marilyn, moved to Detroit where Judge Howard worked for Gar Wood Industries for a short time and then joined a small firm in Royal Oak, Michigan. In 1964, he accepted a position as Assistant City Attorney for Grand Rapids, a part-time job that allowed him to have a private practice as well. In 1966, he left the city job and continued his general law practice full time.

Howard was always interested in politics and the Democratic Party. In 1968, he agreed to run for Congress as a Democrat against the incumbent Congressman, Gerald Ford. He lost but received 37.5 percent of the vote. He found his involvement in the turbulent campaigns of that year to be the experience of a lifetime, including serving as a delegate to the Democratic National Convention in Chicago. He remained active in Democratic politics. In 1975, he heard that Edward Benson, bankruptcy referee for the Western District of Michigan, was going to retire and that the District Court was seeking applicants to succeed him. Howard applied and, after a short process and background check, District Judges Fox and Miles appointed him to the position on January 14, 1976. After the passage of the Bankruptcy Code, he remained in office as a Bankruptcy Judge for the U.S. Bankruptcy Court of the Western District of Michigan.

Judge Howard had not practiced in bankruptcy much before his appointment as a referee, and at the beginning of his tenure he relied heavily on advice from Judge Nims. He quickly absorbed the necessary statutes and case law, although the enormous changes involved in the 1978 Code left both judges, for a while, scrambling to decide what the new statute meant. Judge Howard served as a referee and judge for twenty-three years before he retired on February 28, 1999. In February 2003, while he was vacationing with his family at their winter home on Marco Island, Florida, his doctors discovered an aneurysm and operated, but Judge Howard died at the hospital on February 22, 2003. He was sixty-nine years old and was survived by Marilyn, his wife of more than forty years.

Like Judge Nims, Judge Howard ran a courtroom that was comfortable for litigants and that was emblematic of his easygoing temperament and his ready sense of humor. He accepted without apology his label as a pro-debtor judge who wanted to give debtors a second chance. He explained that being poor and losing the family home were among the worst things that can happen so that he always gave debtors as much time as he could to try to avoid such a loss. He had great sympathy for all struggling debtors, and he never forgot about the real consequences of his decisions. During his years as a referee and Bankruptcy Judge, he handled thousands of cases, and he handled each one as if it was the single most important case before him. He is remembered for his compassion, fairness, humility, and integrity. He was a role model for bankruptcy attorneys and judges.[43]

U.S. Bankruptcy Judge Marvin Lee Heitman

Judge Marvin L. Heitman was born on July 7, 1930, in Marquette, Michigan, to Ernest C. and Emma (Boese) Heitman. He graduated from Marquette High School in 1948, and he attended Northern Michigan University for one year. In July 1949, he left school and enlisted in the U.S. Air Force, which trained him as an electronics specialist. When his enlistment ended in 1953, he returned to Northern Michigan and graduated in 1956 with a bachelor of arts degree. Although his major was pre-law, he initially followed his interest in electronics and worked for Michigan Bell Telephone from 1956 to 1964. While working for Michigan Bell, he also began to study law. After one year at Wayne State University Law School, he transferred to the Detroit College of Law where he earned his juris doctor degree in 1963.

Not long after graduating from law school, Heitman returned to Marquette to practice bankruptcy law with George and Edward Quinnell. George was already a long-serving bankruptcy referee, and his son, Edward, would inherit the referee position in 1972. On November 8, 1974, after Edward Quinnell was elected Marquette County's Circuit Court judge, District Judges Miles and Engel appointed Heitman to succeed him as the Northern Division's part-time referee. When the bankruptcy code went into effect in 1979, Heitman became a U.S. Bankruptcy Judge, although still on a part-time basis.

The 1978 Code allowed the appointment of both full-time and part-time Bankruptcy Judges. In the Western District of Michigan, Judges Nims and Howard had full-time appointments, but Judge Heitman was still part-time. Nationally, most Bankruptcy Judges/Referees did serve part-time, so most of the first Bankruptcy Judges were appointed as part-timers. This proved to be inefficient, and the 1984 amendments to the Code specified that all Bankruptcy Judges "shall serve on a full-time basis"[44] and could not otherwise practice law.

Congress provided transitional relief for part-time judges sitting at the time of the enactment of the 1984 amendments by allowing them to serve for two years after the amendments' effective date (i.e., until July 10, 1986)[45] and to practice law other than bankruptcy. On July 2, 1986, Congress further extended the term of part-time Bankruptcy Judges to the earlier of the date of the appointment of a full-time judge in their place or to December 31, 1986. This extension applied to part-time Bankruptcy Judges in three districts, the Western District of Michigan, the District of Oregon, and the Eastern District of Oklahoma.[46] The Sixth Circuit did not name a full-time judge for the Northern Division, and Judge Heitman retired on December 31, 1986, at the age of fifty-six. Judge Heitman died in Marquette on September 25, 2007, at the age of seventy-seven. He was considered to be learned and efficient, and, as one attorney noted, he was not particularly partial to ceremony or formality. Upon Heitman's retirement without the appointment of a full-time successor, the Northern Division's resident Bankruptcy Judge position expired, and the remaining Bankruptcy Judges, all residing in the Southern Division, added Marquette to the destinations they travel to and hold court.

U.S. Bankruptcy Judge James D. Gregg

James D. Gregg was born in Detroit on December 6, 1947. He graduated from
Livonia Bentley High School and from Michigan State University where
he earned a degree in divisional social science (BS, 1969) and where he met
his wife, Elizabeth Holmes. They both taught school for several years, and
he obtained his masters degree in education administration from Central
Michigan University. However, after scoring very high on the Law School
Admissions Test, he decided to try the law as a career. He entered Wayne
State University Law School in Detroit and graduated with high honors (JD,
1978, magna cum laude). After graduation, Judge Gregg moved with his family to Grand Rapids to practice law. He joined the firm of Schmidt, Howlett,
Van't Hof, Snell & Vana, which in 1983 merged with another firm and be-
came Varnum, Riddering, Schmidt & Howlett. He specialized in commercial
law, bankruptcy, and corporate reorganizations. He was first appointed to a
fourteen-year term as judge on the U.S. Bankruptcy Court for the Western
District of Michigan by the U.S. Court of Appeals for the Sixth Circuit on
June 1, 1987, and in 2001 he was reappointed to a second fourteen-year term.
He served as Chief Judge of the court from 1997 to 2005 and then again, after
Judge Stevenson retired, from 2007 to 2013. Recognized as one of the nation's
leading Bankruptcy Judges, Judge Gregg was on the Bankruptcy Appellate
Panel for the Sixth Circuit from 2004 to 2007. From 1997 to 1999 and again
in 2001, he was a visiting judge in the United States Bankruptcy Court for
the Southern District of Florida. He also served two stints as a visiting Bankruptcy Judge for the Eastern District of Michigan from 1997 to 1999 and
from 2001 to 2003. He taught at the Thomas Cooley Law School and served
as President of the National Conference of Bankruptcy Judges, on the executive committee of the American Bankruptcy Institute, and as a Class VIII
Fellow in the American College of Bankruptcy. Judge Gregg retired from the
Western District's Bankruptcy Court on June 27, 2014.

U.S. Bankruptcy Judge Jo Ann Cacavio Stevenson

On December 23, 1987, Jo Ann C. Stevenson became the first woman to be appointed judge of any federal court in the Western District of Michigan when
she was appointed to the Bankruptcy Court. She was also the first woman
to serve as chief judge of a Western District federal court, from March 2005
until October 2007, when she retired from the Bankruptcy Court. Judge Ste-

venson was born on October 2, 1942, in Seattle, Washington. She grew up in Hamilton Square, New Jersey, and she graduated in 1960 from Hamilton High School East, Joseph Steinert Memorial. She was the first person in her family to attend college, graduating in 1964 from Douglass College, the Rutgers University, with majors in French and political science. After graduating, she worked at several jobs in New Jersey, including the Gallup Organization and Educational Testing Service, got married, and had a child, Kenneth Stevenson. It was not until 1976 that she began law school at the Detroit College of Law (now Michigan State University College of Law) from which she graduated cum laude in 1979. After leaving law school, she worked for the prehearing division of the Michigan Court of Appeals and as law clerk for the Hon. Vincent J. Brennan of that court. She also clerked for one year with the Hon. Cornelia G. Kennedy, Judge of the U.S. Court of Appeals for the Sixth Circuit. She then entered private practice with the business bankruptcy practice group at the firm of Hertzberg, Jacob & Weingarten in Detroit. She practiced there until 1997 when the Sixth Circuit authorized a third full-time judge for the U.S. Bankruptcy Court for the Western District of Michigan. She applied, and after a long vetting process, she won the appointment. She began her judgeship on December 23, 1987, and retired almost twenty years later, on October 2, 2007. In the course of her career, Judge Stevenson authored several hundred opinions, of which approximately 95 percent were affirmed on appeal. During the time Judge Stevenson was on the bench, she also taught bankruptcy reorganization and debtor/creditor relations at her alma mater. She has given numerous presentations and speeches and participated in many panels, including conferences for the Federal Bar Association Bankruptcy Seminar, the Conference for Chief Bankruptcy Judges, the American Bankruptcy Institute, the Grand Rapids Bar Association, the University of Michigan Institute of Public Policy Studies, and the Sixth Circuit Judicial Conference. Judge Stevenson has published articles in the *American Bankruptcy Law Journal* and the *Detroit College of Law Review*.

U.S. Bankruptcy Judge Jeffrey Raymond Hughes

Jeffrey R. Hughes was born on November 16, 1954, in St. Joseph, Michigan, the son of the Hon. Julian and Evelyn Hughes. He grew up in nearby Benton Township and graduated from Benton Harbor High School in 1973. He earned his undergraduate degree (BA, 1977) and his law degree (JD, 1980) at the University of Michigan. From 1980 until 2000, he also practiced in

Grand Rapids with the law firm of Schmidt, Howlett, Van't Hof, Snell & Vana, which merged with the Varnum Riddering firm in 1983 to become Varnum, Riddering, Schmidt, & Howlett, LLP. He was appointed to the bench of the U.S. Bankruptcy Court for the Western District of Michigan in September 1999 and was sworn in on January 6, 2000, to succeed Bankruptcy Judge Laurence Howard. Judge Hughes is married to Sharon Hughes, and they have three children. He retired from the Bankruptcy Court on September 13, 2013, and was succeeded by John T. Gregg.

The U.S. Bankruptcy Court for the Western District of Michigan in 2020

As of 2020, the Bankruptcy Court for the Western District of Michigan has three U.S. Bankruptcy Judges, Chief Judge Scott W. Dales and Judges James W. Boyd and John T. Gregg.

Chief U.S. Bankruptcy Judge Scott W. Dales

Judge Dales graduated from George Washington University Law School and served as a law clerk for U.S. District Judge Constantine G. Cholakis of the Northern District of New York. After practicing law for several years in Albany, New York, in 1998 he moved to Grand Rapids to clerk for Bankruptcy Judge James D. Gregg. After his clerkship, he practiced law with the Dykema law firm in Grand Rapids and then served as in-house counsel to National City Corporation's insolvency practice group and its bank and nonbank subsidiaries until October 2007 when he was appointed to the Bankruptcy Court to succeed Judge Stevenson. He became Chief Judge in October 2013 upon the retirement of Judge James Gregg.

U.S. Bankruptcy Judge James Wesley Boyd

James W. Boyd was born on March 15, 1955, in Yale, St. Clair County, Michigan. He grew up in Croswell, Sanilac County, Michigan. He graduated from Croswell-Lexington High School in 1973, Michigan State University in 1977, and from Thomas M. Cooley Law School, now Western Michigan University/Thomas M. Cooley Law School, in 1981. While attending law school, he worked for the Michigan House of Representatives Committee on Corrections. In 1984, he moved to Traverse City where he worked for local governments. In 1988, he began a law practice specializing in bankruptcy and insolvency matters, and he also served as a Chapter 7 and Chapter 11 bankruptcy trustee. For twenty-five years, he continued his law practice, alone and as a partner in a Traverse City firm, as well as his trustee work. From 1999 to 2012, he was a board member of the National Association of Bankruptcy Trustees, serving as its President from 2009 to 2010. On May 30, 2014, he was appointed to be a U.S. Bankruptcy Court Judge for the Western District of Michigan, succeeding Bankruptcy Court Chief Judge James Gregg.

U.S. Bankruptcy Judge John T. Gregg

John T. Gregg, the son of retired Chief Bankruptcy Judge James Gregg and Elizabeth (Holmes) Gregg, was born in Big Rapids, Michigan, on April 3, 1974, and grew up in Rockford, Michigan. He graduated from Rockford High School in 1992, the University of Michigan in 1996, and, DePaul University College of Law in 2002. After working in Chicago for three years, he joined the Grand Rapids office of the law firm Barnes & Thornburg in 2005. He practiced at that firm until he was appointed to the bench of the Bankruptcy Court on July 17, 2014, to succeed Judge Jeffrey Hughes. He is married to Korie Gregg, and they have a son.

Bankruptcy Court Locations

As has been the case since the end of the separate slot for a Bankruptcy Judge in the Northern Division, all three of the present Bankruptcy Judges have their chambers in the court's headquarters, at 1 Division Avenue N, in Grand Rapids, where the court moved in October 2005 from the Gerald R. Ford Federal Building.[47] Each Bankruptcy Judge holds court periodically in all five locations in which Congress has authorized the District Court to preside: Grand Rapids, Kalamazoo, Marquette, Lansing, and Traverse City. In Marquette, the Bankruptcy Court shares a courtroom on the second floor of the U.S. Post Office and Courthouse with the District Court. There are judicial chamber facilities for each Bankruptcy Judge when he is holding court, which occurs about once each month. In Lansing, the Bankruptcy Court has a courtroom in the Charles E. Chamberlain Federal Building and Post Office, the building where the District Court also has its courtroom. As in Marquette, Traverse City, and Lansing, there is no resident staff of the Bankruptcy Court in Kalamazoo, but the court does use facilities in the federal courthouse for hearings and meetings. Traverse City has never had a federal courthouse of any kind. Although Congress has authorized the District Court to sit there since 1970, it has yet to do so. The Bankruptcy Court rents a court facility in an office park in Traverse City at 3249 Racquet Club Drive.

Because the Bankruptcy Court is allotted three Bankruptcy Judges and has five court locations to cover, the Bankruptcy Judges engage in a more complex version of the old judicial custom of riding circuit, holding court a number of days each month in the venues outside of Grand Rapids. Currently, Judge Dales is assigned to cases in Grand Rapids, Kalamazoo, and Lansing. The other two judges hold court in Grand Rapids; Judge Gregg also sits in Marquette and Kalamazoo, and Judge Boyd sits in Traverse City.

CHAPTER 10

The Offices of the U.S. Attorney and the Federal Public Defender

The U.S. Attorneys for the Western District of Michigan

IN THE JUDICIARY ACT of 1789, Congress created the first U.S. federal court system as well as other federal officers necessary for that system's operations, including an attorney in each judicial district to represent the interests of the United States. Section 35 of that first judiciary act provided that, for each judicial district, the President was to nominate and the Senate confirm "a meet person learned in the law to act as attorney for the United States" in both criminal and civil cases.[1] These "meet persons" were at first called United States District Attorneys, but they were often also referred to in government documents and elsewhere simply as United States Attorneys. For clarity, this book will generally use the latter title, which became official in 1948, regardless of the time period being discussed. Each U.S. Attorney and U.S. Attorney's Office is further identified by its judicial district, such as the Office of the U.S. Attorney "for the Western District of Michigan," or sometimes "Michigan." Each district's U.S. Attorney is the highest ranking federal law enforcement officer in the district who, with the office's Assistant U.S. Attorneys and the other staff, represents the United States in legal matters, both civil and criminal, arising in or concerning matters within the geographical confines of the district.

President George Washington described the essential qualities that he believed would characterize an attorney to be a meet person: "The high importance of the judicial system in our national government makes it an indispensable duty to select such characters to fill the several offices in it as would discharge their respective duties in honor to themselves and advantage to their country."[2] About 150 years later, in his opinion in *Berger v. United States,*

U.S. Supreme Court Justice George Sutherland expressed that ideal thusly: "The United States Attorney is the representative not of an ordinary party to a controversy, but of a sovereignty whose obligation to govern impartially is as compelling as its obligation to govern at all; and whose interest, therefore, in a criminal prosecution is not that it shall win a case, but that justice shall be done."[3]

Until 1870, U.S. Attorneys acted with considerable independence from the rest of the federal government, although they theoretically answered, at different times and for different purposes, to the Secretary of State, the Secretary of the Interior, the Secretary of the Treasury, and the Attorney General. Attorneys appointed U.S. Attorneys were usually prominent members of their community who were used to acting without supervision and who, in most districts, spent as much time or more on their private practice and businesses as they did on their duties as U.S. Attorneys. As early as 1791, President George Washington recommended that Congress give the U.S. Attorney General superintendence over U.S. Attorneys, but nothing happened.[4] In 1820, Congress did appoint an "agent" of the Treasury Department to superintend and give instructions to the U.S. Attorneys regarding suits for money or property involving the United States and regarding debts owed to the United States. However, problems of distance, communication, and resources made it difficult for any "agent" in Washington to even attempt supervision of those cases. In 1829, President Andrew Jackson renewed President Washington's request that the Attorney General supervise suits being handled by the U.S. Attorneys, but once again Congress refused. Instead, the legislators created the office of the Solicitor General to instruct the U.S. Attorneys, court clerks, and Marshals in the conduct of all civil litigation in which the United States was a party, but most U.S. Attorneys ignored that advice if it displeased them.

In practice, then, the U.S. Attorneys continued to enjoy independence, a situation which led to some problems. For example, like federal court clerks and U.S. Marshals, U.S. Attorneys were compensated by fees paid by the opposing parties in each civil case filed and by the United States in criminal cases. This arrangement gave rise to a frequent complaint that U.S. Attorneys had an incentive, which they too often gave in to, to file a large number of civil and criminal cases of questionable merit and to perform other tasks of doubtful usefulness simply to generate fees. To deal with those complaints, in 1849 Congress created the Interior Department, which, among other responsibilities, was authorized to oversee the financial accounts of the U.S. Attorneys, clerks, and Marshals, but for all other purposes, U.S. Attorneys remained stubbornly independent. In 1854, U.S. Attorney General Caleb Cushing again proposed a new department that would consolidate all federal legal business, but congressional opposition, led by Michigan Senator Lewis Cass, killed that proposal once more.

In August 1861, in order to increase control over the enforcement of federal laws during the "present insurrection," Congress finally did transfer to the Attorney General the "general superintendence and direction of the attorneys and Marshals in all of the districts in the United States and the Territories as to the manner of discharging their respective duties."[5] That law also imposed on the U.S. Attorneys and Marshals a duty "to report to the Attorney-General an account of their official proceedings, and the state and condition of their respective offices, in such time and manner as the Attorney-General shall direct." Furthermore, the law authorized the Attorney General to hire up to two additional clerks "to discharge the increased duties . . . occasioned by this act." Congress may have expected that this Act would reduce the independence of the U.S. Attorneys, but it was passed at a time when the Attorney General was both the President's chief legal counsel and a member of the cabinet setting policy for war operations and thus had many more pressing responsibilities than disciplining U.S. Attorneys. Besides, even with two new clerks, the Attorney General faced the same problems affecting earlier efforts to oversee U.S. Attorneys, and any attempt at "superintendence" was just as ineffective as ever.

True oversight of the U.S. Attorneys did not begin until June 1870, when Congress finally decided to unify federal legal business by creating the U.S. Department of Justice, headed by the Attorney General.[6] Among its many provisions dealing with establishing the new department's structure, assets, and responsibilities, the 1870 Act mandated that the Attorney General "shall have supervision of the conduct and proceedings of the various attorneys for the United States in the respective judicial districts who shall make report to him of their proceedings. . . ."[7]

The 1870 law also directed the Attorney General to report annually to Congress "of the business of the said Department of Justice and any other matters pertaining thereto that he may deem proper. . . ."[8] The first such annual report, submitted by Attorney General Amos T. Akerman in January 1871,[9] included information reported by U.S. Attorneys such as the number of terminations in 1870 of criminal cases and of civil cases in which the United States was a party, as well as the number of cases pending at the end of the year. Although several District Attorneys did not file reports for 1870, John H. Standish, U.S. Attorney for Western Michigan, did so, and after a few years all of the districts submitted reports, although the accuracy of the reports during the remainder of the nineteenth century was often dubious. In 1886, Attorney General Augustus Garland complained that most federal court records were in such disarray that no accurate statistics were possible. For example, many District and Circuit Court clerks did not bother to determine whether cases that were settled or abandoned should be classified as closed. Thus, by 1900 a District Court clerk might tell the U.S. Attorney that a hundred new cases of all kinds were filed the previous year, but that the court's docket showed several hundred cases still open and "pending."

Although the Department of Justice and the Attorney General had finally secured control over the U.S. Attorneys, they faced another lengthy struggle with the legal staffs of other departments to control all litigation involving the federal government. Before the creation of the Department of Justice, Congress had authorized the employment of many attorneys by other departments and offices of the federal government for matters related to their areas of interest. In 1913, more than forty years after the creation of the Department of Justice, the legal affairs of the federal government, including litigation, were still dispersed among the independent legal staffs of the Departments of Justice, State, Treasury, Interior, Commerce, Labor, Agriculture, and Navy, the Post Office, and the Internal Revenue Service.[10] Except for a brief consolidation of jurisdiction during World War I, all of those agencies acted independently until 1930, when President Franklin D. Roosevelt finally issued an executive order transferring to the Department of Justice the authority to handle all litigation for the United States and the exclusive right to supervise the U.S. Attorneys. As a result, the other departments and agencies reluctantly transferred more than thirteen thousand cases to the Department of Justice. The Attorney General, in turn, transferred most of those cases, of which a great majority were then assigned to various U.S. Attorneys across the country. Almost ninety years later, U.S. Attorneys are accepted as the chief federal law enforcement officers of their district. They and their more than five thousand Assistant U.S. Attorneys conduct the great majority of the Justice Department's criminal prosecutions and civil litigation in federal courts.

The Western District of Michigan's U.S. Attorneys

Since the creation of the Western District of Michigan in 1863, the district has had thirty-eight U.S. Attorneys (See Appendix F). The first, appointed by President Lincoln, was Frederick O. Rogers, the county prosecutor for Berrien County, who served as U.S. Attorney from 1863 to 1865. Each U.S. Attorney brings his or her own experience and sense of service to the district, but there have also been several common themes.

At least ten of the Western District's U.S. Attorneys, as well as at least one attorney who resided in western Michigan and who served as U.S. Attorney for the District of Michigan, served in the armed forces at some time during their lives. William L. Stoughton, of St. Joseph County, was appointed U.S. Attorney for the District of Michigan by President Lincoln, in March 1861, but he resigned a few months later to become colonel of the 11th Michigan Volunteer Infantry Regiment. He fought in several Civil War battles, and he was awarded the rank of major general upon his resignation from the army for ill health. Irish-born Andrew T. McReynolds, the district's third U.S. Attorney (1866–1867), was a decorated cavalry officer in both the Mexican-American and Civil Wars. He took part in headlong cavalry charges in both wars, one to the gates of Mexico City and one in Virginia galloping at the head of his brigade at the age of fifty-seven. Another Union veteran, Lewis Palmer (1890–1894), saw service as a drummer boy at the age of eleven. U.S. Attorney Wendell Miles (1953–1960), a future Chief U.S. District Court Judge, served as an officer and lawyer in the U.S. Army in the European theater during and after World War II. Recently, Charles R. Gross (2007–2008) served as a colonel in the U.S. Marine Corps in Iraq in 2006. Donald A. Davis (2008–2012) also served in the Marine Corps, and Robert G. Quinn (1964–1965) and Phillip J. Green (2001) served in the U.S. Navy.

Several of the district's U.S. Attorneys enjoyed politics and served as lawmakers before or after their appointment. Stoughton, McReynolds, and John W. Stone (1882–1886) all served as legislators before their U.S. Attorney appointments. Stoughton represented Michigan's second congressional district, Stone represented Michigan's fifth congressional district, and McReynolds served as a state senator. Lewis Palmer became a state senator after serving his term as U.S. Attorney, while Augustus Griswold (1865–1866) was both a state representative before his appointment and a state senator afterward.

Five of the district's U.S. Attorneys became judges after their federal prosecutorial service. Among these are Wendell Miles, who served on three courts: Michigan's twentieth circuit court, the Western District of Michigan's U.S. District Court, and the federal Foreign Intelligence Surveillance Court. After John Stone completed his time as U.S. Attorney, he was elected judge of Michigan's twenty-fifth circuit court, and after sitting in that court for nineteen years, he was elected in 1909 to the Michigan Supreme Court. Robert J. Danhof (1960–1961) was appointed to the Michigan Court of Appeals in 1969 where he served as judge and then chief judge for twenty-three years. Former U.S. Attorney Phillip Green has served as a U.S. Magistrate Judge since 2014. Robert G. Quinn, Jr. became a U.S. Commissioner in 1969.

Assistant U.S. Attorneys

Many Assistant U.S. Attorneys for the Western District have gone on to assume positions on the bench. In the Western District, these include U.S. District Judge Janet T. Neff, U.S. Magistrate Judges Hugh W. Brenneman, Jr., Phillip J. Green, Maarten Vermatt, Sally J. Berens, and U.S. Commissioner Robert G. Quinn, Jr., as well as U.S. District Judge John (Jay) E. Steele of the Middle District of Florida. Former assistants who have moved to a state court bench include former Kent County, Michigan, Circuit Court Judge and presently Michigan Court of Appeals Judge James Redford, and Kent County Circuit Judges Joseph Rossi, Roman J. Snow, and H. David Soet as well as Michigan State District Judges Carol A. Husum, Jeanine LaVille, and Michael Schipper.

Since 1863, the number of Assistant U.S. Attorneys in the Western District has grown from none to three dozen. In 1863, U.S. Attorney Frederick O. Rogers operated from his private law office with no official assistant; he was paid a small salary plus fees. In 1876, U.S. Attorney John H. Standish, still being compensated with $200 and fees, had one assistant, William D. Fuller, whom he paid from the fees the office collected. In 1910, U.S. Attorney Fred C. Wetmore still had just one official assistant, William K. Clute, who received a salary from the government of $2,000 per year. The U.S. Attorney continued to serve with just one assistant until September 1925, when an additional assistant position was added to handle matters in the Northern Division. The first assistant assigned to the U.S. Attorney's office in Marquette was John Jones.

Ella Mae Backus, First Female Assistant U.S. Attorney in the Western District[11]

Born in April 1863 in Oakland County's Royal Oak Township, Ella Mae Backus was raised on her parents' farms in various locations in western Michigan. After graduating from a one-room school, she taught in a similar school in Harbor Springs, and then she attended Northern Indiana Normal School and the Ferris Industrial School to train for work as a stenographer. It was only when she was hired at the Pratt & Davis law firm in Traverse City that she began to consider becoming a lawyer. With her employers' support, she studied law on her own and became a member of the Traverse City bar in August 1895. Although she did try cases, often won them for her clients, and developed a reputation as a fine trial attorney, she found that she preferred office legal work. When the position of clerk opened up in the office of the U.S. Attorney in Grand Rapids in 1903, she applied and was hired. She would spend the rest of her long life in that office.

In 1903, clerks for U.S. Attorneys were almost all men. The clerk was responsible for keeping the office's financial records and the files and records of cases opened, closed, and pending. The clerk also prepared the detailed reports that the U.S. Attorney sent to the Justice Department each year, and the clerk drafted and typed correspondence and other documents. Few of the clerks had a legal education, but Ella Mae Backus's legal background and her experience in her law practice made her exceptionally helpful to the office she joined. On some occasions she appeared in court representing the United States, based on her bar membership, even though she was not an official assistant, but her profound knowledge of the office work she preferred was invaluable.

In 1922, Ms. Backus found that the value of her annual salary, then $1,500, was being threatened by postwar inflation. Her new boss, U.S. Attorney Edward J. Bowman, wanted to pay her $1,800, the amount paid to clerks in very large districts. He went to Washington and met with Assistant Attorney General Rush L. Holland to explain that Ms. Backus was a clerk of nineteen years' service with extraordinary legal and clerical skills who was well worth the higher salary. As a result of Bowman's request, Backus not only received a raise, she was also appointed to the dual position of clerk and Assistant U.S. Attorney, effective September 1, 1923. With this promotion, she became the first woman to serve as an Assistant U.S. Attorney in Michigan.

Ella Mae Backus continued to be a great asset of the U.S. Attorney's office for the rest of her life, working through seven U.S. Attorneys and more than a dozen assistants. She spent much of her time when she was away from work serving in many community organizations, including the Grand Rapids Bar Association. When Ms. Backus did not appear at work on July 28, 1938, a clerk was sent out to investigate and found her dead in her apartment. Her service to the court and community was extolled at a special court ceremony attended by District Judge Fred Raymond, U.S. Attorney Francis T. McDonald, and many former U.S. Attorneys and assistants. In her obituary, *The Grand Rapids Herald* noted that, in an office with high turnover, she lasted for thirty-five years "[b]ecause she was hard working, faithful, able, and attended to her business, because she had become an institution in the U.S. District Court, because none felt they cared to try to get on without her."

When Ms. Backus died, she was not replaced, and the U.S. Attorney made do with just two assistants until February 1942 when a third position was authorized. By the mid-1970s, the number had increased marginally to just four assistants, but forty-five years later, the number has risen to about thirty-six.

The Caseload of the U.S. Attorney

In the decades before the creation of the Western District of Michigan in 1863, the types of cases, criminal or civil, involving the United States were small. Consequently, so was the caseload of the U.S. Attorney for the District of Michigan, who often filed fewer than fifty criminal and civil cases each year, and in some years fewer than ten. The subject matter of those cases did not vary much from year to year. Typical criminal cases were prosecutions for smuggling, counterfeiting, postal theft, and cutting timber on federal land. Civil cases involving the United States primarily involved customs disputes, suits to collect debts owed to the United States, and foreclosure on the fidelity bonds of defaulting federal employees. As late as 1857 and 1858, a total of only twenty-one cases involving the United States were filed in the District and Circuit Courts, as contrasted to almost nine hundred new private civil cases.

However, the Western District of Michigan and the position of its U.S. Attorney came into being at a time when the caseload of federal trial courts and of the U.S. Attorneys was increasing tremendously. During the Civil War, Congress enacted a flood of new federal tax laws and other laws involving issues arising from the war, and the caseloads of the U.S. Attorneys in both of Michigan's federal District Courts rose to unprecedented heights. That caseload did not decrease at the war's end, because many of the taxes were maintained, particularly taxes on the various aspects of the alcohol business.

In January 1871, when Attorney General Amos Akerman submitted the first report to Congress under the 1870 Act, he stated that, according to the reports of the U.S. Attorneys who had responded to his call for information, about half of their civil and criminal cases in 1870 involved the war taxes. Almost all of the rest of their cases were under the customs laws.[12] John H. Standish, U.S Attorney for the Western District of Michigan, was among those who responded to Akerman. He reported that, at the end of 1870, his district had pending six civil cases, all for customs violations, and twenty-nine criminal cases, of which sixteen were for internal revenue violations and four involved the post office. Despite the end of most of the war taxes in 1872, taxes were still a large portion of the caseload of the U.S. Attorneys nationally in 1881. Acting Attorney General S. F. Phillips reported that 69 percent of the criminal cases pending in the federal trial courts involved violations of the tax laws, presumably all involving taxes on alcohol. The U.S. Attorney for the Western District, Mardsen C. Burch, reported that sixteen of the district's forty-five pending criminal cases were internal revenue violations.[13] A decade later, in 1891, only 718 of the 10,325 criminal cases pending nationally (7 percent) involved the traditional staples of the U.S. Attorneys' dockets, customs and post office violations; 4,861 were tax cases (47 percent), while 4,003 (39 percent) were "miscellaneous prosecutions."[14] Lewis G. Palmer, U.S. Attorney for the Western District, reported thirteen of the forty-seven criminal cases pending in the Western District were tax cases, but twenty-two were miscellaneous; of the twelve civil cases, one was a postal case, none involved taxes, and eleven were miscellaneous. For 1900, nationally tax cases were 43 percent of pending criminal cases (4,379 of 10,047), and in the Western District they were 41 percent (26 of 68).

The forty-one criminal cases pending at the end of fiscal year 1910 were principally the same postwar bag of crimes, including two customs cases, fifteen tax cases, and thirteen postal cases. On the other hand, the fifty pending U.S. civil cases included none relating to customs, postal matters, or taxes. Instead, thirteen cases sought damages for "timber trespass" on federal land, and thirty-three sought to cancel naturalization certificates. More notably, the labels on the form on which the U.S. Attorneys reported their cases that year were evidence of laws that Congress had passed in the spirit of the Progressive Era, laws that would impose new duties on the U.S. Attorneys over the next decades: the Railroad Safety Appliance Act, the eight-hour labor law, the Food and Drug Act, the Sherman Antitrust Act, the Interstate Commerce Act, and the Meat Inspection Act. The events and laws that would place the greatest burden on the federal courts and the offices of the U.S. Attorney were yet to come—World War I, Prohibition, and the Great Depression.

As prosecutions for violations of the prohibition laws (discussed in chapter 5) faded with the repeal of prohibition in 1933, the country was in the midst of the Great Depression, and other criminal problems arose in the Western District of Michigan. The farming communities of the Western District as well as the Upper Peninsula, which relied upon agriculture and lumbering, were hard hit at the beginning of the depression. Prices on farm products fell as much as 40 percent, and many could not meet their mortgage payments. Soon the cities—Grand Rapids, Lansing, Kalamazoo—felt the Depression as wages for industrial workers flattened and many people were forced to buy on credit and reduce their spending. With a decrease of the amount of money in circulation, counterfeiting increased.

The image of the federal government also improved as the public found some economic hope in Franklin Roosevelt's New Deal. But it was the outbreak of World War II that most affected the U.S. Attorney's Office in Grand Rapids. The office was faced with issues concerning internal security, war-risk insurance coverage, the Selective Service, and enemy aliens. During the war, the office was on duty twenty-four hours a day to handle issues involving interned Japanese and German aliens. Fortunately for the office, the number of prosecutions of draft dodgers was considerably less than in the neighboring Eastern District. In 1943, for example, the Western District reported only 133 cases of the 3,284 cases in the state. Significant developments in the 1940s, aside from Selective Service Act enforcement, included enforcement of the Emergency Price Control Act of 1942 by which Congress intended to check speculative and expensive price increases and inflation for agricultural commodities, goods and services, and even real estate, to help the country weather the war. Also on the U.S. Attorney's plate were land condemnation cases. The War Department acquired 225,739 acres of land in the Western District to be used for training sites and other war-related purposes.

In the early 1950s, the U.S. Attorney General placed the U.S. Attorney for the Western District, Joseph F. Deeb, in charge of a special grand jury to travel the country in an effort to suppress organized crime. When Deeb was appointed U.S. Attorney in 1940, at the age of thirty-one, he was the youngest U.S. Attorney in the country. Asked then about his accomplishments, he said "I haven't lived long enough to do much of anything." During his tenure, he was elected president of the U.S. Attorneys' Conference. When he left the office in 1953, he was the longest-serving U.S. Attorney in the District's history. Notwithstanding a significant effort by the grand jury, however, the problem of organized crime had already grown too great. But the racketeering investigations in Michigan would continue.

In one racketeering investigation, Deeb was able to report that he had found no organized crime in Grand Rapids. Deeb's investigation and grand jury presentation began in 1950 when Robert Faulkner, a Republican state representative from Coloma in Berrien County, charged in the House of Representatives that "Grand Rapids is a city of sin and in the clutches of organized rackets."[15] In several following speeches, Faulkner asserted that the city was home to two thousand prostitutes and that organized gambling was "wide open" and dominated by the Chicago syndicate. But having made these charges, Faulkner refused to show any proof publicly. He also refused to appear before a Kent County Circuit Judge who sought his appearance. Faulkner did testify, however, when Deeb called him before a federal grand jury in 1951. Grand Rapids reform mayor Paul Goebel, an All-American football player for the University of Michigan and prominent Grand Rapids businessman, and others also testified. After months of work, the grand jury released its final report on April 3, 1953, finding that "whatever local criminal element may exist, there appears to be no connection or affiliation between them and any of the so-called interstate syndicates, nor do any local criminal elements appear to exert any political control." The local press read the report with approval, and Faulkner expressed pleasure at how well Grand Rapids had been "cleaned up."

The 1950s saw a substantial increase in a number of other criminal cases brought by the Western District's U.S. Attorney's Office, including prosecutions under the Dyer Act for transportation of stolen cars across state lines. The office brought thirty-nine such cases in 1955 alone. During the 1950s, there was also an increase in the prosecutions against people sending obscene matter through the mail.

During the 1960s and the following decades, drug prosecutions made up an increasingly large proportion of the federal criminal caseload in Western

Michigan, as demand for more and different kinds of drugs, from marijuana, heroin, cocaine, crack cocaine, methamphetamines, and later opioids, grew throughout the country. The U.S. Attorney's Office prosecuted many of those drug cases in conjunction with prosecutions of federal firearms offenses. Il- lustrative of the scope of the drug problem was a case brought in this district in 2014, spearheaded by Assistant U.S. Attorney Brian P. Lennon, which re- sulted in forty-seven people being convicted, with some receiving a sentence of life in prison. Taken down were two major drug trafficking organizations in Los Angeles who flooded western Michigan with tons of cocaine, heroin traffickers from New Jersey and New York, and a notorious Lansing street gang. U.S. District Judge Paul Maloney ordered the forfeiture of more than $170 million in drug sale proceeds, including eleven houses in California and Michigan and fifty-five motor vehicles, boats, motorcycles, firearms, jewelry, and furs.

A prominent case began in November 1978 when a man walked into the office of Drug Enforcement Agency (DEA) in Grand Rapids. He said that, in exchange for a few thousand dollars and new identities for himself and his wife, he would reveal how massive amounts of cocaine were being smuggled by organized crime figures from Peru to Grand Rapids in hollowed-out furni- ture. Notwithstanding the irony that anyone would send furniture to Grand Rapids, then the furniture capital of the country, the agent pursued the case and arrested several people who were charged and brought to trial in Grand Rapids. Trial was scheduled to begin on June 18, 1979, before Chief Judge Wendell Miles. Before the trial began, however, the U.S. Attorney's Office received a call from an inmate at the Lompoc, California, federal prison who said that he had read about the case. The inmate claimed that he had worked for the same smugglers in the past. In fact, he said, he had been represented by the same attorneys now representing his former bosses. Judge Miles ad- journed the trial, and the Assistant U.S. Attorney prosecuting the case, Don- ald A. Davis, and the DEA agent flew to Lompoc to interview the prisoner. They decided to make this man their star witness and brought him to Grand Rapids. In a surprising twist, the witness hanged himself, or so it seemed, in the Kent county jail on the Sunday before the trial, and he died the following Wednesday. Now it was necessary to bring in the two protected persons, hus- band and wife, who had first informed the authorities about the case, as sub- stitute witnesses. These two individuals had to be brought to Grand Rapids with special U.S. Marshals from New York for heightened security. To complicate the matter, the wife suffered from myasthenia gravis, which required her to travel with suitcases full of medicine and which made her unable to speak when she was upset, such as when she was being cross-examined. Nevertheless, the U.S. Attorney's Office was able to able to overcome all of these hurdles. The defendants were convicted and given the maximum sentence.

Another case that captured nationwide public attention occurred in 1982, when an extortion letter arrived at the office of the President of the Kellogg Company in Battle Creek, Michigan, threatening to poison thousands of Kellogg products throughout a twenty-state area if a very large amount of gold was not deposited in the Cayman Islands by April 22. The extortionist sent similar letters to all of the major television and syndicated news outlets, causing considerable apprehension. Kellogg heightened its security. Although the deadline passed without incident, tension remained, and the case was unfortunately not solved until the extortionist, a man from Kalamazoo, was arrested on a bad check charge and bragged to a cellmate about writing the letter. The defendant was convicted of extortion in the District Court for the Western District and sentenced to twenty-five years in prison. The defendant later testified against an accomplice who, he said, had pressured him into working with her. The pair had gone to the library in Royal Oak, Michigan, to research potential targets and discovered that Kellogg had $32 million in cash reserves. But, he testified, he never planned to mail his letter because "that's against the law." U.S. District Judge Richard Enslen sentenced the accomplice to ten years in federal prison.

More recently, crimes involving guns and violent crimes, child pornography, sexual assault, and fraud have also markedly increased, facilitated, indeed propelled, by the growth of the Internet. This has lead to such programs as Project Safe Neighborhoods, the Western District of Michigan Environmental Crimes Task Force, Project Safe Childhood, and the Attorney General's Obscenity Prosecution Task Force, to name a few. Additionally, the complicated and ever-evolving federal sentencing guidelines have greatly increased the burden in bringing each felony prosecution, as has the need for detention hearings and asset forfeiture proceedings in many cases.

The Office of the Federal Public Defender

Located prominently in the Western District of Michigan's Office of the Federal Public Defender is a quotation from the 1963 opinion of the U.S. Supreme Court in its landmark decision in the case of *Gideon v. Wainwright*[16]: "reason and reflection require us to recognize that in our adversary system of criminal justice, any person who is haled into court, who is too poor to hire a lawyer, cannot be assured a fair trial unless counsel is provided for him. This seems to us to be an obvious truth." That decision and others led Congress to pass the Criminal Justice Act of 1964 (CJA),[17] which paved the way for a system in which counsel appointed to represent indigent defendants in federal criminal trials would be paid.[18]

Before the CJA, indigent federal defendants were represented by private attorneys working pro bono because the courts had no way to pay their fees. In major cases, these attorneys might be among the best, most experienced criminal attorneys in the local bar, but in less notable cases, they might have little criminal trial experience. Following the passage of the CJA, the Western District of Michigan and many other federal courts created a voluntary panel of attorneys, known as CJA panel attorneys, whom the court could appoint to represent indigent defendants. The compensation rate authorized by the CJA was so low that it discouraged experienced criminal attorneys, although their reluctance afforded an opportunity for young attorneys to gain trial experience in federal courts. However, this dichotomy created concerns in the court and the bar about guaranteeing the rights of indigent defendants. In the late 1980s, at the urging of newly appointed District Judge Robert Holmes Bell, the original CJA panel list was converted to a shorter list of experienced criminal counsel evaluated and selected by the court.

In 1970, Congress amended the CJA to allow the creation of a public defender office in any judicial district in which at least two hundred defendants annually qualified for appointed counsel. In 2018, more than eighty-one of the ninety-four federal judicial districts have Federal Defender programs, some organized as Federal Defender offices (FDO) and others as community defender organizations (CDO). FDOs are federal offices headed by a Federal Public Defender appointed by the relevant U.S. Court of Appeals for four-year terms. CDOs are nonprofit organizations incorporated under state law, supervised by a board of directors rather than by the judiciary, and funded by federal grants. The Western District of Michigan has an FDO while the Eastern District has a CDO.

The Federal Public Defender office of the Western District of Michigan was established in 1995 when the Sixth Circuit appointed Howard W. Gillingham, an attorney practicing in California, as the district's first Federal Public Defender. The defender office began accepting appointments in the district's Southern Division in early 1996, but CJA panel attorneys continued to cover cases in the Northern Division. Among his other duties, the new Federal Defender was responsible for training CJA panel attorneys throughout the district to assure the availability of appointed counsel in cases in which the federal defender office could not represent defendants due to conflicts or scheduling. Even in 2020, approximately one-third of the appointments are handled by a panel attorney.

When Gillingham assumed office in Grand Rapids in October 1995, his new organization had no physical office. He opened a temporary office in the Waters Building, a block south of the Gerald R. Ford Federal Building and U.S. Courthouse. His initial staff included one office manager and one Assistant Public Defender, Sharon E. Turek. In June 1996, the Federal Defender's office moved from the Waters Building to 50 Lewis NW in an old Masonic Temple, where it is still located as of this writing. In 2003, as the responsibilities of the Public Defender Office in the Northern Division grew, a branch office was established in Marquette.

In May 1997, Gillingham resigned as the Federal Defender. As a temporary successor, the Sixth Circuit named Henry Martin, the long-time Federal Defender for the Middle District of Tennessee. In June 1997, Christopher P. Yates, then an Assistant U.S. Attorney in the Eastern District of Michigan, joined the Western District's Federal Defender office as an Assistant Federal Defender, and in September 1998 he was appointed the Federal Public Defender. Yates served in that position until March 2004, when he entered private practice as a partner in the Grand Rapids criminal defense firm of Willey & Chamberlain. In 2006, he left there to form the firm Yates, LaGrand & Denenfeld. In 2008, Yates was appointed, and subsequently elected and reelected, a judge of the Kent County Circuit Court. Paul Denenfeld, who had previously been an Assistant Federal Public Defender in Grand Rapids, followed Judge Yates to the Kent County circuit bench in 2009 by appointment and was subsequently elected in 2010 and reelected in 2016.

After Yates's departure from the Western District's FDO, Assistant Public Defender Paul L. Nelson became Acting Public Defender. In January 2005, Raymond S. Kent of Grand Rapids was sworn in as the Federal Public Defender. Kent served until 2015 when he was appointed a U.S. Magistrate Judge for the Western District. Sharon Turek succeeded him as Acting Defender, and in 2016, after serving as Assistant Defender for twenty years, Ms. Turek was appointed the permanent Federal Public Defender.

The Federal Defender office began operation in 1996 with just two attorneys, an office manager, and a budget of $750,000, including $152,000 for start-up costs. In 2018, the Federal Defender office had grown to nineteen employees in its Grand Rapids facility (the Defender, six Assistant Defenders, two research and writing attorneys, and ten support staff), as well as two employees in the Marquette office (an Assistant Defender and a paralegal), and an annual budget of $4.1 million. The support staff includes a panel administrator who, with the Defender, administers the Western District's panel of nearly fifty CJA attorneys, maintaining daily contact with the panel members, lending support, and providing multiple training opportunities each year.

Throughout the years, the Western District has seen a steady increase in criminal cases. During the first year after the establishment of the Defender office, 371 criminal cases were filed. Over the next twenty-one years, the average number of criminal cases filed in the Western District has been approximately 450 per year, with drug prosecutions usually accounting for the most prosecutions. Firearm, fraud, and immigration offenses are also some of the most commonly prosecuted cases.

In the Western District, as across the country, the workload of a Federal Defender office and the CJA panel attorneys often reflects the emphasis that the U.S. Attorney and the Department of Justice have placed on certain types of criminal activity, newly passed legislation, and evolving caselaw. For example, beginning in 2000, an initiative was started to combat gun violence in the Western District. The feeling was that focusing on offenders carrying guns during crimes would remove the more dangerous, and often repeat, offenders from the streets. The Western District's U.S. Attorney's Office joined forces with Michigan's Attorney General, Jennifer Granholm, and the Kent County Prosecuting Attorney office to focus on gun violence. Initially called Project Exile, this initiative later morphed into a program called Project Safe Neighborhoods (PSN), which resulted in an increase of federally prosecuted firearm offenses from a low of forty-nine in 2000 to highs of ninety-three in 2003 and ninety-two in 2010. After a decline in firearms prosecutions between 2010 and 2016, firearm prosecutions once again increased in 2018.

A significant part of any federal defense attorney's work revolves around the federal sentencing guidelines. These guidelines came into effect in 1987 following the passage of the Sentencing Reform Act of 1984,[19] which created the U.S. Sentencing Commission. The guidelines' primary goal was to end disparities in sentencing among federal judges and to provide determinate sentences, as opposed to indeterminate sentences with the actual time served to be determined by a parole board. The federal sentencing guidelines abolished parole as part of federal sentences and established a specific range within which a judge would normally sentence a defendant. Each guideline range was determined by considering both a defendant's criminal history and the conduct involved in the crime for which the defendant was being sentenced.

Two decisions by the U.S. Supreme Court twenty years later changed the landscape dramatically. In 2004's *Blakely v. Washington*,[20] the Court held in a state case that sentencing guidelines could violate the Sixth Amendment's right to a jury trial where mandatory sentences were concerned. Six months later, in 2005's *United States v. Booker*,[21] the Court held that a provision of the federal sentencing guidelines that was treated as mandatory violated a defendant's Sixth Amendment right to a trial by jury. Instead, the Court ruled, the guidelines were to be considered to be advisory, not mandatory, and it directed federal appeals courts to review sentences for reasonableness.

Over the years, other changes in the law impacted tens of thousands of defendants who had been convicted of drug offenses. The first change dealt with what came to be known as the "100 to one rule." Believing that crack cocaine was more dangerous than powder cocaine, federal drug laws mandated a ten-year sentence for a defendant responsible for fifty grams of crack cocaine while a defendant would have to be responsible for five thousand grams of powder cocaine to receive the same sentence. Although it took years to address this disparity, amendments to the sentencing guidelines in 2007 and 2011 sought to address this injustice. The Western District's Public Defender office opened 288 files for defendants seeking relief under those amendments. In 2014, Amendment 728 of the sentencing guidelines adjusted the drug quantity tables used in calculating sentence ranges. The Public Defender office represented another 573 defendants who sought to have their sentences reduced retroactively under another sentencing guideline amendment.

Beginning in 2005, another priority for the district's Public Defender office was its involvement in the Western District Court's "reentry court."

This project, known as the Accelerated Community Entry Program (ACE), helped individuals reestablish themselves back into their communities after incarceration. For thirteen years, the Public Defender office, the District Court, the office of the U.S. Attorney, and the court's probation department joined together in this program to help many individuals reenter their community as positive members of society.

CHAPTER 11

The Western District's Federal Bar Association and Historical Society

The Western Michigan Chapter of the Federal Bar Association

A COURT IS KNOWN BY its cases and the quality of its judges. But these do not operate in a vacuum. In the Western District of Michigan, the Federal Bar Association has played a prominent role in enhancing the quality of modern practice for forty years and in making the Western District a desirable place to practice law.

The Western District underwent a transformation at the end of the 1970s. It had been founded more than a century earlier as a single judge court, then slowly became an overburdened two-judge court, with an overcrowded courthouse. By the 1970s, it was barely able to meet the exigencies of the day. Criminal cases had to be processed, but civil complaints were often met with a motion to dismiss, and then those cases just sat there unheard and undecided.

The cornerstone for a new courthouse was laid in 1972, and increased space would soon be available. When Washington, D.C., decided in the late 1970s that the district would gain two additional judgeships, and Judge Fox, one of the two sitting judges, decided to take senior status, thus opening up his seat for a third new judge and bringing the number of judges in the district from two to five, it finally became apparent that the court would now be able to accomplish more than simply keeping its head above water. There would be changes.

It seemed apparent to some that an invigorated new court and an active bar would mutually benefit from being able to share their concerns about the practice of law in the federal court. This required a vehicle of communication, open to all of those interested. Unfortunately, no bar association was paying much attention to the federal court in Grand Rapids. Local county bar groups focused their interest on city and county courts, while the State Bar of Michigan in Lansing had its hands full with the statewide practice of law. This left a place for a regional bar association dedicated to enhancing practice in a growing federal court on the western side of the state, but without stepping on the toes of the existing bar associations.

Accordingly, on November 7, 1978, an organizing committee convened at the law offices of Bergstrom, Slykhouse & Shaw, PC, in Grand Rapids to form a new bar association for this purpose.[1] Honorary members of the committee were the Hon. Albert J. Engel, Sixth Circuit Court of Appeals, and both Western Michigan District Judges, Noel P. Fox and Wendell A. Miles. Importantly, the judiciary was on board.

The committee decided that bringing the new organization under the auspices of an established bar association would give this fledgling group both legitimacy and credibility in the eyes of local attorneys, and provide it with the organizational tools necessary to accomplish its goals. The national Federal Bar Association (FBA) was deemed an appropriate entity. The FBA is a voluntary professional association for attorneys who maintain a federal practice and for the federal judges before whom they appear. Although the FBA was then composed primarily of federally employed attorneys, of whom there were likely fewer than ten in Grand Rapids, the FBA also permitted as members attorneys who had merely expressed an interest in federal practice. This opened the door to any west Michigan lawyer practicing before the federal district and bankruptcy judges. The FBA itself was happy to encourage creation of a new chapter.

The FBA's nascent western Michigan chapter launched its inaugural meeting on February 17, 1979, with a high-profile speaker, the Hon. George C. Edwards, Jr., the new Chief Judge of United States Court of Appeals for the Sixth Circuit and a former justice of the Michigan Supreme Court. The significance of that first meeting cannot be overstated. Along with all of the federal judges, bankruptcy referees, and the clerk of the court of appeals, the president of the State Bar of Michigan, Leo Farhat of Lansing, was also in attendance. The Grand Rapids Bar Association and its president, Gordon Boozer, were, in typical west Michigan fashion, quite supportive of the new organization, and attorneys turned out in large numbers to hear Judge Edwards give his initial address. An admissions ceremony was also held for attorneys wishing to be admitted to practice before the Sixth Circuit, a ceremony normally only held in Cincinnati, Ohio. The evening was a success, and on January 26, the chapter received interim approval of its charter by the national association.

The chapter continued to bring headliners to Grand Rapids to raise its profile. Later that year, on September 18, 1979, the Solicitor General of United States, the Hon. Wade McCree, spoke to the chapter at Adrian's Ramona Terrace on the outskirts of Grand Rapids.[2] General McCree took the opportunity to suggest a plan to reduce the heavy workload of the Supreme Court by consolidating several special courts handling tax appeals, environmental appeals, and patent appeals into one court with exclusive jurisdiction. The presence of the distinguished Solicitor General was an honor to the members of the bar generally, and the local firms turned out a sizable audience for the luncheon.[3] The new chapter had established its legitimacy, and its membership was swelling.[4] By August 1983, the Western Michigan chapter was recognized as the fastest-growing FBA chapter in the country, and a year later it had grown from 122 members to 212.

Also in the audience to hear General McCree were the three new federal judge-designees, Douglas Hillman, Benjamin Gibson, and Richard Enslen. Douglas Hillman would not be a judge-in-waiting for long. A week later, on September 25, 1979, his nomination was confirmed by the Senate. Three days later, as a mark of its growing stature, the fledgling FBA chapter cohosted, with the Grand Rapids Bar Association, Judge Hillman's investiture at the Grand Rapids federal courthouse and a reception at the Peninsula Club.

McCree would not be the only Solicitor General the young chapter would host. On May 18, 1983, Solicitor General Rex Lee came to town at the invitation of Chapter Vice President and U.S. Attorney John Smietanka, to speak at the chapter's annual dinner held in the Ambassador Ballroom of the Amway Grand Plaza Hotel. More than 230 persons attended. Rex Lee was a hot ticket, both locally and nationally, and the following month he was featured on the cover of the *ABA Journal*.[5]

The local FBA chapter proved to be of service to the court from the beginning, thus fulfilling its purpose. For example, when it became evident to several of the new judges, experienced litigators themselves, that many attorneys did not have adequate courtroom skills, the FBA instituted a trial skills workshop. Later renamed the Hillman Advocacy Program in honor of the Hon. Douglas W. Hillman, who was the driving force behind it, the workshop has been in existence ever since its inception in 1981, improving the courtroom skills of more than two thousand attorneys. This two-and-a-half-day learning-by-doing seminar, run by experienced trial attorneys, was the first of its type in the country conducted in a federal courthouse. The faculty is not compensated except by the satisfaction of giving back to the profession. On the contrary, the program is underwritten by generous contributions from west Michigan law firms.

The trial skills workshop was one of a countless number of educational programs the chapter has hosted almost from its inception. The chapter has sponsored day-long seminars as well as activities, now known as "brown bag lunches," which focus on an extensive range of topics on federal practice. A luncheon meeting on bankruptcy evolved into a widely acclaimed annual seminar in northern Michigan, hosted by the chapter's bankruptcy section, which draws a regional audience reaching outside the district.

The largest general-purpose seminars conducted by the chapter, which have become known as the Shanty Creek, or Bench-Bar, Conferences in the last decade or so, are now held on Mackinac Island in conjunction with the court every three years. Modeled after the judicial conferences of the federal courts of appeals originally mandated by Congress to bring attorneys and federal judges together on an informal basis to exchange ideas and concerns, these retreats provide many substantive sessions and opportunities for interaction between the court and the bar. But the chapter has undertaken numerous other projects to enhance federal practice in the Western District, to build collegiality between the lawyers and the judges, and to enhance professionalism generally.

Recognizing the underlying importance of communication, in December 1982, the chapter launched the *Bar & Bench*, a national award-winning newsletter featuring substantive articles by local practitioners and judges.[6] In 1983, the publication began annotating recent federal decisions, which were prepared courtesy of the Thomas M. Cooley Law School. Arguably as a result, the *Michigan State Bar Journal* began publishing annotations of new federal cases as well. This, in turn, was followed by a separate and brand-new statewide publication, the *Michigan Lawyers Weekly (MLW)*, which offered annotations on a subscription basis. Once the *MLW* was firmly in place, the FBA could stand down from this labor-intensive annotation service. But the *Bar & Bench* continued, and in 1988, the chapter also began a successful second newsletter aimed at its bankruptcy practitioners.

In 1983, in what the court described as a "joint bench and bar experiment," the chapter was instrumental in persuading the District Court to adopt a common motion day, drafting the initial rule. The chapter also provided an ad hoc committee to assist the court in preparing its alternative dispute resolution arbitration rules and has routinely assisted with the implementation of other alternative dispute resolution procedures. In January 1984, the court also invited the chapter to establish a special committee to study the issue of peer review. In a related vein, the chapter regularly sponsors federal District Court admission ceremonies, and on one occasion, in 2012, arranged for the admission of forty-two attorneys to the U.S. Supreme Court when the clerk of that court, General William K. Suter, came to Grand Rapids to address the FBA's annual meeting. For many years, the chapter published an annual desktop directory of local federal offices. Routinely, chapter members sit on screening committees for judicial candidates and court executive personnel.

The chapter also was essential in forming a program for pro bono attorneys to serve in civil docket cases, particularly civil rights cases, where no attorney was otherwise available. Growing out of an FBA conference concerning the "Poor and Underrepresented in Federal Court," the goal was to provide litigation costs and training to help recruit attorneys to meet the needs of the underrepresented. Appointments are at the discretion of the court, and the chapter maintains a fund to reimburse costs of the program. Another important area in which the chapter was active and successful was the campaign, described in chapter six, for a federal court facility in Lansing, which is coincidentally now named after the father of one of the chapter's past Presidents, Charles E. Chamberlain, Jr.

Throughout its existence, the chapter, like the federal court, has recognized, indeed emphasized, the importance of civility in the Western District. Together, the chapter and the court adopted a Civility Code, which both attorneys and judges were encouraged to sign. This was not in reaction to a lack of civility but to heighten the concept of civility in everyone's mind. Recognizing the continuous influx of new members to the bar, the chapter continues to underwrite countless court-related receptions for a wide variety of occasions and ceremonies and has started a Young Lawyers Section, all of which have contributed to a strong sense of rapport among attorneys and cooperation between the attorneys and the court. In tribute to the extensive involvement by western Michigan attorneys in court-related endeavors, the chapter has created several awards to recognize significant achievements in relevant areas.[7] And the FBA has recognized the rapidly increasing role of women in the profession. Since naming its first female president, Katherine Smith Kennedy, in 2010, three more women have held that position, Jennifer McManus, Sarah Riley Howard, and Sharon Turek.

The chapter has also provided financial assistance to projects of general benefit to the court when it can properly do so, whether it is the purchase of an electronic evidence cart or framing portraits of retired judges, which now grace courtroom walls. But not all of the financial assistance provided by the chapter has been within the court. The chapter also aided in establishing an American Inns of Court in Grand Rapids and was instrumental in starting the court's historical society.

The preceding discussion is not exhaustive, but it may safely be said that the efforts of the FBA's Western Michigan chapter, with the welcoming encouragement of the court, have greatly benefited those attorneys practicing in federal court in the Western District of Michigan.

The Historical Society for the U.S. District Court for the Western District of Michigan

The foundation of the Historical Society for the U.S. District Court for the Western District of Michigan was an outgrowth of a project undertaken by District Judge Wendell A. Miles, the Western District's first official Court Historian, to write the history of the court, going back to the earliest days of the Northwest Ordinance.[8] While Judge Miles was unable to complete that project before he passed away, his efforts inspired others, such as one of his former law clerks, Charles E. "Chip" Chamberlain, Jr., who decided "to capture tomorrow's history today" by obtaining professional interviews by historian Gordon Olson of Judge Miles and other District Judges in order to record their oral histories while the judges were still available. The involvement of other volunteers, to interview attorneys and court staff to advance the oral history project, in turn led to the creation of a historical society for the court.

The Historical Society was incorporated in 2002 according to the laws of the State of Michigan and Internal Revenue Code section 501(c)(3) as an educational and charitable organization operating under an independent board of trustees. The Society's purpose is to research, collect, and preserve documents and other physical memorabilia of significance to the court's history, together with the oral histories of judges and attorneys who have been part of the fabric of the federal court in west Michigan, and to disseminate that history in a meaningful way to the public so as to promote a better understanding of the involvement of the rule of law across the Western District's many communities within its vast geography.

The District Court and the Western Michigan Chapter of the Federal Bar Association each initially contributed $10,000 to the undertaking. In a foreshadowing of the Court's future history, attorney (and future U.S. District Judge and Chief District Judge) Robert J. Jonker and his firm, Warner, Norcross & Judd, donated their time and services to do the necessary legal work to establish the Society. The incorporators of the Society were District Judge Robert Holmes Bell, also a future Chief Judge, Senior Judge Miles, Magistrate Judge Hugh W. Brenneman, Clerk of the Court Ron Weston, and attorneys Stephen Bransdorfer, Chip Chamberlain, Jamie Geary, Michael MacDonald, Jan Mann, Patrick Mears, and Michael Puerner. The inaugural President of the Society was Judge Brenneman, followed by Chip Chamberlain, Mike MacDonald, John H. Logie, James A. Mitchell, and David J. Gass. The first annual meeting of the Society was held, fittingly, in a courtroom of the old 1909 federal courthouse, which at that time was a museum.

In gathering its oral histories, the Society was fortunate to have the services of past Grand Rapids City Historian and author Gordon Olson, a past president of the Michigan Oral History Society and a veteran of some two hundred such interviews. The histories were digitally recorded and transcripts were made; other members of the Historical Society recorded histories from attorneys and court employees, and all of the histories were placed in an archive established for all of the physical items collected.

In 2003, the Society began publishing *Stereoscope: Journal of the Historical Society*. Its first editor was Patrick Mears, a longtime editor of the FBA chapter's *Bar & Bench* newsletter. The *Stereoscope* reports the proceedings of the Historical Society and provides in-depth articles about the Court's colorful past. This publication is highly regarded. The Society has also produced video and DVDs about the history of the federal court in west Michigan.

On March 12, 2013, the Society threw a gala banquet at the Amway Grand Plaza Hotel, which sits on the site of the court's first permanent courtroom (opened on July 1, 1863, see chapter 3), to celebrate the 150th anniversary of the creation of the Western District and the appointment by Abraham Lincoln of Solomon Withey as the new district's first judge. The creation of the district in February 1863, the midpoint of the Civil War, was a bright spot

amid a time of uncertainty and worry for the Union-faithful people of Grand
Rapids. Six months earlier, on September 17, 1862, the Battle of Antietam was
fought in Maryland. This was celebrated in the Northern states as a Union
victory, because the Confederate army of Robert E. Lee had retreated back
south, but it was also the bloodiest day of the Civil War. On March 3, 1863,
eight days before Withey's appointment on March 11, President Lincoln
signed the controversial Union military draft into law, and ten weeks earlier,
on January 1, 1863, his Emancipation Proclamation took effect. On July 1, the
armies met again in the three-day Battle of Gettysburg, which would be the
bloodiest battle of the war.

More than four hundred people attended the black-tie gala, which was re-
plete with reenactors in period dress, a Civil War military band, video displays
of photos of Grand Rapids in the 1860s, and actors playing President and
Mrs. Lincoln. The invocation was given by Mark S. Gurley, the great-great
grandson of Lincoln's D.C. pastor, Phineas D. Gurley. Master of Ceremony
David J. Gass introduced the guest of honor, Harold Becker—the ninety-
five-year-old son of a Union veteran who was born when his father, who had
enlisted at the age of seventeen, was seventy years old. The gala was favored
with a talk by nationally known American historian Richard Norton Smith,
the first Executive Director of the Abraham Lincoln Presidential Library and
Museum. A special challenge coin was minted. It was a historical moment
come to life, captured on videotape for the benefit of future generations. The
latest project of the Historical Society is . . . this book.

Judges of the Supreme Court of the
Territory of Michigan

Judge	In Office	Appointed by
Augustus B. Woodward	1805–1824	Thomas Jefferson
Frederick Bates	1805–1806	Thomas Jefferson
John Griffin	1806–1824	Thomas Jefferson
James Witherell	1808–1828	Thomas Jefferson
John Hunt	1824–1827	James Monroe
Solomon Sibley	1824–1836	James Monroe
Henry C. Chipman	1827–1832	John Quincy Adams
William D. Woodbridge	1828–1832	John Quincy Adams
George Morell	1832–1836	Andrew Jackson
Ross Wilkins	1832–1836	Andrew Jackson
"Additional" Federal Judges of the Territory of Michigan		
James Duane Doty	1823–1832	James Monroe
David Irvin	1832–1836	Andrew Jackson

Succession of the U.S. District Judges for the Western District of Michigan

I (12 Stat. 660): 2/24/1863
Solomon L. Withey (1863–1886)
Henry F. Severens (1886–1900)
George P. Wanty (1900–1906)
Loyal E. Knappen (1906–1910)
Arthur C. Denison (1910–1911)
Clarence W. Sessions (1911–1931)
Seat Abolished: 4/1/1931

II (43 Stat. 949): 2/17/1925
Fred M. Raymond (1925–1946)
Raymond W. Starr (1946–1961)*
Noel P. Fox (1962–1979)*
Richard A. Enslen (1979–2005)*
Paul L. Maloney (2007–Present)

III (68 Stat. 8): 2/10/1954
W. Wallace Kent (1954–1970)
Albert J. Engel, Jr. (1971–1974)
Wendell A. Miles (1974–1986)*
Robert Holmes Bell (1987–2017)*

IV (92 Stat. 1629): 10/20/1978
Douglas W. Hillman (1979–1991)*
David W. McKeague (1992–2005)
Janet T. Neff (2007–Present)

V (92 Stat. 1629): 10/20/1978
Benjamin F. Gibson (1979–1996)*
Seat Abolished: 7/13/96

VI (104 Stat. 5089): 12/1/1990
temporary judgeship, became
permanent on 7/13/1996
Gordon J. Quist (1992–2006)*
Robert J. Jonker (2007–Present)

* Judge assumed senior status.

Clerks of the U.S. District and U.S. Circuit Courts for the Western District of Michigan

Court		Appointed by
District and Circuit Court		
Lewis Porter	5/18/1863–5/31/1865	Solomon L. Withey
Isaac H. Parrish	6/1/1865–12/31/1875	Solomon L. Withey
Chester B. Hinsdill	12/31/1875–10/31/1878	Solomon L. Withey
Circuit Court		
Henry M. Hinsdill	10/31/1878–2/1/1887	Solomon L. Withey
Charles L. Fitch	2/1/1887–12/31/1911	Henry F. Severens
District Court		
Chester B. Hinsdill	10/31/1878–1/1/1886	Solomon L. Withey
John McQuewan	1/2/1886–12/18/1900	Solomon L Withey
Charles J. Potter	1/2/1901–4/30/1926	George P. Wanty
Orrie J. Sluiter	5/1/1926–6/30/1957	Fred R. Raymond
Howard T. Ziel	7/1/1957–6/30/1972	District Judges
Arthur Langeveld	7/1/1972–7/31/1972	District Judges
Jack E. Frost	8/1/1972–7/11/1975	District Judges
Gerald H. Liefer	10/14/1975–5/9/1986	District Judges
C. Duke Hynek	5/12/1986–9/30/1995	District Judges
Ronald C. Weston	10/1/1995–2/6/2009	District Judges
Tracey Cordes	2/9/2009–8/7/2015	District Judges
Thomas L. Dorwin	1/11/2016–Present	District Judges

Chief Judges of the U.S. District Court for the Western District of Michigan

Raymond W. Starr	(1954–1961)
W. Wallace Kent	(1961–1970)
Noel P. Fox	(1971–1979)
Wendell A. Miles	(1980–1986)
Douglas W. Hillman	(1986–1991)
Benjamin F. Gibson	(1991–1995)
Richard A. Enslen	(1995–2001)
Robert Holmes Bell	(2001–2008)
Paul L. Maloney	(2008–2015)
Robert J. Jonker	(2015–Present)

Circuit Court Commissioners and U.S. Commissioners for the Western District of Michigan

Name	Residence	Appointed
Circuit Court Commissioners		
Ebenezer McIlvain	Berrien	1847
John Bean Upton	Big Rapids	1863
Jonathan G. Ramsdell	Traverse City	1863
Isaac H. Parrish	Grand Rapids	1863
Charles Jewett	Niles	1863
George S. Clapp	St. Joseph	1863
William W. Mitchell	Ionia	1863
Germain H. Mason	Kalamazoo	1863
John W. Stone	Allegan	1863
John C. Fitzgerald	Calhoun	1863
Galin A. Graves	Calhoun	1863
Ashman A. Knappen	Schoolcraft	1863
H. H. Holt	Muskegon	1863
James M. Spencer	Kalamazoo	1863
Charles S. May	Kalamazoo	1863
Robert W. Duncan	Grand Haven	1864
Edward A. Foote	Charlotte	1864
Elias O. Rose	Big Rapids	1864
Albert Williams	Ionia	1864
Dewitt C. Leach	Traverse City	1866
Joseph B. Clark	Dowagiac	1866
Edwin E. Benedict	Manistee	1866
John N. Hiller	Escanaba	1866
Holmes A. Patterson	Muskegon	1866

Name	Residence	Appointed
L. D. Grove	Pentwater	1866
Haley C. Akeley	Grand Haven	1866
George Ray	Glen Arbor	1867
Charles A. Thompson	Kalamazoo	1868
Benjamin Vosper	Ionia	1868
Charles Holbrook	Hastings	1868
Isaac D. McCutcheon	Charlotte	1870
Edward H. Wylie	Muskegon	1870
David S. Hurley	Manistee	1870
George M. Buck	Kalamazoo	1871
Thomas B. Rice	Menominee	1871
Frederick J. Russell	Hart	1871
Albert G. Day	Newaygo	1871
Lyman C. Moore	Stanton	1872
Calvin W. Nottingham	Big Rapids	1872
Henry D. Post	Holland	1872
Carlos J. Beerstachen	Centerville	1873
Dexter T. Sapp	Greenville	1873
Silas S. Fallass	Clam Lake	1874
Aaron C. McAlvay	Manistee	1874
Stephen H. Ballard	Grand Rapids	1875
David R. Joslin	Petoskey	1875
Edwin Baxter	Grand Haven	1875
Chester B. Hinsdill	Grand Rapids	1875
Charles K. Latham	Eaton Rapids	1876
Darius C. Warner	Baldwin	1876
Joseph Sayles	Evart	1876
Lovell H. Gage	Traverse City	1876
William Hudson	Pentwater	1876
John Wood	Eaton Rapids	1877
Henry F. Walch	Grand Rapids	1877
James B. McMahon	Ludington	1877
Seymour M. Sadler	Centerville	1877
E. S. Ingalls	Menominee	1878
Robert F. Judson	Kalamazoo	1878

Name	Residence	Appointed
William H. Fuller	Pentwater	1878
William Y. Gilbert	Niles	1878
Charles J. Pailthorpe	Petoskey	1878
Joseph Thew	Allegan	1878
Gad Smith	Marquette	1878
Gershom Jones	Negaunee	1878
Michael Finn	Hancock	1878
Joseph H. Steere	S. Ste. Marie	1878
Henry M. Hinsdill	Grand Rapids	1878
Clay E. Call	Petoskey	1878
John J. Sherman	Decatur	1879
Loyal E. Knappen	Hastings	1880
Orlando J. Fast	Mendon	1881
S. C. Coffinbury	Constantine	1887
John A. Colwell	S. Ste. Marie	1887
Ransom Cooper	Reed City	1887
James E. Dalliba	Marquette	1887
James M. Davis	Kalamazoo	1887
Nathaniel A. Hamilton	St. Joseph	1887
E. Eugene Haskins	Cadillac	1887
William S. Hill	Marquette	1887
Coy W. Hendryx	Dowagiac	1887
R. J. Macdonald	Muskegon	1887
Frank D. Mead	Escanaba	1887
John McQuewan	Grand Rapids	1887
John M. Opsahl	Menominee	1887
Vivian Prince	Champion	1887
Lorin Roberts	Traverse City	1887
Thomas Smurthwaite	Baldwin	1887
Robert W. Shriner	Charlotte	1887
James Snow	Muskegon	1887
Daniel W. Thompson	Manistique	1887
William H. Tuller	Pentwater	1887
Charles L. Fitch	Grand Rapids	1887
A. A. Hammond	Ironwood	1887

Name	Residence	Appointed
William Stacey	Newberry	1887
Thomas B. Wilson	Bessemer	1888
Charles J. Grier	Charlevoix	1888
Isaac M. Turner	Grand Rapids	1888
Edward P. Lott	Irson River	1889
Sidney M. Constantine	Three Rivers	1889
Silas Goodale	Houghton	1889
Charles H. McGurrin	Kalamazoo	1889
Lon B. Winsor	Reed City	1890
Arch B. Eldredge	Ishpeming	1891
Francis M. Moore	Stanton	1891
Ceylon C. Fuller	Big Rapids	1891
Frank G. Baker	Charlotte	1891
Edgar L. Gray, Jr.	Newaygo	1894
John G. Hill	Petoskey	1894
John Phelan	Ludington	1894
J. B. Abbott	Iron River	1895
Albert E. McCafe	Petoskey	1895
Louis E. Morris	Manistee	1895
Jerome E. Turner	Muskegon	1895
George A. Coe	Branch County	1895

U.S. Commissioners

Name	Residence	Appointed
James R. Bishop	Cadillac	1897
John A. Colwell	S. Ste. Marie	1897
Sidney M. Constantine	Three Rivers	1897
Michael Finn	Hancock	1897
Albert E. McCabe	Petoskey	1897
Charles H. McGurrin	Kalamazoo	1897
John McQuewan	Grand Rapids	1897
Frank D. Mead	Escanaba	1897
Francis M. Moore	Marquette	1897
Louis E. Morris	Manistee	1897
James O'Harra	St. Joseph	1897
Lorin Roberts	Traverse City	1897
E. S. B. Sutton	S. Ste. Marie	1897

Name	Residence	Appointed
Jerome E. Turner	Muskegon	1897
Henry Hoffman	St. Ignace	1910
Ira C. Jennings	Escanaba	1910
David Knox	Manistique	1910
Charles S. Olivier	Hancock	1910
John J. Shea	Ironwood	1910
Charles N. Belcher	Manistee	1910
E. G. Hackney	Petoskey	1910
Benjamin H. Halsted	Petoskey	1910
William P. Harvey	Benton Harbor	1910
E. Eugene Haskins	Cadillac	1910
Robert W. Kane	Charlevoix	1910
Addison A. Keiser	Ludington	1910
Charles H. McGurrin	Kalamazoo	1910
Joseph W. Stockwell	Kalamazoo	1910
Amil F. Nerlinger	Traverse City	1910
Charles J. Potter	Grand Rapids	1910
John Q. Ross	Muskegon	1910
Edward C. Farmer	Muskegon	1912
Henry Hatch	Marquette	1919
George C. Quinnell	Marquette	c. 1938
William E. Myers	Traverse City	c. 1938
Dean S. Face	Grand Rapids	c. 1938
M. Robert Deo	Escanaba	c. 1938
Charles O. Oliver	Hancock	c. 1938
John D. McDonald	Grand Rapids	c. 1938
James Joseph Fenlon	S. Ste. Marie	1938
Max C. Hamlin	Manistee	c. 1941
Lawrence P. Walsh	Ontonagon	1943
Robert W. Dilley	Grand Rapids	1946
Wilfred J. Lewis	Manistee	1950
William J. Howard	Kalamazoo	1950
David E. Nims, Jr.	Kalamazoo	1950
Charles H. Miltner	Cadillac	1950
Stephen W. Karr	Grand Rapids	1950

Name	Residence	Appointed
Lloyd R. Fayling	Kalamazoo	1952
Elizabeth H. Forhan	Benton Harbor	1953
James R. Davis	Lansing	1954
Theodore H. Elferdink	Grand Rapids	1954
James M. Sullivan	Battle Creek	1955
(never qualified by sending in Oath)		
Collins Eddy Brooks	Grand Rapids	1955
John G. Erickson	Escanaba	1955
Hugh T. Nowak	Grand Rapids	1955
Charles H. Mullen, Jr.	Kalamazoo	1956
Ormond S. Danford	Traverse City	1956
David E. McDonald	Ironwood	1956
Garry E. Brown	Kalamazoo	1957
Roscoe W. Baldwin	Marquette	1960
Thomas J. Fagan	Lansing	1962
Arthur Staton, Jr.	Kalamazoo	1963
Robert M. Bordeau	Marquette	1964
John T. Peters, Jr.	Kalamazoo	1967
Robert G. Quinn, Jr.	Grand Rapids	1969
John R. Weber	Marquette	1970

U.S. Attorneys for the Western District of Michigan

Frederick O. Rogers, 1863–1865

Augustus D. Griswold, 1865–1866

Andrew T. McReynolds, 1866–1867

Augustus D. Griswold, 1867–1869

John H. Standish, 1869–1877

Mardsen C. Burch, 1877–1882

John W. Stone, 1882–1886

G. Chase Godwin, 1886–1890

Lewis G. Palmer, 1890–1894

John Power, 1894–1898

George G. Covell, 1898–1910

Fred C. Wetmore, 1910–1914

Edward J. Bowman, 1914

Myron Walker, 1914–1922

Edward J. Bowman, 1922–1930

Fred C. Wetmore, 1930–1933

Joseph M. Donnelly, 1933–1937

Fred C. Wetmore, 1937

Francis T. McDonald, 1937–1940

Joseph F. Deeb, 1940–1953

Wendell A. Miles, 1953–1960

Robert J. Danhof, 1960–1961

George E. Hill, 1961–1964

Robert G. Quinn, Jr., 1964–1965

Harold D. Beaton, 1965–1969

John P. Milanowski, 1969–1974

Frank Spies, 1974–1977

James S. Brady, 1977–1981

Robert C. Greene, 1981

John A. Smietanka, 1981–1993

Thomas J. Gezon, 1993

Michael H. Dettmer, 1993–2001

Phillip J. Green, 2001

Margaret M. Chiara, 2001–2007

Brian K. Delaney, 2007

Charles R. Gross, 2007–2008

Donald A. Davis, 2008–2012

Patrick Miles, Jr., 2012–2017

Andrew B. Birge, 2017–Present

APPENDIX G

U.S. Magistrates and U.S. Magistrate Judges for the Western District of Michigan

Magistrate/Judge	Term of Service	Chambers
Stephen W. Karr	July 20, 1971–October 1, 1973 (#) October 2, 1973–December 31, 1987	Grand Rapids
Lloyd R. C. Fayling	July 26, 1971–November 8, 1982 (#)	Kalamazoo
John R. Weber	March 13, 1972–January 10, 1988 (#)	Marquette
Stuart D. Hubbell	June 23, 1972–October 23, 1973 (#) January 30, 1974–July 31, 1979 (#)	Traverse City
Hugh W. Brenneman, Jr.	April 1, 1980–July 31, 2015	Grand Rapids
Doyle A. Rowland	July 23, 1984–January 15, 1985 (#) January 16, 1985–February 29, 2000	Kalamazoo
Timothy P. Greeley	January 11, 1988–December 20, 1989 (#) December 21, 1989–March 15, 2019	Marquette
Joseph G. Scoville	January 28, 1988–July 31, 2014	Grand Rapids
Ellen S. Carmody	October 10, 2000–November 1, 2019	Grand Rapids
Phillip J. Green	August 1, 2014–Present	Grand Rapids
Raymond S. Kent	August 1, 2015–Present	Grand Rapids
Maarten Vermaat	March 15, 2019–Present	Marquette
Sally J. Berens	November 2, 2019–Present	Grand Rapids

= Part-Time

U.S. Referees in Bankruptcy
for the Western District of Michigan

Referees Appointed 1898–1938

Southern Division, Grand Rapids Region

Charles B. Blair	1898–1901; 1924–1939
Alfred H. Hunt	1901–1903
Kirk E. Wicks	1903–1916
Benn M. Corwin	1916–1924

Southern Division, Kalamazoo Region

Henry C. Briggs	1898–1912
Willard J. Banyon	1912–1925

Northern Division

Benjamin O. Pearl	1898–1910
Richard T. Looney	1910–1938

Referees Appointed 1938–1978

Southern Division

Chester C. Woolridge	1939–1960
David E. Nims, Jr.	1955–1978*
Edward H. Benson	1961–1976
Laurence E. Howard	1976–1978*

Northern Division

George C. Quinnell	1938–1972
Edward A. Quinnell	1972–1974
Marvin L. Heitman	1974–1978*

---

* Indicates referees subsequently appointed Bankruptcy Judges under the 1978 bankruptcy code.

Judges of the U.S. Bankruptcy Court for the Western District of Michigan

Judges	Dates of Service	Vice	Location
David Erwin Nims, Jr.	4/15/1955–9/30/1986	Referee	Grand Rapids
	10/1/1986–10/1/1992	Recall	Grand Rapids
Marvin L. Heitman	11/8/1974–12/31/1986	Referee	Marquette
Laurence E. Howard	1/14/1976–2/28/1999	Referee	Grand Rapids
James D. Gregg	6/1/1987–6/27/2014	Nims	Grand Rapids
Jo Ann C. Stevenson	12/23/1987–10/2/2007	New Full-Time	Grand Rapids
Jeffrey R. Hughes	1/6/2000–9/13/2013	Howard	Grand Rapids
Scott W. Dales	10/3/2007–Present	Stevenson	Grand Rapids
James W. Boyd	5/30/2014–Present	James Gregg	Grand Rapids
John T. Gregg	7/17/2014–Present	Hughes	Grand Rapids

Chief Judges of the U.S. Bankruptcy Court for the Western District of Michigan

Laurence E. Howard	
James D. Gregg	January 2005, October 2007–October 2013
Jo Ann C. Stevenson	March 2005–September 2007
Scott W. Dales	October 2013–Present

Clerks of the U.S. Bankruptcy Court for the Western District of Michigan

Clerks	Dates of Service	Appointed By
Richard Jackson	10/1/1979–12/31/1988	David E. Nims
Mark Van Allsburg	3/23/1989–1/9/1999	Laurence E. Howard
Daniel L. LaVille	2/15/1999–7/31/2019	James D. Gregg
Michelle M. Wilson	8/1/2019–Present	Scott W. Dales

Federal Public Defenders for the Western District of Michigan

Federal Public Defender	Term of Service
Howard W. Gillingham	October 1995–May 1997
Henry Martin (acting)	May 1997–September 1998
Christopher P. Yates	September 1998–March 2004
Paul Nelson (acting)	March 2004–February 2005
Raymond S. Kent	February 2005–July 2015
Sharon A. Turek	August 2015–Present

Chief U.S. Probation Officers for the Western District of Michigan

Chief Probation Officer	Appointment as Probation Officer
John Veneklasen	September 29, 1930
Martin Brown	October 30, 1935
William Page White	March 16, 1940
Richard Anderson	April 17, 1957
Ted O. Wisner	April 1, 1955
Robert E. Brent	January 8, 1973
Valerie A. Martin	September 5, 1989
Rebecca A. Howell	June 16, 2014

Presidents of the Western Michigan Chapter of the Federal Bar Association

Hugh W. Brenneman, Jr.	1979–1980
Bruce W. Neckers	1980–1981
James S. Brady	1981–1982
Steven L. Dykema	1982–1983
Steven C. Bransdorfer	1983–1984
John L. Coté	1984–1985
Joseph G. Scoville	1985–1986
Robert J. Eleveld	1986–1987
Paul T. Sorensen	1987–1988
Richard A. Kay	1988–1989
W. Fred (Fritz) Hunting, Jr.	1989–1990
William W. Jack, Jr.	1990–1991
Jon G. March	1991–1992
Fred Dilley	1992–1993
Donald A. Davis	1993–1994
Brett N. Rodgers	1994–1995
Douglas E. Wagner	1995–1996
Robert D. VanderLaan	1996–1997
Charles E. Chamberlain, Jr.	1997–1998
James H. Geary	1998–1999
John E. Anding	1999–2000
Michael W. Puerner	2000–2001
Patrick E. Mears	2001–2002
James R. Redford	2002–2003
David J. Gass	2003–2004

Bradley K. Glazier	2004–2005
John Allen	2005–2006
Geoffrey Fields	2006–2007
Kevin O'Dowd	2007–2008
Timothy P. VerHey	2008–2009
Raymond S. Kent	2009–2010
Katherine Smith Kennedy	2010–2011
Scott Brinkmeyer	2011–2012
Jennifer McManus	2012–2013
Ron DeWaard	2013–2014
D. Andrew Portinga	2014–2015
Sarah Riley Howard	2015–2016
Bryan Walters	2016–2017
Sharon Turek	2017–2018
Matthew G. Borgula	2018–2019
Brian P. Lennon	2019–2020

Officers and Directors of the Historical Society for the U.S. District Court for the Western District of Michigan (2003–2020)

Anding, John E.

Andrews, Mary (Archivist)

Bell, Hon. Robert Holmes

Botsford, Jon D.

Brady, James S.

Bransdorfer, Stephen C.

Brenneman, Jr., Hon. Hugh W.

Byerly, Joan (Archivist)

Chamberlain, Jr., Charles E.

Coey, David C.

Cordes, Tracey

Davis, Donald A.

Denenfeld, Hon. Paul J.

Dilley, Thomas R.

Dorwin, Thomas

Farr, William S.

Gass, David J.

Geary, James H.

Goebel, Margaret E. (Meg)

Green, Hon. Phillip J.

Gruszka, Elliot

Hurwitz, Mark S.

Jonker, Hon. Robert J.

Kent, Hon. Raymond S.

Latterman, Mark A.

Loeschner, Raymond B.

Logie, Hon. John H.

Lubbers, Arend D. (Don)

MacDonald, Michael A.

MacGuidwin, Stephen F.

Makens, Hugh H.

Maloney, Hon. Paul L.

Mann, Janice Kittel

Mears, Patrick E.

Miles, Hon. Wendell A.

Mitchell, James A.

Nolan, Jahel H.

Olson, Gordon L.

Puerner, Michael W.

Redford, Hon. James R.

Smary, Eugene E.

Smietanka, John A.

Smith, Webb A.

Stevens, Ruth S.

Weston Sr., Ronald C.

Whitney, Gleaves

Willis, Myra L.

CHAPTER I

1. Under Vergennes's plan, the western land south of the Ohio River would become an Indian nation controlled by Spain.

2. Willis F. Dunbar and George S. May, *Michigan: A History of the Wolverine State,* 3rd rev. ed. (Grand Rapids, MI: W. B. Eerdmans Pub. Co., 1995), map on 111.

3. However, both Virginia and Connecticut reserved land in what became Ohio to compensate their veterans of the Revolution—the Virginia Military District and the Connecticut Western Reserve.

4. *Journal of the Continental Congress* 18 (October 10, 1780): 915.

5. "Revised Report, Plan for Government of the Western Territory," *The Papers of Thomas Jefferson,* Julian P. Boyd ed. (Princeton: Princeton University Press, 1950-) 6 (March 22, 1784): 607–09.

6. "The Ordinance of 1784," *Journal of the Continental Congress* 26 (April 23, 1784): 275–79. This ordinance set out the boundaries of numerous new states and proposed that each state's residents would, soon after settling, form a temporary government, based on the constitution and laws of one of the original states. When a state reached 20,000 "free inhabitants," they would form a permanent government, and when that population was equal to that of "the least numerous of the thirteen original states," the state would be admitted "into the Congress of the United States, on an equal footing with the said original states." Congress did, however, delete a provision that would have banned slavery in the Northwest Territory after 1800.

7. "An Ordinance for the Territory of the United States north-west of the River Ohio," *Journal of the Continental Congress* 32 (July 13, 1787): 334–43.

8. 1 *United States Statutes at Large* (hereafter Stat.) 50 (August 7, 1789).

9. Treaty of Amity, Commerce, and Navigation, between his Britannic Majesty and the United States of America, by Their President, with the Advice and Consent of Their Senate, 8 Stat. 116, 117, Article II (November 19, 1794).

10. A Treaty of Peace between the United States of America and the Tribes of Indians Called the Wyandots, Delawares, Shawonoes, Ottawas, Chipewas, Putawatimes, Miamis, Eel-river, Weea's, Kickapoos, Piankashaws, and Kaskaskias, 7 Stat. 7, 49 (August 3, 1795).

11. At first there was only one U.S. citizen in Michigan: Peter Audrain, born in France and more recently from Pennsylvania.

12. *Territorial Papers of the United States* (hereafter *TPUS*) Book (Washington: [s.n.], 1937) 7 (March 20, 1803): 100.

13. 2 Stat. 2 (May 7, 1800).

14. 2 Stat. 173 (April 30, 1802).

15. *TPUS* 7 (March 20, 1803): 99.

16. *TPUS* 7 (December 6, 1804): 240–41.

17. 2 Stat. 309 (January 11, 1805).

18. 2 Stat. 514 (January 31, 1809).

19. The effect of this isolation may have been nil because that part of the Upper Peninsula was still Indian country and there is no evidence that the Indiana Territory ever exercised its sovereign power there.

20. 3 Stat. 289 (April 19, 1816).

21. 3 Stat. 428 (April 18, 1818).

22. 3 Stat. 428, 431 (April 18, 1818).

23. 4 Stat. 701 (June 28, 1834).

24. 5 Stat. 10 (April 10, 1836), effective on July 3, 1836.

25. 5 Stat. 144 (January 27, 1837).

26. 5 Stat. 49 (June 15, 1836).

27. Jefferson actually appointed Samuel Huntington to be a Michigan judge one day earlier than Woodward, but Huntington, a judge on the Ohio Supreme Court, declined the appointment.

28. Frank B. Woodford, *Mr. Jefferson's Disciple: A Life of Justice Woodward* (East Lansing: Michigan State Press, 1952).

29. For more on the Northwest Territory, the Territory of Michigan, and the Supreme Court of the Territory of Michigan, see David G. Chardavoyne and Paul Moreno, *Michigan Supreme Court Historical Reference Guide*, 2nd ed. (East Lansing: Michigan State University Press, 2015); David G. Chardavoyne, *The United States District Court for the Eastern District of Michigan: People, Law, and Politics* (Detroit: Wayne State University Press, 2012); David G. Chardavoyne, "The Northwest Ordinance and Michigan's Territorial Heritage," in *The History of Michigan Law*, Paul Finkelman and Martin J. Hershock, eds. (Athens: Ohio University Press, 2006).

30. As it turned out, Michigan was not much more to Griffin's liking, and he conducted a campaign for a federal job elsewhere during most of his nineteen-year tenure in Detroit. Like Woodward, he was a lifelong bachelor.

31. Charles Lanman, *The Life of William Woodbridge* (Washington, D.C.: Blanchard & Mohun, 1867), 32–34.

32. For more detail, see Chardavoyne, "The Northwest Ordinance and Michigan's Territorial Heritage," 19–22.

33. James Grant v. Thomas, the Earl of Selkirk, in William Wirt Blume, *Transactions of the Supreme Court of the Territory of Michigan, 1805–1836* (hereafter *TSCM*), 6 vols. (Ann Arbor: University of Michigan Press), vol. 4, 431–51.

34. 1 Stat. 50 (August 7, 1789).

35. 3 Stat. 428, 431 (April 18, 1818).

36. *Laws of the Territory of Michigan* (Lansing:W. S. George &Co., 1871 1 (October 26, 1818): 327.

37. For example, see "Brown County," *Laws of the Territory of Michigan* 1 (October 26, 1818): 327.

38. Fifth U.S. Census, Michigan Territory (1830). For the census results by county, see Wirt Blume, *TSCM*, vol. 5, liv.

39. 3 Stat. 722 (January30, 1823)

40. U.S. Congress, *Senate Exec. Journal*, 18th Congress, 1st Sess. (January 20 and 21, 1824).

41. Robert W. Shank, "The Odyssey of David Irvin," *East Texas Historical Journal* 4, no. 2 (Oct. 1966): 116.

42. Between 1829 and 1833, the additional judge for the Michigan Territory (Judge Doty, 1824–1832; Judge Irvin, 1832–1836) sentenced six men to death under federal law who were executed in what was then the Michigan Territory. Five of the defendants were U.S. soldiers who were convicted and executed under federal law: Sgt. John Renaca, hanged in Prairie du Chien in 1829 for killing a Lt. McKenzie; Pvt. James Brown, hanged on Mackinac Island in 1830 for killing Cpl. Hugh Flinn; Pvt. Daniel Hempstead, hanged in Green Bay in 1830 for killing a civilian boat builder at Duck Creek; Pvt. Matthew Beckwith, hanged in Prairie du Chien in 1832 for shooting an officer; and Pvt. Patrick Doyle, hanged in Green Bay in 1833 for killing a Lt. Foster. In the sixth case, the defendant was a Chippewa named Wau-ben-e-micki, also known as White Thunder, who was convicted and hanged, under federal law, on Mackinac Island in 1833 for killing Jean Baptiste Brunet in Indian country along Lake Superior. Wisconsin Historical Society, "Executions in Wisconsin," *Dictionary of Wisconsin History*, accessed December 4, 2019, https://www.wisconsinhistory.org/Records/Article /CS2319; Keith Widder, *Justice at Mackinac: The Execution of Private James Brown* (Mackinaw City, MI: Mackinac Island State Park Commission, 1974); David G. Chardavoyne, *A Hanging in Detroit: Stephen Gifford Simmons and the Last Execution under Michigan Law* (Detroit: Wayne State University Press, 2003), 144.

43. The original statements taken by Irwin from Katakah and the soldiers are in the Solomon Sibley Papers, Burton Historical Collection, at the Detroit Public Library, in the correspondence files for May–July 1821 ("Ka-ta-kah, an Indian of the

Chippewa tribe") and August–November 1821 ("Barkin Atkinson, George Johnson, and Elijah McCray").

44. "Letter, James Duane Doty to Henry R. Schoolcraft," *TPUS* 11 (November 17, 1821): 175.

45. For example, in June 1806, Judge Bates did travel to Mackinac Island to charge a grand jury. *Michigan State Bar Journal* 14 (1934–1935): 344, 353.

46. An Act to Provide for the Punishment of Crimes and Offences Committed within the Indian Boundaries, 3 Stat. 383 (March 3, 1817).

47. The three judges argued for days among themselves and with the defense counsel about how to swear in the grand jurors. The *Detroit Gazette*, whose owner despised the judges, particularly Woodbridge, later published alleged summaries of the proceedings during those arguments that depicted the judges as pompous, foolish, and pedantic.

48. *Detroit Gazette*, November 18, 1822 through January 3, 1823, in Wirt Blume, *TSCM*, vol. 5, 484–96.

49. *Detroit Gazette*, December 28, 1821.

50. The constitutional status of territorial judges remained in dispute until the U.S. Supreme Court held that such judges were administrative judges created under Article I of the Constitution rather than judges created under Article III. Thus, territorial judges lacked jurisdiction over matters exclusive to the Article III courts, including admiralty and bankruptcy. American Insurance Company v. 356 Bales of Cotton, 26 U.S. 511 (1828).

51. 3 Stat. 769, § 3 (March 3, 1823).

52. See Chardavoyne and Moreno, *Michigan Supreme Court Historical Reference Guide*, 20–21.

53. Solomon Sibley (1769–1846), a graduate of what is now Brown University, was the second American attorney to settle in Detroit after the British left. He served as mayor of Detroit (1806), U.S. Attorney for the Territory of Michigan (1815–1823), and the Michigan Territory's delegate to Congress (1820–1823). John Hunt (c. 1788–1827) arrived in Detroit in 1818 or 1819. Other facts about him are lost except that after his wife died in September 1826, Hunt's mind deteriorated. Hunt left Detroit in late 1826, and he died in New Hartford, New York, in June 1827. Chardavoyne and Moreno, *Michigan Supreme Court Historical Reference Guide*, 24.

54. Henry C. Chipman (1784–1867) was born in Vermont but spent fifteen years practicing law in South Carolina. After his service on the Supreme Court, he served as a criminal judge in Detroit and then became a writer. A Whig when he arrived in Detroit, he became a Democrat in reaction to the creation of the Republican Party. Chardavoyne and Moreno, *Michigan Supreme Court Historical Reference Guide*, 25.

55. William Woodbridge (1780–1861), born in Norwich, Connecticut, left a successful law practice in Ohio in 1814, at the urging of Lewis Cass, to become secretary of the Michigan Territory, devastated by the War of 1812. After his service on Michigan's Supreme Court, Woodbridge was elected Michigan state senator (1838–1839), governor of Michigan (1840–1841), and U.S. senator (1841–1847). Chardavoyne and Moreno, *Michigan Supreme Court Historical Reference Guide*, 26.

56. Chardavoyne and Moreno, *Michigan Supreme Court Historical Reference Guide*, 27.

57. Beginning in 1825, murder trials were tried by three judges of the county Circuit Courts. However, in Wayne County, the Circuit Court judges were the same persons as the Supreme Court judges. So, technically, the judges presided over the Simmons murder trial as the Wayne County Circuit Court, not as the Supreme Court. However, in practice the distinction really made little or no difference because appeals from the Circuit Court were heard by the Supreme Court.

58. See Chardavoyne, *A Hanging in Detroit*.

59. The Saginaw Treaty of 1819, 7 Stat. 203 (September 24, 1819), and the Chicago Treaty of 1821, 7 Stat. 218 (August 21, 1821).

60. The descendants of many New Englanders migrated to newly opened land in western New York after the Revolution. For discussions of the roles of both Yankee groups in Michigan's development, see Brian C. Wilson, *Yankees in Michigan* (East Lansing: Michigan State University Press, 2008); Susan E. Gray, *The Yankee West: Community Life on the Michigan Frontier* (Chapel Hill: University of North Carolina Press, 1996).

61. 5 Stat. 49, 50 (June 15, 1836). Congress did award Michigan a consolation prize. By 1835, the Territory of Michigan included what is now Wisconsin, Iowa, Minnesota, and parts of North Dakota, but it was understood during all of this turmoil that the state's northern and western boundaries would be those set out in the law creating the territory: the Lower Peninsula and that small part of the Upper Peninsula east of Mackinac Island. To replace Toledo, Congress granted Michigan the rest of the Upper Peninsula, a trackless wilderness that did not console many residents of the Lower Peninsula in 1836 but that became crucial to the state's development over the next century.

62. 5 Stat. 144 (January 26, 1837).

Chapter 2

1. The Articles did provide for arbitration of boundary disputes and conflicting land claims, and appeals of admiralty, maritime, and prize decisions by temporary arbitration boards.

2. Erwin C. Surrency, *History of the Federal Courts* (New York: Oceana Publications, Inc., 1987), 9.

3. W. B. Allen and Gordon Lloyd, *The Essential Antifederalist* (Lanham, MD: University Press of America, 1985), 11–12.

4. Russell R. Wheeler and Cynthia Harrison, *Creating the Federal Judicial System*, 2nd ed. (Washington, D.C.: Federal Judicial Center, 1994), 2.

5. U.S. Const. art. III, § 1: "The judicial Power of the United States, shall be vested in one Supreme Court, and in such inferior Courts as the Congress may from time to time ordain and establish."

6. An Act to Establish the Judicial Courts of the United States, 1 *United States Statutes at Large* (hereafter Stat.) 73 (September 24, 1789).

7. 1 Stat. 126 (June 4, 1790), North Carolina; 1 Stat. 128 (June 23, 1790), Rhode Island.

8. In 1838, the first year that the District of Michigan held a Circuit Court session, its appointed justice, John McLean, traveled 2,500 miles circuit-riding through Illinois, Ohio, Indiana, and Michigan. His colleague John McKinley covered ten thousand miles circuit-riding through the deep South that year. Frankfurter, 49.

9. U.S. Const., Article art. II, §sec. 2

10. The drafters recognized the importance of lifetime tenure, which had become the norm for judges in the new states, in isolating judges from politics. See Surrency, *History of the Federal Courts*, 14.

11. 18 Stat. 470 (March 3, 1875).

12. 1 Stat. 73, 88 (September 24, 1789).

13. I. Scott Messinger, *Order in the Courts: A History of the Federal Clerk's Office* (Washington, D.C.: Federal Judicial Center, 2002), 1.

14. 1 Stat. 73, 76 (September 24, 1789).

15. 1 Stat. 216, 217 (March 3, 1791).

16. 5 Stat. 321, 322 (February 28, 1839).

17. 1 Stat. 73, 87.

18. 1 Stat. 275, 277.

19. 1 Stat. 626.

20. 1 Stat. 73, 91, § 33 (September 24, 1789).

21. An Act in Addition to the Act, Entitled "An Act to Establish the Judicial Courts of the United States," 1 Stat. 333, 334, § 4 (March 2, 1793).

22. An Act for the More Convenient Taking of Affidavits and Bail in Civil Causes, Depending in the Courts of the United States, 2 Stat. 679, 680–81, § 1 (February 20, 1812).

23. An Act in Addition to an Act, Entitled "An Act for the More Convenient Taking of Affidavits and Bail in Civil Causes, Depending in the Courts of the United States," 3 Stat. 350 (March 1, 1817).

24. 5 Stat. 61.

25. Although some sources identify Senator Wilkins as Judge Wilkins's brother, he was, in fact, the youngest brother of General Wilkins. Ross Wilkins' appointment to the Michigan Supreme Court in 1832 was Jackson's attempt to influence then-Senator William Wilkins to vote against the Second Bank of the United States.

26. John Snowden to Andrew Jackson, November 5, 1835, Record Group 59 (State Department Records), National Archives and Records Administration.

27. Stevens T. Mason to Ross Wilkins, July 12, 1836, 1830–1837 Folder, Ross Wilkins Papers, Burton Historical Collection, Detroit Public Library.

28. *Acts of the Legislature of the State of Michigan Passed at the First and Extra Sessions of 1835 and 1836*, 30–34 (Lansing: 1836).

29. 5 Stat. 61 (July 1, 1836).

30. Mich. Const. of 1835, art. VI, § 2.

31. *Acts of the Legislature of the State of Michigan Passed at the First and Extra Sessions of 1835 and 1836*, 30–34.

32. Ross Wilkins to William Seward, October 2, 1851, 1850–1851 Folder, Ross Wilkins Papers, Burton Historical Collection, Detroit Public Library.

33. He was an early member of the Washingtonian Movement, which sought out drinkers and tried to bring them to abstinence by counseling and discussion, much like today's Alcoholics Anonymous.

34. Robert B. Ross, *Early Bench and Bar of Detroit: From 1805 to the End of 1850* (Detroit, 1907)217.

35. Robert B. Ross, *Early Bench and Bar of Detroit: From 1805 to the End of 1850* (Detroit, 1907)13.

36. Alexander D. Frazer, quoted in *Detroit Free Press*, December 3, 1869.

37. George I. Reed, *Bench and Bar of Michigan: A Volume of History and Biography* (Chicago: Century Publishing & Engraving Co., 1897), 160.

38. Even before he was sworn in as District Judge, he wrote to John Norvell, Michigan's first U.S. senator, asking for his help in getting a raise in pay, but Norvell had to report that Congress would not agree. John Norvell to Ross Wilkins, January 30, 1837, 1830–1837 Folder, Ross Wilkins Papers, Burton Historical Collection, Detroit Public Library.

39. 14 Stat. 468, 471 (March 2, 1867).

40. The 1860 census, for example, records a Wilkins household of eleven people, including two daughters, four grandchildren, and four servants, one of whom, twelve-year-old Louis Parker, was reported as "Black."

41. 5 Stat. 321, 322, § 2 (February 28, 1839).

42. Surrency, *History of the Federal Courts*, 374.

43. Asst. Secretary of State to Ross Wilkins, January 28, 1837, 1837 Folder, Ross Wilkins Papers, Burton Historical Collection, Detroit Public Library. Note on verso of letter states it was received on February 6, 1837.

44. According to one legend, his tavern was also the source of calling Michigan residents "wolverines." When he told one settler that he had fed her wolf steaks, she replied that she must then be a wolverine, the only animal that eats wolves. Friend Palmer, *Early Days in Detroit* (Detroit: Hunt & June, 1906), 906.

45. 5 Stat. 62 (July 1, 1836).

46. U.S. Senate Journal, 24th Cong., 1st Sess., 236 (March 22, 1836); U.S. House Journal, 24th Cong., 1st Sess., 427 (March 1, 1836). Indeed, the petitioners could not seriously have expected a positive response because, at that time, there was only one federal courthouse in the nation, on Royal Street in New Orleans. The building is now the Andrew Jackson French Quarter Hotel.

47. Alfred Conkling, *Treatise on the Organization, Jurisdiction and Practice of the Courts of the United States* (Albany, NY: William A. Gould & Co., 1831), 107.

48. U.S. District Court, Eastern District of Michigan, Journal A (hereafter, "Journal A"), February 23, 1837, Records Group 21.24.2, Chicago Federal Records Center; *Detroit Daily Advertiser*, February 21–24, 1837.

49. W. Hawkins Ferry, *The Buildings of Detroit: A History* (Detroit: Wayne State University Press, 1968), 32.

50. William Wirt Blume, 1 *Transactions of the Supreme Court of the Territory of Michigan, 1805–1836* (hereafter *TSCM*), 6 vols. (Ann Arbor: University of Michigan Press 1935–1940)6:385.

51. Blume, 385, 411.

52. See "The First Session and First Local Rules," *The Court Legacy* 11, no. 1 (February 2003): 10.

53. Journal A. In 1837, the District Court sat on February 23, March 15, May 1 to 6 and 7 to 13, June 22, July 6, October 2 to 5 and 10, and November 9 to 11.

54. 5 Stat. 176.

55. Journal A, May 5, 1837.

56. Dred Scott v. Sandford, 60 U.S. 393 (1857).

57. *New York Times*, April 18, 1860.

58. John McLean, *Reports of Cases Argued and Decided in the Circuit Court of the United States for the Seventh Circuit*, 6. vols. (Cincinnati: H. W. Darby & Co., 1840–1856).

59. John McLean to Ross Wilkins, June 10, 1838, 1838–1839 Folder, Ross Wilkins Papers, Burton Historical Collection, Detroit Public Library. McLean explained that: "Should any indictments grow out of the Canada insurrection, I presume the defendants will not be ready until the fall term."

Chapter 3

1. The states with more than one district and one District Judge in 1862 were: Alabama (1824), Arkansas (1851), Florida (1847), Georgia (1848), Illinois (1855), Louisiana (1849), Mississippi (1838), Missouri (1857), New York (1814), Ohio (1855), Pennsylvania (1818), Texas (1857), and Virginia (1819). Three states had more than one district but just one District Judge: North Carolina (1802), South Carolina (1823), and Tennessee (1839).

2. At the same time, he gave notice that he would introduce a bill to limit the jurisdiction of the United States courts to cases arising under the laws and Constitution of the United States, but abolishing diversity jurisdiction. U.S. House Journal, 29th Cong., 1st Sess., 143 (December 19, 1845).

3. U.S. House Journal, 29th Cong., 1st Sess., 450 (February 24, 1846).

4. U.S. House Journal, 29th Cong., 1st Sess., 595 (March 27, 1846).

5. [1857] Acts *of the Legislature of the State of Michigan, Joint Resolution No. 28* (1857) Lansing: Hosmer & Fitch, 1857), 493 (February 17, 1857).

6. U.S. House Journal, 35th Cong., 1st Sess., 639 (April 17, 1858).

7. Michigan's congressmen at that time were Bradley F. Granger, Fernando C. Beaman, Francis W. Kellogg, and Rowland E. Trowbridge, all Republicans.

8. *Congressional Globe*, 37th Cong., 3rd Sess., 1018 (February 17, 1863).

9. *Congressional Globe*, 37th Cong., 3rd Sess., 1018 (February 17, 1863).

10. *Congressional Globe*, 37th Cong. 3rd Sess., 1019 (February 17, 1863).

11. *Congressional Globe*, 37th Cong., 3rd Sess., 1155 (February 21, 1863).

12. *Congressional Globe*, 37th Cong., 3rd Sess., 1156 (February 21, 1863).

13. *Congressional Globe*, 37th Cong., 3rd Sess., 1156 (February 21, 1863).

14. *Congressional Globe*, 37th Cong., 3rd Sess., 1156 (February 21, 1863).

15. Kentucky did not receive a second district until 1901.

16. 12 *United States Statutes at Large* (hereafter Stat.) 660 (February 24, 1863): "The western district shall embrace all the territory and waters within the following boundaries, to wit: Commencing at the southwest corner of Hillsdale county, in the State of Michigan, and running from thence north, on the west line of said county, to the south line of Calhoun county; thence east, on the south line thereof, to the southeast corner of said last-named county; thence north, on the east boundary of said county, to the south line of Eaton county; thence east, on said south line, to the southeast corner of Eaton county; thence north, on the east boundary of Eaton county, to the south line of Clinton county; thence west, on the south boundary of said county, to the southwest corner thereof; thence north, on the west boundary of Clinton and Gratiot counties, to the south boundary of Isabella county; thence west, on its south boundary, to the southwest corner of said last-named county;

thence north, on the west line of Isabella and Clare counties, to the south boundary of Missaukee county; thence east, on its south boundary, to the southeast corner of Missaukee county; thence north, on the east line of Missaukee, Kalcasca [*sic*], and Antrim counties, to the south boundary [of] Emmet county; thence east to the southeast corner of Emmet county; thence north, on the east boundary of Emmet county, to the Straits of Mackinac; thence north to midway across said straits; thence westerly, in a direct line, to a point on the shore of Lake Michigan where the north boundary of Delta county reaches Lake Michigan; thence west, on the north line of Delta county, to the northwest corner of said Delta county; thence south, on the west boundary of said county, to the dividing line between the States of Michigan and Wisconsin in Green Bay; thence northeasterly, on the said dividing line, into Lake Michigan, and thence southerly, through Lake Michigan, to the southwest corner of the State of Michigan, on a line that will include within said boundaries the waters of Lake Michigan within the admiralty jurisdiction of the State of Michigan; thence east, on the south boundary of the State of Michigan, to the intersection of the west line of Hillsdale county." Congress would change the boundaries of the districts from time to time. See Robert Holmes Bell and Avern Cohn, "The Federal Districts of Michigan," *Michigan Bar Journal* (May 1988).

17. 12 Stat. 660, 661 (February 24, 1863).

18. Senate Executive Journal, 37th Cong., 3rd Sess., 282 (March 11, 1863).

19. *Detroit Free Press*, March 14, 1863.

20. *Detroit Free Press*, March 14, 1863. From the article it seems that this source was the Eastern District's long-time clerk, John Winder, who doubtless feared losing some of his income, which depended on the number of cases filed.

21. U.S. House Journal, 38th Cong., 1st Sess., 264 (February 15, 1864).

22. 13 Stat. 143 (June 20, 1864).

23. The major sources of the details of Judge Withey's life and death are *History of Kent County, Illustrated* (Grand Rapids, MI: Charles C. Chapman & Co., 1881), 1171–73; "Solomon L. Withey Memorial," 59 Mich. xxxii (1886); "Judge Withey Dead: Dropped Away Suddenly at San Diego, California—Biographical Sketch," *Grand Rapids* (Michigan) *Daily Eagle*, April 26, 1886; Albert Baxter and Willard I. Brigham, *History of the City of Grand Rapids, Michigan* (Grand Rapids, MI: Munsell & Company, Publishers, 1891), 747. The family name was originally McWithey, but Judge Withey's grandfather, a veteran of the Revolution, dropped the "Mc."

24. Withey's Vermont heritage was important to him. In 1877, he became the first President of the Vermont Society, a Grand Rapids social association, later named the New England Society, whose members had all been born in New England.

25. John Ball was a legendary figure in Grand Rapids. He had been the first white teacher in Oregon and one of its first farmers. When Michigan became a state, he settled in Grand Rapids, aided in the rapid development of its river valley, served in

the legislature, and, on his death in 1884, donated the land that became the John Ball Zoo on the city's west side.

26. Marion Withey, like her husband, became very involved in the Grand Rapids community. She was a leader in founding the forerunners of several prominent city institutions such as Blodgett Memorial Hospital, a nursing school, the public library, and the Ladies' Literary Club.

27. In 1869, he tried another tactic. Sitting as circuit judge in the Eastern District, he ruled that under Michigan law a promissory note used to buy liquor was void and unenforceable. *St. Joseph* (Michigan) *Herald*, July 3, 1869.

28. "Solomon L. Withey Memorial," xxiii.

29. "Solomon L. Withey Memorial," xxiii.

30. *Grand Rapids* (Michigan) *Daily Democrat*, April 27, 1886; *Grand Rapids* (Michigan) *Daily Eagle*, April 26, 1886. In the absence of Judge Withey, court was held by judges from other districts, principally District Judge George Reed Sage from the Southern District of Ohio. *Grand Rapids* (Michigan) *Daily Eagle*, May 5, 1886.

31. *Grand Rapids* (Michigan) *Daily Democrat*, May 4, 1886.

32. *Grand Rapids* (Michigan) *Daily Eagle*, May 16, 1863.

33. David J. Gass, "Our First District Judge and the Civil War," *Stereoscope* 5, no. 4 (Winter 2007): 7–8.

34. *Grand Rapids* (Michigan) *Daily Eagle*, July 1, 1863.

35. *Grand Rapids* (Michigan) *Daily Eagle*, September 8, 1863. Some records and documents identify this deserting soldier of Company A of the 21st Michigan Volunteer Infantry as George W. Champlin, others as George W. Champlain.

36. 5 Stat. 676 (August 1, 1842).

37. 16 Stat. 44 (April 10, 1869).

38. Withey's change of mind upset an intricate political deal between the President and the state's Republicans. With Judge Wilkins about to retire and Withey made a circuit judge, the path would have been open to reward two Republicans with a district judgeship, with Emmons fingered for the Eastern District judgeship. Instead, Emmons "settled" for the circuit judgeship, which involved much more travel and work, even if with more pay. *Detroit Advertiser and Tribune*, January 10, 1870.

39. Solomon L. Withey, *Address to the Graduating Class of the Law Department of the University of Michigan, March 29, 1871* (Ann Arbor: E. B. Pond, 1872), 13. For more on this speech and the Law Department of the University of Michigan, see David J. Gass, "Solomon Withey's March 29, 1871 Commencement Address to the University of Michigan Law School," *Stereoscope* 16, no. 1 (Fall, 2018).

40. See Christian R. Burset, "The Messy History of the Federal Eminent Domain Power: A Response to William Baude," *California Law Review Circuit* 4, (December, 2013): 187.

41. Avery v. Fox, 2 F. Cas. 245 (C.C. W.D. Mich. 1868).

42. U.S. Lake Survey, Detroit Office, *Bulletin of the Northern and Northwestern Lake Survey*, Issues 19–20 (May 22, 2012) 206.

43. 14 Stat. 418, 419 (March 2, 1867).

44. Avery v. Fox, Circuit Court Journal A, 228 (C.C. W.D. Mich. January 21, 1868).

45. Avery v. Fox, 2 F. Cas. 245.

46. For more on this case, see Michael W. Puerner, "The Taxing Journey of the *Daniel Ball*," *Stereoscope* 2, no. 1 (Summer 2004).

47. 5 Stat. 304 (July 7, 1838) and 10 Stat. 61 (August 30, 1852).

48. See Barbara Voulgaris, *From Steamboat Inspection Service to U.S. Coast Guard: Marine Safety in the United States from 1838–1946* (United States Coast Guard, 2009).

49. Identified by Withey as a "manuscript" opinion involving *The Forest Queen* and *The Pontiac*, "pronounced in 1856 or 1857."

50. Augustus Griswold (1823–1890) served as District Attorney for the Western District from 1865 to 1869 except for six months in 1866–1867 when he was removed and then reinstated by President Andrew Johnson.

51. The *Daniel Ball*, 1 Brown Admin. 193, 6 F. Cas. 1161 (D.C. W.D. Mich. 1868).

52. The United States v. the Steamer Daniel Ball, Circuit Court Journal A, 268–70 (C.C. W.D. Mich. November 6, 1868). Justice Swayne, apparently considering his duty complete, did not tarry but left the district and did not appear again on the Circuit Court that term.

53. Benjamin H. Bristow (1832–1896) was the nation's first Solicitor General and a relentless prosecutor of the Ku Klux Klan. He was also known for his advocacy of the rights of African Americans. Andrew T. McReynolds (1808–1898), a cavalry officer decorated for his reckless charges in both the Mexican-American War and Civil War, was then a private attorney but had been U.S. Attorney for the Western District from 1866 to 1867.

54. The *Daniel Ball*, 77 U.S. (10. Wall.) 557 (1870).

55. *New York Times*, October 18, 1871.

56. *Grand Rapids Gazetteer* (1873).

57. 17 Stat. 470 (February 21, 1873).

58. 18 Stat., 204, 228, part 3 (June 23, 1874); Jackson D. Dillenback, *Grand Rapids in 1874*(Grand Rapids: 1875) 15.

59. Payments authorized by 18 Stat., 395, part 3 (March 3, 1875); 19 Stat. 110 (July 31, 1876); 19 Stat. 351 (March 4, 1877); 20 Stat. 210 (June 20, 1878).

60. *American Architect and Building News*, February 12, 1876, 49.

61. *American Architect and Building News*, July 22, 1876, 236–37.

62. H.R. Bill 209, 41st Cong., 1st Sess. See also U.S. House Journal, 41st Cong., 1st Sess., 88 (March 22, 1869).

63. U.S. House Journal, 41st Cong., 2nd Sess., 41 (December 10, 1869).

64. 20 Stat. 175, 177, § 9 (June 19, 1878).

65. Born in New York State in 1841, Uhl came to Ypsilanti with his family in 1844, graduated from the University of Michigan in 1862, and read law in Ypsilanti where he partnered with Lyman Norris and then followed Norris to Grand Rapids in 1876. A staunch Democrat, Uhl served as mayor of Grand Rapids (1890–1891) and ambassador to the German Empire (1896–1897). He died in Grand Rapids in 1901. Ernest B. Fisher, ed., *Grand Rapids and Kent County, Michigan: Historical Account of Their Progress from First Settlement to the Present Time* (Chicago: Robert O. Law Company, 1918), 377–78.

66. *Grand Rapids Daily Democrat*, April 28, 1886; *Grand Rapids Daily Democrat*, May 2, 1886.

67. *Detroit Free Press*, May 5, 1886.

68. (Chicago) *Inter Ocean*, May 15, 1886.

69. *Detroit Free Press*, May 15, 1886.

70. Middlebury College, *Catalogue of Officers and Students of Middlebury College in Middlebury, Vermont, and All Others Who Have Received Degrees, 1800 to 1889* (1890) 110.

71. James W. Ellis, *The History of Jackson County, Iowa*, vol. 1 (Chicago: S. J. Clarke Publishing Co., 1910), 89, 487.

72. *History of St. Joseph County, Michigan, with illustrations descriptive of its scenery, palatial residences, public buildings* . . . (Philadelphia: L. H. Everts & Co., 1877), 39.

73. St. Joseph County Genealogical Society, *Cemeteries of St. Joseph County* (n.p., n.d.), vol. 4, 206.

74. Township of New Buffalo v. Cambria Iron Co., 105 U.S. 73 (1881).

75. *Kalamazoo Gazette*, May 15, 1886.

76. *Grand Rapids Herald*, February 10, 1900.

77. *Kalamazoo Gazette*, June 9, 1923.

78. Letter, William Howard Taft to Henry F. Severens, July 11, 1911, Severens Papers, Bentley Historical Library, University of Michigan.

79. *Grand Rapids Herald*, June 10, 1923.

80. 226 Mich. xxxi (1924).

81. 17 Stat. 283 (June 8, 1872).

82. 17 Stat. 283, 302, § 148 (June 8, 1872).

83. 17 Stat. 283, 302, § 149 (June 8, 1872).

84. United States v. Reid, 42 F. 134 (W.D. Mich. 1890).

85. 1890 Case Journal, U.S. District Court for the Western District of Michigan, Records Group 21, National Archives at Chicago, Illinois.

86. "The Todd Farm," accessed December 3, 2019, http://fennville.memorieshop.com/History/Maps/Todd-Farm.html.

87. United States v. Staples, 45 F. 195 (W.D. Mich. 1890).

88. United States v. Staples, 45 F. 195, 198.

89. 22 Stat. 177 (July 27, 1882).

90. *Annual Report of the Supervising Architect to the Secretary of the Treasury for the Year Ending September 30, 1885 (Washington: U.S. Printing Office, 1885)*, 34, 75.

91. *Annual Report of the Supervising Architect of the Treasury Department for Fiscal Year Ending June 30, 1904 (Washington: U.S. Printing Office, 1904)*, 108.

92. *Detroit Free Press*, July 17, 1889.

93. 26 Stat. 826 (March 3, 1891). The Evarts Act also established a uniform annual salary of $5,000 for all U.S. District Judges. Previously, Congress set the salary for each District Court separately.

94. The main purpose of the Evarts Act was to relieve the Supreme Court of its historic duty of hearing every appeal of a civil case from every district, a burden which, in 1890 alone, added 623 new appeals to the Court's docket. The act did this by providing that decisions of the Circuit Courts of appeals were to be final for diversity, patent, and admiralty cases unless that court or the Supreme Court certified the case for further appeal. This change reduced the appeals filed in the Supreme Court to 275 in 1892.

95. I. Scott Messinger, *Order in the Courts: A History of the Federal Clerk's Office* (Federal Judicial Center, 2002), 36–37, quoting Felix Frankfurter and James M. Landis, *The Business of the Supreme Court: A Study in the Federal Judicial System* (New York: MacMillan, 1928), 100.

96. U.S. Const. art. I, § 8.

97. 1 Stat. 103 (March 26, 1790). The Naturalization Law of 1802, 2 Stat. 153 (April 11, 1802), revised the 1790 Act but did not change the racial limitation.

98. U.S. Const. amend. XIV, § 1.

99. 16 Stat. 254 (July 14, 1870).

100. The Burlingame Treaty, 16 Stat. 739 (July 28, 1868).

101. 18 Stat., 477, part 3 (March 3, 1875).

102. As commonly used, the term Chinese Exclusion Acts included the Chinese Exclusion Acts of 1882, 22 Stat. 58 (May 6, 1882), and of 1884, 23 Stat. 115 (July 5, 1884); the Scott Act of 1888, 25 Stat. 476 (September 13, 1888); the Geary Act of 1892, 27 Stat. 25 (May 5, 1892); the McCreary Act of 1893, 28 Stat. 7 (November 3, 1893); the Chinese Exclusion Act of 1902, 32 Stat. 176 (April 29, 1902); and the Chinese Exclusion Extension Act of 1904, 33 Stat. 394, 428 (April 27, 1904).

103. 57 Stat. 600 (December 17, 1943).

104. Section 13 of the Scott Act authorized "any justice, judge, or commissioner of any United States court" to issue arrest warrants, hold hearings, and order deportations. 25 Stat. 476, 479 (September 13, 1888).

105. Roger Daniels, *Coming to America: A History of Immigration and Ethnicity in American Life*, 2nd ed. (New York: Harper Perennial, 2002), 271.

106. These may or may not have been their names. Not only did apprehended Chinese people often give false names, arresting officers generally had no experience with Chinese names so that translating the sounds of Chinese names into English was usually a matter of rough approximation.

107. In re Sing Lee, In re Ching Jo, 54 F. 334 (D.C. W.D. Mich. 1893).

Chapter 4

1. *Grand Rapids Herald*, March 1, 1900.

2. *Grand Rapids Herald*, March 2, 1900.

3. *Grand Rapids Herald*, March 3, 1900.

4. *Grand Rapids Daily News*, July 9, 1906.

5. Albert Baxter, *History of the City of Grand Rapids, Michigan* (New York and Grand Rapids, MI: Munsell & Co., 1891), 714.

6. *Detroit Free Press*, July 5, 1901.

7. *Cincinnati Enquirer*, January 14, 1906.

8. *Cincinnati Enquirer*, January 14, 1906; *St. Joseph Weekly Press*, July 12, 1906.

9. *St. Joseph Weekly Press*, July 12, 1906.

10. *Grand Rapids Daily News*, July 9, 1906.

11. Article 14 of Michigan's 1850 constitution had authorized the legislature to levy "specific taxes" on various types of corporations, including railroads. The legislature created such a specific tax on railroads and related corporations based on their gross revenue.

12. Pingree v. Auditor General, 120 Mich. 95 (1899).

13. The proposal became Article XIV, section 10 of the 1850 constitution.

14. Mich. Pub. Act [1901], No. 173.

15. *Appendix to the Journals of the Senate and Assembly of the 37th Session of the Legislature of the State of California*, vol. 2 (1907), 131–35.

16. The original twenty-four plaintiffs included Pere Marquette Railroad Co.; Detroit & Mackinac Railroad Co.; Chicago & Northwestern Railway Co.; Toledo, Saginaw & Muskegon Railway Co.; Michigan Air Line Railway Co.; Grand Trunk Western Railway Co.; Michigan Central Railroad Co.; Ann Arbor Railroad Co.; Cincinnati Saginaw & Mackinac Railroad Co.; Chicago, Detroit & Canada Grand Trunk Junction Railroad Co.; Munising Railway Co.; Lake Superior & Ishpeming Railway Co.; Marquette & Southeastern Railway Co.; Chicago, Milwaukee & St. Paul Railway Co.; Mineral Range Railroad Co.; Pontiac, Oxford & North-

ern Railroad Co.; Minneapolis, St. Paul & Sault Ste. Marie Railway Co.; Copper Range Railroad Co.; Gogebic & Montreal River Railroad Co.; Manistee & Northeastern Railroad Co.; Escanaba & Lake Superior Railroad Co.; Grand Rapids & Indiana Railway Co.; Detroit, Grand Haven & Milwaukee Ry. Co.; and Wisconsin & Michigan Railway Co.

17. "Retiring Message of Governor Aaron T. Bliss," *Bessemer* (Michigan) *Herald*, June 14, 1905.

18. Among the attorneys arguing on behalf of the auditor general was Loyal Knappen, Judge Wanty's former partner who would succeed him on the Western District court within a year.

19. Michigan Railroad Tax Cases, 138 F. 223 (C.C. W.D. Mich. 1905).

20. Michigan Central Railroad Co. v. Powers, 201 U.S. 245 (1906). One railroad did, however, prevail, but on a contractual rather than constitutional point of law. In a separate opinion, Judge Wanty decided that the Detroit, Grand Haven & Milwaukee Railway Co. was allowed to rely on a limitation on tax assessment found in a predecessor railroad's 1834 charter as a contract between the state and the railroad. Detroit, Grand Haven & Milwaukee Ry. Co. v. Powers, 138 F. 264 (C.C. W.D. Mich. 1905). Like Wanty's main decision, this decision was affirmed by the U.S. Supreme Court in Powers v. Detroit, Grand Haven & Milwaukee Ry. Co., 201 U.S. 543 (1906).

21. "Judge Wanty Memorial," 146 Mich. xxxvii–xlii (October 16, 1906).

22. *Grand Rapids Daily News*, July 11, 1906.

23. "It is known that Mr. Knappen was offered the position about two months ago but owing to having signed the petition in favor of Mr. Denison he declined to allow his name to be used but the entrance later of more candidates into the field brought about a complicated situation and Senator Burrows reverted to the early choice of Mr. Knappen." *Grand Rapids Daily News,* December 3, 1906.

24. *Grand Rapids Press*, May 15, 1930.

25. Withey was appointed to the Sixth Circuit, and he accepted, but he changed his mind and never served on the appeals court.

26. President Coolidge established the board because of the crash of the U.S. Navy dirigible U.S.S. *Shenandoah* and statements by Army General William "Billy" Mitchell, an ardent proponent of air power, that both the Army and the Navy were guilty of "criminal negligence" with respect to that crash and in their flight operations generally.

27. *Grand Rapids Press*, May 28, 1942.

28. 34 *United States Statutes at Large* (hereafter Stat.) 772 (June 30, 1906).

29. 34 Stat. 772, 785 (June 30, 1906).

30. 34 Stat. 772, 796 (June 30, 1906).

31. 34 Stat. 772 (June 30, 1906).

32. "Judge Denison maintained a modest office in the temporary federal building on Division-av. [*sic*], N, across the street from the present post office building which was being constructed at that time." *Grand Rapids Press*, May 28, 1942.

33. 35 Stat. 317 (May 27, 1908), $6,000 for rent; 35 Stat. 950 (March 4, 1909), $340,000 to complete the building; 36 Stat. 207 (February 25, 1910), $6,000 for rent; 36 Stat. 889 (December 23, 1910), $7,300 for rent. In March 1931, Congress authorized the "extension and remodeling" of what was then a twenty-two-year-old building, "under an estimated total cost of $300,000." 46 Stat. 1552, 1593 (March 4, 1931). However, two years later, Congress repealed that appropriation along with those for many other building projects. 47 Stat. 1602, 1613 (March 4, 1933).

34. *Grand Rapids Herald*, August 21, 1910.

35. *Detroit Free Press*, August 21, 1909.

36. *Grand Rapids Herald*, May 3, 1910.

37. *Detroit Free Press*, February 2, 1911.

38. *News-Palladium* (Benton Harbor, Michigan), June 23, 1954.

39. *Herald-Palladium* (St. Joseph, Michigan), December 30, 1908.

40. *Detroit Free Press*, January 1, 1909.

41. *Detroit Free Press*, January 4, 1909.

42. *Herald-Palladium* (St. Joseph, Michigan), February 8, 1909.

43. Although the cornerstone laying took place on February 12, the cornerstone carries the date February 19.

44. The dead postal employees were Ernest Roth, a postal truck driver, and Herman Pettersch, a dock man. Dale Newhouse, employed at Bulman Manufacturing Co., which supplied the post office with twine and paper dispensers, died the next day of a fractured skull. The seriously injured men were Charles Butler, the supervisor of mails; A. A. Weston, assistant supervisor of mails; St. Clair Vetter and Hoy Bush, dockhands; Lawrence Yarrington and Edwin Annatoyn, postal clerks; and C. R. Mackley, a manager at the American Weatherstrip Company, who was struck on the head by flying debris while standing across the street. *Detroit Free Press*, November 13, 1924.

45. *Detroit Free Press*, November 13, 1924.

46. *Detroit Free Press*, March 23, 1924.

47. 46 Stat. 1552, 1593 (March 4, 1931).

48. 47 Stat. 1602, 1613 (March 4, 1933).

49. 24 Stat. 128 (July 8, 1886).

50. *Sault Ste. Marie Evening News*, June 28, 1906.

51. 34 Stat. 772, 777 (June 30, 1906).

52. 34 Stat. 190 (May 12, 1906).

53. 34 Stat. 772, 791 (June 30, 1906).

54. 34 Stat. 1303 (March 4, 1907).

55. 35 Stat. 521 (May 30, 1908).

56. $30,000 appropriated at 35 Stat. 945, 957 (March 4, 1909); $40,000 appropriated at 36 Stat. 703, 707 (June 25, 1910).

57. Congress had dissolved the Circuit Courts as of January 1, 1912.

58. 37 Stat. 190 (July 9, 1912). The District Court judge was required to hold terms in Grand Rapids beginning on the first Tuesdays of March, June, October, and December; in Marquette on the second Tuesdays of April and September; and in Sault Ste. Marie on the second Tuesdays of January and July.

59. *Sault Ste. Marie Evening News*, January 14, 1913.

60. *Sault Ste. Marie Evening News*, January 13, 1913.

61. 28 *United States Code* 102(b)(2).

62. *Weekly Press* (St. Joseph Michigan), August 2, 1906.

63. *Indianapolis News*, March 4, 1910.

64. *Indianapolis News*, March 7, 1910.

65. *Grand Rapids Press*, April 1, 1931.

66. Among publications discussing the Federal League and this case in particular, see Daniel R. Levitt, *The Battle that Forged Modern Baseball: The Federal League Challenge and Its Legacy* (Lanham, MD: Ivan R. Dee, 2012); Sean Deveney, *Before Wrigley: The Inside Story of the First Years of the Cubs' Home Field* (New York: Sports Publishing, 2014); Patrick E. Mears, "The Catcher, 'The Quick Lunch King,' and Baseball's Reserve Clause: Major League Litigation in Grand Rapids," *Stereoscope* 1, no. 1 (Winter 2003). For a study of the overall battle over the baseball reserve clause, see Nathaniel Grow, *Baseball on Trial: The Origin of Baseball's Antitrust Exemption* (Urbana: The University of Illinois Press, 2014).

67. In the press and in the courts, the correct spelling of Killefer's surname was confused. Most newspapers contemporary with his career spelled it Killifer, as did the U.S. Court of Appeals for the Sixth Circuit. On the other hand, other newspapers and pleadings in the U.S. District Court for the Western District of Michigan spelled it Killefer as does Major League Baseball. I have used the MLB version.

68. (Chicago) *Day Book*, March 20, 1914. Although the plaintiffs could have based their case on the Sherman Antitrust Act by claiming that the agreement of the National League teams to require the reserve clause in all player contracts was an illegal restraint on interstate commerce, they instead relied simply on their contract with Killefer.

69. John Norton Pomeroy, *A Treatise on Equity Jurisprudence* (San Francisco: Bancroft-Whitney Co., 1907), secs. 398, 400, 404.

70. (Chicago) *Inter Ocean*, April 5, 1914.

71. Weeghman v. Killefer, 215 F. 168 (W.D. Mich. 1914).

72. Weeghman v. Killifer [*sic*], 215 F. 289 (6th Cir. 1914).

73. Federal Baseball Club of Baltimore, Inc. v. National League of Professional Baseball Clubs, 259 U.S. 200 (1922).

74. In December 1975, at the end of hearings on a grievance filed by the players association against the league on behalf of Andy Messersmith and Dave McNally, the neutral arbitrator on a three-arbitrator panel, Peter Seitz, agreed with the players association arbitrator, Marvin Miller, that because Messersmith and McNally had played for their teams for a year without signing a new contract, they were free of any "contractual bond" with their teams. MLB appealed unsuccessfully through the U.S. District Court for the District of Missouri and the U.S. Court of Appeals for the Eighth Circuit. Finally, in 1976, MLB and the players association signed a new collective bargaining agreement that allowed players with six years' experience to become free agents.

75. There are several recent publications dealing with the sinking and its aftermath, including Jay Bonansinga, *The Sinking of the* Eastland: *America's Forgotten Tragedy* (New York: Citadel Press, 2004); John A. Farrell, *Clarence Darrow: Attorney for the Damned* (New York: Knopf Doubleday Publishing Group, 2012); George W. Hilton, Eastland, *Legacy of the* Titanic (Palo Alto, CA: Stanford University Press, 1995); Michael McCarthy, *Ashes Under Water: The SS* Eastland *and the Shipwreck that Shook America* (Guilford, CT: Lyons Press, 2014); Bill Jack, "The *Eastland* Tragedy and the Western District of Michigan," *Stereoscope* 12 no. 1 (Spring 2014): 2–9. They disagree with each other on various points.

76. George T. Arnold, President of the ship line; William H. Hull, its vice President; Harry Pederson, the ship's captain; Joseph Erickson, the ship's engineer; and Robert Reid and Charles Eckliff, federal steamship inspectors.

77. James A. Scott, *The Law of Interstate Rendition: Erroneously Referred to as Interstate Extradition* (Chicago: Sherman Hight, 1917), sec. 219–220, 325.

78. The LaFollette Seamen's Act, 38 Stat. 1164 (March 4, 1915), applicable to all ships exceeding 100 gross tons.

79. *Chicago Daily Tribune*, February 19, 1916.

80. For a well-researched and incisive discussion of the Newberry case and the social context of the time, see Patrick E. Mears, "On the Road to Watergate: The Criminal Prosecution of Senator Truman H. Newberry," *Stereoscope* 2 no. 2 (September 2004). For an overview of the history of campaign finance in senatorial campaigns, see Anne M. Butler and Wendy Wolff, *United States Senate Election, Expulsion, and Censure Cases, 1793–1990* (Washington, D.C.: Government Printing Office, 1995).

81. 34 Stat. 864 (January 26, 1907).

82. 36 Stat. 822 (June 26, 1910).

83. 37 Stat. 25 (August 19, 1911).

84. Mich. Pub. Acts [1913], No. 109.

85. Newberry v. United States, 256 U.S. 232 (1921).

86. Newberry v. United States, 256 U.S. 232, 250 (1921).

87. United States v. Grovey, 313 U.S. 299 (1941).

88. *Grand Rapids Press*, February 6, 1946.

Chapter 5

1. *News-Palladium* (Benton Harbor, Michigan), December 3, 1924.

2. *Escanaba* (Michigan) *Daily Press*, January 1, 1925.

3. 43 *United States Statutes at Large* (hereafter Stat.) 949 (February 17, 1925).

4. *Grand Rapids Press*, April 1, 1931.

5. The university's regents renamed the Law Department the University of Michigan Law School in 1915, at which time the admission requirements changed from a high school diploma to two years of college. Elizabeth Gaspar Brown, *Legal Education at Michigan, 1859–1959* (Ann Arbor: The University of Michigan Law School, 1959), x.

6. *News-Palladium* (Benton Harbor, Michigan), May 11, 1925. Other attorneys seeking the nomination included Sherman T. Handy and W. W. Potter, both on the state's public utilities commission.

7. *Escanaba* (Michigan) *Daily Press*, April 1, 1925.

8. *News-Palladium* (Benton Harbor, Michigan), May 8, 1925.

9. *News-Palladium* (Benton Harbor, Michigan), May 11, 1925.

10. *Times-Herald* (Port Huron, Michigan), May 16, 1925, quoting the *Grand Rapids Press*, the *Muskegon Chronicle*, and the *Saginaw News-Courier*.

11. Raymond often joked that he became a judge because of "the untimely passing of a President of the United States, the daytime doze of a Vice President during a tie vote on confirmation of an Attorney General, and a sudden fatal illness of the leading aspirant." The joke is incomprehensible today unless you know that: (1) Without the intervention of U.S. Attorney General John G. Sargent, Raymond would not have been nominated to the District Court; (2) President Warren Harding died in 1923, two years into his first term, and he presumably would have been nominated for a second term in 1924 with Calvin Coolidge continuing as Vice President; (3) Instead, Coolidge became President and won the election in 1924 with Charles G. Dawes as his Vice President; (4) A few days after the inauguration, Dawes was presiding over the Senate during the confirmation proceedings for Charles B. Warren to be United States Attorney General; (5) The vote on Warren was expected to be close, and Dawes knew he might have to be a tie-breaker; (6) At noon, Dawes was sleepy

and asked if any votes would take place soon; (7) Assured by both parties there would not be, Dawes went home for a nap; (8) In fact, there was a vote in Dawes's absence, the vote was tied, and Dawes would have voted to confirm Warren; (9) Before Dawes was rushed back to the Senate, a second vote resulted in Warren failing confirmation by one vote, and there was no longer a tie to break; and (10) Coolidge next nominated Sargent who was easily confirmed.

12. *Grand Rapids Press*, February 6, 1946.

13. 41 Stat. 305 (October 28, 1919).

14. In April 1919, the Michigan legislature added possession and importation to the state prohibition law, essentially making Michigan "bone dry" in advance of the effective date of the Volstead Act. Michigan Public Laws [1919], No. 53.

15. Carroll v. U.S., 267 U.S. 132 (1925).

16. *News-Palladium* (Benton Harbor, Michigan), March 14, 1930.

17. Husty v. U.S., 282 U.S. 694 (1931).

18. Records Group 21.24.4, Records of the U.S. District Court for the Western District of Michigan, Commissioner Records, Hatch, 2 vols., National Archives and Records Administration, Chicago.

19. For example, in October 1927, Judge Raymond, sitting in the federal court in Marquette, sentenced five bootleggers from Escanaba to eighteen months in Leavenworth. *Escanaba Daily Press*, October 16, 1927.

20. Canadian-born Red Hamilton first met Dillinger when Hamilton was sentenced to twenty-five years in the Indiana State Prison for a failed bank robbery in South Bend. At the time, Hamilton was also wanted in Michigan for robbing a branch of the Kent State Savings Bank of $22,500 two months earlier. He agreed to stand trial for the Indiana robbery to avoid Michigan's mandatory life sentence. *Lansing* (Michigan) *State Journal*, March 17, 1927.

21. The following facts and Judge Raymond's opinion and ruling on ownership of the Ford are from U.S. v. One Ford V-8 Sedan, 7 F. Supp. 705 (W.D. Mich. N.D. 1934).

22. U.S. v. One Ford V-8 Sedan, 7 F. Supp. 705.

23. *Lansing* (Michigan) *State Journal*, June 7, 1935.

24. *Ironwood* (Michigan) *Daily Globe*, June 8, 1935.

25. 96 Stat. 52 (April 2, 1982).

26. Russell R. Wheeler, *Origins of the Elements of Federal Court Governance* (Washington, D.C.: Federal Judicial Center, 1992), 11–12.

27. Emergency Relief and Construction Act, Title III, sec. 301(a)(10), 47 Stat. 709, 718 (July 21, 1932).

28. H.R. Document 788, 71st Cong.

29. 48 Stat. 22 (March 31, 1933).

30. Emergency Appropriation Act for Fiscal Year 1935, 48 Stat. 1021 (June 19, 1934).

31. H.R. Report 1879, 73rd Cong, accompanying H.R. 9830, Statement 2 (June 2, 1934).

32. 49 Stat. 571 at 599 (August 12, 1935).

33. (Marquette) *Daily Mining Journal*, February 14 and 20, 1936.

34. *Escanaba Daily Press*, April 13, 1937.

35. The landlord of the Marquette federal building is the U.S. Postal Service, unlike the Grand Rapids federal building where the landlord is the General Services Administration.

36. As many people have remarked, Albinson (1898–1971) painted Marquette standing up straight in the canoe, a highly unsafe posture. A Minnesota native, the artist surely knew better. Other of his works are in the Smithsonian American Art Museum, the San Diego Museum of Art, the University of Michigan Museum of Art, and the Frederick R. Weisman Art Museum at the University of Minnesota.

37. 56 Stat. 765 (October 2, 1942).

38. Woods v. Boyle, 77 F. Supp. 881 (W.D. Mich. 1948), aff'd, 173 F.2d 224 (6th Cir. 1949).

39. At its peak, there were thirty-seven cigar manufacturers in the city. Minnie Eseleen Johnson's brother Tunis was active in the industry; he later was elected mayor of the city.

40. Attorney General Starr hired as an assistant G. Mennen Williams who later became both the governor of Michigan and a justice of the Michigan Supreme Court.

41. *Ironwood* (Michigan) *Daily Globe*, March 28, 1946.

42. Governor Kelly appointed John R. Dethmers, a Republican, who served on the supreme court for twenty-five years.

43. *Holland* (Michigan) *Evening Sentinel*, November 4,1968.

44. *Escanaba Daily Press*, November 4, 1968.

45. [1935] Mich. Pub. Act 127, codified as M.C.L.A. 551.301 (1948), since repealed.

46. 68 Stat. 8, part 1 (February 10, 1954). The law created twenty-one new permanent district judgeships and six new temporary district judgeships while making permanent three existing temporary district judgeships.

47. H. Rep. 1005, 83rd Cong., 1st Sess., 74.

48. *News-Palladium* (Benton Harbor, Michigan), January 30, 1954.

49. *Holland* (Michigan) *Evening Sentinel*, February 20, 1954.

50. On appeal, the Sixth Circuit set aside the contempt judgments, ruling that criminal contempt proceedings involving a court order should be conducted by a different judge. U.S. v. Bradt, 294 F.2d 879 (6th Cir. 1961).

51. Before his appointment to the Sixth Circuit, Kent was on President Nixon's

short list for appointment to the U.S. Supreme Court to succeed Justice Abe Fortas, but Harry Blackmun received the appointment instead.

52. Deal v. Cincinnati Board of Education, 369 F.2d 55 (6th Cir. 1966).

53. *News-Palladium* (Benton Harbor, Michigan), February 2, 1970.

54. Berry v. School District of the City of Benton Harbor, 505 F.2d 238 (6th Cir. 1974).

55. Milliken v. Bradley, 48 U.S. 7717 (1974).

56. Congressman Clardy was known as "Michigan's McCarthy," and when Mc-Carthy lost his popularity, Clardy did as well. He became a one-term representative when he lost reelection in November 1954.

57. 2 *United States Code* 192.

58. 52 Stat. 942 (June 22, 1938).

59. Barenblatt v. United States, 252 F.2d 129 (D.C. Cir. 1958), cert. granted, 356 U.S. 929 (1958).

60. Davis v. U.S., 269 F.2d 357 (6th Cir. 1959), cert. den'd, 361 U.S. 919 (1959).

61. *Escanaba Daily Press*, February 2, 1960.

Chapter 6

1. Until 1869, federal judges had no retirement benefits, and, consequently, they worked until they dropped. In 1869, Congress passed a law that dealt with the dilemma of elderly U.S. District Judges who felt they could no longer perform their duties but who could not afford to leave the bench. 16 *United States Statutes at Large* (hereafter Stat.) 44, 45 (April 10, 1869). Judges who had been ten years in service and were at least seventy years old could resign and receive full pay for the rest of their lives. In 1919, another law created a new status for federal judges (except Supreme Court Justices), who, although eligible to resign with pay, were not ready to do so. 40 Stat. 1156 (February 25, 1919). Instead, such judges could retire, with the same pay, and be eligible to be assigned by the Chief Judge of the corresponding Circuit Court to perform judicial duties. The seat of a judge who retired was considered vacant, and the President could nominate a new candidate to take that seat. In 1954, Congress added a retirement option for judges aged at least sixty-five with fifteen years of service. 68 Stat. 8 (February 10, 1954). In 1958 Congress provided that judges retired under either option would be called senior district or circuit judges.

2. He attended church every day, and on days he was on the bench, his secretary and law clerks made sure that he adjourned in time to attend a noon Mass.

3. *Holland Evening Sentinel*, July 12, 1962.

4. Oliver v. Kalamazoo Board of Education, 368 F. Supp. 143 (W.D. Mich. 1973);

NAACP v. Lansing Board of Education, 429 F. Supp. 583 (W.D. Mich. 1976); Berry v. School District of the City of Benton Harbor, 442 F. Supp. 1280 (W.D. Mich. 1977).

5. U.S. v. State of Michigan, 471 F. Supp. 196 (W.D. Mich. 1979).

6. *Detroit Free Press*, January 11, 1985.

7. *Detroit Free Press*, January 11, 1985. In his fifty-thousand-word opinion in favor of tribal fishing rights in *U.S. v. State of Michigan*, Judge Fox first addressed the sixty thousand petition signatures against the tribal rights presented to him by a sportsmen's group: "That it is a passionate issue is exemplified by a recent wholly improper attempt to influence this Court through the circulation of petitions amongst sports fishermen which urged that the court rule against the Indians. . . . This was a corruption of the concept of the Federal Judicial system. In a democracy, many times people violate Constitutional and Inalienable rights. The United States Courts exist to ensure guaranteed constitutional rights against the TYRANNY OF POPULAR MAJORITIES. Federal Court Judges are, or ought to be, custodians of secured constitutional right." U.S. v. State of Michigan, 471 F. Supp. 192 (W.D. Mich. 1979).

8. House Bill 209, 42nd Cong., 1st Sess.

9. 47 Stat. 709 (July 21, 1932).

10. *Kalamazoo Gazette*, November 12, 1939.

11. On the date of the dedication of the new post office in 1939, there were only two Union veterans alive in Kalamazoo County. *Kalamazoo Gazette*, November 12, 1939.

12. Mason was the architect for Detroit's Masonic Temple and Gem Theater as well as the Grand Hotel on Mackinac Island.

13. https://www.fjc.gov/history/courthouse/kalamazoo-michigan.-1939. Web site accessed February 25, 2020.

14. 68 Stat. 11 (February 10, 1954).

15. *Detroit Free Press*, July 23, 1954.

16. *News-Palladium* (Benton Harbor, Michigan), February 5, 1960.

17. 28 *United States Code* (hereafter U.S.C.)142.

18. 28 U.S.C. 142 was repealed on April 2, 1982, by 96 Stat. 32, title I, §115(c)(3).

19. 75 Stat. 80, 83.

20. "A new bench for the United States District Court for Western Michigan was established in Kalamazoo last week." *News-Palladium* (Benton Harbor, Michigan), October 31, 1963.

21. *News-Palladium* (Benton Harbor, Michigan), November 23, 1963.

22. *News-Palladium* (Benton Harbor, Michigan), April 20, 1966.

23. 92 Stat. 1629 (October 20, 1978).

24. For more on Judge Miles, see Gordon L. Olson, Oral History Interview Series, Judge Wendell Miles (February 7 and 15, 2002), transcripts and video tapes located

in the archives of the Historical Society for the U.S. District Court in the Gerald R. Ford Federal Building in Grand Rapids; "Memorial: A Celebration of the Life of Honorable Wendell A. Miles, United States District Judge, 1916–2013," *Stereoscope: Journal of the Historical Society of the United States District Court for the Western District of Michigan vol. 11 (* Spring 2013).

25. *Holland* (Michigan) *Evening Sentinel*, June 17, 1953.

26. *Herald Press* (St. Joseph, Michigan), December 8, 1973.

27. Oral History of Wendell A. Miles (February 7 and 15, 2002), 43.

28. Lewis v. City of Grand Rapids, 222 F. Supp. 349 (W.D. Mich. 1963).

29. Lewis v. City of Grand Rapids, 356 F.2d 276 (6th Cir. 1966).

30. Oral History of Wendell A. Miles (February 7 and 15, 2002), 75.

31. 92 Stat. 1629 (October 20, 1978) provided for the Western District's third and fourth judgeships. Judges Gibson and Hillman were nominated and confirmed on the same day.

32. When Judge Gibson assumed senior status on July 13, 1996, his district judgeship seat was abolished, and the temporary seat created in 1990 became permanent, reducing the district's active judgeships from five to four. 104 Stat. 5089 (December 1, 1990).

33. *Grand Rapids Press*, c. April 17, 1979; Feb 8, 1991.

34. The first African American law clerk to serve in the Western District was Thomas O. Martin, who began working for Magistrate Judge Brenneman on March 1, 1982. Martin received his undergraduate degree from the University of Michigan and his law degree from the University of Houston. He was an Assistant U.S. Attorney for the Western District of Michigan for twelve years before becoming assistant chief counsel at Immigration and Customs Enforcement in Detroit.

35. *Grand Rapids Press*, October 10, 1996.

36. *Grand Rapids Press*, October 16, 1996, and March 24, 2002.

37. *Grand Rapids Press*, February 3, 1991.

38. Many of the facts in this section are taken from the interview of Judge Enslen taken by Gordon L. Olson on May 22, 2003 for the court's Oral History Interview Series, transcripts and video tapes located in the Historical Society archives the Gerald R. Ford Federal Building in Grand Rapids.

39. Enslen's Senate confirmation hearing was held in July 1979 along with those for Hillman and Gibson even though Judge Fox had not yet taken senior status. However, Fox was in the audience at the hearing, and Senator Riegle was able to represent to the committee that Fox intended to retire by year's end.

40. Z. Z. Lydens, *The Story of Grand Rapids* (Grand Rapids, MI: Kregel Publications, 1966), 213–14.

41. Lydens, *The Story of Grand Rapids*, 213.

42. Not all of the new courtrooms were ready for their new tenants. Judge Gibson and Magistrate Brenneman were moved between temporary spaces several times. In Brenneman's case it took the General Services Administration eight years to build his courtroom, during which time period he shared the courtroom assigned to Magistrate Karr.

43. 120 *Congressional Record* 4998 (January 5, 1975); Gerald R. Ford Presidential Papers, 1975, No. 17 (January 5, 1975). Because Congress was adjourned on January 4, 1975, and continued in adjournment for more than ten days, the President could not return the bill to Congress, and officially this was a pocket veto.

44. 91 Stat. 60 (May 4, 1977).

45. Count I: 18 U.S.C. 241; Count II: 18 U.S.C. 1584 and 2.

46. Judge Hillman granted the defendants' motion in which they asserted that a trial by jury would violate their religious beliefs. *Detroit Free Press*, June 12, 1986.

47. U.S. v. Lewis, 644 F. Supp. 1391 (W.D. Mich. 1986).

48. *Detroit Free Press*, December 20, 1986.

49. U.S. v. King, 840 F.2d 1276 (6th Cir. 1988), cert. den'd sub nom. Lewis v. U.S., 488 U.S. 894 (1988).

50. See Noel P. Fox, "Settlement: Helping the Lawyers to Fulfill Their Responsibility," 53 F.R.D. 1 (1971).

51. In 1990, District Judge Richard Enslen described to the U.S. Senate Judiciary Committee some of the civil causes of action that increased the dockets of the Western District in the 1970s and 1980s: "The Civil Rights Act of 1964 was, perhaps, a harbinger for the legislation which followed. Statutes prohibiting discrimination in employment, in housing, in public accommodations, in the school setting, in federal and state-financed construction and support, in licensing, in labor, and even in the private sector contributed greatly to increased filings in our federal courts in the 1970s and 1980s. Legislation affecting our environment, our economy, our retirement rights, our social security entitlements, state and local revenue sharing, and our federal tax obligations are examples of how legislation has increased the filings in our federal District Courts." Statement of Hon. Richard A. Enslen, before the Judiciary Committee, U.S. Senate Hearing 1097, 101st Cong., 2nd Sess., regarding the Civil Justice Reform Act of 1990 and the Judicial Improvements Act of 1990 (March 6, 1990), 235–36 (cited hereafter as *Enslen Statement*).

52. Unless otherwise cited, data references in this section are taken from the relevant year's *Federal Court Management Statistics*, compiled and published by the Administrative Office of the U.S. Courts.

53. *Enslen Statement*, 227.

54. For example, in 1984, he was interviewed extensively about the Western District's early ADR procedures in a special supplement to the journal *Alternatives to*

the High Cost of Litigation 2, no. 10 (October 1984); in March 1985, he spoke about ADR to a select gathering at the Brookings Institution's Seventh Annual Administrative Justice Congress where he received an enthusiastic response from the audience, which included then Chief Justice of the United States Warren Burger, then Attorney General Edwin Meese, Senator Strom Thurmond, and the legendary law professor Charles Alan Wright. Besides his master's thesis, he also contributed to a publication by the CPR Institute for Dispute Resolution, *ADR and the Courts—A Manual for Judges and Lawyers* (New York: Butterworth Legal Publishers, 1987).

55. *Enslen Statement*, 229.

56. Western District Local Rules (hereafter W.D.L.R.), Rule 16.8.

57. *Standard Instruction to All Attorneys at FRCP 16 Scheduling Conferences.*

58. W.D.L.R. 16.7. In the court's first ADR local rules issued in 1983, summary jury trials were authorized under W.D.L.R. 44(b).

59. "SJT, 'Mediation,' and Mini Trials in Federal Court: An Interview with Judge Richard A. Enslen," *Alternatives to the High Cost of Litigation* 2, no. 10 (October 1984).

60. "SJT, 'Mediation,' and Mini Trials in Federal Court: An Interview with Judge Richard A. Enslen.".

61. W.D.L.R. 16.7(a).

62. "SJT, 'Mediation,' and Mini Trials in Federal Court: An Interview with Judge Richard A. Enslen," 4–8.

63. Hugh W. Brenneman, Jr. and Edward Wesoloski, "Blueprint for a Summary Jury Trial," *Michigan Bar Journal* 65, no. 888 (September 1986).

64. W.D.L.R. 16.3.

65. Case evaluation began in the 1970s as Wayne County Circuit Court Local Rule 403, which the judges of that court named mediation. In 1980, the Michigan Supreme Court adopted the program, using the same title for all state district and Circuit Courts as Michigan General Court Rule 316, which in 1985 became Michigan Court Rule (hereafter M.C.R.) 2.403. In 1983, the Western District adopted a slightly altered version of the program, still with the title mediation, as W.D.L.R. 42, which is now W.D.L.R. 16.5. In 2000, the Michigan Supreme Court recognized that the provisions of M.C.R. 2.403 were not traditional mediation and changed the rule's title to case evaluation. Later, the Western District did the same for W.D.L.R. 16.5.

66. "Special Supplement, Alternate Dispute Resolution in Court," *Alternatives to the High Cost of Litigation* 2, no. 10 (October 1984): 5.

67. W.D.L.R. 16.5.

68. Many sophisticated attorneys volunteer to serve as mediators despite the minimal compensation available under the court rule, because they find it instructive to learn how their fellow mediators analyze cases.

69. M.C.R. 2.403(O)(1) & (3).

70. "More favorable" means that the verdict amount, plus assessable costs and interest on the amount of the verdict from the filing of the complaint to the date of the case evaluation, is 10 percent better for the rejecting party than the case evaluation amount. M.C.R. 2.403(O)(3).

71. Tiedel v. Northwestern Michigan College, 865 F.2d 88 (6th Cir. 1988), reversing Tiedel v. Beech Aircraft Corp., 118 F.R.D. 54 (W.D. Mich. 1987).

72. The U.S. District Court for the Eastern District of Michigan has adopted a different approach. In *Mencer v. Princeton Square Apartments*, 228 F.3d 63 (6th Cir. 2000), the court affirmed an award of attorney fees as mediation sanctions entered by the Eastern District of Michigan, but did so only because the plaintiffs had stipulated to the state rule on case evaluation, including, specifically, the attorney fee sanctions. Consequently, under Eastern District Local Rule 16.5, a judge may refer a civil case to case evaluation, "but only if the parties consent to be bound by . . . the sanctions provisions."

73. The 1983 rule cited Douglas M. Parker and Phillip L. Radoff, "The Mini-Hearing: An Alternative to Protracted Litigation of Factually Complex Disputes," *The Business Lawyer* 38, no. 1 (November 1982): 35–44.

74. W.D.L.R. 16.6 (1988), deleted 2012.

75. 102 Stat. 4642 (November 19, 1988), title IX, sec. 658.

76. *Enslen Statement*, 265.

77. W.D.L.R. 16.4.

78. *Detroit Free Press,* March 12, 1987.

79. *Detroit Free Press,* June 30, 1987.

80. *Detroit Free Press,* July 2, 1987. On August 14, the Michigan Court of Appeals reversed Judge Bell's decision and held that the ban could not go into effect until April 1988. *Detroit Free Press,* August 14, 1987.

81. 44 Stat. 630 (May 25, 1926).

82. 46 Stat. 1552, 1595 (March 4, 1931). Other approved projects in Michigan included post offices in Ann Arbor, Boyne City, Calumet, Iron Mountain, Lapeer, Marshall, and South Haven, as well as extensions and renovations of the existing post office/courthouses in Grand Rapids and Port Huron.

83. *Ironwood* (Michigan) *Times*, April 7, 1933.

84. *Marshall Evening Chronicle*, November 7, 1932.

85. *Detroit Free Press*, May 15, 1933.

86. 68 Stat. 8, 11 (February 10, 1954).

87. 75 Stat. 80, 83 (May 19, 1961).

88. 101 Stat. 893 (November 9, 1987).

89. *Lansing State Journal*, April 19, 1988.

90. *Lansing State Journal*, April 14, 1988.

91. *Detroit Free Press*, March 12, 1987.

92. U.S. District Court for the Western District of Michigan, Admin. Order 07-90 (August 8, 2007).

93. U.S. District Court for the Western District of Michigan, Juror Selection Plan (November 19, 2013).

94. Bryan v. Itasca County, Minnesota, 426 U.S. 373 (1976).

95. U.S. v. Dakota, 666 F. Supp. 989 (W.D. Mich. 1985).

96. U.S. v. Dakota, 796 F.2d 186 (6th Cir. 1986).

97. U.S. v. Bay Mills Community, 692 F. Supp. 777 (W.D. Mich. 1988), vacated by consent, 727 F. Supp. 1110 (W.D. Mich. 1989).

98. 102 Stat. 2467 (October 17, 1988).

99. Michigan v. Bay Mills Indian Community, 695 F.3d 406 (6th Cir. 2012).

100. Michigan v. Bay Mills Indian Community, 695 F.3d 406 (6th Cir. 2012).

101. Michigan v. Bay Mills Indian Community, 134 S. Ct. 2024 (2014). Justice Kagan wrote the majority opinion. Justices Scalia, Thomas, Ginsberg, and Alito dissented.

Chapter 7

1. Robert L. Haig, ed., *Business and Commercial Litigation in Federal Courts* (Chicago: American Bar Association, Section of Litigation, 1998).

2. The delay in Judge McKeague's appointment to the Sixth Circuit was caused by a larger political struggle over judicial appointments discussed in the text infra.

3. 104 *United States Statutes at Large* (hereafter Stat.) 5089, 5101 (December 1, 1990).

4. 104 Stat. 5089, 5101 (December 1, 1990).

5. While temporary seats have customarily, in recent years, become permanent because of the continuing growth of the federal courts' caseload, in this rare instance the judges of the Western District court advised that the additional seat was unnecessary.

6. Helene White was a judge in Michigan trial courts and the state's court of appeals for almost three decades. From 1999 to 2006, she was married to former Michigan Supreme Court Justice Charles Levin, the cousin of Senator Carl Levin.

7. The fourth nominee, Ms. Neilson, had been diagnosed with myelodysplastic syndrome, a rare blood disorder and her nomination was on hold. She was confirmed in November 2005, but she died in January 2006.

8. *New York Times*, December 19, 2006. At one point, Brownback offered to stop blocking the confirmations if Neff agreed to recuse herself from all cases involving same-sex unions. She did not agree.

9. Reynolds v. Sims, 377 U.S. 533, 586 (1964).

10. On August 2, Republicans filed a petition in the Michigan Supreme Court asking that court to do the same for electoral districts for seats on the Michigan House and Senate. *Detroit Free Press*, August 3, 1991.

11. Richard Austin, Michigan's secretary of state, was named as the defendant in both cases, but that was a formality. The real adversaries were the two sets of plaintiffs representing the interests of the Democratic and Republican parties in Michigan.

12. 28 *United States Code* (hereafter U.S.C.) 2284(a).

13. Wesberry v. Sanders, 376 U.S. 1 (1964).

14. Karcher v. Daggett, 462 U.S. 725, 732 (1983).

15. Kirkpatrick v. Preisler, 394 U.S. 526 (1969).

16. The plan under the 1980 census, also established by a federal three-judge court, had seventeen districts with 514, 560 residents and one district with 514,559 residents. That panel consisted of Judges Newblatt and Philip Pratt of the Eastern District and Judge Damon Keith of the Sixth Circuit.

17. 79 Stat. 437 (August 6, 1965), codified at 42 U.S.C. 1973 et seq.

18. Beer v. United States, 425 U.S. 130 (1976).

19. Good v. Austin, 800 F. Supp. 557 (E.D. & W.D. Mich. 1992), 560, citing United Jewish Organizations of Williamsburgh, Inc. v. Carey, 430 U.S. 144 (1977).

20. Good v. Austin, 800 F. Supp. 557, 560–61.

21. *Detroit Free Press*, March 24, 1992.

22. Good v. Austin, 800 F. Supp. 551[stet, it is cited as an opinion of both courts and there are two decisions, one at p. 551, one at p. 557.].

23. The witness testified that he preferred that test over a "proportionality" test that determines whether a redistricting plan is likely to produce, statewide, a congressional delegation that is proportional in its partisan makeup to the overall partisan makeup of the state.

24. Stupak-Thrall v. U.S., 843 F. Supp. 327 (W.D. Mich. 1994).

25. U.S. Const. art. IV, § 3, cl. 2.

26. Stupak-Thrall v. U.S., 70 F.3d 881 (6th Cir. 1995).

27. Stupak-Thrall v. U.S., 89 F.3d 1269 (6th Cir. 1997).

28. Stupak-Thrall v. Glickman, 988 F. Supp. 1055 (W.D. Mich. 1997).

29. Herr v. United States Forest Service, 2014 WL 11309766 (W.D. Mich. 2014), rev'd, 803 F.3d 809 (6th Cir. 2015).

30. Herr v. United States Forest Service, 212 F. Supp. 2d 720 (W.D. Mich. 2016).

31. Herr v. United States Forest Service, 865 F.3d 351 (6th Cir. 2017).

32. This section is based in large part on the written opinions of Judge McKeague and of the Sixth Circuit in this case, as well on an article by Judge McKeague, "The Medical Mile: A Health Care Revolution in GR," in *Judging in West Michigan: Cel-*

ebrating the Community Impact of Effective Judges and Courts, Nelson P. Miller, ed. (Lake Mary, FL: Vandeplas Publishing, 2011), 141.

33. Clayton Antitrust Act, 38 Stat. 730 (October 15, 1914), codified at 15 U.S.C. 12–27, and 29 U.S.C. 52–53.

34. FTC v. Butterworth Health Corp., 946 F. Supp. 1285, 1294 (W.D. Mich. 1996).

35. FTC v. Butterworth Health Corp., 946 F. Supp. 1285 (W.D. Mich. 1996).

36. The court accepted the FTC's assertion that for the purposes of the summary judgment hearing, the geographic market was "approximately 70 zip code areas and consist[ing] essentially of all of Kent County, northwest Montcalm County, southern Newaygo County, eastern Ottawa County, northeast Allegan County, northwest Barry County and northwest Ionia County." FTC v. Butterworth Health Corp., 946 F. Supp. 1285, 1293 (W.D. Mich. 1996).

37. For example, the hospitals presented evidence that mergers of nonprofit hospitals tended to reduce prices because many of the directors of nonprofits are local businessmen with an interest in keeping prices down.

38. FTC v. Butterworth Health Corp., 121 F.3d 708 (6th Cir. 1997).

39. The penalty imposed by the Michigan statute also provided for hard labor, but the prison authorities informed the legislature that there were no facilities capable of enforcing that provision.

40. 18 U.S.C. 1111 (b).

41. For a more detailed story of the case, see L. C. Timmerman and John H. Timmerman, *The Color of Night: A Young Mother, a Missing Child, and a Cold-Blooded Killer* (Fair Hills, NJ: New Horizons Press, 2011). Note that the authors are Rachel's father and her uncle, a journalist.

42. In their book, the Timmermans state that Rachel said she had a date with Ian, and that this was likely Ian Decker who was working with Rachel Timmerman and had been a handyman for Gabrion. The U.S. District Court and subsequently the Sixth Circuit, in their opinions, identified that person as John Weeks. E.g., U.S. v. Gabrion,719 F.3d 911 (6th Cir. 2013). Whatever his name, that person disappeared very soon after Rachel's death and has never been seen since.

43. Gabrion appealed, but the Sixth Circuit affirmed on all issues without an opinion on July 27, 2000.

44. 18 U.S.C. 1111(b) makes it a federal crime to commit murder "within the special maritime and territorial jurisdiction of the United States." The penalty for first-degree murder within that jurisdiction is death or imprisonment for life. Gabrion's attorneys attacked federal jurisdiction in this case because land in the Manistee National Forest was returned to the United States by the state of Michigan with the provision that Michigan retained civil and criminal jurisdiction and the United States received concurrent jurisdiction only as necessary for the administration, con-

trol, and protection of such lands. Judge Bell held that federal jurisdiction was not so limited and did include this murder case. The Sixth Circuit affirmed this ruling and the U.S. Supreme Court denied review. U.S. v. Gabrion, 2006 WL 2473978 (W.D. Mich. 2006), aff'd, 517 F.3d 839 (6th Cir. 2008), cert. den'd, 556 U.S. 1168 (2009).

45. The Federal Death Penalty Act, 18 U.S.C. 3591 et seq.

46. With the change in administrations, Green replaced Michael Dettmer who had been in office when the decision to charge Gabrion in federal court was made.

47. 18 U.S.C. 3592.

48. U.S. v. Gabrion, 2006 WL 2473978 (W.D. Mich. 2006), aff'd, 517 F.3d 839 (6th Cir. 2008), rehearing and rehearing en banc denied (6th Cir. 2008), cert. den'd, 556 U.S. 1168 (2009).

49. U.S. v. Gabrion, 648 F.3d 307 (6th Cir. 2011).

50. U.S. v. Gabrion, 719 F.3d 511 (6th Cir. 2013) (District Court aff'd on reh'g en banc).

51. U.S. v. Gabrion, 134 S. Ct. 1934 (2014) (certiorari denied).

52. 42 U.S.C. 2000e et seq.

53. Waldo v. Consumers Energy Co., 2010 WL 2302305 (W.D. Mich. 2010).

54. Waldo v. Consumers Energy Co., 726 F.3d 802 (6th Cir. 2013). The majority ruled that: "1. the District Court did not abuse its discretion in finding that employee was subjected to severe or pervasive harassment sufficient to create a hostile work environment; 2. the District Court did not abuse its discretion in finding that employer could be held liable for coworkers' harassing behavior; 3. the District Court did not err by considering the full span of harassing behavior, even the conduct that occurred prior to the 300-day filing period; 4. the District Court's determination that $400 was a reasonable hourly rate for employee's lead counsel was within its discretion; 5. the District Court did not abuse its discretion in declining to reduce the fee award based on the fact that employee succeeded on only one of the seven claims asserted in her complaint; and 6. the District Court acted within its discretion in finding that employee's requested costs for focus groups, mock trials, jury-selection services, and mediation were reasonable and necessary."

55. *United States v. Playboy Entm't Grp., Inc.,* 529 U.S. 803, 811 (2000).

56. *Turner Broad. Sys., Inc. v. F.C.C.,* 512 U.S. 622, 642 (1994).

57. Planet Aid v. City of St. Johns, 2014 WL 11309765 (W.D. Mich. 2014).

58. Planet Aid v. City of St. Johns, 782 F.3d 318 (6th Cir. 2015).

59. Speet v. Schuette, 889 F. Supp. 2d 969 (W.D. Mich. 2012).

60. Speet v. Schuette, 726 F.3d 867 (6th Cir. 2013).

Chapter 8

1. Charles A. Lindquist, "The Origin and Development of the United States Commissioner System," *American Journal of Legal History* 14, no. 1 (January 1970): 9.

2. Big Rapids, Traverse City, Grand Rapids, Niles, St. Joseph, Ionia, Kalamazoo, Allegan, Calhoun, Schoolcraft, Grand Haven, Charlotte, and Muskegon.

3. See U.S. Department of Justice, *Register of the Department of Justice and the Judicial Officers of the United States* (Washington, D.C.: U.S. Government Printing Office), for the years referred to.

4. Hugh W. Brenneman, Jr., "Discreet Persons Learned in the Law," in *Judging in West Michigan: Celebrating the Community Impact of Effective Judges and Courts*, Nelson P. Miller, ed. (Lake Mary, FL: Vandeplas Publishing, 2011), 57, 63.

5. Lindquist, "The Origin and Development of the United States Commissioner System."

6. Brenneman, "Discreet Persons Learned in the Law," 61.

7. Brenneman, "Discreet Persons Learned in the Law," 61.

8. Department of Justice Appropriations, 29 *United States Statutes at Large* (hereafter Stat.) 184, § 19 (May 28, 1896).

9. The relevant passage stated: "That no Marshal or Deputy Marshal, attorney or assistant attorney of any district, jury commissioner, clerk of Marshal, no bailiff, crier, juror, janitor of any Government building, nor any civil or military employee of the Government, except as in this Act provided, and no clerk or employee of any United States justice or judge shall have, hold, or exercise the duties of the United States commissioner" 29 Stat. 184, § 20.

10. See U.S. Department of Justice, *Register of the Department of Justice and the Judicial Officers of the United States* for the years referred to.

11. *Annual Report of the Director, Administrative Office of the U.S. Courts* (Washington, D.C.: U.S. Government Printing Office, 1967), 151.

12. The Federal Magistrates Act: "An Act to abolish the office of United States commissioner, to establish in place thereof within the judicial branch of the Government the office of United States magistrate, and for other purposes," 82 Stat. 1107 (October 17, 1968).

13. The Judicial Conference of the United States was created by Congress in 1922 to frame policy guidelines for the administration of the federal courts. Its members include the Chief Justice of the United States, the Chief Judges of each U.S. Court of Appeals, District Judges from various U.S. District Courts, and the Chief Judge of the U.S. Court of International Trade.

14. 90 Stat. 2729 (October 21, 1976).

15. 93 Stat. 643 (October 10, 1979).

16. The Michigan Court of Appeals affirmed the jury verdict, rejecting Souter's claim that the twelve-and-a-half-year delay between Ringler's death and Larry's arrest denied him due process of law. On March 19, 1996, in lieu of granting leave to appeal, the Michigan Supreme Court remanded the case to the trial court to conduct an evidentiary hearing to address Souter's claim that he was prejudiced by the delay. People v. Souter, 450 Mich. 546 (1996). On September 3, 1996, the trial court issued its opinion, finding that though Souter was prosecuted "with essentially the same evidence that was available in 1983," the delay was not deliberate and it did not prejudice his case." The Michigan Supreme Court denied Larry's motion for leave to appeal on December 30, 1996. People v. Souter, 453 Mich. 978 (1996).

17. Souter v. Jones, 395 F.3d 577 (6th Cir. 2005).

18. 28 *United States Code* 2254(d)(1).

19. Taylor v. Louisiana, 419 U.S. 522 (1975); Duren v. Missouri, 439 U.S. 357 (1979).

20. A month after Smith's voir dire, the county reversed its policy and began supplying prospective jurors to the Circuit Court first.

21. People v. Smith, 1999 WL 33445050 (Mich. App.), rev'd, 463 Mich. 199 (2000).

22. "(1) that the group alleged to be excluded is a 'distinctive' group in the community; (2) that the representation of this group in venires from which juries are selected is not fair and reasonable in relation to the number of such persons in the community; and (3) that this underrepresentation is due to systematic exclusion of the group in the jury selection process." Duren v. Missouri, 439 U.S. 357, 364 (1979).

23. Smith v. Berghuis, 2006 WL 461248 (W.D. Mich.).

24. Berghuis, Warden v. Smith, 559 U.S. 314 (2010).

25. In re Letter of Request from the Local Court of Pforzheim, Division AV, Federal Republic of Germany, 130 F.R.D. 363 (W.D. Mich. 1989).

26. Hugh W. Brenneman, Jr., "Reflections at the Service of Remembrance and Celebration for the Hon. Stephen W. Karr (November 2, 2007), reprinted in *Stereoscope, vol. 6, no.1 (July 2008)*.

27. Christopher E. Smith, *United States Magistrates in the Federal Courts: Subordinate Judges* (Santa Barbara, CA: Praeger Publishing, 1990), 82–83.

28. Michigan Canners and Freezers Ass'n, Inc. v. Agricultural Marketing and Bargaining Bd., 467 U.S. 461 (1984).

29. Baum Research and Development Co. v. University of Massachusetts at Lowell, 587 F. Supp. 2d 840 (W.D. Mich. 2008).

Chapter 9

1. U.S. Const. art. I, § 8, cl. 4.

2. Sturges v. Crowninshield, 17 U.S. 122 (1819).

3. For comprehensive explanations of the history of bankruptcy legislation, see Kevin M. Ball, *Adversity and Justice: A History of the United States Bankruptcy Court for the Eastern District of Michigan* (Detroit: Wayne State University Press, 2016); and Charles Jordan Tabb, "The History of the Bankruptcy Laws in the United States," *American Bankruptcy Institute Law Review* 3 (1995): 5.

4. An Act to Establish a Uniform System of Bankruptcy throughout the United States, 2 *United States Statutes at Large* (hereafter Stat.) 19 (April 4, 1800).

5. The statute defines merchant broadly as a person "buying or selling in gross, or by retail, or dealing in exchange, or as a banker, broker, factor, underwriter or marine insurer." 2 Stat. 19, § 1.

6. 2 Stat. 19, § 34, 30.

7. An Act to Repeal an Act, [entitled] "An Act to Establish a Uniform System of Bankruptcy throughout the United States," 2 Stat. 248 (December 19, 1803).

8. An Act to Establish a Uniform System of Bankruptcy throughout the United States, 5 Stat. 440 (August 19, 1841).

9. An Act to Repeal the Bankrupty Act, 5 Stat. 614 (March 3, 1843).

10. An Act to Establish a Uniform System of Bankruptcy throughout the United States, 14 Stat. 517 (March 2, 1867).

11. 14 Stat. 517, § 3.

12. An Act to Repeal the Bankruptcy Law, 20 Stat. 99 (June 7, 1878).

13. An Act to Establish a Uniform System of Bankruptcy throughout the United States, 30 Stat. 544, part 1 (July 1, 1898).

14. 30 Stat. 544, 555, ch. V, § 33.

15. "Report on Bankruptcy Matters," *Annual Report of the Attorney General of the United States* (Washington, D.C. Government Printing Office, 1903), 122–26.

16. 30 Stat. 544, 556, part 1.

17. *Detroit Free Press*, October 12, 1898.

18. Although some historical and biographical resources state that Charles B. Blair is a graduate of Michigan's Law Department, he is not on the Michigan Law School's official list of graduates. "Yearly Index of Law School Graduates," accessed January 7, 2020, http://www.law.umich.edu/historyandtraditions/students/Pages/Graduate ListByYear.aspx.

19. In October 1906, after Judge Wanty died, he was one of the unsuccessful candidates to succeed as district judge. *Detroit Free Press*, October 25, 1906.

20. The details of Pearl's life up to 1894 are taken from *Memorial Record of the Northern Peninsula of Michigan* (Chicago: The Lewis Publishing Company, 1895), 612–14.

21. The exact timing of the change in office between Banyon and Blair is cloudy. In 1926, the *Journal of the National Association of Referees in Bankruptcy* stated that Blair was appointed in 1924. However, hearing notices published in the Benton Harbor

News-Palladium during the first three months of 1925 indicate that both men were holding hearings as referees on bankruptcy cases that arose in the former Kalamazoo bankruptcy region.

22. The Chandler Act, 52 Stat. 840 (June 22, 1938).

23. Referees' Salary Act, 60 Stat. 323 (June 28, 1946).

24. All of the caseload data in this chapter is based on a fiscal year, so that, for example, 1901 means the period from July 1, 1900, to June 30, 1901. The data are from the annual reports to Congress by the U.S. Attorney General and the Administrator of the Office of the United States Courts.

25. 60 Stat. 323 (June 28, 1946).

26. "Reflections by Referee Chester C. Woolridge," *Bankruptcy Law Newsletter* (May 1989).

27. An Act to Establish a Uniform Law on the Subject of Bankruptcies, 92 Stat. 2549 (November 6, 1978).

28. Northern Pipeline Construction Co. v. Marathon Pipe Line Co., 458 U.S. 50 (1982).

29. Bankruptcy Amendments and Federal Judgeship Act of 1984, 98 Stat. 333 (July 10, 1984).

30. Bankruptcy Judges, United States Trustees, and Family Farmer Bankruptcy Act, 100 Stat. 3088 (October 27, 1986).

31. Bankruptcy Abuse Prevention and Consumer Protection Act of 2005, 119 Stat. 23 (April 20, 2005).

32. An Act to Establish a Uniform Law on the Subject of Bankruptcies, 92 Stat. 2549, 2662 (November 6, 1978).

33. The ten districts and groups of districts chosen for the pilot program were: (1) District of Maine, District of New Hampshire, District of Massachusetts, and District of Rhode Island; (2) Southern District of New York; (3) District of Delaware and District of New Jersey; (4) Eastern District of Virginia and District of District of Columbia; (5) Northern District of Alabama; (6) Northern District of Texas; (7) Northern District of Illinois; (8) District of Minnesota, District of North Dakota, and District of South Dakota; (9) Central District of California; and (10) District of Colorado and District of Kansas.

34. Bankruptcy Judges, U.S. Trustees, & Family Farmer Bankruptcy Act of 1986, 100 Stat. 3088 (October 27, 1986). Bankruptcy cases filed in the six judicial districts in Alabama and North Carolina are not under the jurisdiction of the United States Trustee Program. Instead, those districts have a "bankruptcy administrator" who performs similarly to a U.S. Trustee.

35. In re Revco D.S., Inc., 898 F.2d 498, 500 (6th Cir. 1990).

36. A U.S. Trustee may not serve as the case trustee in Chapter 11.

37. The 1986 Act also added fifty-two new positions for U.S. Bankruptcy Judges across the nation, usually increasing one slot to a district. 100 Stat. 3088 (October 27, 1986). Some districts added more than one, such as the Central District of California, which added seven Bankruptcy Judge positions to bring its roster to nineteen. The Western District of Michigan received one additional slot, bringing its total to three. On December 23, 1987, Jo Ann C. Stevenson was appointed to fill that third judgeship.

38. 28 *United States Code* (hereafter U.S.C.) 158(b)(1), added by the Bankruptcy Reform Act of 1994, 108 Stat. 4106, 4109–11 (October 22, 1994).

39. 119 Stat. 23 (April 22, 2005).

40. Statement of one of the bill's sponsors, Senator Chuck Grassley of Iowa.

41. For the preceding, I am indebted to the skill and research expertise of Dean E. Reitberg, Esq., Trial Attorney for the Office of the U.S. Trustee.

42. For more about Judge Nims, see "Interview with Former Bankruptcy Judge David E. Nims, Jr., Part I," *Bar & Bench, Your Western Michigan Chapter Federal Bar Association Newsletter* 11, no. 11 (November 1999), and "Interview with Former Bankruptcy Judge David E. Nims, Jr., Part II," *Bar & Bench, Your Western Michigan Chapter Federal Bar Association Newsletter* 11, no. 12 (December 1999). Additionally, several of his fellow attorneys and judges discussed both Judge Nims and Judge Howard in depth in Volume 1, Issue 2 of *The Stereoscope.*

43. Much of this biographical information on Judge Howard comes from "Interview with Retiring Bankruptcy Judge Laurence E. Howard," *Bar & Bench, Your Western Michigan Chapter Federal Bar Association Newsletter* 11, no. 1 (December 1998).

44. 98 Stat. 333, 338 (July 10, 1984), codified at 28 U.S.C. 153(a).

45. 98 Stat. 333, 342, codified at 28 U.S.C. 106(b)(1).

46. 100 Stat., Part 1, 718 (July 2, 1986).

47. One of the courtrooms in the Ford Building used by the Bankruptcy Judges was reassigned to the U.S. Magistrate Judges.

Chapter 10

1. 1 *United States Statutes at Large* (hereafter Stat.) 73, 92 (September 24, 1789).

2. 1789 letter from President George Washington to the inaugural class of U.S. Attorneys.

3. Berger v. U.S., 295 U.S. 78 (1935).

4. Ross Parker, *Carving Out the Rule of Law: The History of the United States Attorney's Office in Eastern Michigan* (Bloomington, IN: Author House, 2009), xiv.

5. 12 Stat. 285, § 1 (August 2, 1861).

6. 16 Stat. 162 (June 22, 1870).

7. 16 Stat. 162, 164, § 16. However, even under this control, problems regarding the abuse of fees for compensation continued. "The Evils of the Fee System," *Annual Report of the Attorney General of the United States for the Year 1891* (Washington, D.C.: Government Printing Office, 1891), xxvi. Consequently, in 1896 Congress changed the compensation of U.S. Attorneys to a straight salary. 29 Stat. 140, 180, § 7 (May 28, 1896).

8. 16 Stat. 162, 164, § 12.

9. *Annual Report of the Attorney General of the United States for the Year 1870* (Washington, D.C.: Government Printing Office, 1870).

10. Parker, *Carving Out the Rule of Law*.

11. "A Woman Who Made Good," *Grand Rapids Herald*, July 30, 1938. See Ruth S. Stevens, "Assistant US Attorney Ella Mae Backus: 'A Most Important Figure in the Legal Profession in the Western District of Michigan,'" *Michigan Historical Review* 42, no. 2 (Fall 2016): For additional information on female attorneys in the Western District, see Ruth S. Stevens, "Claiming Their Place: Pioneering Women of the Law in the Western District of Michigan," *Stereoscope*, 15, no. 1 (Summer 2017).

12. *Annual Report of the Attorney General of the United States for the Year 1870*.

13. *Annual Report of the Attorney General of the United States for the Year 1881* (Washington DC: Government Printing Office, 1881).

14. *Annual Report of the Attorney General of the United States for the Year 1891*, xxviii.

15. *Battle Creek* (Michigan) *Enquirer*, April 3, 1953.

16. Gideon v. Wainwright, 372 U.S. 335 (1963).

17. 78 Stat. 241 (July 2, 1964), codified at 18 *United States Code* 3006A.

18. The judicial branch of the federal government administers the CJA. The Judicial Conference of the United States established policies and procedures as guidelines for administering the requirements of the CJA. The Defender Services Office of the Administrative Office of the U.S. Courts ensures the day-to-day operation of, and compliance with, the CJA.

19. 98 Stat. 1987 (October 12, 1984).

20. Blakely v. Washington, 542 U.S. 296 (2004).

21. U.S. v. Booker, 543 U.S. 220 (2005).

Chapter 11

1. The members of the organizing committee were:

> Chairman: Hugh W. Brenneman, Jr., Bergstrom, Slykhouse & Shaw
> Secretary/Treasurer: Larry Willey, Varnum, Riddering, Schmidt & Howlett

Bar Liaison: Sam Ford Massey, Jr., Allaben, Massie, Vander Weyden & Timmer
Bylaws: Margaret Cook, Old Kent Bank & Trust Co.
Court Liaison: U.S. Magistrate Stephen W. Karr
Education: Stephen C. Bransdorfer, Miller, Johnson, Snell & Cummiskey
Facilities: Hugh H. Makens, Warner, Norcross & Judd
Membership: Bruce W. Neckers, Mohney, Goodrich & Titta; and Robert G.
    Quinn, Jr., Bergstrom, Slykhouse & Shaw
Programs: U.S. Attorney James S. Brady; and John D. Tully, Warner, Norcross
    & Judd

2. The location is significant only in that this was not the usual venue, the Pantlind Hotel, which was being remodeled into the Amway Grand Plaza. The city, like the federal court, was in the midst of transition.

3. Obtaining the highly sought-after Solicitor General as a speaker for the new bar association, only weeks before the Supreme Court commenced its next term, was directly attributable to the efforts of U.S. Attorney James Brady who was in charge of programming for the chapter.

4. Indeed, chapter chairman Hugh W. Brenneman, Jr. was invited to speak at the National Convention of the Federal Bar Association in San Antonio, Texas, on September 25, 1979, to explain how such recruitment was being accomplished. And the fortunes of the FBA nationwide were on the rise. On November 5, 1979, Attorney General Benjamin R. Civiletti sent a letter to all attorneys of the Department of Justice suggesting that they consider the benefits of membership in the FBA.

5. Not all speaking engagements for the local FBA chapter went as smoothly. On September 11, 2001, Attorney General John Ashcroft was slated to speak to the Western Michigan Chapter of the Federal Bar Association. Ashcroft was in the Upper Midwest, and it had been arranged for him to fly to Grand Rapids in a private plane to speak at noon before the FBA chapter, before returning to Washington, D.C. However, when the second plane hit the Twin Towers in New York City, it became evident that Ashcroft was not coming to lunch. Indeed, he had difficulty even returning to Washington, D.C., due to the grounding of all aircraft throughout the country.

6. The initial award was presented in October 1989 to the newsletter's first editor, U.S. Magistrate Hugh Brenneman, and its publication committee, Donald Daniels and Thomas G. Demling. Its second award was accepted in 2002 by editor Patrick Mears, and the third in 2011 by editor Joseph A. Kuiper.

7. There are three awards. The first is the Service to the Profession Award, which is given from time to time to a practicing attorney, legal educator, or judge who has rendered outstanding service in the improvement of the administration of justice in the federal courts or to the perfecting of the skills of those who serve as advocates in those courts. The second is the Hillman Award, given in recognition to an individual

for their contribution and commitment to developing trial lawyers through the Hillman Advocacy Program. The third is the Thomas J. McNamara Scholarships to assist young attorneys whose financial circumstances would have made it difficult to attend the Hillman Advocacy Program. The scholarships were named after an attorney who was a devoted and tireless teacher of trial skills and who played a leading role in the development of the workshop.

8. Judge Miles was appointed as the first official Court Historian by the court's Administrative Order 0/00-41 on July 5, 2000. Judge Enslen signed the administrative order. Judge Brenneman was appointed by the court as his successor.

INDEX

Page references in italics indicate illustrations, and t *indicates a table. "WD" refers to the West-ern District of Michigan.*

art deco federal buildings, 122, 140
Articles of Confederation, 2, 21–22, 337n1
Ashcroft, John, 213–14, 217, 371n5
Assimilative Crimes Act, 182–83
Assistant U.S. Attorneys, 290–92
Audrain, Peter, 334n11
Austin, Richard, 362n11
Avery v. Fox, 48–49

Backus, Ella Mae, 86, 291–92
Backus, Henry T., 32
Bailey, Norman, 45
Baldwin, Augustus C., 41
Ball, Byron, 50
Ball, John, 42, 342–43n25
Ball, Martin, & Withey, 42
bank robber gangs, 115–16, 210, 353n20
bankruptcy administration, 250–84
  Bankruptcy Abuse Prevention and
    Consumer Protection Act (2005;
    BAP/CPA), 270, 273–74
  Bankruptcy Act (1800), 250–51, 367n5
  Bankruptcy Act (1841), 250–52
  Bankruptcy Act (1867), 250, 252–54
  Bankruptcy Act (1898; Nelson Act), 250,
    254–56, 260–61, 276
  Bankruptcy Amendments and Federal
    Judgeship Act (1984), 267
  Bankruptcy Appellate Panels (BAPs), 272
  Bankruptcy Judges, United States Trust-
    ees, and Family Farmer Bankruptcy
    Act (1986), 269–70
  Bankruptcy Judges, U.S. Trustees, &
    Family Farmer Bankruptcy Act of
    1986, 270, 368n34
  Bankruptcy Reform Act (1978; U.S.
    Bankruptcy Code), 266–71, 276
  Bankruptcy Reform Act (1994), 272
  caseload/operations of bankruptcy court,
    273–75
  Chandler Act (1938), 260–62
  Chapter 7 cases, 268–71, 273–74
  Chapter 11 cases, 269–71, 275, 369n36

  Chapter 12 cases, 269–71
  Chapter 13 cases, 269–71, 273–74
  Chief Judges, 325*t*
  clerks, 326*t*
  judges, 275–83, 324*t*, 369n37
  locations of bankruptcy court, 283–84
  overview of, 250
  referees, duties/number/qualifications
    of, 255–57
  referees, list of, 323*t*
  referees' changing status, 260–62
  referees in the Grand Rapids region,
    257–58
  referees in the Kalamazoo region, 259
  Referees in the Northern Division,
    259–60, 264–65
  Referees in the Southern Division,
    262–64
  Referees' Salary Act (1946), 261–62
  registers in bankruptcy, 252–54
  U.S. Trustees, 270–71, 368nn33–34,
    369n36
  World War II's impact on filings, 263–64,
    266
Banyon, Willard Johnson, 259–60,
  367–68n21
Bar & Bench, 306, 309, 371n6
baseball's reserve clause, 93–100, 350n68,
  351n74
Bass, John, 217
Bates, Asher B., 32
Bates, Frederick, 7–8, 336n45
Bates, George C., 29
Bauckham, Jack, 159
Baxter, John, 55, 57
Bay Mills Indian Community, 183–86
Beaman, Fernando C., 341n7
Becker, Harold, xi, 310
Beckwith, Matthew, 335n42
begging, 222–24
Bell, Helen Mortensen, 176
Bell, Jonathan, 176
Bell, Mifflin E., 66

prohibition law in, 353n14
statehood of, 1, 7, 19–20, 27
territorial governments/judges of, 5
unemployment rates in, 255
See also Michigan Territory
Michigan Lawyers Weekly (MLW), 306
Michigan State Bar Journal, 306
Michigan Territory
 boundaries of, 20, 337n61
 capital punishment in, 13–15, 17–18, 210,
  335n42, 337n57
 Congress extends boundaries of, 6–7, 11
 creation of, 6
 government of, 7
 impediments to statehood, 19
 Indian title to land in, 11
 New Englanders' migration to, 19–20,
  41–42, 337n60
 population of, 19–20
 slavery in, 9–10
 See also Michigan
Michilimackinac County (Michigan Territory), 11–12
Milburn, Herbert Theodore, 197
Miles, Fred Thomas and Dena Del Alverson, 147
Miles, Lorraine, 151
Miles, Mariette Bruchert, 148, 151
Miles, Michele, 151
Miles, Thomas, 151
Miles, Wendell A., *148*
 bankruptcy judge appointed by, 277, 279
 as Chief Judge, 151
 childhood/background of, 147
 as Circuit Judge, 149, 290
 as Court Historian, 308, 372n8
 death and funeral of, 151–52
 as District Judge, 144, 149–50, 290
 on the FBA committee, 304
 vs. Noel P. Fox, 150–51
 as general counsel for Ferris State University, 127
 Historical Society incorporated by, 309

 on Indian sovereignty, 182–83
 law practice of, 148–49
 marriage of, 148
 military career of, 147–48, 289
 referee appointed by, 279
 as Senior District Judge, 151
 on *United States v. Horace Chandler Davis*,
  134
 as U.S. Attorney, 149, 289–90
 on the U.S. Foreign Intelligence Surveil-
  lance Court, 151, 290
Miller, Lewis M., 92
Miller, Marvin, 351n74
Miller, Richard, 214
Miller, Shackleford, Jr., 134
Milliken, William, 149
Milliken v. Bradley, 131–32
Minnesota, statehood of, 7
Missouri, statehood of, 8
Missouri Territory, 8
Mitchell, James A., 309
Mitchell, William ("Billy"), 348n26
MLB, 351n74
Monroe, James, 12, 16, 33
Montgomery, Robert M., 92
Morell, George, 16–17
Murphy, Frank, 210
Muzzy, Franklin, 46

National Bank Robbery Act (1934), 210
National League of Professional Baseball
  Clubs, 93–95, 97, 99, 350n68, 351n73
National Prohibition (Volstead) Act. *See*
  Prohibition
National Wilderness Preservation System, 203
Naturalization Act (1790), 67, 346n97
Naturalization Act (1870), 67
Naturalization Law (1802), 346n97
Navajo Nation Reservation, 181
Nebiolo, Pauline J. and Lino, 195
Neff, David, 195
Neff, Janet T., 190–92, *195*, 195–96, 218–22,
  361n8

—JUSTICES
Alito, 361n101
Harry Blackmun, 355n51
Abe Fortas, 355n51
Ginsburg, 361n101
Horace Gray, 239
Kagan, 185–86, 361n101
Horace Harmon Lurton, 78
John McLean, 33–34
James Clark McReynolds, 105
William H. Rehnquist, 151
John Roberts, 177
Scalia, 361n101
Potter Stewart, 134
Stone, 113
George Sutherland, 285–86
William Howard Taft, 60, 66, 78, 80, 92,
    104, 107, 111–12
Thomas, 361n101
Robert Trimble, 33
U.S. Trustees, 270–71, 368nn33–34, 369n36
U.S. v. Bay Mills Indian Community, 183
U.S. v. Dakota, 182–83

Van Arman, Christopher, 77
Vande Velde, George, 212, 214
Van Wagoner, Murray D., 125
Vergennes, Charles Gravier, comte de, 1–2,
    333n1
VerHey, Timothy P., 214
Vermaat, Maarten, 238–39, 243, 248–49, 290
Vetter, St. Clair, 349n44
Virginia, 2, 35
Virginia Military District, 333n3
Voting Rights Act (1965), 200–201

Waldo v. Consumers Energy Co., 217–19,
    364n54
Walker, Henry N., 32
Walker, William M., 94–95
Wanty, Emma M. Nichols, 70–72
Wanty, George Proctor, 69–76, *71*, 78–80,
    92, 257–58, 348n19

Wanty, Samuel and Elizabeth Proctor, 70
Wanty, Thomas Cooley, 70
War Department, 294
Warner, Norcross & Judd, 244, 309
War of 1812, 19
Warren, Charles B., 352–53n11
Washington, George, 285–86
Washingtonian Movement, 339n33
Washington Treaty (1836), 19
Watson, Samuel G., 32
Wau-ben-e-micki (White Thunder), 335n42
Wayne, Anthony, 4
Weber, John R., 238
Weeghman, Charles, 94–96, 99–100
Weeks, Jonathon, 210, 217, 363n42
Welsh, J. W., 116
Western District of Michigan
    counties and boundaries of, 129,
        341–42n16, xiii
    creation of, 35–41, *39*, 309, 341–42n16,
        ix, xi, xiii
    dispute resolution in (*see* ADR)
    150th anniversary of, 309–10, xi–xii
    population of, 129
    Southern and Northern Divisions of,
        56–57, 64, *89*, 113–15, *126*
Western Electric Manufacturing, 100
Weston, A. A., 349n44
Weston, Ron, 309
Wetmore, Fred C., 290
Whales (*formerly* Chi-Feds), 94–97, 99
Wheeler Upham, 70
Whig Party, 251
Whiskey Rebellion (1791), 26
White, Alpheus, 31
White, Helene, 191–92, 361n6
White Lake, eminent domain on, 48–49
Whitney, Gleaves, 310
Wicks, John H. and Mary, 258
Wicks, Kirk E., Sr., 258
Wilderness Act (1964), 203–4
Wilkins, Catherine Stevenson, 27
Wilkins, John, Jr., 27–28

David Gardner Chardavoyne is a veteran Michigan lawyer and a legal educator who is a graduate of the University of Michigan and the Wayne State University Law School where he has been an adjunct professor of law for more than two decades. He is the author of many books and articles dealing with the history of the law in Michigan, including *The United States District Court for the Eastern District of Michigan* (Wayne State University Press, 2012) and frequent contributions to *The Court Legacy*, the journal of the Historical Society for the United States District Court for the Eastern District of Michigan. He lives with his family in Oakland County, Michigan.

Hugh W. Brenneman, Jr., is a retired United States Magistrate Judge for the U.S. District Court for the Western District of Michigan, having served for thirty-five years on that court. He is presently the Court Historian. He is a graduate of Alma College and the University of Michigan Law School and lives with his wife in West Michigan.